Principles of World Trade Law

Principles of World Trade Law presents a comprehensive and balanced picture of the legal framework underpinning the modern world trading system – covering the law of the WTO but also drawing on bilateral and regional instruments. It acknowledges the shifting relevance of the WTO in world trade law in favour of regionalism, particularly in relation to new fields such as digital trade.

While drawing heavily on the law of the WTO as a source of legal rules, this concise text also engages with elements found in preferential Free Trade Agreements (FTAs) (such as Rules of Origin) and mutual recognition agreements (such as recognition of professional qualifications in the case of services). Practical in nature, it blends straightforward descriptive explanations of the legal concepts with critical inquiry, directing readers to the key debates in the field as well as the source materials themselves. It also offers guidance with discussion questions for the reader to consider for each chapter.

Principles of World Trade Law is an ideal introductory textbook for advanced undergraduate and postgraduate students taking courses in world trade law, international trade law, and international economic law as well as a valuable guide for scholars, legal practitioners, and policymakers.

David Collins is Professor of International Economic Law at The City Law School, City St George's, University of London, UK.

"This volume provides a needed overview of the state of the field today. Covering topics at the forefront of current trade policy agendas, the book expertly reviews these issues in an accessible and thoughtful way that will be useful to students and experienced researchers alike."

— **Kathleen Claussen**, *Georgetown University, USA*

"I had long been seeking a book on the principles of world trade law that is succinct yet comprehensive in terms of its coverage and am pleased that Professor David Collins has produced such an excellent book that I can happily recommend to my students. It is intellectually interesting, accessible and provides an impressive analysis of the principles of world trade law."

— **Surya P. Subedi**, *Professor, KC, University of Leeds, UK*

"Prof. Collins masterfully combines an exploration of world trade law principles with pressing global issues such as digital trade, the challenge of China's state capitalism, and the competing claims of non-trade concerns. This insightful book is an essential read for scholars and practitioners engaged in trade."

— **Henry Gao**, *Professor of Law,*
Singapore Management University, Singapore

Principles of World Trade Law

David Collins

Routledge
Taylor & Francis Group
LONDON AND NEW YORK

Designed cover image: rikkyal / iStock / Getty Images Plus / Getty Images ®

First published 2025
by Routledge
4 Park Square, Milton Park, Abingdon, Oxon OX14 4RN

and by Routledge
605 Third Avenue, New York, NY 10158

Routledge is an imprint of the Taylor & Francis Group, an informa business

British Library Cataloguing-in-Publication Data
A catalogue record for this book is available from the British Library

ISBN: 978-1-032-73733-1 (hbk)
ISBN: 978-1-032-73732-4 (pbk)
ISBN: 978-1-003-46567-6 (ebk)

DOI: 10.4324/9781003465676

Typeset in Times New Roman
by Apex CoVantage, LLC

Contents

Table of Cases

Disputes under Preferential Free Trade Agreements

GATT / WTO cases

Table of Treaties

1 Introduction

History and Rationale for Trade Liberalization

1.1 International Trade

The complexity of the interconnectedness of people and societies around the world today is astounding relative to previous centuries. The consequences of globalization are now so well entrenched in the daily lives of most people that it makes no sense to frame economic issues in terms of the nation-state, much as the boundaries between countries are artificial constructs rather than natural features of geography. Thanks to advances in technology, such as telecommunications and shipping containerization, in the 21st century there is no longer any such thing as a national economy. Although there can be some downsides to this – something which politicians are often all too quick to point out – economic globalization has overwhelmingly raised standards of living around the world.

Few successful companies have business models focused entirely on serving home markets, and even fewer source their goods exclusively locally. While the pace of globalization may have slowed in recent years in tandem with geopolitical events such as Covid-19 and regional wars, it is still thriving. Since virtually all economic activity has taken on an international dimension, the legal problems that arise in the delivery of goods and services around the world require internationally focused solutions. As international law has grown in importance along with globalization, the erosion of nationalism in law-making means that some regulatory control and judicial oversight is surrendered by nation-states to the international arena.

Nowhere has this transition been more acute than in the field of international trade. Countries which pride themselves on self-sufficiency in agriculture and manufacturing have, in pursuit of efficiencies and ensuing increases in the quality of life, become dependent on foreign trading partners. Imported foreign goods and services, while often cheaper and in some cases of superior quality, have meant that many of the people who were employed in the production of these goods have seen their livelihoods suffer as jobs literally moved overseas. Consequently much of the activity of government, in terms of the legislative, executive, and judicial branches of the state, has become the purview of global institutions. This transformation has found expression in the anxieties of national legislators who see their role in the law-making process diminishing.

DOI: 10.4324/9781003465676-1

The benefits of international trade, such as a greater variety of affordable products and services, cannot be taken for granted. Protectionist tendencies, mistakenly aimed at furthering the interests of the nation-state, have a tendency to reappear at the moments when progress either falters generally or is enjoyed unequally. The world appears to be witnessing yet another flirtation with policies that are antithetical to free trade, including not only tariffs and quotas but also wide-ranging subsidization for inefficient producers. The standards of living that we have enjoyed in recent decades may well go into reverse. The obligations owed by states to each other under world trade law may help guard against these outcomes.

1.2 Terminology

In this introductory chapter, it is useful to set out the main concepts upon which this book is based, as reflected in its title. These are: "world trade" and "principles." Law, specifically international law, will be explained further.

1.2.1 World Trade

The subject of this book is the laws governing international trade. Trade itself simply means the voluntary exchange of objects of subjectively different value. One party values the thing that it surrenders to the other party less than the thing that it acquires from them. In civilized stable societies, laws are required to ensure that such transactions are enforceable – this can be a problem where the actual exchange of objects is not simultaneous or where a symbolic store of value, such as money, is used to "purchase" the item rather than in a traditional barter situation (item for item).

International trade describes this phenomenon as it occurs between parties located in two different countries. But the book's title is not *International Trade Law* because that term is, in a sense confusingly, associated with the private law of international trade, such as the laws governing international shipping, bills of lading and transnational commercial contracts. This book is about the international legal framework governing states, essentially another word for countries. These are international legal commitments, typically in the form of treaties, which bind countries to act in a certain way – often restricting their capacity to regulate their own domestic economies because of the impact this will have on their trading partners. If you are hoping for information on marine insurance or the United Nations Convention on Contracts for the International Sale of Goods (CISG), you are reading the wrong book.

For the sake of distinguishing this body of law from international trade law, this subject is sometimes called *world* trade law. Traditionally world trade law has concerned itself exclusively with the law of the World Trade Organization (WTO). Indeed, the WTO has had a foundational role in establishing the key principles governing trade at the international level. Many of these will be explored in this book. But, the importance of the WTO in the universe of world trade law is diminishing as bilateral and regional trade treaties grow in breadth and reach. Unlike

WTO law, these instruments do not have global reach – the WTO is truly a "world" organization, now comprising 166 member states. But many of the legal principles being developed in these bilateral and regional trade treaties are beginning to adopt a universal character in that they are reappearing, in some cases in different forms, across a range of trade treaties, often reflecting or in some cases enhancing the original principles established at the WTO.

As a final point on the terminology of "world trade" – this body of law forms the basis of the larger subject of international economic law,[1] which traditionally also comprises international investment law[2] along with monetary law and developmental law.

1.2.2 Principles

The book's title captures the importance of legal *principles* as opposed to bright-line *rules*. While provisions of trade treaties will be referred to directly, and in some cases quoted, this book will focus primarily on the concepts that are at the heart of world trade law – the ideas that form the basis of the technical trade rules from which participating states benefit and to which they are held accountable.

The distinction between a principle and a rule is a fundamental concept in legal theory and practice, with significant implications for how laws are interpreted and applied. While both principles and rules serve to guide behaviour and decision-making, they differ in their nature, application, and flexibility. A rule is typically a specific, clearly defined directive that prescribes or prohibits certain conduct.[3]

Rules are characterized by their precision and are often formulated in an "if-then" structure. For example, a rule might state that "if a driver exceeds the speed limit, then they must pay a fine." Rules are designed to be applied in a straightforward manner, with little room for interpretation. They provide clear guidance on how to act in specific situations and are often associated with predictable outcomes. In contrast, a principle is a broader, more general norm that embodies a fundamental value or policy. Principles are less specific than rules and often require interpretation and balancing against other principles when applied to specific situations. For instance, the principle of "freedom of speech" is broad (although not universal) and can be applied in various contexts. But its exact application may vary depending on the circumstances and competing interests. "Free trade" is probably the most basic principle of world trade law – one that underpins many other principles as well as many rules that manifest as articles in trade treaties. Free trade is by no means always unconditional, as will be seen throughout this book.

The application of rules tends to be more straightforward and binary – either the rule is followed or it is not. Principles, on the other hand, allow for more flexibility

1 See D Collins, *The Foundations of International Economic Law* (2nd ed. Elgar, 2024)

2 See D Collins, *An Introduction to International Investment Law* (2nd ed. Cambridge University Press, 2023)

3 See generally J Raz, "Legal Principles and the Limits of Law" 81 Yale Law Journal 823 (1971–72)

and can be applied with varying degrees of weight depending on the context. This can be particularly useful in the context of a diplomatic setting in which two countries are negotiating outcomes based on compromise. When principles conflict, they can be balanced against each other, whereas conflicting rules typically require one to be chosen over the other.

Another key difference lies in their origin and development. Rules are often explicitly created by legislative bodies or other authorities, while principles may evolve over time through judicial decisions, societal norms, or philosophical reasoning. Principles often underpin the creation of specific rules and can guide the interpretation of rules when their application is unclear. Again, since international law has multiple sources of authority, including international tribunals and numerous treaties, the notion of principles is more apposite. In legal reasoning, principles play a crucial role in filling gaps where specific rules do not exist or in guiding the interpretation of rules in complex or novel situations. They provide a framework for understanding the purpose and intent behind specific rules and can help ensure that the application of rules aligns with broader legal and societal values. In this book, the tension between the goals of trade and other societal values, such as the protection of the environment, often relies on the use of principles.

Understanding the difference between principles and rules is crucial for legal practitioners, policymakers, and anyone engaged in legal reasoning in the field of world trade. It allows for a more nuanced approach to law-making and interpretation, ensuring that legal systems, both nationally and internationally, can maintain both the clarity and predictability provided by rules, and the flexibility and adaptability.

1.3 History of World Trade

1.3.1 Ancient Times

Trade is almost as old as civilization itself, in fact, it is difficult to separate the two. One of the consequences of the beginning of farming and domestication of animals 10,000 years ago was the capacity of people to achieve a surplus of food which they could store for later consumption. As tribes travelled between early settlements, they were able to exchange these excess crops for different ones produced by other peoples. With incremental advances in agriculture and in the fabrication of tools, early humans discovered that trading for higher-valued goods was less exhausting than conquest, and in the long run, was more reliable.

There was already a flourishing jewellery trade in Mesopotamia in 3000 BCE (before the Common Era). This bartering (object for an object for a different object rather than object for money) was facilitated by the creation of money. Simply put, money is merely a store of value which allowed for transactions that could be delayed (selling crops produced the next month) rather than those which were instantaneous. Money enabled greater and more varied kinds of trade. The first coins are thought to have originated in Turkey around 600 BCE. As trade between different peoples became commonplace, trading routes were established between the cities of the Ancient World like Athens, Constantinople, and Babylon. These later became roads. The most important of these was the Great Silk Road which crossed Asia, linking the Far East to the Roman Empire, and through which valuable commodities like exotic spices found their way into medieval Europe. Cities such as Uruk and Samarkand (the remains of which are located in modern Iraq and Uzbekistan, respectively) grew up as settlements along the Silk Road, evincing the role of trade in the spread of humanity. Constructed over centuries, China's Grand Canal system connected major waterways that led to a vast expansion of trade across China and remains the world's largest artificial waterway.

1.3.2 The Pre-Modern Era

During the Renaissance international trade became dominated by sailing ships delivering cargo from around the world across the ocean back to Europe. The Age of Exploration, spanning from the 15th to the 17th centuries, was a period of significant expansion in international trade that reshaped global economic and political relationships. European nations, driven by a desire for wealth and new trade routes, embarked on voyages of discovery that connected previously isolated parts of the world and established new trade networks.

One of the primary motivations for exploration was the search for direct access to the lucrative spice trade of Asia. Spices were in high demand in Europe for both culinary and medicinal purposes but the existing trade routes through the Middle East were controlled by Arab and Italian merchants, making spices expensive and sometimes difficult to obtain. Portuguese explorers like Vasco da Gama sought to find a sea route to India by sailing around Africa while Spanish-sponsored voyages, such as those of Christopher Columbus, attempted to reach Asia by sailing west across the Atlantic.

These explorations led to the discovery of new lands and the establishment of colonial empires. The Spanish and Portuguese were the first to establish vast overseas territories, followed later by other European powers such as England, France, and the Netherlands. These colonies served as sources of raw materials and new commodities as well as markets for European manufactured goods, fundamentally altering the nature and scale of international trade. The Columbian Exchange, named after explorer Christopher Columbus, was a significant outcome of this era. It involved the transfer of plants, animals, culture, human populations, technology, and diseases between the Old and New Worlds. Crops like potatoes, tomatoes, and corn were introduced to Europe, while wheat, sugar cane, and domesticated animals were brought to the Americas. This exchange had profound effects on agriculture, diets, and populations worldwide.

The influx of precious metals, particularly silver from the Americas, into Europe, had a substantial impact on the global economy. It led to increased trade with Asia, as European traders now had the means to purchase large quantities of Asian goods. However, this also contributed to inflation in Europe and economic disruptions in China and other parts of Asia. The Age of Exploration also saw the rise of new economic systems and institutions. Mercantilism became the dominant economic theory, emphasizing the accumulation of wealth through a favourable balance of trade. Joint-stock companies, such as the Dutch East India Company and the British East India Company, were formed to finance and manage long-distance trade, becoming powerful entities in their own right. New railway and canal networks penetrating inland enabled the movement of goods at lower cost and greater speed. This was especially significant in England, the birthplace of the Industrial Revolution.[4]

The expansion of trade during this period also had darker aspects. The transatlantic slave trade, which forcibly transported millions of Africans to the Americas, was established to provide labour for plantations producing cash crops for European markets. This horrific trade had long-lasting demographic, economic, and social consequences for Africa, the Americas, and Europe. Some of the vast wealth of the British Empire was subsequently spent in the prevention of slavery, following its abolition by the United Kingdom in 1834.[5]

While economic globalization is sometimes seen as a recent phenomenon, international trade remained vibrant until the early twentieth century. Neo-mercantilist theories reflected in the imposition of protectionist tariffs to restrict imports had generally failed in practice in Britain, France, and Germany throughout the 16th and 18th centuries. Belief in the effectiveness of isolationist policies began to fade as the writings of Adam Smith, who advocated liberalization of the economy rather than protectionism, took hold and the Industrial Revolution unlocked the transformative potential of the mass production of goods which could be consumed in larger quantities. This not only raised the standard of living – it meant that surplus goods could be traded overseas, creating huge profits. The virtues of free trade were embraced by many across the political spectrum, including many holding what might today be described as socialist views.[6]

Britain's repeal of the Corn Laws in the mid-nineteenth century, eliminating tariffs on imports of grain, reflected the increasing acceptance of free trade. The Suez Canal, opened in 1869, dramatically reduced travel distances between Europe and Asia. A journey from Rotterdam to Mumbai that previously required rounding Africa was shortened by nearly 50 per cent, saving more than a week of shipping time. This allowed ships to make more trips per year and reduced fuel consumption. For the route between London and Shanghai, the distance was cut by almost a third. The Panama Canal, completed in 1914, had an even more dramatic impact on certain routes. It shortened the voyage from New York to Los Angeles by 60 per cent, eliminating the need to sail around South America. This saved approximately up to five months for ships making that journey. Economically, these shortened routes translated into substantial cost savings for shipping companies and traders. Sea freight became four to six times cheaper than air or land transport options. The

4 M Koyama and J Rubin, *How the World Became Rich* (Polity, 2022)
5 N Biggar, *Colonialism: A Moral Reckoning* (William Collins, 2023)
6 MW Palen, *Pax Economica: Left-Wing Visions of a Free Trade World* (Princeton University Press, 2024)

canals allowed larger quantities of goods to be shipped at once, reducing the overall number of shipments needed. This was especially impactful for bulk commodities like oil, which still accounts for a quarter of Suez Canal traffic. Today disruptions in Suez and Panama Canal traffic still are felt across the world in shortages and higher prices.

It was not all smooth sailing for international trade. While the aftermath of the First World War ultimately led to a period of sustained prosperity and wealth, this was followed by the Great Depression of the 1930s, characterized instead by widespread poverty and unemployment on both sides of the Atlantic. Misguidedly, both the United States and the United Kingdom enacted a series of protectionist tariffs on a range of products with the aim of protecting farms and factories from international competition. The United States Smoot-Hawley Tariff Act of 1930 led to an almost total collapse in global trade. Mercantilism had once again reared its head. Retaliatory tariffs were imposed by other countries and food became unaffordable or unavailable. Trade protectionism had achieved the exact opposite of what it had been intended to do – it only made the depression deeper and longer. Higher tariffs led to retaliatory measures from other countries, reducing global trade and further hurting American exporters. United States imports decreased by two-thirds and exports fell by more than 50 per cent between 1929 and 1933, exacerbating the economic contraction. For the United Kingdom, the impact of trade barriers was more complex. The United Kingdom abandoned its longstanding free trade policy in 1931 and implemented a system of imperial preference, favouring trade with its empire. This shift in policy contributed to about a quarter of the decline in United Kingdom imports between 1929 and 1931. More significantly, it dramatically altered the geographic pattern of United Kingdom trade, with the share of imports from the British Empire rising by a third between 1929 and 1938.

The rise in protectionism hindered international economic cooperation and contributed to the contraction of world trade, which fell by approximately two-thirds between 1929 and 1934. This dramatic reduction in global commerce deepened and prolonged the economic crisis in both nations. The scarcity of food and other products meant people could not afford the basic staples of life. Trade barriers made it more difficult for countries to export their way out of the depression, limiting opportunities for economic recovery. Furthermore, the protectionist policies of the 1930s contributed to increasing international tensions. As nations viewed trade policy as a tool to frustrate geopolitical rivals, it led to a breakdown in international cooperation, contributing to political instability. Interruptions in trade may well have played a role in both world wars.

1.3.3 The Modern Era

In July 1944, representatives of the world's leading economies met to establish the first system of global economic management with a view, amongst other things, to prevent another economic depression through ill-advised trade protectionism. The Bretton Woods system, as it is often known (named after the location of the resort in New Hampshire where the meeting took place), led to the establishment of the

General Agreement on Tariffs and Trade (the GATT). This later became the World Trade Organization (WTO) the rules of which are one of the main subjects of this book. GATT, to be discussed further in the next chapter, was designed to prevent the imposition of tariffs and quantitative restrictions on imports, which were understood to lead to an escalation of prices as well as tension between countries.

Shipping containerization further revolutionized international trade in the 20th century by dramatically reducing shipping costs and times. Introduced in the 1950s, standardized shipping containers allowed cargo to be easily transferred between ships, trucks, and trains without needing to be unloaded and reloaded at each step. This intermodal transport system greatly improved efficiency compared to previous break-bulk cargo methods. The adoption of containerization led to significant reductions in cargo handling time and labour costs at ports. Loading and unloading ships became much faster, allowing vessels to spend less idle time in port and more time at sea transporting goods. Standardized container sizes also enabled ships, ports, and transport vehicles to be optimized for handling containers, further improving efficiency. The introduction of ever-larger container ships throughout the late 20th century allowed for increasing economies of scale in ocean shipping. This continued to drive down per-unit transport costs, further fuelling the growth of global trade. Containerization also improved cargo security and reduced losses from damage and theft. The sealed containers were harder to pilfer from and protected goods from the elements during transport and handling. This made international shipping more reliable and reduced insurance costs.

Telecommunications technology has played a crucial role in facilitating the dramatic increase in global trade over the past few decades. By enabling instant communication and data transfer across vast distances, first through the telephone and then the Internet, telecommunications have fundamentally transformed how international business is conducted. One of the primary ways telecommunications have boosted global trade is by dramatically reducing the costs and barriers to international transactions. In the past, coordinating trade deals across borders was slow, expensive, and prone to miscommunication. Now, businesses can instantly connect with partners and customers around the world via phone, email, video conferencing, and other digital channels. This allows for real-time negotiation, order placement, and problem-solving, greatly increasing the speed and efficiency of global commerce.

Much of modern trade is characterized by e-commerce and digital marketplaces that facilitate cross-border transactions. Online platforms allow even small businesses to reach global customer bases, while electronic payment systems make international purchases quick and convenient. This has opened up new export opportunities for businesses of all sizes and expanded consumer access to global products. Additionally, advanced telecommunications infrastructure has improved supply chain management and logistics coordination for international trade. Companies can now track shipments in real-time, quickly adjust to disruptions, and optimize their global operations. This has made complex, multinational supply chains more feasible and efficient. The availability of instant global communication has also expanded trade in services. Many professional and technical services can now be delivered remotely via telecommunications networks. This has created new export industries in areas like business process outsourcing, software development, and consulting. Real-time data on prices, demand, and economic conditions helps companies make more informed decisions about global trade strategies. Telecommunications have furthermore facilitated the global spread of knowledge and innovation, indirectly supporting trade growth. The rapid exchange of ideas and technical information across borders accelerates the development of new products and production methods that can then be traded internationally.

Throughout the latter part of the 20th Century, trade liberalization efforts, including reductions in tariffs and other trade barriers through multilateral agreements like GATT and the WTO, as well as regional trade agreements, opened up markets and encouraged greater cross-border commerce. The average tariff rates in industrialized countries fell from about 40 per cent in 1947 to just under 4 per cent today. The growth of global exports rose commensurately during this period (**See Figure 1.1**). The rise of intra-industry and intra-firm trade became increasingly prominent, with companies establishing global production networks and trading intermediate goods across borders. This led to more complex and interconnected global value chains.

China has played an increasingly dominant role in international trade in the 21st century, becoming a global economic powerhouse and the world's largest exporter. Since joining the World Trade Organization in 2001, China's share of

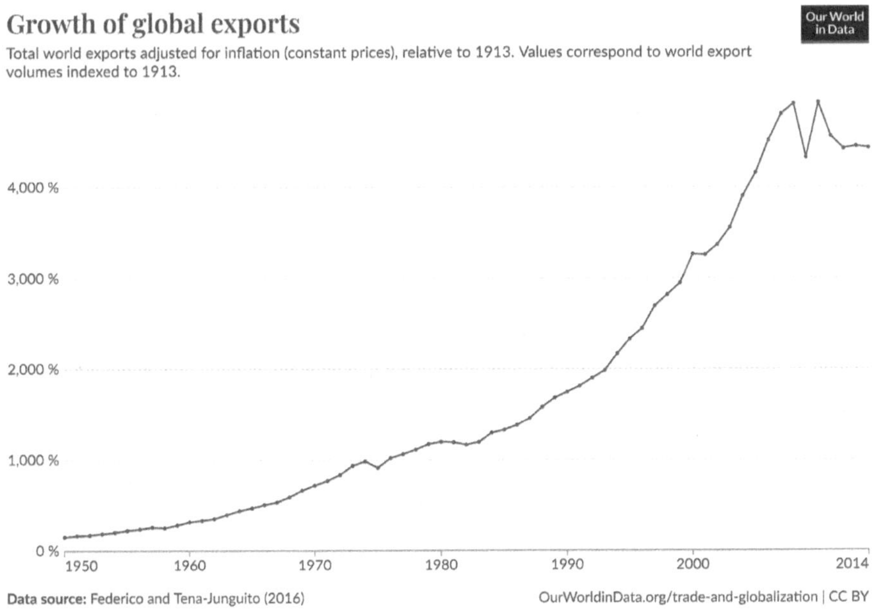

Figure 1.1 Growth of Global Exports Relative to 1913, 1950–2014

Source: Our World in Data

global trade has risen dramatically, accounting for nearly 15 per cent of global exports by 2022. This meteoric rise has reshaped global supply chains and trade patterns, with China becoming the largest trading partner for many countries around the world. However, China's trade practices have faced criticism from some quarters, with accusations that it does not always adhere to free trade principles fairly. Concerns have been raised about issues such as state subsidies, intellectual property rights violations, and currency manipulation. These practices have led to trade tensions, particularly with the United States, resulting in tariffs and other trade barriers being imposed on Chinese goods in recent years. Today China is often accused with over-producing electric vehicles (EVs) and exporting them to Europe and North America at prices far below what domestic producers can compete with.

China's economic growth has also made it a key driver of global economic expansion. Its GDP now accounts for over 18 per cent of the global total, making it the world's second-largest economy. This economic heft means that any significant downturn in China's economy could have major ripple effects on global trade and growth. There are some indications that China's role as the engine of global growth may be approaching its peak. A sustained slowdown in China could lead to reduced demand for imports from other countries and potentially disrupt global supply chains that have become heavily reliant on Chinese manufacturing. Furthermore, geopolitical tensions and efforts by some countries to reduce dependence on China could lead to a reconfiguration of global trade patterns. There are signs of some companies diversifying their supply chains away from China to countries like Vietnam and India. Some countries, such as the United States, are building up their production of critical components of electronic goods, especially microchips in order to strengthen their economic independence. This trend, if it continues, could result in more regionalized trade networks and potentially lower overall levels of global trade.

Today the expansion of international trade and globalization is associated with several controversies. Critics argue that trade liberalization has contributed to job losses and wage stagnation in developed countries, particularly for low-skilled workers in manufacturing sectors. This has fuelled political backlash against globalization in some nations. Concerns have been raised about the environmental impacts of increased global trade, including higher carbon emissions from transportation and the potential for regulatory arbitrage leading to pollution havens. Some argue that the benefits of trade have been unevenly distributed, exacerbating inequality both within and between countries. Developing countries have often struggled to compete in higher value-added industries. The growth of trade has led to debates about labour standards, with critics arguing that companies exploit workers in countries with weaker protections. On the other hand, manufacturing unemployment probably owes more to automation than it does to free trade. The high price of energy has also hurt manufacturing in many developed countries seeking to reduce carbon emissions. Climate change is at least in part due to natural cycles rather than the industrialization associated with economic expansion. Inequality, while unquestionably pervasive, is arguably a natural condition of humanity and therefore difficult to eradicate without dubious value judgements about who is most deserving.[7]

1.4 Rationales for International Trade

An important question to ask when embarking on a study of the principles of world trade law is why do nations trade with one another? There are two main rationales underpinning this strategy.

1.4.1 Efficiency Gains

The economic purpose for fostering international trade by eliminating unnecessary legal barriers is grounded in the theory of comparative advantage, first identified by the British political economist David Ricardo in the 18th century.[8] The theory posits that a country should specialize in the production of a given commodity and establish a cost advantage in its production because of the efficiencies engendered by expertise, then export it to other countries. That country should furthermore import other products where its cost advantage is relatively smaller, meaning products in which it does not have a specialism.

Ricardo outlined his theory using the example of England and Portugal producing shirts and bottles of wine. He showed that even if Portugal is *absolutely* better than England at producing both shirts and bottles of wine, it is still in Portugal's interest to produce the commodity where its cost advantage is greater to the exclusion of the other product, and import that other product from England. Portugal should produce wine if it is *more better* (meaning better to a more significant degree) than England at producing wine than it is at producing shirts, even if it is absolutely better at producing both. In other words, it should specialize in the production of the product where its *relative* advantage is greater. The demonstration that this strategy of comparative advantage leads to gains in terms of efficient productivity – greater output per unit of cost – is the theoretical basis of international trade.

Comparative advantage is open to the criticism that not all commodities are readily substitutable. It can also be risky to rely on your neighbour for essential goods, such as food and commodities like steel, oil or in today's world, semi-conductors. If there is a war, then countries that are not able to source these materials domestically can be vulnerable. This concern became a reality following Russia's invasion of Ukraine in 2022 when energy costs increased dramatically in Europe and elsewhere. The security of supply chains may be one of the reasons that free trade has become less popular in recent times.

Ricardo's insight into the value of trade, echoing Adam Smith's earlier work on the value of specialization and competition within an economy generally, was instrumental in encouraging politicians to abandon the mercantilist practices

7 See T Sowell, *Wealth, Poverty and Politics: An International Perspective* (Basic Books, 2016)
8 D Ricardo, *On the Principles of Political Economy and Taxation* (John Murray, 1817)

predicated on self-sufficiency and isolation. With borders that are open to trade, consumers are able to purchase the best goods and services at the lowest prices. This strategy has allowed people to enjoy all kinds of exotic commodities from around the world that would have been unimaginable in an era of protectionism because these things would have been either too expensive for an ordinary consumer or would have been simply unavailable.

Figure 1.2 shows the value of exported goods as a share of GDP since 1989 for four major economies and the world. With the exception of China, which began to derive growth from serving its own domestic economy after about 2005, exports steadily increased as a component of GDP with slight variations due to the global financial crisis of 2008–2009 and its aftermath. Trade is the lifeblood of many countries' economies.

The expansion of international trade must also be credited with declines in global inequality. While the gap in living standards between the rich and poor has increased in some countries in the past few decades, particularly in the developed world, the gap between rich and poor across the world continues to gently decline [See **Figure 1.3** Global Income Inequality 1913–2022]. This is due not only to lower-priced goods as imports but also to expanded overseas markets for exports. Some believe this has led to greater social harmony and a sense of personal well-being. The situation is somewhat different for the suppliers of goods and services and those who they employ. Producers face ever tougher competition because there

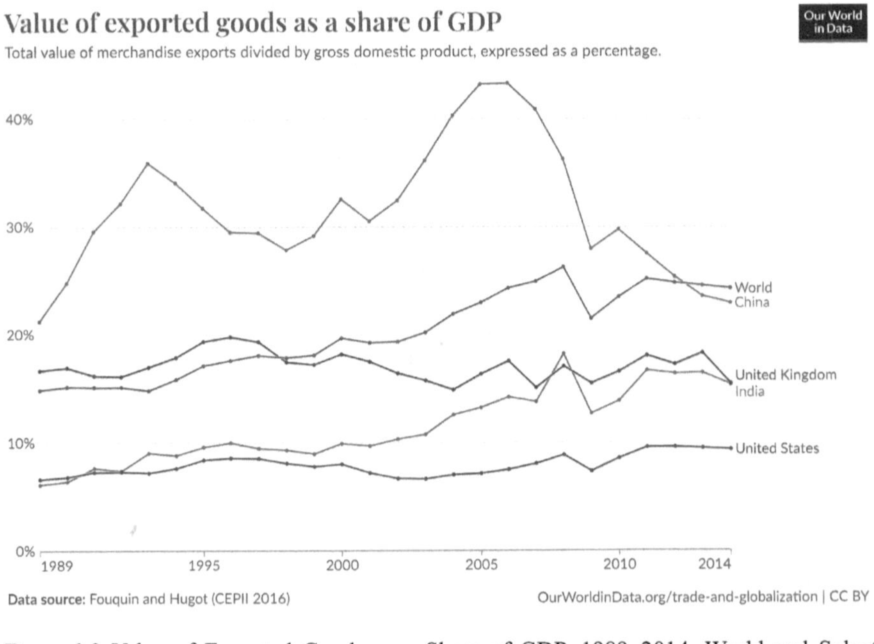

Figure 1.2 Value of Exported Goods as a Share of GDP, 1989–2014, World and Select Economies

Source: Our World in Data

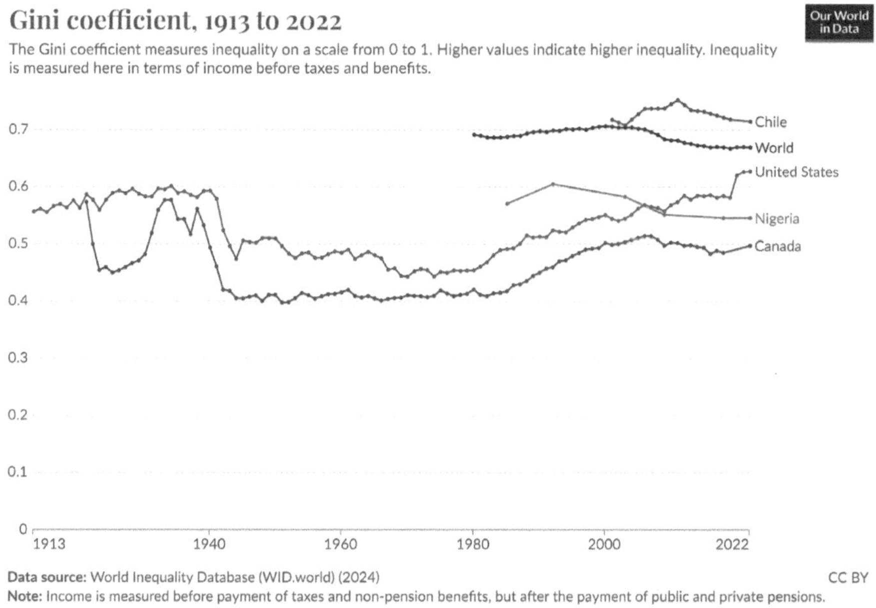

Figure 1.3 Inequality as Measured by the Gini Coefficient, 1913–2022, World and Select Economies

Source: Our World in Data

are no legal obstacles to the markets in which they once reigned unchallenged. Of course, this is precisely what Adam Smith wanted. It should keep prices down and ensure quality. Trade accounts for 25 per cent of United States economic activity and the average American gains about a quarter of their purchasing power from trade. Nearly half of imports are also inputs for United States businesses. Exporting firms also pay higher wages.[9]

But employees are also consumers and, if their employer, unshielded by tariffs, cannot withstand international competition, these people can see their wages collapse. This will mean that they are no longer able to act as market participants as purchasers, potentially leading to a downward economic spiral. While Ricardo and Smith were correct that trade can lead to efficiency gains, they perhaps did not appreciate or did not care, that there are losers from international trade. The hollowing out of the so-called working class in the West due to the decline in manufacturing employment is perhaps the most obvious casualty of trade although automation may be the real culprit here[10] [See **Figure 1.4**]. Manufacturing jobs as

9 J Wallar, "Misperceptions and Misplaced Perceptions: Time to Turn the Page on International Trade" Council on Foreign Relations (September 2024)

10 Declines in employment in the United States, the United Kingdom, and the world suggest that this trend does not exclusively capture manufacturing moving from these countries to other ones, but a decline in manufacturing employment generally.

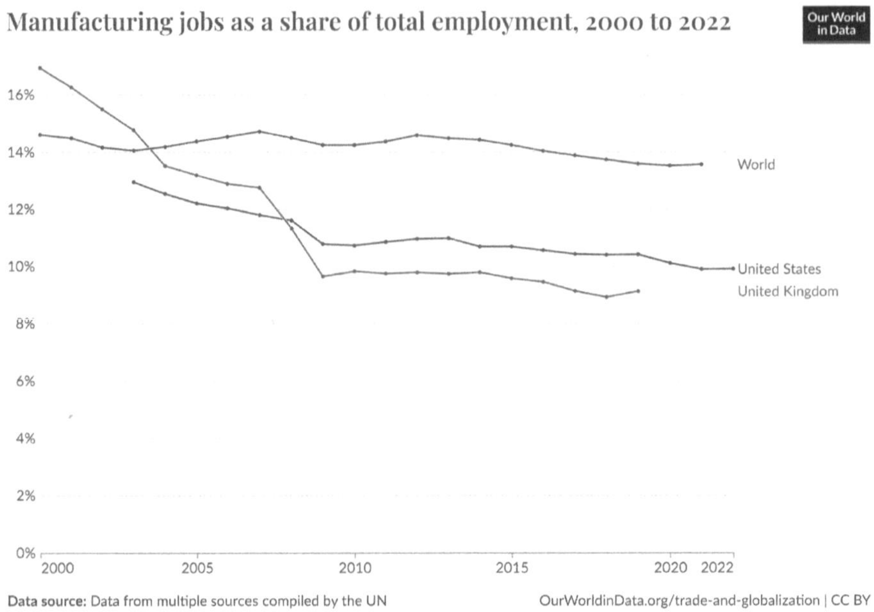

Figure 1.4 Manufacturing as a Share of Total Employment, 2000–2022, World, United States, and United Kingdom

Source: Our World in Data

a share of total employment]. These events have contributed to political developments in recent years premised on the harm inflicted to ordinary people by companies in pursuit of global profits and the seeming indifference of our leaders. The people who gain from international trade tend to be the consumers who enjoy a wider variety of goods and lower prices than they would have done otherwise; however, these consumers do not organize themselves as well and consequently are often underappreciated in the political process. Trade unions can be quite vocal and influential.

More work needs to be done by governments to address the harm suffered by those who have seen their wages decline or their employment disappear because of more efficient production in foreign markets, typically in developing countries where labour costs are lower, as are the costs of raw materials. Retraining, or reskilling as it is sometimes known, has been explored in a number of contexts with varying degrees of success. But labour is often not as mobile as economists think it should be in theory (workers do not move across international borders as easily as the goods they produce), and older workers often struggle to acquire new skills, especially when they are tied to technology.

This is why some countries, especially the United States, have expressed derision for the multilateral trading system and imposing tariffs on a wide range of goods, often justified on the basis of a wide understanding of national security. This response has been exacerbated by the perception that other countries, especially

China, have not played by the rules, providing state support to manufacturers to enable them to lower costs. Rising geopolitical tensions in recent years have only intensified these issues.

Shifting production and supply chains closer to home or to allied nations, known by various terms like "reshoring" or "friendshoring," is becoming increasingly commonplace. Global events such as the heightened United States-China tensions, the Covid-19 pandemic, and the Ukraine conflict have prompted nations to reconsider their economic ties, particularly with countries that don't share their values or pose significant trade imbalances. Government policies, including tariffs, subsidies, and geopolitical considerations, are now compelling multinational companies to re-evaluate their production locations and supply sources. This shift, which began subtly during the first administration of United States President Trump and has since involved other major economies, is now becoming apparent in various global economic indicators. It is thought that countries with strong bilateral free trade agreements, of which more below, are experiencing less trade diversion, even when their geopolitical stances differ. Efficiency gains are not always the most important consideration.

1.4.2 Trade and Peace

States may also choose to trade with one another because this is one of the best ways of avoiding militaristic conflict. The theory that international trade promotes peace is often referred to as the "liberal peace" or "commercial peace" theory. It posits that economic interdependence through trade reduces the likelihood of conflict between nations. Put simply, countries are less likely to attack those upon which they are economically dependent. Moreover, since trade promotes wealth, this abundance means that people are less needful of obtaining material goods from others by force. One of the earliest and most influential proponents of this theory was Immanuel Kant who argued in his 1795 essay "Perpetual Peace" that commercial ties between nations would create incentives for peaceful relations.[11] In the modern era, this concept has been further developed and empirically tested by numerous scholars. Countries with greater trade relations were less likely to engage in conflict, concluding that a doubling of trade on average leads to a 20 per cent diminution of belligerence.[12] The effect is thought to be particularly strong for neighbouring countries. One interesting permutation of this theory is that multilateral trade openness may actually increase the likelihood of war because it reduces the opportunity cost of bilateral conflict.[13]

There are numerous historical examples that seem to support the trade-peace theory. The European Union, which began as the European Coal and Steel Community, is often cited as a prime example of how economic integration can foster

11 I Kant, Perpetual Peace: A Philosophical Sketch in HS. Reiss (Ed.), *Kant: Political Writings* (H. B. Nisbet, Trans., 2nd ed. Cambridge University Press, 1991) 93–130

12 S Polachek, "Why Democracies Cooperate More and Fight Less: The Relationship Between International Trade and Cooperation" 5:3 Review of International Economics (1997/98)

13 P Martin, T Mayer, and M Thoenig, "Make Trade Not War" 75:3 The Review of Economic Studies 865–900 (2008)

peace. The deep economic ties between member states have been credited with helping to maintain peace in a region that had previously been torn apart by two world wars. Another example is the relationship between China and Taiwan. Despite political tensions, their strong economic ties have been seen as a stabilizing factor. Today, cutting off trade via trade sanctions in the form of embargoes is the preferred method for placing geopolitical pressure on non-allied countries. Under international law, these are seen as provisional measures before resorting to the use of force.[14] Russia and Iran to name but two countries are currently the target of trade restrictions by the West. While the effectiveness of these measures is debatable, it is much less costly in terms of lives lost than actual war.

1.5 International Law and World Trade

It is important to have a basic grasp of international law in order to appreciate the nuances of world trade law. International trade tends to be regulated domestically but supervised by international rules. To the extent that the principles upon which these laws rest are becoming standardized globally, we can now speak of world trade law and why a book such as this can exist. This body of law consists of measures, effectively meaning laws, both at the border (tariffs and quotas) and behind the border (all other regulations). The principles of world trade law are characterized by treaty-based rules and case law, primarily that which has been produced by the WTO dispute settlement system.

Importantly, the rules governing world trade are rooted in pragmatism. This includes diplomacy rooted in negotiation that itself is often linked to reciprocal concessions. The diplomatic nature of world trade law is partly the consequence of the need to adapt the regime to suit each country as well as each sector of economic activity. The Statute of the International Court of Justice specifies that treaties are one of the primary sources of international law.[15] This is the main variety of international law that will be explored in this book.

Treaties must be interpreted according to the Vienna Convention on the Law of Treaties (VCLT) which sets out that treaties should be interpreted "in good faith in accordance with the ordinary meaning to be given to the terms of the treaty in their context and in the light of its object and purpose."[16] The object and purpose can be discerned, in part, from the preamble of the treaty in question. Many trade treaties have preambles which make statements about improving economic conditions of signatory parties.

Customary international law, the other primary source of international law, operates at the same time as treaties, but in the background. Unlike treaties, customary international law is not based on written rules, but rather on the behaviour of states over time. It consists of rules that have emerged from the consistent practice of

14 Chapter 7 Charter of the United Nations
15 Article 38
16 Article 31(1)

states, accompanied by a sense of legal obligation. Customary international law is binding on all states, except for those that have persistently objected to a particular rule during its formation. The formation of customary international law requires two key elements: state practice and *opinio juris*. State practice refers to the general and consistent behaviour of states, which can be evidenced through various acts such as diplomatic correspondence, policy statements, national legislation, and judicial decisions. *Opinio juris*, on the other hand, is the belief that such practice is required by law, rather than mere courtesy or political expediency. Identifying customary international law can be a complex process, often requiring careful examination of state behaviour and expressions of legal conviction. International courts and tribunals, particularly the International Court of Justice, play a crucial role in recognizing and applying customary international law. Scholars and jurists also contribute to the identification and development of customary rules through their writings and analyses. One of the distinctive features of customary international law is its dynamic nature. Unlike treaties, which are static unless formally amended, customary rules can evolve over time as state practice and *opinio juris* change. This flexibility allows customary international law to adapt to new global challenges and emerging norms.

General principles of law are another primary source of international law. General principles of law are basic legal concepts and rules that are widely accepted across different legal systems around the world. These principles serve as essential tools for filling gaps in international law when treaties or customary rules do not provide clear guidance on a particular issue. While traditionally they were thought to derive primarily from domestic legal systems, there is growing recognition that general principles can also emerge within the international legal system itself. Identifying general principles of law typically involves a two-step process: first, ascertaining the existence of a principle common to various legal systems worldwide and second, determining whether that principle can be transposed to the international legal system. This process requires careful analysis of national legal systems, international jurisprudence, and scholarly writings to determine whether a principle has gained widespread recognition and acceptance. In the context of world trade law, general principles could include concepts such as good faith (being open and honest) and estoppel (not going back on your promise once someone has relied on it).

The two subsidiary sources of international law are judicial decisions and the teaching of publicists (otherwise known as academics). The most important juridical decisions in world trade law are those of the Appellate Body and panels of the WTO. There are a number of leading scholars in the field of world trade law and numerous well-respected topic-specific journals. In theory, all of these kinds of international law can establish rights and obligations in world trade law and can be challenged and enforced through dispute settlement procedures, again chiefly the WTO panels and Appellate Body.

As with any system of international law, world trade law can be accommodated into domestic legal systems in various ways. Some countries give international law direct effect in their courts, essentially meaning that it has the same legal validity as domestic legislation (an approach sometimes described as monism). Much more commonly, other countries require the enactment of separate legislation in order to give force to the international treaties to which the state has committed itself (sometimes described as dualism). For example, the United Kingdom Parliament enacted the European Union (Future Relationship) Act 2020 to ratify the Trade and Cooperation Agreement (the trade treaty between the United Kingdom and the European Union) which had been negotiated and signed months before. These different approaches can be problematic where international law comes into conflict with domestic law – a situation which can occur quite readily in the context of world trade given its reach and the range of trade barriers in existence. Generally speaking, most domestic courts will aim to construe domestic laws in a manner that is compatible with the state's international obligations wherever possible.[17]

1.5.1 The World Trade Organization (WTO)

The WTO was established on 1 January 1995 as a result of international negotiations under the multilateral GATT treaty, concluded during the Uruguay Round of trade negotiations. WTO-covered agreements and FTAs are therefore part of the larger body of international law. WTO law is sometimes described as a *lex specialis* a special body of law which applies to WTO members in relation to the subject of world trade. Many of the principles developed in WTO law have become the basis for laws found in FTAs and, in that sense, they have contributed to this special body of law. Indeed, this book is premised on the idea that there are well-established principles of world trade law, many of which have their origin in the laws of the WTO. Even as the WTO declines in relevance as the source of rights and obligations under world trade law, its residual influence is undeniable. Were the WTO to disappear tomorrow, the principles contained in its agreements and honed through its dispute settlement procedures would continue to shape world trade law for years to come.

The purposes of the WTO are outlined in the preamble to the agreement establishing the World Trade Organization, also known as the Marrakesh Agreement. These are: raising the standards of living of the world; ensuring full employment; ensuring a steady and growing volume of real income; expanding production of trade in goods and services; and finally optimal use of the world's resources. When evaluating the WTO for its effectiveness or applying criticisms for its alleged failures, it is therefore important to be mindful of these aims. The WTO should not be condemned for failing to do something which it was never designed to do. It is important to recognize that many of these objectives may also be found in the preamble of RTAs, demonstrating the wide-reaching acceptance of these types of goals as illustrative of principles of world trade law.

It is illuminating to consider each of the aforementioned aspects of the WTO's "mission" in turn. With respect to raising living standards of the world – this may be assessed by measures such as GDP, ideally on a global level. Other measures of living standards could include life expectancy and literacy levels. On most of these

17 For example, in the case of the United States, this is sometimes described as the 'Charming Betsy Doctrine': *Murray v Charming Betsy* 6 United States (Cranch), 118, 2 L Ed 208 (1804)

measures, the WTO has performed well in that world GDP, life expectancy, and literacy levels have all risen since the 1990s and even more so since the GATT in the 1940s. While global poverty has not disappeared entirely, it is not as pervasive as it has been in the past. Of course, the WTO's role here may be minimal. Full employment is a more variable measure, prone to fluctuations from year to year. It is also much more closely tied to policies implemented at the domestic level.

Still, the rise of emerging markets, especially in Asia over the last two decades suggests that more people are working than in the past. This indicator is tied to the next one – a steady and growing volume of real income. The expansion of the "middle class" in China and elsewhere in Asia suggests that more people earn enough money to buy not only the necessities of life but also things that at one point might have been viewed as luxuries.

The metric of expanding production in trade for goods and services is perhaps the one which is most closely tied to the main objectives of the WTO – eliminating barriers to international trade. Here the WTO has performed quite well, as the volume of trade has essentially increased steadily since 1995, with a slight downturn during the period of the financial recession in 2009–2010 and during the Covid-19 pandemic and its aftermath 2020–2022.

The final factor, optimal use of the world's resources, is often thought to cover environmental sustainability. This is difficult to measure and arguably drifts slightly outside the WTO's core mandate. While the WTO aims to address the need to safeguard the environment, it is by no means an environmental agency. Some of these issues will be explored later in Chapter 6 on non-trade values.

There are other goals which the WTO arguably seeks to attain. While it is not stated expressly, the promotion of fair competition is arguably one of the purposes of the WTO. As classic economics informs us, it is through the competition of suppliers for consumers that the highest quality goods (and services) are obtained at the lowest prices. Competition also spurs innovation – the development of new products which enrich our lives. There is an argument to be made that competition within free markets is strongly linked to democracy and freedom, although this may be more of a cause of fair competition than an effect of it. On that point, it is sometimes suggested that the WTO has encouraged domestic reforms in the sense of reducing bureaucracy and improving competition. Economic reform is certainly something which the WTO has fostered simply because many countries, notably China and Russia, were required to modify their economic system in order to be able to join the WTO, for example by curtailing corruption and by establishing robust protection for IP.

1.5.2 Governance and Structure of the WTO

The institutional elements of the WTO are not hugely important when it comes to understanding the principles that the organization has promulgated. Still, a basic outline is instructive. The WTO is a negotiating forum rather than an entity which has its own will. The WTO's actions are those of the expressed preferences of its members. It merely provides a setting in which members can interact with each other in a formal setting to reach a decision collectively on their own behalf. As discussed earlier, the modern institution was born out of the negotiations pursued under the GATT during the Uruguay Round, so named because of the location in which the negotiations began.

Most importantly, the WTO also comprises a set of rules. These are contained in the agreements which were negotiated by the organization's members, essentially the world's trading nations. In setting out these rules, the ultimate purpose of the WTO is to eliminate unnecessary barriers to trade, allowing goods and services to flow freely across international borders. In many cases, the obstacles to international trade will simply be a lack of transparency regarding trade-oriented laws. In other instances, there will be actual types of protectionism, the most common of which has historically been tariffs.

The WTO also incorporates judicial processes. It has a dispute settlement facility which renders binding rulings regarding the meaning of the various agreements. The purpose of this part of the WTO is to provide confidence that the rules of the international trading system do indeed carry obligations. The more predictable the system is the more likely there will be compliance and therefore greater flow of trade around the world. WTO disputes are something akin to "caselaw" of the common law in the sense that they give shape and substance to the WTO rules.

While the WTO was created by the Marrakesh Agreement, the substantive commitments are found in four separate annexes. Annex 1 consists of the Multilateral Trade Agreements, which are mandatory and binding on all members. These include the GATT, the GATS, and many of the other agreements which will be explored in this book. Annex 2 contains the procedural rules on dispute settlement. Annex 3 establishes the Trade Policy Review Mechanism through which the WTO monitors each member's trade policies as well as their compliance with WTO obligations on a regular basis. Annex 4 comprises the plurilateral (meaning optional) agreements.

The highest organ within the WTO is the Ministerial Conference, which must meet at least every two years. This body is composed of representatives of all WTO members and takes decisions on all matters relating to the multilateral trade agreements. Directly under the Ministerial Conference is the General Council. This body also consists of representatives of all WTO members and possesses overall supervisory authority, carrying out many of the functions of the Ministerial Conference between meetings. In practice, it meets at least monthly at the WTO's headquarters in Geneva, Switzerland. The General Council also acts as the Dispute Settlement Body, which meets at least monthly to adopt formally the judicial decisions of the panels and the Appellate Body. The General Council's third iteration is the Trade Policy Review Body, which as mentioned previously carries out monitoring and review of each member's trade policy on a regular basis to ensure compliance. The General Council further directs the activities of the three other councils – the Council for Trade in Goods, the Council for Trade in Services, and the Council for Trade-Related Aspects of Intellectual Property Rights. Finally, there is the WTO Secretariat which provides technical support to the members and has very limited power. [See **Figure 1.5** Organizational Chart of the WTO].

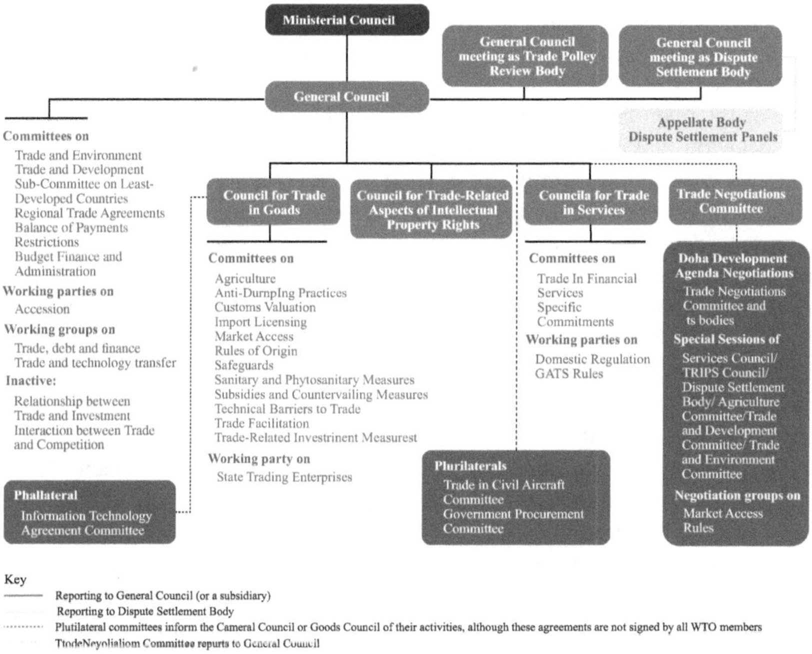

Figure 1.5 The World Trade Organization Organizational Structure

Source: The World Trade Organization (reproduced with permission)

1.5.3 WTO Membership

The WTO is a member-driven organization which implements a consensus approach to decision-making. This avoids problems associated with majority voting (which might be viewed as an affront to the sovereignty of a member) and weighted voting, which would give preference to larger countries, and which could also compel a member to act in a manner which is against its own wishes. The WTO's membership currently consists of 166 countries, covering all of the world's major economies and more than 99 per cent of all trade. Two-thirds of the WTO's membership are developing countries, including its newest member Timor-Leste. While each member has a vote, power is wielded by the largest countries – these are the United States, the European Union (which acts collectively on behalf of its member states), and China. Traditionally Canada, Japan, and Australia have also carried much weight in terms of the WTO's strategic direction. India has also often been viewed as the most influential of the developing countries.

Membership of the WTO requires acceptance of all of the WTO's agreements – it is not an à la carte menu. Still, newly joining members must go through the process of accession, which in some cases requires special treatment consisting of greater or lesser obligations than those of other members, often for a limited time period. These obligations are outlined in accession "protocols" which are legally binding documents which are often interpreted by WTO panels and the Appellate Body to clarify members' obligations towards the rest of the WTO.

One of the main problems faced by the WTO today is the requirement of consensus decision-making, which is increasingly difficult to achieve as WTO membership has grown significantly, far beyond the original signatories of GATT. The practical result of the rule of consensus is that there is a built-in veto – any member can prevent a decision from being operationalized by resisting. This makes it nearly impossible to effect changes at the WTO, including where reform is badly needed, for example in relation to dispute settlement. On the other hand, consensus is often depicted as one of the system's great strengths. If every member does not agree, then a change is not implemented. There have been discussions over the years about altering the consensus requirement, perhaps in favour of a super-majority or even a simple majority for decisions, but these have not been forthcoming. It is unlikely that the United States or China would surrender their capacity for veto over the world trading system, as these countries have the most at stake when changes work to undermine their economic dominance in negotiations.

The rules on WTO membership are found in the WTO Agreement itself. This reiterates some of the original GATT. Under GATT Article XXX it is established that Articles I and II of GATT (Most Favoured Nation and Tariff Commitments) and a handful of provisions of other WTO treaties cannot be amended without consent of all WTO members. The rest of GATT/WTO rules can be amended with consent of two-thirds of the membership. WTO Accession by a country is covered by Article XII of the WTO Agreement (XXXIII of GATT): accession will be permitted if two-thirds of members support it. For some new members, accession comes with additional or specialized obligations contained in what is known as "Accession Protocols." The Accession Protocol for China was particularly onerous, notably in relation to the use of trade remedies against China. Russia's Accession Protocol had phase-in periods for certain tariff and subsidy obligations. This is designed to cushion the shock of accepting full WTO obligations at once.

Regarding withdrawal from the WTO, GATT Article XXXI states that any country can withdraw from GATT/WTO six months after tendering written notice. Regarding expelling members from the WTO, there is no specific expulsion process. A two-thirds majority would be needed to create such a process and a three-fourths majority to remove the relevant member. The WTO typically reaches decisions by consensus among its members rather than through voting. This is one of the reasons that expelling Russia from the WTO, debated following its invasion of Ukraine in 2022, is unlikely to materialize.

1.6 Bilateralism

Virtually all of the trading countries of the world are bound by the rules of the WTO. But countries can adopt additional rules which apply only between them and other countries. Historically, bilateralism has a much older pedigree in trade relations than multilateralism, which only appeared in the second half of the 20th century. It may transpire that multilateralism was merely a brief period of internationally law and we are witnessing a return to its original bilateral origins.

1.6.1 Free Trade Agreements

Versions of preferential Free Trade Agreements (FTAs) can be found in the 18th century but became more common in the 20th century. There are currently approximately 350 in force. Almost 60 per cent of world trade in goods is covered by FTAs and every WTO member is a party to at least one FTA. FTAs are also treaties, and like those of the WTO, they are therefore objects of international law, to be interpreted by the VCLT.

Negotiations of FTAs have accelerated as multilateral negotiations have failed. There is a varying degree of "depth" in terms of coverage of FTAs. The modern trend is for comprehensive coverage, sometimes described as WTO-plus. Many additional issues include recognition of professional qualifications for services suppliers and for health and safety inspections of food and goods (often set out in their own Mutual Recognition Agreement (MRA)), digital trade, and material on state-owned and small- and medium-sized enterprises (SOEs and SMEs, respectively). While the negotiation and signing of FTAs is undoubtedly an important aspect of many countries' trade policy and economic strategy, it must be acknowledged that international trade does not require FTAs. Trade can and does still occur between countries that do not have an FTA in place, or even which are not members of the WTO. Like the WTO agreements, FTAs merely make such trade easier and less costly.

Some of the most significant bilateral trade agreements include the United States-Mexico-Canada Agreement (USMCA), which replaced NAFTA in 2020, and the EU-Japan Economic Partnership Agreement which entered into force in 2019. The USMCA modernized trade relations in North America, adding new provisions on digital trade, intellectual property, and labour standards. The EU-Japan agreement eliminated most tariffs and created the world's largest open trade zone.

On the regional level, the Comprehensive and Progressive Agreement for Trans-Pacific Partnership (CPTPP) stands out as a major plurilateral trade pact. Signed in 2018 by 11 Pacific Rim countries after the United States withdrew from the original Trans-Pacific Partnership (TPP), CPTPP substantially reduces tariffs and sets common standards in areas like labour and the environment. Another significant regional agreement is the African Continental Free Trade Area (AfCFTA), which aims to create a single market for goods and services across Africa.

The European Union represents the deepest form of regional economic integration, with its single market allowing for the free movement of goods, services, capital, and people among member states. The European Union has also pursued an ambitious agenda of bilateral trade agreements with partners worldwide. For their part, China has been actively pursuing bilateral and regional trade agreements as part of its economic diplomacy. It has signed bilateral free trade agreements with countries like Chile, Pakistan, and New Zealand, while also joining the Regional Comprehensive Economic Partnership (RCEP), a major Asia-Pacific trade pact.

These bilateral and regional agreements generally aim to be WTO-compliant and build upon WTO rules. They often go beyond WTO commitments in liberalizing trade and setting standards in areas not fully covered by WTO agreements, sometimes described as WTO-plus. However, the proliferation of these agreements has raised concerns about the fragmentation of global trade rules and potential discrimination against non-members.

The WTO allows for these preferential agreements under certain conditions through exceptions to its most-favoured-nation principle. Regional trade agreements must be notified to the WTO and are subject to certain transparency requirements. The WTO also provides a forum for discussing how these agreements interact with the multilateral system. In recent years, as multilateral negotiations at the WTO have stalled, many countries have turned to bilateral and regional agreements as a faster way to liberalize trade with key partners. However, there is ongoing debate about how to better integrate these agreements with the WTO framework to ensure a coherent global trading system. Some experts argue for greater harmonization of rules across agreements, while others call for multilateralizing regional innovations through the WTO.

1.6.2 Regionalism

Some of the preferential FTAs, like the CPTPP or the USMCA, have more than two parties and are associated with a particular region of the globe. Regionalism is therefore an expanded variety of bilateralism, falling short of multilateralism in its scope. There are some regional FTAs (or Regional Trade Agreements, RTAs) that have many parties and as such comprise, collectively, significant GDP. These arrangements are particularly important from the perspective of establishing principles of world trade law because of their breadth. The CPTPP is now an existing free trade treaty which is open for other countries to join, rather than to be negotiated from scratch, as in the case of a conventional bilateral free trade agreement. We therefore speak of "joining" or "acceding" to the CPTPP, much as a country would do with regard to the WTO.

Since the CPTPP is poised to grow in importance in the world economy, it is worthwhile to consider the rules governing its accession process, which is outlined in its Accession Process, an annexe to the CPTPP itself. The CPTPP is open to accession by any state or separate customs territory that is prepared to comply with its obligations, subject to terms and conditions agreed between the original signatories and the acceding state.

A country interested in joining submits a formal request to the depositary of the agreement, which is New Zealand. The CPTPP Commission, consisting of representatives from all member countries, establishes a working group to negotiate the terms and conditions for accession. The working group conducts negotiations with the aspiring member, which typically involve discussions on tariff schedules, service commitments, and compliance with CPTPP rules. Once negotiations are complete, the Commission decides by consensus whether to approve the terms of accession. If approved, the acceding country then needs to complete its domestic procedures for ratification. The country officially becomes a member 60 days after it deposits its instrument of accession with the depositary. The United Kingdom became the first country to join the CPTPP following this process.

One of the main controversies surrounding CPTPP accession is the potential membership of China. While China has formally applied to join, its state-led economic model and practices have raised concerns among some existing members about its ability to comply with CPTPP's high standards, particularly in areas such as state-owned enterprises, labour rights, and digital trade. The accession of new members to the CPTPP could have significant implications for global trade patterns and geopolitical dynamics. Expanding CPTPP membership could increase the agreement's economic impact and potentially influence the development of future trade rules. Managing the accession process while maintaining the CPTPP's high standards presents a challenge.

1.6.3 Trade Governance and Institutional Provisions in FTAs

FTAs commonly include provisions regarding cooperation and dialogue, often in conjunction with the creation of numerous committees covering various specialized topics. This mirrors the WTO's emphasis on transparency and negotiation. Such discussions are not limited to tariff reductions on goods but all kinds of trade issues, including services and digital, along with regulatory cooperation generally. Regular meetings constituted under these committees are often pivotal in the review or upgrading of these RTAs, in some cases by integrating the input of civil society and other stakeholders. For example, the Australia-India FTA includes a side letter which creates a Whisky Working Group to consider rules relating to market access for whisky and other alcoholic beverages. The group meets every six months. Since some countries form trade agreements with limited democratic scrutiny (in Parliament or Congress), such committees can be a way of injecting democratic accountability into trade policy.

The institutional provisions in FTAs, particularly those establishing committees and other administrative bodies, play a crucial role in the implementation and ongoing management of these agreements. These provisions are increasingly recognized as essential components of modern FTAs, going beyond mere tariff reductions to create mechanisms for ongoing cooperation and dispute resolution. The institutional provisions in FTAs further serve to enhance transparency, accountability, and stakeholder participation in trade governance. Committees established under FTAs can provide forums for regular dialogue between parties, allowing for the discussion of implementation issues and potential trade irritants before they escalate into formal disputes. Institutional provisions facilitate regulatory cooperation between FTA partners. Committees created under FTAs can serve as platforms for harmonizing standards and regulations, potentially reducing non-tariff barriers to trade over time. This aspect is particularly important in modern FTAs, which often deal with complex behind-the-border issues that cannot be addressed through tariff reductions alone.

These institutional mechanisms contribute to the "living" nature of FTAs, allowing FTAs to evolve and adapt to changing economic circumstances and emerging trade issues, rather than remaining static documents.[18] They further enhance the effectiveness of FTAs by creating mechanisms for monitoring implementation and compliance. Regular meetings of committees can help identify and address implementation challenges early, potentially preventing trade disputes.

1.7 Conclusion

International trade is one of the major means of wealth-enhancement today much as it was centuries, even millennia ago. By exchanging goods and services across borders, companies and the people they serve are able to access a range of products and experiences far beyond what they could at home and at much lower prices. The potential of international trade has contributed, not only to the reduction in poverty but also to the expansion of a middle class of people who are not merely surviving but thriving – enjoying more of what the world has to offer. Trade has also helped contribute to the maintenance of peace between nations – foreign countries are perceived more as markets to be served than lands to be conquered. While the oceans and mountains continue to make trading across countries and continents challenging, the legal barriers to trade, many of which will be explored in this book, can be managed and suppressed through thoughtful negotiation and compromise. Precisely how this has been achieved has been one of the triumphs of international law over the past hundred years.

This book will examine the major principles of international law that have contributed to the rise and continued success of international trade. As the most important source of these principles because of its history and its multilateral nature, the laws of the WTO will be front and centre, followed by developments observed at the regional and bilateral levels. Chapter 2 will introduce trade in goods, outlining the main features of GATT including tariff reduction and the elimination of quotas, both of which have been taken further in preferential FTAs. Chapter 3 will take this discussion further by focusing on the two non-discrimination standards in world trade law: National Treatment and Most Favoured Nation, designed to ensure equality of competitive conditions for goods. Chapter 4 explores dispute settlement in world trade law, specifically the dispute settlement system of the WTO, including its panels and now dysfunctional Appellate Body. This chapter will also touch on the arbitration systems found in FTAs. The contentious issue of trade remedies will be examined in Chapter 5. The associated rules on subsidies, dumping and safeguards developed at the WTO, have taken on a new dimension in the context of the rise of industrial policy.

The conflicts at the heart of world trade law will be confronted in Chapter 6 on non-trade values, such as the protection of the environment, human rights, and the maintenance of security. While again the laws of the WTO have been foundational in addressing these tensions, modern FTAs have gone much further. Chapter 7 will

18 B Hoekman and PC Mavroidis, "MFN Clubs and Scheduling Additional Commitments in the GATT: Learning from the GATS" 28:2 European Journal of International Law 387–407 (2017)

penetrate more deeply into one particular sphere of social policy which can operate as a barrier to trade – health and safety, both of which have received new attention in the era of a global pandemic. The vital area of services trade is the focus of Chapter 8. A facet of trade that has been weakly liberalized at the multilateral level, trade in services has been enhanced by wider and deeper commitments in FTAs, especially in relation to the recognition of qualifications. Chapter 9 evaluates the importance of intellectual property protections in facilitating world trade, again building upon the principles established by the WTO. Lastly, the emerging field of digital trade will be examined in Chapter 10. The liberalization of rules covering digital trade in goods and services, initially absent from the WTO framework, has been a major achievement of bilateral and regional arrangements with progress still unfolding.

Discussion Questions

1. Why do countries engage in international trade?
2. What is the role of international law in fostering world trade?
3. Is there a backlash against free trade? What has caused this and how can this be resolved? Should it be?
4. What is regionalism/bilateralism and is it a better way to conduct free trade?
5. Why is the WTO important? Will it remain so?

2 Trade in Goods

Quotas, Tariffs, Rules of Origin, and Trade Facilitation

2.1 Introduction

World trade began with the exchange of basic commodities like wood and spice. While commodities are still an important aspect of international trade, today's goods are complex, multi-component products like electric vehicles, solar panels, and cell phones assembled in multiple jurisdictions. It is now commonplace to speak of a "supply chain" in the context of trade in goods, referring to the interconnected network of organizations, people, activities, and resources involved in producing and delivering a product from suppliers to end consumers. Supply chains often span multiple countries, driven by cost efficiencies, specialization, market access, and advancements in technology. Global supply chains offer opportunities for economic growth, especially for developing countries, but they also present challenges such as vulnerability to disruptions and cumbersome procedures. Recent global events have prompted discussions on enhancing supply chain resilience through strategies like reshoring and diversification.

This chapter will examine these issues as they pertain to trade in goods by introducing the prohibition on quantitative restrictions (both import and export) found in the WTO's General Agreement on Tariffs and Trade (GATT) and most FTAs. It will explain tariffs and look at how these have been reduced, in some cases to zero in modern FTAs. Tariff Rate Quotas which set different tariff levels for certain quantities of imports, will also be explained. Trade facilitation, as found variously in the WTO Trade Facilitation Agreement and regional initiatives like the USMCA and the CPTPP will be discussed along with the foundational principle of transparency. This chapter will further consider, at a general level, how the principles governing trade in goods have responded to the needs of developing countries.

2.2 GATT Basic Principles

First drafted in the 1940s, GATT is the WTO's basic agreement covering trade in goods and remains the most important trade treaty in the world. GATT is mandatory for all 166 WTO members. It also encapsulates some of the central principles of world trade law which are reiterated in some of the other more specific WTO agreements, in some cases as expansions of more generic provisions of the GATT itself.

DOI: 10.4324/9781003465676-2

As discussed in the previous chapter, the GATT was originally a stand-alone agreement, and its signatories were referred to as Contracting Parties. These parties later became WTO members when the WTO was created in 1995. The GATT has been the source of the greatest number of disputes among the WTO's covered agreements and is the bedrock of the world's trading system of manufactured goods.

While recent years have witnessed the growth of bilateral and regional trade agreements, many of which are developing new principles in world trade law, it is difficult to overstate the importance of the GATT. Its contribution to lowering trade barriers may be regarded as one of the 20th century's great achievements in international law and diplomacy. Its articles contain the very foundations of world trade law that are echoed in the most cutting-edge trade treaties, even those that do not deal directly with goods. This chapter will now turn to the key principles of GATT which are the prohibition on quantitative restrictions (quotas), tariff reductions, and transparency. The equally important concept of non-discrimination will be discussed in the next chapter.

From the outset, it is important to establish that the main subject of GATT, namely quotas and tariffs, are "border" measures. This means that they are restrictions applied as a good enters (or leaves) a country. They are not imposed internally within a market once a good has entered the stream of commerce of that country. While quotas and tariffs have been successfully controlled, if not eliminated, by the WTO and FTAs over the years, many are still in place and remain harmful instruments of protectionism.

2.2.1 Prohibition on Quantitative Restrictions (GATT Article XI)

GATT begins by addressing one of the key barriers to a functioning international market for goods – supply. In other words, it deals with legal barriers that prevent the availability of foreign goods to consumers who wish to purchase them. Section 1 of GATT Article XI reads as follows:

> No prohibitions or restrictions other than duties, taxes or other charges, whether made effective through quotas, import or export licences or other measures, shall be instituted or maintained by any contracting party on the importation of any product of the territory of any other contracting party or on the exportation or sale for export of any product destined for the territory of any other contracting party.

The prohibition of quantitative restrictions on imports or exports is a fundamental principle of world trade law that is replicated in many if not all, FTAs. Under this provision of GATT, it is illegal to set a quota, meaning a numerically measurable limit in terms of value, quantity, weight, etc. on imported goods.

WTO regulations forbid quotas due to their severe economic impact, which exceeds that of other trade restrictions like tariffs. While tariffs are discouraged, they remain permissible. Quotas artificially limit product availability, causing price increases in line with supply and demand principles. This scarcity-induced price hike can lead to unfulfilled consumer needs, potentially impacting quality of life. The quota ban aims to preserve free market benefits, including the competitive advantages of improved quality and reduced prices. Although tariffs also increase prices, their effect is typically less dramatic than quotas. Additionally, tariffs provide governments with a source of income, unlike quotas.

WTO members are also prohibited under GATT Article XI from restricting the amount of goods exported into the international stream of commerce. This rule, which so far has had less relevance in terms of WTO disputes, accomplishes the same goal as the import quota prohibition via different means. By reducing the volume of a good which is available in foreign markets, its price abroad is artificially inflated. Article XI a) permits temporary quantitative restrictions applied to essential products to relieve critical shortages. There are additional exceptions to the import and export quota prohibition in order for members to fulfil their IMF obligations relating to the balance of payments. Quotas may also be permitted if they fall within the GATT's General Exceptions, which will be considered in Chapter 6. The complainant bears the initial burden of establishing a prima facie case that a measure violates Article XI:1. Once this is done, the burden shifts to the respondent to prove that the measure falls within one of the exceptions.

There have been several significant disputes regarding export quotas and restrictions. These cases have helped clarify the interpretation and application of Article XI of the GATT, which generally prohibits quantitative restrictions on imports and exports. Here are some of the key disputes.

In *Japan – Semi Conductors,*[1] the panel found that Japan's measures to restrict the export of semiconductors below a certain price constituted a violation of Article XI:1. The panel emphasized the broad scope of GATT's quota prohibition. It stated that it applies to all measures instituted or maintained by a contracting party prohibiting or restricting the importation, exportation, or sale for export of products other than measures that take the form of duties, taxes or other charges.

Two more recent cases dealing with China illustrate the breadth of the prohibition on quotas contained in GATT. In *China – Raw Materials,*[2] the WTO Appellate Body held that China's export quotas on certain raw materials were inconsistent with Article XI:1. The Appellate Body rejected China's attempt to justify these measures under Article XX(g) of the GATT, which allows for measures relating to the conservation of exhaustible natural resources, a topic which will be explored further in Chapter 6. Similarly, in *China – Rare Earths,*[3] concerning China's export restrictions on rare earth elements, the panel and Appellate Body found that China's export quotas on these materials violated Article XI:1. China's attempts to

1 Japan – Trade in Semi-Conductors, BISD 35S/116, adopted 4 May 1988

2 China – Measures Related to the Exportation of Various Raw Materials, Appellate Body Report, WT/DS394/AB/R, WT/DS395/AB/R, WT/DS398/AB/R, adopted 22 February 2012

3 China – Measures Related to the Exportation of Rare Earths, Tungsten, and Molybdenum, Appellate Body Report, WT/DS431/AB/R, WT/DS432/AB/R, WT/DS433/AB/R, adopted 29 August 2014.

justify these measures under Article XX were again rejected. Furthermore, the panel in *Indonesia – Raw Materials,*[4] found that Indonesia's export prohibition on nickel ore and domestic processing requirements were inconsistent with Article XI:1 of the GATT. The panel emphasized that the broad scope of Article XI:1 includes measures that limit export opportunities and create uncertainties in export opportunities.

In *India – Iron Ore Export Prohibitions*[5] Japan requested consultations with India regarding prohibitions on the export of iron ore. The European Union and Japan separately requested consultations with Russia regarding its export restrictions on wood products. These cases are still in the consultation phase at the time of writing.[6]

These cases indicate that the prohibition on quotas by GATT will be interpreted broadly to cover all forms of import and export restrictions other than duties, taxes, or other charges. The prohibition extends to both *de jure* (legally mandated) and *de facto* (effectively implemented but often harder to pinpoint) restrictions.

A number of countries have implemented import bans (zero quotas) for non-economic reasons. The United States implemented import quotas in relation to tuna[7] and shrimp[8] ostensibly due to concerns about the sustainability of other marine species (dolphins and turtles, respectively) arising from various types of commercial fishing. Brazil imposed an import restriction on recycled tyres out of concern that these tyres contributed to the spread of disease-carrying mosquitoes.[9] While these aims may have been laudable, the effect of these bans was that consumers were compelled to purchase local equivalents, creating a trade distortion. Some of these issues will be explored in the chapter on non-trade values.

2.2.2. Import/Export Restriction Cases Under FTAs

While the GATT/WTO disputes under Article XI are more widely known, there have been some import/export restriction disputes brought under the dispute settlement mechanisms of FTAs as well. In 2011, Costa Rica initiated a dispute against El Salvador regarding restrictions on imports of Costa Rican avocados under the Dominican Republic-Central America Free Trade Agreement (CAFTA-DR). Costa Rica claimed that El Salvador's phytosanitary measures (essentially food health,

4 Indonesia – Measures Concerning the Importation of Nickel Ore and Nickel Pig Iron, Panel Report, WT/DS577/R, circulated 30 August 2022.

5 India – Certain Measures Relating to the Exportation of Iron Ore, Panel Report, WT/DS471/R, adopted 7 January 2015

6 Russia – Measures Concerning the Exportation of Wood, Panel Reports, WT/DS462/R, WT/DS463/R, adopted 7 November 2018.

7 United States – Restrictions on Imports of Tuna, GATT Panel Report, DS21/R – 39S/155, adopted 3 September 1991

8 United States – Import Prohibition of Certain Shrimp and Shrimp Products, Appellate Body Report, WT/DS58/AB/R, adopted 6 November 1998.

9 Brazil – Measures Affecting Imports of Retreaded Tyres, WT/DS332/AB/R, adopted 17 December 2007

a topic which will be examined in Chapter 7) effectively banned avocado imports and were not based on scientific evidence, violating the agreement's provisions on sanitary and phytosanitary measures. This dispute was resolved through bilateral negotiations. Under the EU-South Korea Free Trade Agreement, there was a dispute in 2018 regarding Korea's restrictions on imports of EU pork products. The European Union argued that Korea's import ban, which was implemented due to African swine fever concerns, was disproportionate and not based on international standards. This issue was addressed through the agreement's dispute settlement mechanisms and bilateral discussions.

Export quotas are becoming an increasing element of many countries' economic and geopolitical strategies. This is especially true of "critical" minerals such as nickel, cobalt, and lithium which have important industrial applications. Securing supply chains for these minerals has become an objective of standalone agreements, such as the Japan-United States Critical Minerals Agreement, to specialized provisions in FTAs, such as the innovative Energy and Raw Materials chapter of the Chile-EU trade agreement. These new approaches to restricting supply in the face of fraught geopolitics reflect a shift in world trade law in relation to traditional understandings of the roles of states and markets.[10]

In 2015, Ukraine implemented a ten-year moratorium on the export of unprocessed timber, primarily affecting pine and valuable hardwoods. The European Union challenged this as a violation of the EU-Ukraine Association Agreement's prohibition on quantitative restrictions. The ban was intended to protect Ukraine's forests and boost its domestic wood processing industry. The dispute was handled through the bilateral dispute settlement mechanism provided in the EU-Ukraine Association Agreement. In this case, the European Union initiated the dispute settlement procedure in 2019, marking the first time the European Union had used this mechanism under a bilateral trade agreement.

The panel recognized Ukraine's right to regulate the management of its forest sector sustainably, including with an export ban, for certain wood species. Specifically, the panel allowed Ukraine to maintain its 2005 export ban for rare and valuable wood species. However, the panel ruled that Ukraine's 2015 export ban on pine and other wood species was incompatible with Ukraine's commitment to allow such exports under the EU-Ukraine Association Agreement. This ruling arguably demonstrated a more deferential approach to the respondent (Ukraine) compared to typical WTO panel decisions, illustrating greater consideration of sustainability and regulatory autonomy in trade disputes under bilateral agreements.

2.2.3 GATT Article II: Preservation of Tariff Commitments

Tariffs are a tax imposed on goods when they cross international borders and are sometimes referred to as customs duties or simply duties. Practically speaking,

10 See further L Cotula, "'Critical Minerals': International Economic Law in a Global Resource Rush" 15:2 Trade, Law and Development (Winter 2023–2024)

most tariffs are paid to the government by the importing party, in most cases the buyer of the foreign goods. Tariffs are a classic form of protectionism designed to protect domestic goods from foreign competitors by raising prices to consumers. Unfortunately, the cost of tariffs is often borne by the consumer in the form of higher prices, although in some cases importers internalize the cost of tariffs themselves by lowering their profit margins.

While developed countries nowadays rely less on tariffs for revenue, favouring income tax instead, many developing nations still depend heavily on tariff income. Revenue generated from tariffs is often depicted as a way of reducing a country's deficit for example. Tariffs have another advantage over quotas: they are more transparent. Consumers often struggle to notice quotas, which can lead to corruption. Tariffs, on the other hand, are easier to track and consumers clearly see them as an added cost. This visibility makes it more likely for governments to reduce tariffs over time.

Unlike quotas, however, tariffs are not illegal. The only commitment in the GATT is that members must honour the tariff commitments which they have made. The operative provision in the GATT states as follows:

> 1(b) The products described in Part I of the Schedule relating to any contracting party, which are the products of territories of other contracting parties, shall, on their importation into the territory to which the Schedule relates, and subject to the terms, conditions or qualifications set forth in that Schedule, be exempt from ordinary customs duties in excess of those set forth and provided therein. Such products shall also be exempt from all other duties or charges of any kind imposed on or in connection with the importation in excess of those imposed on the date of this Agreement or those directly and mandatorily required to be imposed thereafter by legislation in force in the importing territory on that date.

Departures from these negotiated tariffs (as negotiated through various WTO meetings) are illegal. Negotiated tariffs are called "bound" tariffs, which are set for each individual product in enormous schedules. Members are free to charge tariffs lower than the bound rate, indeed they often do. But they cannot go above this level. Tariffs are set out in each country's Schedule of Tariff Concessions.

The difference between bound and applied tariff rates has led to disputes under the GATT/WTO system. One notable example is *Argentina – Textiles and Apparel*[11] brought by the United States against Argentina in 1997. Here the United States challenged Argentina's specific duties on textiles, apparel, and footwear. The United States argued that these specific duties, in many instances, exceeded Argentina's bound rate of 35 per cent *ad valorem* (meaning by value). Argentina contended that as long as the applied rate did not exceed the bound rate there was

11 Argentina – Measures Affecting Imports of Footwear, Textiles, Apparel and Other Items, WT/DS56/AB/R, adopted 22 April 1998

no violation. The panel and Appellate Body disagreed with Argentina's interpretation. They found that Argentina's system of specific duties was inconsistent with Article II:1(b) of GATT 1994 because it resulted in the possibility of duties being applied in excess of the bound rate specified in Argentina's Schedule. This case is significant because it clarified that WTO members cannot impose a system of duties that creates the potential for exceeding bound rates, even if the applied rates are generally below the bound rates. The mere possibility of exceeding the bound rate was deemed sufficient to constitute a violation of GATT Article II:1(b).

As noted in the previous chapter, the GATT/WTO's success in lowering tariffs on manufactured goods throughout the latter half of the 20th century is astounding. Average tariffs dropped from more than 40 per cent in the 1940s to less than 4 per cent today, making a wide range of products more affordable for consumers around the world and opening up a planet of diverse goods to be enjoyed that were beyond the reach of previous generations. Tariff reduction is often done in stages, allowing parties to acclimatize to the increase in foreign competition. To be fair, the role that the GATT/WTO played in the reduction of tariffs throughout the last 80 years is debatable. As countries recognized the harmful effects of tariffs, many would have chosen to reduce them unilaterally, even without the sanction of international law.

Tariffs are still the most widely used form of protectionism, granting an artificial advantage to domestic over imported goods. Although they are clearly a cost to consumers, tariffs raise revenue for importing governments. They may therefore be viewed as an essential policy tool for countries which are unable to secure significant revenue from their citizens' income taxes. Developing countries in particular may rely on tariffs to raise revenue. This is why the WTO does not prohibit them but rather encourages members to reduce them where possible. In fact, the lowering of tariffs, typically on a reciprocal basis, between WTO members was at one point the primary diplomatic activity of international trade representatives of governments at the WTO.

While tariffs distort prices, leading to market inefficiencies on a global scale, they are thought to be less harmful than quotas. The product is still available, even if it is more expensive, which is not the case for a quota where supply is constricted. This is why the WTO instructs its members who feel the need to protect domestic industry from foreign competition in some sectors to convert their quotas into tariffs – a process called "tariffication." Most of the case law generated by Article II of GATT concerns the precise manner in which tariffs are levied by members with respect to certain products as well as customs classification methodology.[12] Differences in approaches to these issues may lead to disagreements regarding the tariff commitments which have been made.

The imposition of tariffs, while raising the price of goods for domestic consumers and therefore self-harmful, is thought to place pressure on other countries to modify their behaviour if they are believed to be engaging in unfair trade practices.

12 For example European Communities – Customs Classification of Certain Computer Equipment, WT/DS62/AB/R, WT/DS67/AB/R, WT/DS68/AB/R, adopted 22 June 1998

Tariffs are sometimes described as retaliation and can be authorized by the WTO Dispute Settlement Body in the event that a country fails to fulfil its WTO obligations, as determined by a WTO panel or Appellate Body (to be discussed further in Chapter 4). Generally, though, there is a lack of evidence that retaliatory tariffs actually effect change in the behaviour of other countries in terms of their own unlawful trade practices. The application of tariffs, or the threat to do so, has less leverage even when wielded by large economies such as the United States.[13]

2.2.4 Tariffs and FTAs

Many FTAs contain provisions similar to that of GATT Article II. For example, RCEP contains an equivalent provision, phrased in simplified language:

> Article 2.4: Reduction or Elimination of Customs Duties
>
> 1. Except as otherwise provided in this Agreement, each Party shall reduce or eliminate its customs duties on originating goods of other Parties in accordance with its Schedule in Annex I (Schedules of Tariff Commitments)

FTAs have significantly lowered tariffs between participating countries, often reducing them well below the rates bound under GATT. This is often one of the main purposes of FTAs. The extent of tariff reductions in FTAs varies widely depending on the specific agreement and the sectors involved. However, many FTAs aim for comprehensive tariff elimination on substantially all trade between partners.

NAFTA, replaced by USMCA, eliminated approximately 99 per cent of tariff lines between the United States, Canada, and Mexico. This agreement went well beyond the parties' WTO commitments, particularly in sensitive sectors like agriculture and automobiles. For instance, while Mexico's bound tariff rate for automobiles under the WTO is 35 per cent, NAFTA (and now USMCA) provides for duty-free treatment.

The European Union has many FTAs which reduce tariffs below that achieved by GATT. For example, the EU-South Korea FTA, which entered into force in 2011, abolished duties on nearly all trade in goods. For industrial goods, the European Union eliminated 98.7 per cent of duties within five years, while South Korea eliminated 98.1 per cent. For agricultural goods, the European Union eliminated 94.5 per cent of duties within five years, while South Korea eliminated 91 per cent. Many of these tariffs were significantly higher under WTO commitments. Although not yet ratified, the EU-Mercosur agreement aims to eliminate tariffs on 91 per cent of goods that EU companies export to Mercosur. This includes sectors where Mercosur countries have traditionally high tariffs, such as cars (35 per cent), car parts (14–18 per cent), and machinery (14–20 per cent).

13 E Boehm, "Biden's Top Trade Official Just Admitted Tariffs Haven't Changed China's Behavior" Reason (15 October 2024)

Japan has also made progress in lowering tariffs via its FTAs. Under the Japan-Australia Economic Partnership Agreement, Japan eliminated or reduced tariffs on many agricultural products that were previously highly protected. For example, the tariff on frozen beef was reduced from 38.5 per cent to 19.5 per cent over 18 years, with a significant upfront cut. Under WTO rules, Japan's bound tariff for beef remains at 38.5 per cent.

The CPTPP mega-regional abolishes 95–100 per cent of tariff lines among its members. To take just one example, Malaysia's average bound tariff rate under the WTO is 23 per cent, but under the CPTPP, it will eliminate tariffs on 85 per cent of tariff lines immediately upon entry into force, with most remaining tariffs phased out over time.

The extent of tariff reductions in FTAs often depends on the level of economic development of the participating countries and the sensitivity of specific sectors. Developed countries typically have lower bound tariffs under the WTO, so the margin for further reductions in FTAs may be smaller. However, even in these cases, FTAs often eliminate remaining tariffs entirely. For developing countries, the difference between WTO-bound rates and FTA preferential rates can be substantial. For instance, India's average bound tariff rate under the WTO is around 50 per cent, but in its FTA with Japan, it agreed to eliminate or reduce tariffs on 90 per cent of tariff lines over ten years.

While FTAs generally lower tariffs below WTO levels, they do not always eliminate them entirely or immediately. Many agreements include phase-out periods for sensitive products, and some products may be excluded from tariff elimination altogether. For example, in the EU-Japan Economic Partnership Agreement, the European Union will eliminate tariffs on 99 per cent of imports from Japan. Rice remains excluded, reflecting its sensitivity in Japanese agriculture.

The proliferation of FTAs and their deep tariff cuts have led to concerns about the erosion of the WTO's Most-Favoured-Nation (MFN) principle of equal treatment with regard to tariffs, which will be examined in depth in the next chapter. The impact of these preferential tariffs on global trade patterns has been significant. It has created complex supply chains that take advantage of the lower tariffs within FTA blocs. On the other hand, preferential rather than universal tariff levels have also led to concerns about trade diversion, where trade shifts from more efficient producers outside the FTA to less efficient producers within it, solely due to the tariff advantage.

Reaching agreement on lowering tariffs remains a daunting task during FTA negotiations. For example, one of the major obstacles to finalizing the United Kingdom-Canada FTA is Canada's notoriously protectionist dairy sector. Canada's dairy farmers continue to put pressure on their government to keep their supply-managed sector out of the United Kingdom FTA. The interim United Kingdom-Canada FTA kept imports of British cheese tariff-free for three years, resulting in annual export growth rates of around 15 per cent, but that arrangement expired last year. Tariffs on British cheese imposed by Canada are now 245 per cent – effectively making British cheese a luxury good.

There have been disputes under FTAs regarding tariff commitments. A notable dispute under NAFTA unfolded between Canada and the United States regarding softwood lumber tariffs. The United States imposed countervailing and anti-dumping duties on Canadian softwood lumber, arguing that Canada was unfairly subsidizing its lumber industry. Subsidies and dumping will be examined in Chapter 5. Canada challenged these tariffs through NAFTA's dispute settlement mechanism multiple times between 1994 and 2006. The dispute remains ongoing, with continued efforts to negotiate a new agreement and pending appeals of the current duties. The situation continues to have significant economic impacts on both Canadian producers and American consumers.

A tariff dispute arose between Costa Rica and El Salvador in 2013 under the CAFTA-Dominican Republic FTA. Costa Rica claimed that El Salvador was not applying the preferential tariff rates agreed upon in the FTA for Costa Rican products, particularly fruit juices and toilet paper. This dispute was addressed through bilateral consultations under the agreement's dispute settlement provisions. Under the United States-Korea Free Trade Agreement (KORUS FTA), there was a dispute regarding the interpretation of tariff commitments for certain auto parts. In 2018, the United States raised concerns that Korea was not properly implementing tariff reductions on United States auto parts as agreed in the FTA. Again, this issue was addressed through bilateral discussions and consultations under the agreement.

Although FTAs are designed to reduce or eliminate tariffs between member countries, disputes can still arise over the interpretation, implementation, or adherence to these commitments. The specific dispute resolution mechanisms provided in FTAs play a crucial role in addressing these issues outside of the WTO framework.

2.2.5 Tariff Rate Quotas (TRQs)

Building upon the aforementioned principles (quota elimination and tariff reduction) leads to a discussion of Tariff Rate Quotas (TRQs). TRQs are a trading arrangement wherein a lower-rate tariff is applied to a good up to a certain quantity ("in quota"); quantities above this amount bear a higher tariff ("out quota"). TRQs are not quotas because they do not restrict the quantity of imported goods. They are used to protect domestic production by restricting imports to levels that domestic industry can deal with competitively (preventing an influx of goods which would lower prices). TRQs are specifically tailored to address the level of competition that a particular good-producing industry can manage in the importing state. They tend to be more commonly used for agricultural products which are not covered by GATT. TRQs were introduced during the Uruguay Round of trade negotiations as a way to maintain some protection for sensitive agricultural products while improving market access.

In the context of the WTO, TRQs are primarily governed by Article XIII of GATT, which deals with the non-discriminatory administration of quantitative restrictions. Additionally, Article II of GATT 1994 allows for the scheduling of TRQs as part of a country's tariff commitments. The Uruguay Round Agreement on Agriculture (AoA), also a WTO agreement, elaborated on the use of TRQs in agriculture. Article 4.2 of the AoA prohibits members from maintaining, resorting to, or reverting to measures that were required to be converted into ordinary customs duties, except as otherwise provided for in Article 5 and Annex 5 of the agreement. TRQs were one of the mechanisms used to implement this tariffication process. The AoA will be considered in more detail in Chapter 5.

FTAs often include additional provisions on TRQs. The CPTPP specifies that parties must administer their TRQs in accordance with Article XIII of GATT (which mandates that any quotas must be applied in a non-discriminatory manner). The CPTPP goes on to add that its procedures for administering its TRQs are made available to the public, are fair and equitable, are no more administratively burdensome than absolutely necessary, and are "responsive to market conditions."[14] In FTAs, TRQs are often used as a transitional measure to gradually liberalize trade in sensitive products. For example, in USMCA, Article 3.A.2 of the agriculture chapter establishes TRQs for certain dairy products.

Despite their widespread use, TRQs have been the subject of several WTO disputes. The method of allocating quota rights can be contentious. In *EC – Poultry*,[15] Brazil successfully challenged aspects of the European Union's administration of its poultry TRQ which had led to misallocations. In *EC – Bananas III*,[16] the Appellate Body found that the European Communities' banana import regime, which included TRQs, violated GATT Article XIII by discriminating among supplying countries. Many TRQs are consistently under filled, leading to questions about whether they truly improve market access. This issue was addressed in part by the Bali Ministerial Decision on Tariff Rate Quota Administration.[17] Clearly, a multitude of different TRQ regimes can create a complex and opaque trading environment, particularly challenging for smaller exporters.

In 2021, the United States requested dispute settlement consultations with Canada under the USMCA regarding Canada's allocation of dairy TRQs. The United States argued that Canada's practices undermined its market access commitments. The panel ultimately ruled in favour of Canada, rejecting the United States arguments that Canada's market-share approach for determining TRQs prohibits retailers, food service operators, and other importers from securing lower tariff rates. The panel noted that the system skews toward Canadian processors but stated this reflects Canada's dairy market rather than a tactic to exclude other types of importers.

A TRQ controversy arose following the United Kingdom's departure from the European Union regarding how the existing EU TRQs would be divided between the United Kingdom and the rest of the EU member states after the United Kingdom's withdrawal. The United Kingdom and European Union agreed in 2017 to split the existing EU TRQs based on historical import data from 2013–2015. This approach was criticized by other WTO members. Major agricultural exporters

14 Article 2.28.1

15 European Communities – Measures Affecting the Importation of Certain Poultry Products, WT/DS69/AB/R, adopted 23 July 1998

16 European Communities – Regime for the Importation, Sale and Distribution of Bananas, WT/DS27/AB/R, adopted 25 September 1997

17 WT/MIN (13/39).

argued that the proposed split would reduce their market access and flexibility. They contended that the changes were more than a simple rectification of schedules and should be compensated with other concessions. The dispute led to delays in finalizing the United Kingdom's WTO schedules and complicated the Brexit process.

TRQs are believed to have a significant impact on global agricultural trade. While they were intended to improve market access, some argue that they have instead become a tool for managed trade, allowing countries to maintain high levels of protection for sensitive products.[18]

2.2.6 GATT Article X: Transparency

While it tends to receive less attention than quotas or tariffs, the GATT's treatment of transparency is in many respects equally important in terms of its role in ensuring free trade. Transparency is now well entrenched in many spheres of international and domestic law-making to the point that it could be viewed as an aspect of customary international law or at least a concept with growing normative force, especially in the context of global governance.[19] Lawyers rightly consider transparency as an essential component of a democratic society governed by the rule of law because it helps guard against the arbitrary imposition of laws.

An obligation of transparency can also be burdensome, especially to developing countries with limited resources. Under certain circumstances, transparency can be weaponized – raising costs of compliance to the point that the regulatory policy behind a measure may not justify the costs involved with implementing it. GATT's central requirement in relation to transparency is found in Article X:

1. Laws, regulations, judicial decisions and administrative rulings of general application, made effective by any contracting party, pertaining to the classification or the valuation of products for customs purposes, or to rates of duty, taxes or other charges, or to requirements, restrictions or prohibitions on imports or exports or on the transfer of payments therefor, or affecting their sale, distribution, transportation, insurance, warehousing inspection, exhibition, processing, mixing or other use, shall be published promptly in such a manner as to enable governments and traders to become acquainted with them. Agreements affecting international trade policy which are in force between the government or a governmental agency of any contracting party and the government or governmental agency of any other contracting party shall also be published. The provisions of this paragraph shall not require any contracting party to disclose confidential information which would impede law enforcement or otherwise be contrary to

18 DW Skully, "Economics of Tariff-Rate Quota Administration" Technical Bulletin No. 1893. Market and Trade Economics Division, Economic Research Service, United States Department of Agriculture, Washington, DC.

19 A Bianchi, "On Power and Illusion: The Concept of Transparency in International Law" in A Bianchi and A Peters (Eds.), *Transparency in International Law* (Cambridge University Press, 2013)

the public interest or would prejudice the legitimate commercial interests of particular enterprises, public or private.

2. No measure of general application taken by any contracting party effecting an advance in a rate of duty or other charge on imports under an established and uniform practice, or imposing a new or more burdensome requirement, restriction or prohibition on imports, or on the transfer of payments therefor, shall be enforced before such measure has been officially published.

The WTO has generally been quite strong in terms of embracing transparency, as seen most obviously on its website. Still, it is sometimes suggested that the WTO needs to improve its transparency. This is especially the case in terms of the WTO's internal transparency in terms of its communications among its members and its committees. The notification procedures required by many committees with respect to various measures implemented by members should be more robust. There is a need for better monitoring in terms of compliance of members with their WTO obligations. Members should be more readily able to submit comments with respect to other members' notifications, these should be reviewable by all members, as should replies. The reputational effects of this "public shaming" on the WTO website and elsewhere might work towards achieving greater compliance, for example with respect to subsidies and safeguards. Some of these issues will be explored in Chapter 5 on Trade Remedies.

The requirement that WTO members must publish all laws, regulations, and judicial decisions regarding international trade could be burdensome to countries at lower stages of development which lack the resources of some of the WTO's larger members. Importantly, though, Article X does not require the publication of any confidential information disclosure which would be contrary to public interests, which may cover matters such as national security, or which is commercially sensitive. Article XI further states that no laws may be enforceable unless they are published and that members must administer their laws in an impartial and reasonable manner with procedures in place for prompt review and correction.

Several WTO disputes have involved the transparency obligations contained in Article X of GATT. In *Dominican Republic – Import and Sale of Cigarettes*[20] Honduras challenged various measures imposed by the Dominican Republic on the importation and sale of cigarettes. The panel found that the Dominican Republic had acted inconsistently with Article X:1 by not publishing the surveys used to determine the tax base for cigarettes. The United States brought a complaint against the European Communities' administration of customs laws and regulations.[21] The panel found that the European Communities had violated Article X:3(a) of GATT by failing to administer its customs laws uniformly throughout its territory. Various countries including the United States and the European Union challenged China's

20 Dominican Republic – Measures Affecting the Importation and Internal Sale of Cigarettes, WT/DS302/AB/R

21 2. EC – Selected Customs Matters (DS315)

export restrictions on various raw materials. The panel found that China had acted inconsistently with Article X:1 by neglecting to publish certain measures relating to export quotas.[22] *Thailand – Cigarettes (Philippines)*[23] involved a complaint by the Philippines against Thailand's customs and fiscal measures on cigarettes imported from the Philippines. The panel found that Thailand had violated Article X:3(a) of GATT by not maintaining an adequate system for the review of customs valuation determinations. The European Union, United States, and Japan challenged Argentina's import requirements and procedures. The panel found that Argentina had acted inconsistently with its GATT obligations by failing to publish certain trade-related requirements promptly.[24]

These cases demonstrate the importance of transparency in international trade and the WTO's role in enforcing these obligations. The disputes often involve complex administrative procedures or unpublished regulations that create barriers to trade. The transparency obligations serve several important functions in the multilateral trading system. They help ensure that traders have access to information about the rules and regulations affecting their business, promote predictability in international trade, and facilitate compliance with WTO commitments. Moreover, transparency can help prevent disguised restrictions on trade and reduce the potential for corruption in customs administration.

These cases also highlight the challenges in implementing and enforcing transparency obligations. It is noteworthy that most of the disputes relating to transparency involve claims by developed countries against developing ones. Many WTO members, particularly developing countries, may face resource constraints in maintaining up-to-date publications of all trade-related measures. Additionally, the increasing complexity of modern trade regulations can make full transparency difficult to achieve.

2.2.7 GATT Article V: Freedom of Transit

In order for the benefits of free trade in goods to be realized, these goods must be able to pass through the territory of a country using the most convenient route when that passage is part of a complete journey beginning and ending beyond that country's borders. The freedom of transit principle in world trade law is reflected in Article V of GATT. This article establishes the fundamental principles for the transit of goods across territories of WTO members. Article V:1 of GATT defines "traffic in transit" as the passage of goods across the territory of a WTO member, with or without trans-shipment, warehousing, breaking bulk, or change in the mode of transport, when such passage is only a portion of a complete journey beginning

22 China – Measures Related to the Exportation of Various Raw Materials, WT/DS394/AB/R, WT/DS395/AB/R, WT/DS398/AB/R, adopted 22 February 2012

23 Thailand – Customs and Fiscal Measures on Cigarettes from the Philippines, WT/DS371/AB/R, adopted 15 July 2011

24 Argentina – Measures Affecting the Importation of Goods, WT/DS438/AB/R, WT/DS444/AB/R, WT/DS445/AB/R, adopted 26 January 2015

and terminating beyond the frontier of the member across whose territory the traffic passes. Article V goes on to read:

2. There shall be freedom of transit through the territory of each contracting party, via the routes most convenient for international transit, for traffic in transit to or from the territory of other contracting parties.
3. Such traffic coming from or going to the territory of other contracting parties shall not be subject to any unnecessary delays or restrictions and shall be exempt from customs duties and from all transit duties or other charges imposed in respect of transit, except charges for transportation or those commensurate with administrative expenses entailed by transit or with the cost of services rendered.

Article V:4 of GATT adds that such charges shall be reasonable. This treatment is required on a Most Favoured Nation (non-discriminatory) basis with regard to the country of origin, a topic to be evaluated in the next chapter. Transit provisions are often replicated in FTAs, particularly those involving landlocked countries, in some cases by direct reference to GATT Article V.[25]

Controversies have arisen regarding the interpretation and application of Article V. One significant dispute that highlighted these issues was *Russia – Traffic in Transit*.[26] In this dispute, Ukraine challenged various measures imposed by Russia that allegedly restricted the transit of Ukrainian goods through Russian territory to third countries. The case raised important questions about the scope of Article V and its relationship with security exceptions under Article XXI, which will be dealt with separately in Chapter 6. The panel affirmed that the obligation of freedom of transit applies to all traffic in transit, regardless of the means of transport. It interpreted "freedom of transit" to mean that traffic in transit should be allowed to pass through the territory of a WTO member unimpeded.

Another controversy related to freedom of transit concerns landlocked countries. These nations are particularly vulnerable to transit restrictions imposed by their coastal neighbours. The United Nations Convention on the Law of the Sea (UNCLOS) complements GATT Article V by providing for the right of access of landlocked states to and from the sea and freedom of transit.[27] However, the practical implementation of these rights remains challenging. Additionally, the WTO Trade Facilitation Agreement (TFA), which entered into force in 2017 and will be dealt with further below, elaborates on and strengthens the provisions of GATT Article V. Article 11 of the TFA provides more detailed rules on freedom of transit, including provisions on fees and charges, formalities and documentation requirements, and customs cooperation.

25 For example, RCEP Article 2.9
26 Russia – Measures Concerning Traffic in Transit, WT/DS512/R, adopted 26 April 2019
27 NM Amerasinghe, "Freedom of Transit and the Right of Access of Land-Locked States: The Evolution of Principle and Law" 52:1 Ocean Development & International Law 1–19 (2021)

2.2.8 Customs Valuation and Rules of Origin

A system of valuation is needed to assess the magnitude of a tariff imposed on an imported good per unit, per value or by weight. GATT helped standardize this process around the world. Article VII of GATT states that the value for customs purposes of imported goods should be based on the actual value of the imported good on which duty is assessed and should not be based on the value of goods of national origin or on arbitrary values. This is the "actual price" on the invoice for the goods.

GATT itself does not contain any specific rules of origin, which are the criteria needed to determine the national source of a product. GATT Article IX merely states that parties must not discriminate when assessing marks of origin. ROOs (Rules of Origin) are most commonly used to assess whether goods deserve preferential treatment under an FTA (or GATT treatment in the case of products which may have components originating from a country outside the WTO's membership). ROOs are also relevant for the application of trade remedies (e.g., anti-dumping or countervailing duties), to be discussed in Chapter 5.

The WTO Rules of Origin (ROO) Agreement, which came into force in 1995, sets out the basic principles and guidelines for non-preferential rules of origin among WTO members. The first of these is transparency. Article 5.1 requires WTO members to provide their non-preferential (meaning applicable to all WTO members) rules of origin to the WTO Secretariat within 90 days of the agreement coming into force for them. Next, the ROO Agreement states that WTO members should not discriminate between WTO members.[28] There is also a predictability requirement – should be administered in a consistent, uniform, impartial, and reasonable manner.[29] Disagreements arising under the ROO Agreement may be resolved through the WTO dispute settlement system.

Importantly, the WTO ROO Agreement covers only non-preferential rules of origin. These are the rules used for the general rule against non-discrimination as to origin (Most Favoured Nation, which will be explored in the next chapter), as well as tariffs imposed on the basis of trade remedies rules, (meaning anti-dumping and countervailing duties, safeguard measures, to be discussed in Chapter 5). Preferential rules of origin, used in preferential FTAs, are not covered by this agreement, although some general principles apply to them as well, contained in Annex II of the agreement.

One of the main objectives of the WTO ROO Agreement is to harmonize non-preferential rules of origin globally. Article 9 of the agreement established a Harmonization Work Programme (HWP) to develop common rules of origin for all WTO members. Unfortunately, this process has been ongoing since 1995 and has faced significant challenges and delays. Harmonization will reappear as a key principle of world trade law throughout this book.

The proliferation of preferential FTAs granting better treatment than is available under the WTO umbrella has led to a complex web of different ROOs, often

28 Article 2(d)
29 Article 2(h)

referred to as the "spaghetti bowl" effect which calls to mind the image of a mess of tangled noodles. The types of criteria used to determine origin across various FTAs include a change in tariff heading, the addition of value or the specific manufacturing process. For example, under the European Union's non-preferential ROOs, the manufacturing process which turns fabric into hats will result in a change in the customs classification heading of the product. This means that the hat will be classified as originating in the country in which its manufacture occurred, rather than taking into account the country of origin of the fabric. In another example, applying the value-added test, the EU-South Korea FTA states that unless a good has been "wholly obtained" (e.g., a fruit has been grown) in South Korea, exporters to the European Union have to prove that the good has been "sufficiently processed" in South Korea to benefit from the preferential rates. This test typically varies according to the type of product being exported.

Turning to the mega-regionals, the USMCA contains some of the most stringent ROO provisions, particularly for the automotive sector. For automobiles, Article 4.1 stipulates that the regional value content (RVC) must be 75 per cent for passenger vehicles and light trucks, a significant increase from NAFTA's 62.5 per cent requirement. Additionally, Article 4.3 introduces a new labour value content (LVC) rule, requiring that 40–45 per cent of auto content be made by workers earning at least United States $16 per hour. CPTPP's ROO provisions are generally more flexible than those in the USMCA. Article 3.2 of the CPTPP outlines the general ROO criteria, which include wholly obtained or produced goods, substantial transformation rules, and RVC requirements. For automobiles, the CPTPP sets a lower RVC threshold compared to the USMCA. Article 3.9 specifies that the RVC for vehicles must be 45–55 per cent, depending on the calculation method used. This is significantly lower than the USMCA's 75 per cent requirement. The CPTPP also introduces more flexible cumulation rules. Article 3.10 allows for "full accumulation," meaning that all production activities undertaken in the CPTPP region can be counted towards meeting the ROO requirements, even if the materials used do not meet the ROO criteria on their own. RCEP's ROO provisions are the most flexible of the three agreements. Article 3.2 of RCEP sets out the general ROO criteria, which include wholly obtained or produced goods, substantial transformation rules, and RVC requirements. One of the key features of RCEP's ROOs is its single rule for the entire bloc. RCEP countries will only require a single certificate of origin. This will allow companies to easily ship products between RCEP countries without needing to satisfy specific rules of origin criteria in each country or for each manufacturing step. RCEP sets a generally lower RVC threshold compared to both the USMCA and CPTPP. For many products, RCEP requires a regional value content of 40 per cent, which is lower than the requirements in the other two agreements. RCEP also introduces more flexible cumulation rules. Article 3.4 allows for regional cumulation, meaning that materials originating in any RCEP country can be used in the production of a good in another RCEP country and counted as originating content.

The USMCA's stricter rules aim to boost North American production and protect domestic industries, particularly in the automotive sector whereas the CPTPP's rules strike a balance between promoting regional integration and maintaining some level of protection for domestic industries. In contrast, RCEP's more flexible rules prioritize facilitating trade within the diverse Asian economic landscape and promoting regional supply chains.

Completing the assessments necessary to achieve preferential treatment under FTAs increases compliance costs for businesses and creates trade distortions – indeed this is one of the principal objections to bilateralism as opposed to multilateralism.[30] The compliance costs associated with identifying and complying with ROO in order to benefit from preferential treatment is sometimes thought to exceed the benefits of the lower tariffs, especially if the preferential treatment is minimal relative to the WTO average. Such traders may not even bother seeking preferential treatment available under an FTA, trading instead on WTO terms. Restrictive ROOs in FTAs have been shown to reduce trade flows by increasing input costs, reducing the welfare gains from trade liberalization.[31]

2.3 Trade Facilitation

The elimination of quotas and the reduction of tariffs are vital principles for the achievement of free trade. Yet even where these are implemented, one of the key remaining barriers to trade concerns the actual procedures which take place at borders which can slow down the movement of goods.

Trade facilitation refers to these practical elements of goods crossing international borders, contemplating the simplification, standardization and harmonization of procedures, and associated information flows required to move goods from seller to buyer and to make payment. These costs can be especially high in developing countries, notably in Africa with its many borders and landlocked countries. Some studies showed that these trade costs can equate to over 100 per cent *ad valorem* tariff in high-income countries and, shockingly, over 200 per cent for developing countries.[32] It is hard to imagine paying three times as much for a product simply because of bureaucracy and paperwork.

2.3.1 The WTO Trade Facilitation Agreement (TFA)

GATT Article XVII touches on trade facilitation by providing that charges or fees in relation to processing goods for importation or exportation must represent the approximate costs of these services and that these fees should be minimized. But, it was the WTO Trade Facilitation Agreement which addressed these issues comprehensively. The Trade Facilitation Agreement contains rules on trade facilitation which are of particular importance to developing countries. It is a landmark

30 For example, J Bhagwati, *Termites in the Trading System* (Oxford University Press, 2008)

31 P Conconi, M García-Santana, L Puccio, and R Venturini, "From Final Goods to Inputs: The Protectionist Effect of Rules of Origin" 108:8 American Economic Review 2335 (2018)

32 T D'Allonnes, "The Trade Facilitation Agreement: A World of Opportunities for MSMEs" United States Agency for International Development (USAID) (2021)

multilateral agreement aimed at simplifying and streamlining international trade procedures. The Trade Facilitation Agreement (TFA) entered into force in February 2017, after two-thirds of WTO members completed their domestic ratification process. It is one of the last significant multilateral success stories of the WTO. It was often cited as evidence that the WTO still "has life in it." The TFA is widely regarded as a significant achievement in global trade governance. Full implementation of the agreement could reduce trade costs by an average of more than 14 per cent and boost global trade by up to United States $1 trillion per year, with the biggest gains in the poorest countries.[33]

The TFA contains provisions for expediting the movement, release, and clearance of goods, including goods in transit. It clarifies and improves the relevant articles (V, VIII, and X) of GATT and sets out provisions for customs cooperation. Key provisions in the TFA include transparency, requiring the publication and availability of information (Article 1); appeal or review procedures to challenge rules (Article 4); various other measures to enhance impartiality, non-discrimination, and transparency (Article 5); disciplines on fees and charges imposed on or in connection with importation and exportation (Article 6); rules on simplifying the release and clearance of goods (Article 7); material on border agency cooperation (Article 8); rules on streamlining the movement of goods intended for import under customs control (Article 9); requirements for minimizing formalities connected with importation, exportation, and transit (Article 10); a reiteration of the principle of freedom of transit (Article 11) and provisions on customs cooperation (Article 12).

While the TFA represents a significant step forward in trade facilitation, its implementation may be challenging for many developing countries due to capacity constraints. Section II of the TFA contains "special and differential treatment" (SDT) provisions that allow developing and least-developed countries to determine when they will implement individual provisions of the agreement and to identify provisions that they will only be able to implement upon the receipt of technical assistance and support for capacity building. This recognizes the reality that given human and financial resource limitations it may not be possible for all WTO members to fully comply with their obligations under the agreement straight away. This topic will be explored further below. Section III of the TFA establishes a permanent committee on trade facilitation at the WTO and requires members to have a national committee to facilitate domestic coordination and implementation of the provisions of the agreement. The effectiveness of SDT provisions depends largely on the availability and quality of technical assistance and capacity-building support provided to developing countries.[34]

33 World Trade Organization, World Trade Report 2015: Speeding Up Trade: Benefits and Challenges of Implementing the WTO Trade Facilitation Agreement (WTO, 2015).

34 B Hoekman, "The Bali Trade Facilitation Agreement and Rulemaking in the WTO: Milestone, Mistake or Mirage?" in J Bhagwati, P Krishna, and A Panagariya (Eds.), *The World Trade System: Trends and Challenges* (MIT Press, 2016)

Some critics have argued that the TFA may limit the ability of developing countries to implement trade policies that they consider necessary for their development strategies. The agreement could therefore reinforce existing power imbalances in the global trading system, potentially benefiting developed countries more than developing ones.[35] There are also concerns about the potential environmental impacts of increased trade facilitation. While the TFA aims to reduce trade costs and increase efficiency, some environmentalists worry that this could lead to increased consumption and transportation, potentially exacerbating environmental problems. More efficient trade procedures could actually reduce environmental impacts by minimizing delays and unnecessary transportation.

Despite these controversies, the TFA represents a significant step towards reducing trade barriers and improving the efficiency of global trade. Its implementation is expected to bring substantial benefits, particularly to small- and medium-sized enterprises (SMSEs) in developing countries. Realizing these benefits will require ongoing commitment from WTO members, as well as substantial technical assistance and capacity-building efforts.

2.3.2 Trade Facilitation in FTAs

Trade facilitation provisions designed to address the practical, bureaucratic impediments to goods crossing borders, can also be found in preferential FTAs. Looking again at the mega-regionals USMCA, RCEP, and CPTPP all contain provisions aimed at facilitating trade among their party countries. These agreements build upon and, in some cases, go beyond the commitments made in the WTO Trade Facilitation Agreement.

The USMCA's trade facilitation provisions are primarily contained in Chapter 7. The "Single Window System" of Article 7.10 requires each party to maintain a single window system, meaning one agency, for the electronic submission of documentation for imports, exports, and transit. The Advance Rulings of Article 7.5 mandates that parties issue advance rulings, meaning before the good actually arrives at the border, on tariff classification, customs valuation, and origin of goods. Article 7.8 on Express Shipments requires expedited customs procedures for express shipments, including release within six hours of submission of customs documents. The Release of Goods provision contained in Article 7.2 stipulates that each party shall adopt or maintain procedures allowing for the release of goods, meaning that they can carry on to their destination, prior to the final determination of customs duties, taxes, and fees. These provisions generally go beyond the TFA requirements. For instance, the USMCA's six-hour release time for express shipments is more specific and stringent than the TFA's general call for expedited release of such shipments.

RCEP's trade facilitation measures are outlined in Chapter 4. Notable provisions include the Release of Goods, found in Article 4.11 which requires parties to

35 R Wilkinson, E Hannah, and J Scott, "The WTO in Bali: What MC9 Means for the Doha Development Agenda and Why It Matters" 35:6 Third World Quarterly 1032 (2014)

adopt or maintain procedures for the prompt release of goods, including pre-arrival processing. Advance Rulings contained in Article 4.10 mandate that parties provide advance rulings on tariff classification and origin of goods. Article 4.13 encourages parties to maintain or establish a single window system for customs procedures and Article 4.15 on expedited customs procedures for express consignments. While RCEP's provisions are generally aligned with the TFA, they are often less prescriptive. For example, RCEP encourages rather than requires the establishment of single window systems, unlike the USMCA's mandatory approach.

CPTPP's trade facilitation measures are found in Chapter 5. Key elements include several of those previously noted such as Article 5.3 requires parties to provide advance rulings on tariff classification, customs valuation, and origin of goods; Article 5.7 on expedited customs procedures for express shipments, including release within six hours where possible; Article 5.2 which requires parties to adopt or maintain procedures allowing for the release of goods prior to final determination of customs duties, taxes, and fees; and the Single Window of Article 5.6 that encourages parties to establish or maintain a single window system. The CPTPP's provisions are generally more detailed than those in the TFA and often go beyond its requirements. For instance, the CPTPP's six-hour target for the release of express shipments is more specific than the TFA's general requirement for expedited release.

At a general level, these mega-regional agreements sometimes cover areas not addressed in the WTO's TFA. For instance, the USMCA includes provisions on the use of information technology (Article 7.12) that are more detailed than those in the WTO Agreement. While the TFA often uses language like "shall endeavour to," the regional agreements more frequently use mandatory language like "shall." Unlike the WTO TFA, which provides for different implementation schedules based on countries' development levels based on the principle of "special and differential treatment," the mega-regional agreements generally require implementation upon entry into force. In some areas, the regional agreements coverage of trade facilitation rules is less prescriptive than that of the WTO. For example, RCEP's approach to single window systems is more flexible than the WTO requirement.

Something should be said of AfCFTA's approach to trade facilitation since issues of border delays have been most acute in Africa. The AfCFTA Protocol on Trade in Goods includes specific provisions on trade facilitation some of which align and build upon the WTO TFA. The AfCFTA implementation will require significant coordination among public and private stakeholders at both national and regional levels reflecting a comprehensive approach to trade facilitation that goes beyond just customs procedures. Part of this is the establishment of National Trade Facilitation Committees (NTFCs) which are expected to play a role in implementing AfCFTA's trade facilitation provisions. Given that AfCFTA aims to create a single market for intra-regional trade, its trade facilitation provisions have a stronger emphasis on harmonizing procedures across African countries. Moreover, as AfCFTA builds upon existing regional integration efforts, its trade facilitation provisions include mechanisms for coordinating with regional initiatives.

Some trade facilitation measures under FTAs can be discriminatory, similar to preferential tariff elimination. This suggests that there is potential for disputes related to trade facilitation in FTAs. Generally, FTAs have been shifting towards being more reciprocal, deeper, broader, and more enforceable. This evolution might increase the likelihood of disputes under dispute mechanisms in FTAs, including those related to trade facilitation.

2.4 Assistance for Developing Countries

Approximately three-quarters of the world's 195 countries, home to more than 85 per cent of the world's population, fall within the category of "developing," characterized by a low GDP per capita (usually something less than US $10,000 income per year) as well as lower life expectancies and levels of literacy and education. Since trade has been shown to be one of the most transformative forces in terms of improving material standards of living, addressing the trade needs of developing countries has been, or at least should be, a fundamental principle of world trade law.

2.4.1 The WTO and Developing Countries

As noted in the previous chapter, two-thirds of WTO membership consists of developing countries. Their concerns should therefore be at the forefront of the WTO's agenda, although this is by no means always the case.[36] GATT contains provisions on special treatment for developing countries known as "special and differential treatment." GATT Article XVIII sets out an objective of assistance for developing countries even where this may transgress some GATT obligations, granting flexibility in tariffs and in the capacity for developing countries to impose quotas. Additionally, Part IV of GATT includes provisions on non-reciprocal preferential treatment for developing countries – when developed countries grant trade concessions to developing ones, they should not expect the developing countries to make matching offers in return. It should be noted that this is not mandatory. The Agreement on Agriculture allows developing countries more flexibility in providing domestic support to farmers. Additionally, the WTO has established the Committee on Trade and Development to focus on issues affecting developing nations.

Perhaps most significantly, the "Enabling Clause" (an addition to GATT) enables developed country WTO members to give more favourable treatment to products originating in developing countries even though this is discriminatory. The Enabling Clause,[37] adopted in 1979, permits developed countries to provide tariff preferences to developing countries without extending the same treatment to other WTO members. It also allows developing countries to enter into regional or global

36 See S Rolland, *Development at the WTO* (Oxford University Press, 2012)

37 GATT Contracting Parties, Decision of 28 November 1979 on Differential and More Favourable Treatment, Reciprocity and Fuller Participation of Developing Countries, L/4903, BISD 26S/203 (1980)

trade arrangements among themselves. The Enabling Clause further provides for special treatment of the least developed among developing countries in the context of any general or specific measures in favour of developing countries. It recognizes that developing countries may not be expected to make contributions inconsistent with their individual development, financial, and trade needs. The Enabling Clause is significant because it provides a legal basis for the Generalized System of Preferences (GSP) and other non-reciprocal preferential schemes that benefit developing countries in the global trading system.

There have been several WTO disputes involving provisions designed to assist developing countries, including the Enabling Clause and GATT Article XVIII. *India – Restrictions on Imports of Agricultural, Textile and Industrial Products*[38] brought by the United States against India in 1997, involved India's use of quantitative restrictions justified under GATT Article XVIII:B. The panel and Appellate Body found that India's balance-of-payments difficulties did not justify the continued use of these restrictions. This case clarified the interpretation of Article XVIII:B and the conditions under which developing countries can use quantitative restrictions for balance-of-payments purposes.

Another dispute, *EC – Conditions for the Granting of Tariff Preferences to Developing Countries*[39] brought by India against the European Communities in 2002, involved the examination of the Enabling Clause and its relationship with GATT Article I:1 (Most Favoured Nation treatment, to be examined in the next chapter). The Appellate Body ruled that the Enabling Clause is an "exception" to Article I:1 and that preferential tariff schemes must be "non-discriminatory" among similarly situated beneficiaries. This case provided important clarification on the scope and application of the Enabling Clause.

While not directly involving the Enabling Clause or Article XVIII, *Brazil – Retreaded Tyres,*[40] brought by the European Communities against Brazil in 2005, touched upon issues relevant to developing countries. The Appellate Body's ruling discussed the balance between trade liberalization and other societal values, including those particularly relevant to developing countries, such as public health and environmental protection.

It is often claimed that the WTO has not made sufficient effort to address the concerns of developing countries and in so doing has not enabled their integration into the world trading system. Critics argue that the various provisions previously discussed have been inadequate in practice.[41] Yet the WTO itself provides technical assistance and capacity-building programs to help developing countries participate more effectively in global trade. This includes the Aid for Trade initiative,

38 India – Quantitative Restrictions on Imports of Agricultural, Textile and Industrial Products, WT/DS90/AB/R, adopted 22 September 1999

39 European Communities – Conditions for the Granting of Tariff Preferences to Developing Countries, WT/DS246/AB/R, adopted 20 April 2004

40 Brazil – Measures Affecting Imports of Retreaded Tyres, WT/DS332/AB/R, adopted 17 December 2007

41 S Rolland, n 36

which aims to help developing countries build trade-related skills and infrastructure. Donor countries have committed an average of US $40 billion annually to trade-related development programs. Still, many developing countries still struggle to fully engage in WTO processes and negotiations due to limited resources and expertise. Developing countries often lack the capacity to effectively utilize WTO dispute settlement mechanisms, putting them at a disadvantage in trade conflicts. Agricultural subsidies in developed countries, which the WTO has struggled to reduce effectively, continue to disadvantage farmers in developing nations. The persistence of high tariffs on processed goods also hinders developing countries' efforts to move up the value chain. There tend to be higher tariffs on processed goods compared to raw materials, meaning that developing countries export their goods virtually tariff-free but pay tariffs on that which they must import. This differential remains a significant obstacle for developing countries seeking to diversify their economies. The costs of implementing the TRIPS Agreement, to be explored further in Chapter 9, have been substantial for many developing countries, often outweighing the perceived benefits.

While the WTO has made efforts to support developing countries through special provisions, technical assistance, and market access initiatives, the outcomes have been mixed. Many developing nations continue to face significant challenges in fully benefiting from the global trading system. Critics argue that more fundamental reforms are needed to address the power imbalances and structural inequities within the WTO system to truly serve the interests of developing countries.

2.4.2 Developing Countries and FTAs

FTAs have become an increasingly popular tool for addressing the trade needs of developing countries, sometimes collectively described as the "Global South." These agreements, typically negotiated between developed and developing nations or among developing countries themselves, aim to provide enhanced market access and foster economic growth. One of the primary benefits of preferential FTAs for developing countries has been improved access to key export markets. As noted earlier, many agreements have resulted in the reduction or elimination of tariffs on goods of particular importance to developing economies, such as agricultural products and textiles.

Furthermore, some FTAs have incorporated provisions specifically designed to address the unique challenges faced by developing countries. These may include longer implementation periods for certain commitments, technical assistance and capacity-building programs, and special safeguard mechanisms to protect sensitive sectors. The European Union's Economic Partnership Agreements (EPAs) with African, Caribbean, and Pacific countries, for instance, have included development cooperation components aimed at supporting trade-related infrastructure and enhancing competitiveness.

Some believe that the benefits of these agreements often accrue disproportionately to more advanced developing countries or to specific sectors within recipient economies. While some countries have successfully leveraged FTAs to boost exports and attract foreign investment, others have struggled to fully utilize the preferences granted due to supply-side constraints and complex rules of origin. Moreover, the proliferation of bilateral and regional FTAs has led to concerns about the "spaghetti bowl" effect mentioned earlier, where overlapping and sometimes conflicting trade rules create administrative burdens and increase transaction costs for developing country exporters. This complexity can be particularly challenging for smaller firms and less developed economies with limited institutional capacity. Preferential FTAs may divert trade away from other developing countries not party to the agreement, potentially undermining broader South-South cooperation. Such trade diversion effects can be significant, particularly for agreements between developed and developing countries. FTAs entered into by developing countries, particularly those with more advanced economies, can restrict developing countries' ability to implement industrial policies or protect nascent industries. The inclusion of provisions on intellectual property rights, investment, and services in many modern FTAs such as the CPTPP or the USMCA (of which Mexico is a signatory) has raised concerns about their potential to limit policy flexibility in key areas of development.

Despite these challenges, many developing countries continue to pursue preferential FTAs as a means of enhancing their integration into the global economy. South-South FTAs, such as AfCFTA, have gained momentum as a way to boost intra-regional trade and create larger markets for domestic producers. Perhaps most notably, AfCFTA includes several provisions aimed at addressing the needs of developing countries, particularly least developed countries (LDCs) and vulnerable economies. AfCFTA incorporates the principle of special and differential treatment, which allows for flexibility and longer implementation periods for less developed countries. This is explicitly mentioned as one of the governing principles in Article 5 of the agreement. LDCs are granted ten years to remove trade barriers, compared to five years for more developed countries. This extended timeline aims to soften the financial impact and allow more time for adjustment. AfCFTA recognizes a group of six member states (Ethiopia, Madagascar, Malawi, Sudan, Zambia, and Zimbabwe) known as the G6. These countries have been granted an even longer implementation period of 15 years due to their specific development challenges. An innovative feature of AfCFTA is the creation of an Adjustment Fund to help countries facing challenges in implementing the agreement. This fund can be used for purposes such as retraining workers, recapitalizing industries, or increasing competitiveness.

AfCFTA seeks to ensure inclusivity for women and youth, including those in rural areas and aims to support the development of SMEs. The agreement further emphasizes the need for technical assistance and capacity-building programs to help developing countries effectively participate in and benefit from the free trade area. Lastly, the agreement aims to balance trade liberalization with the need for developing countries to maintain some policy flexibility for industrial development and economic diversification. These provisions demonstrate that the AfCFTA has been designed with consideration for the varying levels of economic development across the continent, attempting to create a more equitable framework for trade liberalization. However, the effectiveness of these measures in practice will depend on their implementation and the complementary policies adopted by individual countries.

Although preferential FTAs have provided some tangible benefits to developing countries in terms of market access and economic opportunities, their overall impact has been mixed. The effectiveness of these agreements in addressing development needs depends largely on their specific provisions, the capacity of recipient countries to utilize preferences and the broader economic and institutional context in which they are implemented. As the global trade landscape continues to evolve, policymakers and researchers alike are grappling with how to design and implement FTAs that can more effectively support inclusive and sustainable development in less economically prosperous regions.

2.5 Conclusion

This chapter introduced the two main principles of world trade law governing goods, meaning manufactured products. These are the prohibition of quantitative restrictions and the reduction in tariffs, both of which are reflected in the foundational GATT treaty of the WTO. These concepts have been taken further via preferential FTAs which have achieved lower tariffs beyond which were available to the WTO community. The extension of preferential treatment in this regard via FTAs necessitated a discussion of rules of origin, which outline procedures by which products are identified as originating with the territory covered by the preferential agreement. Building upon the other key GATT principle of transparency, this chapter then turned to rules on trade facilitation designed to reduce bureaucratic hurdles at borders. The WTO's TFA is the most noteworthy example of such an initiative in world trade law, but there have been important regional efforts, notably in Africa. This led to an examination of the way in which world trade law has dealt with developing countries, which house almost 90 per cent of the world's population and comprise two-thirds of WTO membership. The principle of special and differential treatment has been pivotal in this regard and has done much to integrate developing countries into the world trading system, although much more needs to be done to ensure that the benefits of free trade are enjoyed by people at all stages of development. The next chapter will consider another important tool in achieving that aim: the principle of non-discrimination.

Discussion Questions

1. Why are quotas preferable to tariffs?
2. What are Rules of Origin and why are they important for preferential Free Trade Agreements?
3. What kinds of trade barriers are rules on trade facilitation designed to address?
4. Does the WTO pay adequate regard to the needs of Developing Countries?
5. In what way is transparency an important aspect of world trade law?

3 Trade in Goods

Non-Discrimination as to National Origin

3.1 Introduction

This chapter will continue the examination of trade in goods by explaining the importance of the two non-discrimination standards: National Treatment and Most Favoured Nation (MFN). GATT rules governing these principles will be considered in depth. Specifically, the chapter will acknowledge the difficulties in interpreting and applying National Treatment, as contained in GATT Article III, examining similar rules in FTAs such as the USMCA and the CPTPP. The concept of MFN will be evaluated, primarily by reference to GATT Article I, but will an expanded discussion of the primary exception to this principle of non-discrimination for trade in goods, found in GATT Article XXIV, and how this has facilitated preferential FTAs, as well as their less common cousins, customs unions.

At the heart of the discussion of the principle of non-discrimination in trade law, as in other spheres of law, is the concept of "likeness" – the idea that there must be some fundamental degree of similarity between traded goods in order for an allegation of discrimination to have any meaning. The twin principles of National Treatment and MFN appear throughout world trade law and while they were conceived in relation to trade in goods, they reveal a fundamental theme at the core of world trade law which is essentially that when it comes to trade, nationality is secondary to the quality and nature of the exchange itself.

3.2 National Treatment

At a basic level, protectionism is the preference for domestic suppliers and their goods over those which originate from abroad in terms of the construction and application of "measures" which is the collective term for laws and regulations as enacted by the state. In theory such treatment gives local firms an advantage because they are subject to less stringent laws, potentially making their products more attractive to domestic consumers because their price will be artificially lower than it should be. Compliance with the stricter law in some way frustrates that goods ability to reach consumers, often because it means that compliance has raised costs. Consumers in the relevant country will be more likely to purchase

DOI: 10.4324/9781003465676-3

these goods rather than the foreign equivalent, even if the foreign good was of higher quality or should have been less expensive.

3.2.1 GATT Article III Overview

Article III of the GATT contains the National Treatment obligation, preventing WTO members from offering better treatment to the domestic product over the foreign one. As a consequence of the wide range of measures to which it can apply inside the borders of the relevant country, the National Treatment obligation is onerous from a sovereignty standpoint – interferes with a state's own internal regulatory capacity. The most important parts of Article III read as follows:

1. The contracting parties recognize that internal taxes and other internal charges, and laws, regulations and requirements affecting the internal sale, offering for sale, purchase, transportation, distribution or use of products, and internal quantitative regulations requiring the mixture, processing or use of products in specified amounts or proportions, should not be applied to imported or domestic products so as to afford protection to domestic production.*
2. The products of the territory of any contracting party imported into the territory of any other contracting party shall not be subject, directly, or indirectly, to internal taxes or other internal charges of any kind in excess of those applied, directly or indirectly, to like domestic products. Moreover, no contracting party shall otherwise apply internal taxes or other internal charges to imported or domestic products in a manner contrary to the principles set forth in paragraph 1.*
3. The products of the territory of any contracting party imported into the territory of any other contracting party shall be accorded treatment no less favourable than that accorded to like products of national origin in respect of all laws, regulations and requirements affecting their internal sale, offering for sale, purchase, transportation, distribution, or use. The provisions of this paragraph shall not prevent the application of differential internal transportation charges which are based exclusively on the economic operation of the means of transport and not on the nationality of the product.

The provision is arguably drafted badly and can be challenging to grasp because it actually contains several obligations. Before examining each of these, it is important to establish first that discrimination under GATT Article III National Treatment is prohibited whether it is *de jure* or *de facto*, essentially meaning expressly based on nationality or covertly linked to nationality but superficially disguised to appear to be based on some other factor. *De jure* discrimination is explicitly codified in law or official policy and is often easier to identify and therefore to challenge legally. *De facto* discrimination is that which occurs in practice, even if it is not officially recognized or sanctioned by law and is therefore often more subtle and harder to prove. Most modern discrimination disputes therefore concern *de facto* discrimination.

The distinction between *de facto* and *de jure* discrimination under GATT Article III has been addressed in several key WTO cases. In the 1996 dispute *Japan – Taxes on Alcoholic Beverages*, concerning differential taxes applied to various spirits, the Appellate Body emphasized that Article III protects expectations of equal competitive relationships, not just formally identical treatment. It stated that Article III of GATT obliges members of the WTO to provide equality of competitive conditions for imported products in relation to domestic products and that this applies to both *de jure* and *de facto* discrimination. The panel report in *Thailand – Customs and Fiscal Measures on Cigarettes from the Philippines*[1] provided a clear explanation of the difference between *de jure* and *de facto* discrimination. It stated that *de jure* discrimination occurs when the measure at issue on its face discriminates between domestic and like imported products. In contrast, *de facto* discrimination covers measures that are origin-neutral on their face, but nevertheless result in less favourable treatment for imported products.

A good example of how the distinction works can be found in the *Korea – Taxes on Alcoholic Beverages*[2] dispute which involved Korea's taxation scheme for distilled spirits. Much as in the Japan case, Korea applied different tax rates to different categories of distilled spirits. The tax categories were based on characteristics like alcohol content and production method, which on the surface appeared to be neutral criteria. The law itself did not explicitly discriminate against imported products. Any product, domestic or imported, that met the criteria for a particular category would be taxed at the same rate. In practice, this system resulted in most imported spirits (like whisky, brandy, gin, vodka) being taxed at higher rates than the domestic Korean spirit soju.

The key point of *de facto* discrimination in *Korea – Alcoholic Beverages* was that while the law didn't explicitly target imports, its practical effect was to impose a much higher tax burden on imported spirits compared to the domestically produced soju. This resulted in imported spirits being put at a competitive disadvantage in the Korean market. The WTO Appellate Body concluded that this system was inconsistent with Korea's obligations under Article III:2, second sentence of GATT, which prohibits members from applying internal taxes so as to afford protection to domestic production. This case illustrates how a seemingly neutral tax classification system can result in *de facto* discrimination against imported products, even when there's no explicit (*de jure*) discrimination in the law itself.

The *Korea – Various Measures on Beef*[3] dispute is another good example of *de facto* discrimination under GATT. This case, brought by the United States and Australia against Korea involved Korea's distribution and sales system for beef. Korea implemented a dual retail system for beef, requiring separate retail outlets

1 *Thailand – Customs and Fiscal Measures on Cigarettes from the Philippines*, Report of the Appellate Body, WT/DS371/AB/R, adopted 15 July 2011

2 *Korea – Taxes on Alcoholic Beverages*, Report of the Appellate Body, WT/DS75/AB/R, WT/DS84/AB/R, adopted 17 February 1999

3 Korea – Measures Affecting Imports of Fresh, Chilled and Frozen Beef, Report of the Appellate Body, WT/DS161/AB/R, WT/DS169/AB/R, adopted 10 January 2001

for domestic and imported beef. The system applied equally to both domestic and imported beef, requiring separate sales channels for each. The law itself did not explicitly discriminate against imported beef. Both domestic and imported beef were subject to the separation requirement. But in practice, this system resulted in significant disadvantages for imported beef because importers faced additional costs to establish new retail stores or persuade existing retailers to convert to imported beef sales. The separation made it less convenient for consumers to compare and choose between domestic and imported beef. Furthermore, the separation implicitly suggested that imported beef was different or inferior, potentially influencing consumer perceptions. While the dual retail system did not explicitly target imports in its language, its practical effect was to create significant market access barriers for imported beef. This put imported beef at a competitive disadvantage in the Korean market. *Korea – Beef* demonstrates how a facially neutral measure (applying equally to domestic and imported products) can still result in *de facto* discrimination against imported products due to its practical effects in the marketplace.

3.2.2 GATT Article III:2 National Treatment and Internal Taxation

Having introduced the principle of National Treatment, the various components of the obligations set out in GATT Article III will now be outlined. Article III:2 sets out the National Treatment test for internal taxation on "like" products or directly competitive and substitutable products. It contains a two-tiered test: whether the imported and domestic products are "like" products, and whether imported products are taxed in excess of the domestic products. It must also be ascertained whether the measure is an internal tax (essentially an extra fee). The tax can be imposed directly (on the profits of the person who sells it) or indirectly (on the consumer as they pay). The regulatory objective of the measure is irrelevant. This is because it would be impossible to verify this; only the effects, that is, the harm that is done to the foreign product from a competitive standpoint, matter.

First, on the issue of "likeness" – in order for National Treatment to have any meaning, the two goods (foreign and local) must be similar to each other in some fundamental way, or else the differential treatment cannot truly be considered discriminatory. "Likeness" is therefore a key legal question in National Treatment analysis, as it is with the other non-discrimination principle, MFN, to be discussed below. Various criteria for "likeness" have been established through WTO jurisprudence.

"Likeness" was famously analysed in the *Japan – Alcoholic Beverages* dispute.[4] The dispute arose when the European Communities, Canada, and the United States challenged Japan's Liquor Tax Law, claiming it discriminated against imported alcoholic beverages. The law imposed a lower tax rate on shochu, a traditional

4 Japan – Taxes on Alcoholic Beverages, Report of the Appellate Body, WT/DS8/AB/R, WT/DS10/AB/R, WT/DS11/AB/R, adopted 1 November 1996

Japanese spirit, compared to other imported spirits like vodka and whisky. The panel concluded that shochu and vodka were "like products" and that Japan violated Article III:2, first sentence, by taxing vodka in excess of shochu. The Appellate Body upheld the panel's conclusions, finding Japan's Liquor Tax Law in violation of Article III of GATT. The case established important criteria for determining "likeness" under Article III:2, first sentence. These criteria include the product's end use; consumer taste (the behaviour and perception of people who buy the product); the product's physical properties (meaning what it looks like or what elements it contains); its tariff classification; and lastly, its quality. Together these are sometimes referred to as the *Japan-Alcohol* Test. Taking the elements of this test a bit further, in the *Mexico – Taxes on Soft Drinks*[5] dispute, the panel examined whether the use of different sweeteners (cane sugar vs. high fructose corn syrup) in otherwise similar soft drinks made them "unlike" for the purposes of Article III:2. The panel found that despite this difference, the products were still "like" due to their similar end-uses and consumer perceptions.

The Process and Production Methods (PPM) of the product, meaning the way in which it was made, are normally seen as irrelevant, unless this affects consumers' tastes, meaning that they would choose to purchase a product because of the way that it was made, even if they had no way of knowing this other than being told. In *United States – Tuna II (Mexico)*[6] the Appellate Body's reasoning suggested that differences in PPMs that don't affect the physical characteristics of the final product might still be relevant in determining "likeness" under certain circumstances. The Appellate Body noted that evidence relating to consumers' tastes and habits could establish that consumers perceive and treat the products differently. It will be seen in Chapter 6 on non-trade values that the way in which a product is made can excuse a breach of WTO law.

If the only difference between the two products is their origin, then the products are most likely "like." "Likeness" is determined on a case-by-case basis. In some cases, it will be construed widely, in others narrowly. This is why, as a concept, it is sometimes descried as an accordion. Generally speaking, it should be interpreted narrowly – the narrowest of the three "likeness" tests in Article III. Indeed, in *Japan – Alcoholic Beverages*, the Appellate Body cautioned against an overly broad interpretation of "likeness" that could undermine the purpose of Article III.

The "likeness" test for internal taxation is complimented, or complicated, by the related "directly competitive or substitutable." Discrimination is not permitted between "directly competitive or substitutable" products. This phrase is not found in GATT itself; it comes from the interpretive note to GATT Article III:2, hence the asterisk at the end of the article. It is understood to apply to the second sentence of GATT Article III:2. Directly competitive or substitutable is a broad category and is easier to satisfy than "like." This concept effectively means that the products are

5 Mexico – Tax Measures on Soft Drinks and Other Beverages, Report of the Panel, WT/DS308/R, adopted 24 March 2006

6 United States – Measures Concerning the Importation, Marketing and Sale of Tuna and Tuna Products, Report of the Appellate Body, WT/DS381/AB/R, adopted 13 June 2012

interchangeable or capable of satisfying a particular need or taste in an alternative way. This concept is sometimes described by economists via the phrase "elasticity of substitution"; the extent to which one product will satisfy the need for another product. For example, if a shopper is looking for butter in the grocery store and it is not there, will they be willing to purchase margarine instead? In order to make this determination, a market analysis may be required involving market conditions and consumers' existing and future preferences and tastes.

In the *Chile – Alcoholic Beverages*[7] dispute, the Appellate Body further refined the interpretation of the second sentence of Article III:2. It emphasized that even small tax differences could be enough to violate the provision if they were applied in a way that afforded protection to domestic production. The case also highlighted that the determination of whether products are "directly competitive or substitutable" should be based on the market situation in the country in question. Another dispute about alcoholic drinks, *Philippines – Distilled Spirits,*[8] provided additional clarity on the concept of "directly competitive or substitutable products" under the second sentence of Article III:2. The Appellate Body confirmed that this determination should be based on a comprehensive analysis of the competitive relationship between the products, including consideration of current and potential competition, meaning the choices of customers who had not yet tried the product.

3.2.3 GATT Article III:4 Any Laws, Regulations, and Requirements

The last part of GATT's National Treatment provision establishes that WTO members cannot discriminate against foreign products with regard to all regulations and requirements. This rule is quite broad, covering regulations of all kinds, some of which may not occur until long after the product has crossed the border and entered the stream of commerce, for example, those affecting the sale, advertising, purchase, transport, distribution, and use. Under this provision, WTO members must regard all products as equal in terms of how they are affected by the internal legal system, whether they are domestic or imported. This means that they must treat imported goods the same way that they treat their own equivalent goods, effectively preventing protectionism in favour of domestic producers. The purpose of this provision is to ensure that there will be equality in competitive conditions between suppliers of goods, irrespective of their national origin, allowing for a proper functioning market where goods compete based on their quality and price, not based on how they have been regulated.

Once again, in order for this provision to take effect, the foreign and local products must be "like." This will be interpreted narrowly and is linked to their competitive relationship. In order to satisfy the "likeness" requirement, effective equality of competitive opportunities is required.

7 Chile – Taxes on Alcoholic Beverages, Report of the Appellate Body, WT/DS87/AB/R, WT/DS110/AB/R, adopted 12 January 2000

8 Philippines – Taxes on Distilled Spirits, Report of the Appellate Body, WT/DS396/AB/R, WT/DS403/AB/R, adopted 20 January 2012

The jurisprudence on the likeness test under GATT Article III:4, which deals with internal regulations, has evolved through several key WTO cases. This test is distinct from the one used for internal taxation under Article III:2. The likeness test under Article III:4 considers four main criteria: the physical characteristics and qualities of the products; the extent to which products can serve the same or similar functions; how consumers perceive and treat the products; how products are classified for customs purposes.

The *EC-Asbestos*[9] case significantly refined the likeness test for Article III:4. The Appellate Body emphasized that all four criteria should be examined, but their relative importance may vary case by case. The health risks associated with a product could be considered under the "physical properties" and "consumer tastes and habits" criteria. Moreover, the competitive relationship between products is crucial in determining likeness. In the *EC – Seal Products*[10] dispute, the Appellate Body confirmed that the determination of likeness in Article III.4 is fundamentally, about the nature and extent of a competitive relationship between products. It explained that the regulatory purpose of the measure is not relevant for determining likeness under Article III:4.

The *United States – Clove Cigarettes*[11] dispute provided insight applicable to GATT Article III:4. The Appellate Body noted that the concept of "likeness" in Article III:4 is broader than in Article III:2, first sentence. It emphasized the importance of examining the competitive relationship between products in the marketplace. In the *China – Publications and Audiovisual Products,*[12] the Appellate Body further refined the understanding of "like products" under Article III:4. It confirmed that the determination of likeness is fundamentally about the nature and extent of the competitive relationship between products. The Appellate Body also clarified that the regulatory purpose of a measure is not relevant to the determination of likeness under Article III:4.

The *Thailand – Cigarettes (Philippines)* dispute provided important clarification on the interpretation of "less favourable treatment" under Article III:4. The Appellate Body emphasized that a formal difference in treatment between imported and like domestic products is not sufficient to establish less favourable treatment. Instead, the analysis must focus on whether the measure modifies the conditions of competition in the relevant market to the detriment of imported products. The *India – Solar Cells*[13] dispute further contributed to the understanding of the phrase "treatment no less favourable" of Article III:4. Here the Appellate Body clarified

9 European Communities – Measures Affecting Asbestos and Asbestos-Containing Products, Report of the Appellate Body, WT/DS135/AB/R, adopted 5 April 2001

10 European Communities – Measures Prohibiting the Importation and Marketing of Seal Products, WT/DS400/AB/R, WT/DS401/AB/R, adopted 18 June 2014

11 United States – Measures Affecting the Production and Sale of Clove Cigarettes, WT/DS406/AB/R, adopted 24 April 2012

12 China – Measures Affecting Trading Rights and Distribution Services for Certain Publications and Audiovisual Entertainment Products, WT/DS363/AB/R, adopted 19 January 2010

13 India – Certain Measures Relating to Solar Cells and Solar Modules, WT/DS456/AB/R, adopted 14 October 2016

that this phrase expresses the general principle of equality of competitive conditions for imported products in relation to like domestic products. It also said that a measure can be found to modify the conditions of competition to the detriment of imported products even if its adverse impact on imports is not yet discernible in trade flows.

Several key principles have emerged for the likeness test under Article III:4 on any regulation or requirement. The fundamental consideration is whether the products are in a competitive relationship in the marketplace. The weight given to each criterion may vary depending on the specific circumstances of each case. No single factor is determinative; all relevant factors must be considered. The regulatory objectives of the measure are not considered in determining likeness under Article III:4. The concept of "like products" under Article III:4 is generally interpreted more broadly than under Article III:2, first sentence. The Article III:4 test is the broadest of the "likeness" tests in GATT Article III because it is also focused on competitive relationships. Still, the Article III:4 test does not consider regulatory purpose, while this can, it would seem, be relevant for the Article III:2 tests.

The expansive scope of GATT Article III:4 has far-reaching implications for domestic policymaking within WTO member countries. This provision's broad applicability extends beyond measures that are explicitly trade-related, potentially affecting a diverse array of internal regulations and policies. For instance, environmental regulations, consumer protection laws, health and safety standards, and even local zoning ordinances could potentially fall under the purview of Article III:4 if they are found to impact the competitive conditions between imported and domestic products. This means that governments must carefully consider the potential trade implications of virtually any domestic policy initiative, even those that may seem entirely unrelated to international commerce. The result is a significant constraint on regulatory autonomy, as policymakers must constantly weigh their domestic objectives against their international trade obligations. This pervasive influence of Article III:4 effectively blurs the line between trade policy and domestic regulation, creating a complex web of considerations for governments as they navigate their economic and social priorities within the framework of their WTO commitments.

3.2.4 Exceptions to GATT National Treatment

There are several exceptions to the National Treatment principle contained within Article III itself. These are apart from the General Exceptions of Article XX and the Security Exception of Article XXI, which will be examined in Chapter 6. It should be mentioned here that the most significant exceptions for National Treatment occur in relation to services, not goods. At the WTO, services are covered by the General Agreement on Trade in Services (GATS) which features prominently in Chapter 8.

There is the government procurement exception of Article III:8(a). This allows governments to discriminate in favour of domestic products when purchasing goods for public purposes. For example, a country may require that all vehicles purchased for its military be domestically produced. It is important to note that there is a WTO Government Procurement Agreement, to which many, but not all, WTO members are signatories.

There is also the domestic subsidies exception contained in Article III:8(b) This provision allows countries to provide subsidies exclusively to domestic producers without violating National Treatment. For instance, a country could offer tax incentives or direct payments to local farmers to support domestic agriculture. Subsidies are now controlled by the Agreement on Subsidies and Countervailing Measures which will be explored in Chapter 5 on Trade Remedies.

The cinematograph films exception (Article III:10) permits countries to establish or maintain internal quantitative regulations relating to exposed cinematograph films. For example, a country might require that a certain percentage of films shown in its theatres be domestically produced. Drafted in the 1940s, this is an early example of culture being used as a justification for trade protectionism – a topic that will be revisited in Chapter 6. Relatedly, while not explicitly mentioned in Article III, the GATT panel in the *Canada – Administration of the Foreign Investment Review Act*[14] dispute recognized that requirements related to local content in television programs could be consistent with Article III:4 if applied equally to foreign and domestic broadcasters.

The existing legislation exception of Article III:1 consists of a "grandfather clause" that enables countries to maintain certain discriminatory measures that were in force on specific dates. For instance, some United States state laws regulating the sale of alcoholic beverages that pre-dated GATT 1947 were allowed to continue under this exception. Some countries have been able to maintain discriminatory practices through agricultural marketing boards under specific circumstances. For instance, Canada's supply management system for dairy, poultry, and eggs has been allowed to continue despite potential conflicts with National Treatment principles. While ostensibly GATT-compliant, this facet of the Canadian economy has operated as an obstacle to the negotiation of preferential FTAs.

3.2.5 National Treatment under FTAs

While many preferential FTAs closely mirror the National Treatment obligations found in GATT Article III, in some cases even incorporating it by reference, some FTAs have introduced variations or additional provisions. In the context of an FTA, the discrimination, which is prohibited, is that which is levied against products from the other treaty partner as opposed to those produced domestically. As noted in the previous section, many of the limits on National Treatment in FTAs relate to services which are generally much less open to international trade than goods.

Article 2.3 of USMCA maintains the NAFTA approach of incorporating GATT Article III but adds more specific language on alcoholic beverages in

14 Canada – Administration of the Foreign Investment Review Act, GATT Panel Report, adopted 7 February 1984

Article 2.3.4, addressing issues not explicitly covered in GATT Article III. USMCA Article 2.3 uses broader language, covering "any measure" related to the sale, offering for sale, purchase, transportation, distribution, or use of goods. The use of "any measure" in USMCA potentially expands the scope beyond just laws, regulations, and requirements to include a wider range of government actions or policies than that even of GATT Article III.4. USMCA Article 2.3 explicitly applies to measures by all levels of government (federal, state/provincial, and local), whereas GATT Article III does not specify this. Perhaps mindful of the poor drafting of GATT Article III, USMCA Article 2.3 uses the broader language of "like, directly competitive or substitutable," combining concepts from both sentences of GATT III:2. This potentially expands the range of products that must receive national treatment.

CPTPP Article 2.3 incorporates GATT Article III, but Article 2.4 adds specific provisions on the treatment of re-manufactured goods, which is not addressed in GATT. Re-manufactured goods are goods that are entirely or partially composed of recovered goods, but they are distinct from used goods as they are restored to a much higher level of functionality. The agreement clarifies that remanufactured goods should not be subjected to import prohibitions or restrictions that could apply to used goods. RCEP contains a National Treatment provision in Article 2.3 which incorporates GATT Article III, however, Article 2.6 adds specific provisions on re-manufactured goods, similar to CPTPP.

Article 2 of the ASEAN-Australia-New Zealand Free Trade Agreement (AANZFTA) has a National Treatment obligation which includes a provision on fees and charges connected with importation and exportation, which goes beyond the scope of GATT III. The Canada-Korea Free Trade Agreement's National Treatment obligation includes a provision on the prohibition of certain performance requirements, which is not present in GATT III. Performance requirements, essentially trade-oriented conditions placed on foreign firms seeking to locate within the territory of another country, are dealt with by the WTO under the Trade-Related Investment Measures (TRIMS) Agreement.[15]

These examples demonstrate that while FTAs generally maintain the core National Treatment obligations of GATT, they often add specific provisions to address particular concerns or sectors not explicitly covered in GATT. The trend towards including specific provisions on remanufactured goods in recent FTAs is a notable example of how these agreements can expand upon GATT obligations. It must be stressed that these additional provisions do not contradict GATT obligations, but rather supplement them or provide more specific guidance in certain areas. The interpretation and application of these provisions in actual disputes under the relevant FTA's dispute settlement mechanism could ultimately determine how they interact with and potentially differ from GATT National Treatment obligations.

15 See further D Collins, *Performance Requirements and Investment Incentives Under International Economic Law* (Elgar, 2016)

3.2.6 Exceptions to National Treatment under FTAs

FTAs often include exceptions to the National Treatment principle to protect certain sectors or national interests. One common exception is in government procurement, where FTAs may allow parties to favour domestic suppliers for specific types of contracts or below certain monetary thresholds. For instance, several United States FTAs exclude government acquisitions set aside for small businesses from National Treatment obligations. The Australia-New Zealand Government Procurement Agreement allows for exceptions in case of urgent procurement of goods and services in emergencies, such as natural disasters or periods of national security. FTAs may include exceptions of this nature for specific government entities or state-owned enterprises. Some agreements exclude procurement conducted by government bodies that trade in substantial competition with the private sector, as they might be placed at a significant commercial disadvantage if required to fully comply with all provisions of the agreement.

Specific goods and sectors are often carved out as exceptions to National Treatment in various FTAs, allowing countries to protect sensitive industries or maintain certain domestic policies. To take a few examples, the ASEAN Free Trade Area (AFTA) agreement includes a "Sensitive List" and "Highly Sensitive List" of products that are exempted from tariff reductions. For example, Malaysia has listed rice and some automotive products on these lists to protect its domestic industries. In the USMCA there are specific exceptions to National Treatment for certain goods. The agreement allows Canada to maintain its supply management system for dairy, poultry, and eggs. This system effectively limits imports of these products, providing protection for Canadian farmers. The CPTPP includes exceptions for certain cultural goods. It allows Vietnam, for example, to maintain quotas on imports of motion picture films to protect its domestic film industry. In the EU-South Korea FTA, there's an exception for agricultural goods. South Korea is allowed to maintain higher tariffs on certain sensitive agricultural products like rice, apples, and pears to protect its domestic farmers. The Australia-United States Free Trade Agreement (AUSFTA) includes an exception for the Australian Wheat Board's export monopoly on wheat. This allowed Australia to maintain its single-desk system for wheat exports for a transitional period. In the Japan-Mexico Economic Partnership Agreement, there are exceptions for certain automotive products. Japan is allowed to maintain tariffs on some auto parts to protect its domestic industry.

Intellectual property rights, the subject of Chapter 9, can also be subject to exceptions in FTAs. Countries may maintain certain preferences for domestic patent holders or copyright owners, particularly in areas related to traditional knowledge or cultural expressions. This allows countries to protect and promote their unique cultural heritage. In the defence sector, FTAs frequently include exceptions for national security reasons. For instance, many United States FTAs exclude acquisitions of arms, ammunition, or war materials as well as purchases indispensable for national security or national defence purposes from National Treatment obligations. This issue will be explored further in Chapter 6.

3.3 Most Favoured Nation (MFN)

The second, and perhaps more important, of the two non-discrimination standards in world trade law is Most Favoured Nation (MFN). The concept of MFN has been around for centuries and is arguably the most important legal principle of all of world trade law. In the case of trade in goods, it requires countries to treat the goods originating from one country the same as any other country. In other words, countries cannot "pick favourites" in terms of how foreign goods are regulated. The MFN principle was designed to prevent alliances, which are not only economically distortive but may also lead to geopolitical tension.

The MFN principle has a long and significant history in international trade law. Its origins can be traced back to the 11th century when it was used in bilateral trade agreements between European nations. Early international trade treaties that included MFN provisions can be traced back several centuries before the GATT. One of the earliest examples is the Anglo-Portuguese Treaty of 1654, which established MFN treatment between England and Portugal. In the 18th century, the United States began incorporating MFN clauses into its commercial treaties, notably in the 1778 Treaty of Amity and Commerce with France. The Franco-British Commercial Treaty of 1860, also known as the Cobden-Chevalier Treaty, was another significant agreement that included MFN provisions and helped spread the use of unconditional MFN clauses in Europe. The MFN principle gained particular prominence in the 19th century as a cornerstone of trade liberalization efforts. It was widely adopted by major trading nations like the United Kingdom as part of their push for free trade policies. The inclusion of MFN clauses in trade agreements helped reduce discriminatory practices and fostered more open international commerce.

3.3.1 GATT Article I

Article I of the GATT contains the MFN provision, applicable to all WTO members. It reads as follows:

1. With respect to customs duties and charges of any kind imposed on or in connection with importation or exportation or imposed on the international transfer of payments for imports or exports, and with respect to the method of levying such duties and charges, and with respect to all rules and formalities in connection with importation and exportation, and with respect to all matters referred to in paragraphs 2 and 4 of Article III,* any advantage, favour, privilege or immunity granted by any contracting party to any product originating in or destined for any other country shall be accorded immediately and unconditionally to the like product originating in or destined for the territories of all other contracting parties.

As with National Treatment, MFN prohibits discrimination in relation to "like" products originating from (or destined for) different members. This means that a

WTO member cannot treat one country better than another one with respect to any restrictions on trade. In other words, WTO members cannot pick favourites with respect to the laws which they levy against traded goods. MFN is therefore the foundation of the international trading "community" that is WTO membership.

Since MFN means that benefits are accorded equally to products originating from all countries, it has the practical consequence of distributing the advantages gained by the shrewdest negotiators to countries which have the weakest negotiators. Once something is offered to one WTO member, it must be offered to all, whether it is a tariff or any other kind of trade advantage. Since MFN applies to all 166 WTO members it is a powerful tool of trade liberalization at the multilateral level. It also contributes to more straightforward customs processes precluding the need to investigate complicated rules of origin of a given good to ascertain whether it deserves to receive the beneficial treatment or not.

GATT Article I is very broad in its scope, covering a wide range of governmental action which impacts trade, whether at the border in terms of tariff commitments or internally, such as with respect to sales taxes. It is most commonly associated with discriminatory tariffs – meaning that the WTO member in question imposes a higher tariff on a good from one country than it does on the same good from another country. It can also apply to the allocation of tariff rate quotas. In *EC – Bananas III,*[16] the Appellate Body upheld the panel's finding that the EC's banana import regime violated Article I:1 of GATT. Specifically, the Appellate Body found that the EC's allocation of tariff quotas to some members but not to others was inconsistent with the MFN principle. The Appellate Body stated that the essence of the non-discrimination obligations is that like products should be treated equally, irrespective of their origin. This case highlighted the broad scope of the MFN principle and its application to both *de jure* and *de facto* discrimination.

In *Canada – Autos,*[17] the Appellate Body found that Canada's measures violated Article I:1 of GATT 1994 by providing an import duty exemption to motor vehicles imported by certain manufacturers, based on their export performance and domestic value-added requirements. The Appellate Body explained that the MFN obligation in Article I:1 is unqualified and applies to any advantage granted by a member to any product originating in or destined for any other country. This case underscored the principle that origin-based discrimination, even if not explicitly stated in a measure, can violate the MFN obligation. Again, like National Treatment, MFN covers both *de jure* and *de facto* discrimination.

In the *EC- Tariff Preferences*[18] case, India challenged the European Communities' Generalized System of Preferences (GSP) scheme, which provided additional tariff preferences to some developing countries based on their compliance with

16 European Communities – Regime for the Importation, Sale and Distribution of Bananas, WT/DS27/AB/R, adopted 25 September 1997

17 Canada – Certain Measures Affecting the Automotive Industry, WT/DS139/AB/R, WT/DS142/AB/R, adopted 19 June 2000

18 European Communities – Conditions for the Granting of Tariff Preferences to Developing Countries, WT/DS246/AB/R, adopted 20 April 2004

certain labour and environmental standards. The Appellate Body found that the EC's drug arrangements under its GSP scheme were inconsistent with Article I:1 of GATT. While the Enabling Clause, discussed in the previous chapter, allows developed countries to provide differential and more favourable treatment to developing countries, such treatment must be "non-discriminatory" among similarly situated GSP beneficiaries. This case provided important guidance on the relationship between the MFN principle and special provisions for developing countries.

In the *Russia – Railway Equipment*[19] dispute from 2020, Ukraine challenged Russia's measures affecting the importation of railway equipment and parts. The Appellate Body upheld the panel's finding that Russia had violated Article I:1 of GATT 1994 by systematically rejecting applications for new certificates and suspending existing certificates for Ukrainian railway products while continuing to accept applications from other countries. This case reaffirmed that the MFN principle applies to both substantive and procedural requirements affecting trade and that systematic differences in treatment can constitute a violation of Article I:1.

One of the most crucial legal issues concerning the MFN obligation relates to the question of "likeness" of products. In Spain – Tariff Treatment of Unroasted Coffee, which was heard in 1981 before the *WTO* came into being, a GATT panel heard a dispute based on Spain's introduction of different tariff rates for various types of unroasted, non-decaffeinated coffee beans. Brazil, which was the main exporter of unwashed Arabica coffee to Spain, complained that this differentiation violated the MFN principle. The GATT panel ruled in favour of Brazil, finding that the different types of unroasted coffee should be considered "like products" for the purposes of Article I:1. The panel in this case considered several factors in determining likeness, including the end-use of the product, consumers' tastes and habits, and the products' properties, nature, and quality. The panel concluded that despite some differences in cultivation methods, characteristics, and prices of various coffee types, they were ultimately used for the same purpose – making coffee for drinking. This case established an important precedent for a relatively broad interpretation of "like products" in the context of MFN treatment.

In *Japan – Tariff on Imports of Spruce, Pine, Fir (SPF) Dimension Lumber* Canada complained about Japan's tariff classification that resulted in higher duties on certain types of dimension lumber typically exported by Canada, compared to other types typically exported by the United States. Although the panel ultimately did not find a violation of Article I:1, it provided important considerations for determining likeness in the context of MFN treatment. The panel emphasized that "like products" for MFN purposes can be quite broad, focusing on factors such as end-use and substitutability rather than minor differences in physical characteristics or production methods.

Although primarily focused on GATT Article III and the Technical Barriers to Trade Agreement (to be examined in Chapter 8), *EC – Seal Products* provided

19 Russia – Measures Affecting the Importation of Railway Equipment, WT/DS499/AB/R, adopted 5 March 2020

some insights relevant to Article I. The Appellate Body emphasized that the determination of likeness under Article I:1 is fundamentally about the nature and extent of the competitive relationship between products. It noted that while the criteria for likeness under Article III:4 can be relevant for Article I:1, the scope and content of these criteria may differ under the two provisions. In the *United States – Tariff Measures on Certain Goods from China*,[20] the panel examined the likeness of products under Article I:1, reaffirming that the determination should be made on a case-by-case basis, considering factors such as physical properties, end-uses, consumer tastes and habits, and tariff classification.

3.3.2 MFN Provisions for Goods in FTAs

Few FTAs include MFN provisions for goods. Aiming to exceed the benefits available under the WTO, FTAs instead focus on eliminating tariffs and quotas that comply with the appropriate rule of origin. The USMCA does include an MFN provision for certain categories of goods, including certain automatic data processing goods and their parts, and certain colour television tubes.[21] FTAs are more likely to include MFN clauses with respect to services trade (the subject of Chapter 8) or for investment than goods. For example, the EU-Canada Comprehensive Economic and Trade Agreement (CETA) contains an MFN provision for services (Article 9.5) and financial services in particular (Article 13.3). The EU's FTAs often include "MFN-forward" provisions. These require parties to extend any better treatment given to future FTA partners to each other. This can be quite risky as it compels treaty partners to think backwards with regard to past concessions they have already made when negotiating new treaties with new partners. It should be noted that an MFN-like effect is achieved through the National Treatment provisions of FTAs which contain more than two parties. For instance, by granting National Treatment (domestic goods treated no better than foreign ones) to all signatories of the CPTPP,[22] each country is promising to treat all signatories the same as each other, which is essentially MFN.

3.4 GATT Article XXIV and Preferential FTAs as an MFN Exception

The key exception to the principle of MFN non-discrimination is in relation to preferential trade agreements, of which there are two chief varieties: customs unions and FTAs or Free Trade Areas. Customs unions, the best-known example of which is that of the European Union, have common external tariffs and low to zero internal tariffs. Conventional FTAs, on the other hand, enable their parties to have their own external tariffs. Their preferential tariff treatment applies only internally

20 United States – Tariff Measures on Certain Goods from China, WT/DS543/R, adopted 26 October 2020
21 Tables 2.10.1–2.10.3
22 Article 2.3

among the parties of the FTA. FTAs are by far more common – there are hundreds of them in existence. Many, such as the CPTPP and the USMCA, have already been mentioned in this book.

GATT Article XXIV and GATS Article V (the services agreement) allow MFN-violating measures to be implemented with a preferential FTA if the formation of the FTA would be impossible without it. This is conditional upon three factors. First, there is an obligation not to raise the overall level of protection and make access for non-FTA members harder. Second, there is an obligation to liberalize substantially all trade among members of the FTA. Finally, the WTO must be notified of the creation of the FTA. These obligations can vary depending on whether the FTA being created is a customs union or a conventional FTA.

With respect to the first obligation, the external trade requirement, for FTAs: members of the FTA may not alter their external protection to affect non-FTA members negatively. For customs unions, members of the customs union may not raise the overall level of external protection. This means that all customs union members must adjust their external protection to the same level. For some members this will be adjusting downwards, for others it may be upwards. If adjusting protection upwards causes harm to non-customs union members, compensation may be required.

A dispute arose between India and Turkey with regard to the interpretation of GATT Article XXIV. In *Turkey – Restrictions on Imports of Textile and Clothing Products*,[23] Turkey was preparing to join Europe's common market. To do so, Turkey was required to impose quotas on clothing products so that it fit the levels imposed by the rest of Europe. The issue for Turkey was that it had never imposed any clothing quotas on any country. When Turkey did this in order to join the customs union, India, with its vibrant textile industry, complained to the WTO. The Appellate Body clarified that Article XXIV can be used as a defence for measures that would otherwise be WTO-inconsistent, but only if two conditions are met. First, the measure at issue is introduced upon the formation of a customs union that fully meets the requirements of Article XXIV; and the formation of that customs union would be prevented if it were not allowed to introduce the measure at issue.

Regarding the second element of GATT XXIV, the internal trade requirement, there is an obligation for all members of a preferential FTA to liberalize substantially all trade among its members. "Substantially all trade" is an ambiguous concept. It might be quantitative – it could be the amount of trade in value per unit of currency, per weight, per unit. It might be qualitative – covering all trade in a given industry. It likely precludes FTAs which are sector specific. For example, there could not be an automobile FTA. Generally speaking, there is a high degree of flexibility with this concept. It seems that it refers to "more than some" of the trade but not necessarily "all." Article XXIV further stipulates that duties and other regulations of commerce imposed at the formation of an FTA shall not be "on the

23 Turkey – Restrictions on Imports of Textile and Clothing Products, WT/DS34/AB/R, adopted 19 November 1999

whole higher or more restrictive" than those previously in force. Measuring this, especially for non-tariff measures, can be complex and contentious.

There have been relatively few WTO disputes directly addressing GATT Article XXIV, which deals with the formation of customs unions and free trade areas. In *Peru – Additional Duty on Imports of Certain Agricultural Products*,[24] the Appellate Body elaborated on the relationship between Article XXIV and other WTO obligations. It emphasized that Article XXIV does not provide a broad exemption from other WTO rules. In *Canada – Certain Measures Affecting the Automotive Industry*[25] the panel noted that the article does not permit the adoption of discriminatory measures against third countries. The relative scarcity of cases directly addressing Article XXIV may be due to the WTO's general acceptance of regional trade agreements, as long as they meet certain criteria. Most disputes related to preferential trade arrangements tend to focus on specific measures rather than challenging the legitimacy of the arrangements themselves under Article XXIV.

3.4.1 Advantages and Disadvantages of Preferential FTAs

As mentioned several times already in this book, bilateral trade relations, often formalized through preferential FTAs that depart from the MFN principle, have become increasingly prevalent in recent decades. These agreements exist alongside the multilateral trading system governed by WTO, which, as we have seen, is the origin of many of the key principles of world trade law. Both approaches have distinct advantages and disadvantages. These are worth exploring in further detail because they challenge the principle of MFN which ensures equality among trading partners. As such, in many ways, they are inimical to world trade law.

Beginning with the advantages of bilateralism/regionalism over multilateralism, the first and perhaps most obvious benefit of FTAs is faster and more flexible negotiations. This is not always the case, as some FTAs take an exceptionally long time to conclude, notably, those of the European Union. This is largely due to the competing interests of its member states and the need for unanimity in ratification (domestic legislative approval). Secondly, bilateral FTAs can be customized to the specific needs and circumstances of the participating countries in a way that is difficult if not impossible at the WTO. This allows for more targeted liberalization and regulatory cooperation in sectors of mutual interest.

A good example of this is the focus on tariff reduction in the automotive manufacturing sector that features strongly in the USMCA as a consequence of the continent-wide supply chains. Third, bilateral trade agreements can be stepping-stones to multilateralism, serving as building blocks for broader multilateral liberalization. Plurilateral agreements, which are preferential FTAs among

24 Peru – Additional Duty on Imports of Certain Agricultural Products, WT/DS457/AB/R, adopted 31 July 2015

25 Canada – Certain Measures Affecting the Automotive Industry, WT/DS139/AB/R, WT/DS142/AB/R, adopted 19 June 2000

several parties which are open to new signatories, are good examples of this phenomena, with the CPTPP as perhaps the best example. Several new members have joined since the agreement's inception. Fourth, there are political and strategic benefits to FTAs which go beyond purely economic considerations. They can strengthen diplomatic ties and enhance cooperation in other areas in a manner that would be diluted at the multilateral level.

The Trade and Cooperation Agreement (TCA) between the United Kingdom and the European Union is an excellent example of this benefit as it represents more than a simple trade agreement but a solidification of ongoing alignment, repairing some of the political damage done in the aftermath of the United Kingdom's departure from the European Union. Lastly and perhaps most significantly of all, bilateral agreements can sometimes address emerging trade issues more quickly than the WTO, which requires consensus among all members. This includes areas like digital trade which the WTO has been notoriously slow to embrace. Many FTAs contain digital trade chapters and there are even dedicated digital trade agreements, such as the Digital Economy Partnership Agreement (DEPA). This issue will be explored further in Chapter 10.

Bilateral trade relations do carry some disadvantages. The most well-known of these is the phenomenon of trade diversion. This is where trade is shifted from more efficient producers outside the agreement to less efficient producers within it. This has a potential negative welfare effect for parties to the FTA. Secondly, there is the complexity and administrative burden of FTAs, an adverse effect which is multiplied by the more FTAs a country joins. The proliferation of bilateral agreements creates a complex web of trade rules, sometimes referred to as the "spaghetti bowl" effect which was mentioned earlier. This can increase transaction costs for businesses navigating multiple sets of rules. A third key problem with bilateral agreements is that they can exclude smaller countries or worse, subject them to worse conditions because of a lack of bargaining power. This can exacerbate global economic inequalities. Preferential access for poorer countries alluded to in the previous chapter, has not proven effective at increasing market access for these countries.

It is not only developing countries which suffer at the hands of developed ones. It has been said that the United Kingdom-EU TCA was one-sided in favour of the larger European Union as it primarily dealt with minimizing barriers to trade in goods (the European Union's export strength) and largely omitted services (the United Kingdom's export strength). Fourth, bilateral agreements may not address systemic issues in global trade as comprehensively as multilateral approaches. They often exclude sensitive sectors and fail to tackle broader issues like agricultural subsidies. Finally, it is arguable that bilateralism has contributed to the weakening of the multilateral system, predicated on the MFN principle. There is only so much time and personnel that countries can devote to trade negotiations and in many cases, the WTO has been neglected in this regard. Indeed, regionalism may be viewed as a threat to the WTO's role as a forum for trade liberalization.

The WTO's near-universal membership allows for truly global trade liberalization and rule-setting, benefiting both large and small economies. Moreover, the

WTO's dispute settlement mechanism, to be examined in Chapter 4, provides a structured, rules-based system for resolving trade conflicts. This is particularly valuable for smaller countries. Multilateral negotiations can achieve broader and more significant trade liberalization in a single undertaking, avoiding the piecemeal, resource-intensive approach of bilateral deals. The WTO is better positioned to tackle global trade issues that require coordinated action, such as fisheries subsidies or e-commerce rules.

Still, the consensus-based decision-making in the WTO can lead to protracted negotiations and watered-down agreements. The stalled Doha Round is often cited as an example of this challenge. WTO agreements may not always account for the diverse needs and circumstances of its heterogeneous membership, particularly developing countries. The WTO has been criticized for being slow to address emerging trade issues, such as digital trade and environmental concerns. While the WTO's dispute settlement system is a strength, enforcement of rulings ultimately relies on member states' willingness to comply, although this criticism is arguably equally applicable to FTAs. Furthermore, many FTAs establish their own dispute settlement mechanisms, which can lead to forum shopping and potentially conflicting interpretations of the principles of world trade law. The large number of participants with diverse interests can lead to political deadlocks and tensions at the WTO, as seen in recent years with conflicts between major powers, especially the United States and China.

Given the strengths and weaknesses inherent in bilateralism and multilateralism, respectively, the challenge for policymakers and trade negotiators is to harness the advantages of both approaches while mitigating their drawbacks. This might involve using bilateral agreements to advance trade liberalization in areas not yet covered by the WTO, while simultaneously working to strengthen and reform the multilateral system to make it more responsive to contemporary trade challenges.[26]

3.4.2 Preferentialism and Border Traffic

The principle of MFN may also be transgressed by WTO members with regard to special trading circumstances which exist in relation to regularly occurring travel across international borders. GATT Article XXIV.3 states that the GATT, in particular the MFN provision shall not be construed to prevent advantages accorded by any contracting party to adjacent countries in order to facilitate frontier traffic.

The border traffic exception to the MFN principle of GATT allows for some flexibility in trade relations between neighbouring countries. It recognizes and accommodates the unique economic and social realities of border regions, acknowledging that communities straddling international borders often have deep historical, cultural, and economic ties that predate modern nation-states and trade agreements. It allows for smoother trade in goods and services between communities on either

26 SJ Evenett and PE Baldwin, Revitalising Multilateralism: Pragmatic Ideas for the New WTO Director-General (Centre for Economic Policy Research, 2020)

side of a border, which can be crucial for local economies. Simplifying customs procedures for small-scale, localized trade, preserves longstanding economic relationships between border communities. The exception can also help stimulate economic activity in often peripheral border regions. By recognizing that strictly enforcing MFN principles in these areas could be impractical and potentially harmful to local communities, the frontier traffic exception helps maintain social and cultural ties between communities separated by international borders.

The exception is typically applied to small-scale trade in a limited geographic area along the border. It might involve simplified customs procedures, reduced tariffs, or other advantages for local traders and consumers. The advantages should be limited to facilitating genuine frontier traffic and not extend to wider preferential treatment that could undermine the MFN principle. There has been no case law which has interpreted this provision, but a more precise meaning may be inferred. In practice advantages likely mean customs procedures and formalities at the border which would be made easier for an adjacent country than would be for other WTO members. With reciprocal trade between the two territories exempted from customs control and other restrictions of trade, other WTO members could not complain that their goods would be subject instead to customs duties when exported to the same territories. The frontier traffic exception most likely referred to cases where a border ran through a city or other populated area. The area affected by this provision was usually limited to a distance of 15 kilometres from the frontier.

3.4.3 Memoranda of Understanding (MOUs)

Preferential FTAs are granted exceptional status, permitting parties which enter into them to breach the MFN obligation of GATT. However, in order to be entitled to do so, the relevant agreement must satisfy the conditions set out in Article XXIV, as discussed earlier. There is therefore a question as to whether a preferential arrangement between two or more WTO members is sufficiently formalized to constitute an FTA for the purposes of that article. This is problematic in the case of agreements that are more aspirational in nature and which lack binding legal obligations. Such agreements, often termed Memoranda of Understanding (MOUs), are economically consequential in terms of their trade implications, however, there is a risk that they could be perceived as violations of MFN.

MOUs for trade in goods are non-binding agreements that countries or trading partners use to outline their intentions for cooperation and trade facilitation. While MOUs are generally not legally binding, they often serve as precursors to more formal agreements and can contain various provisions that guide trade relations. For example, the India-Bangladesh MOU on Border Haats establishes a framework for local border markets (haats) along the India-Bangladesh border. It contains provisions for defining the location and operational guidelines for border haats, specifying the types of goods that can be traded, outlining the maximum value of transactions allowed per person per day and establishing a joint committee to oversee the implementation of the border haats.

Another good example of an MOU for goods is the United States-China MOU on Agricultural Cooperation. This agreement focuses on facilitating agricultural trade between the two countries. It includes provisions for enhancing scientific and technical cooperation in agriculture, promoting the exchange of agricultural information and expertise, facilitating market access for agricultural products, and establishing working groups to address specific issues in agricultural trade. China has an MOU with Canada on canola research which is a sector-specific MOU that focuses on facilitating trade in canola products. It contains material on enhancing scientific cooperation in canola research, sharing information on canola production and processing, and facilitating market access for canola products. It also establishes a joint working group on canola trade issues.

Customs cooperation is often the subject of MOUs. For example, the United Kingdom-India MOU on customs cooperation aims to facilitate trade by improving customs procedures. It contains provisions for exchanging information on customs laws and procedures, cooperating on risk management and trade facilitation measures, sharing best practices in customs administration, and establishing a joint customs cooperation committee. This complements many of the issues featured in the WTO Trade Facilitation Agreement discussed in the previous chapter.

While these MOUs are not legally binding in the strict sense, they often contain language that encourages the parties to make their best efforts to fulfil their commitments. The provisions in these MOUs typically focus on establishing frameworks for cooperation, defining areas of mutual interest, setting up joint committees or working groups, outlining processes for information exchange, encouraging the harmonization of standards and procedures and promoting capacity building and technical assistance.

MOUs signed between governments generally do not satisfy the requirements of GATT Article XXIV for the formation of preferential free trade areas. MOUs are typically non-binding agreements that merely express a convergence of will between parties. Recall also that GATT Article XXIV requires that free trade agreements eliminate duties and other restrictive regulations of commerce on "substantially all the trade" between constituent territories. MOUs generally do not provide for such comprehensive trade liberalization. Full FTAs usually establish institutional mechanisms for implementation and dispute settlement, which are normally lacking in MOUs. WTO members are required to notify free trade agreements under GATT Article XXIV to the relevant WTO committees for review whereas MOUs are generally not notified or reviewed in this manner. GATT Article XXIV envisages the creation of permanent trade arrangements as valid exceptions to MFN. In contrast, MOUs are often temporary or subject to easy termination, lacking the permanence required for free trade areas.

3.4.4. Mutual Recognition Agreements (MRAs) and MFN

Mutual Recognition Agreements (MRAs) for goods between two or more WTO members could potentially raise concerns regarding their compatibility with the MFN principle because an MRA arguably accords special, preferential treatment for a subset of the whole WTO membership. It is important to recognize that MRAs are also associated with trade in services, perhaps even more so than goods. This issue will be examined in Chapter 8.

MRAs typically provide preferential treatment to goods from the participating countries by recognizing their standards or conformity assessment procedures. For example, an MRA between the European Union and the United States on pharmaceutical goods manufacturing practices allows for easier market access for drugs produced in either jurisdiction. This could be seen as discriminating against similar products from non-participating countries, potentially violating the MFN principle. While the principle of non-discrimination is at the heart of MRAs, there is also a good example of another vital principle in world trade law: harmonization. Harmonization, which will reappear later in this book in more depth in relation to health and safety and intellectual property, envisages the alignment between two countries' regulations and processes in order to facilitate international trade by precluding redundant "double regulation" as a good exits one country and enters another.

MRAs often result in reduced technical barriers to trade for participating countries. For instance, an MRA on electrical equipment between Australia and New Zealand allows for mutual acceptance of test reports and certificates, reducing duplicative testing requirements. This advantage is not extended to other WTO members, which could be viewed as inconsistent with MFN obligations. Furthermore, even if MRAs are technically open to all WTO members, the practical difficulties of negotiating and implementing such agreements with multiple partners might result in *de facto* discrimination against countries not party to the MRA.

On the other hand, if the terms of an MRA are applied on a non-discriminatory basis to all like products, regardless of their origin, it could be argued that the MRA does not violate the MFN principle. For example, if an MRA on organic food certification between two countries allows any product meeting the agreed standards to be certified, regardless of its country of origin, it might be considered MFN-compliant.

Moreover, many MRAs include provisions allowing other countries to join the agreement under the same terms. This openness could be seen as satisfying the "unconditional" aspect of the MFN principle. The Trans-Tasman Mutual Recognition Arrangement between Australia and New Zealand, for instance, is open to other countries to join if they meet the necessary conditions. MRAs typically focus on recognizing standards and conformity assessment procedures rather than providing preferential tariff treatment. This distinction might be used to argue that MRAs do not directly conflict with the tariff-focused nature of the MFN principle. If the benefits of an MRA are effectively extended to all WTO members in practice, even if not formally, it could be argued that the MRA does not violate the MFN principle. For example, if a country unilaterally decides to recognize standards or conformity assessment procedures from all countries that meet certain objective criteria, it might be considered as providing *de facto* MFN treatment.

MRAs could be interpreted as falling under the Technical Barriers to Trade (TBT) Agreement, which allows for some flexibility in the application of technical regulations and standards that are not present in the GATT. This issue will be discussed further in Chapter 7.

3.4.5 Plurilateralism and MFN

Plurilateralism is a kind of preferential arrangement in which a group of countries go beyond their WTO commitments with respect to a particular subject matter. Since they can also result in preferential treatment to the other parties which have joined, these types of trade agreements can also operate to violate the MFN principle of non-favouritism with respect to WTO members.

There are both "open" and "closed" plurilateral agreement models. The latter refers to those agreements that have been implemented in accordance with the specific processes outlined in Article II:3 of the WTO Agreement, which defines Plurilateral Trade Agreements as part of the WTO under Annex 4. Plurilateral agreements under Article II:3 are binding only on those members that have signed them. Nonetheless, the adoption and integration of new agreements into Annex 4 requires consensus from all WTO members. There are two Article II:3 plurilaterals currently in force, the Agreement on Civil Aircraft and the Government Procurement Agreement.

In contrast, "open" plurilateral agreements are the result of negotiations and agreements that do not require the participation of all members, nor their unanimous adoption. Open plurilaterals generally enter into force when a "critical mass" of members with a share of trade usually more than 90 per cent have signed the agreement. While operating outside the scope of Article II:3 of the WTO Agreement, open plurilaterals are nonetheless supported by the WTO's highest decision-making body through Ministerial Conference Declarations. The Information Technology Agreement and the Agreement on Basic Telecommunications are examples of a successful application of this model. These agreements have played a role in digital trade, the subject of Chapter 10.

The ITA is worth examining in more detail here since it deals with trade in technology-oriented goods. The ITA was signed by 29 WTO members and states or separate customs territories in the process of acceding to the WTO at the WTO Ministerial Conference in Singapore in December 1996. ITA entered into force in 1997 with a membership of 39 participants accounting for more than 90 per cent of world trade in these products. ITA eliminates import duties for IT products. It is the first agreement to liberalize trade in a specific sector after the establishment of the WTO; it is also the first sectoral agreement negotiated among developed and developing countries. No Least Developed Country has joined the agreement. The commitments on tariff elimination were incorporated into the tariff schedules of individual members. The main product categories covered by the ITA include computers, semiconductors, semiconductor manufacturing equipment, telecommunication apparatus, and data-storage media and software.

Plurilateralism has emerged as an important approach in international trade governance, particularly for trade in goods. This strategy allows like-minded countries to deepen and broaden trade rules and commitments for specific issues while accommodating the diverse preferences and capacities of different countries. Plurilateral agreements can be especially beneficial when dealing with complex trade policy matters that go beyond traditional tariff reductions and involve regulatory cooperation. The rise of plurilateralism in trade governance reflects the evolving nature of global commerce, where negative integration through tariff reduction is increasingly giving way to positive integration through rule convergence – the harmonization alluded to above. This shift makes plurilateral arrangements more suitable for addressing modern trade challenges, as they can better locate mutually agreeable and welfare-maximizing agreements compared to multilateral approaches.

Plurilateral initiatives can also serve as a means to reinvigorate global trade and modernize existing trade frameworks. By allowing subsets of countries to advance on specific trade issues, plurilateralism can help overcome deadlocks in multilateral negotiations and pave the way for broader agreements in the future. This flexibility can be crucial in addressing emerging trade challenges and adapting to the rapidly changing landscape of international commerce. Still, it is important to understand that the rise of plurilateralism in trade governance also presents potential risks to the world trading system. These include the possibility of fragmenting the global trade regime and potentially disenfranchising countries that are not part of specific agreements.

3.5 Conclusion

Non-discrimination is one of the central guiding principles of world trade law. In this chapter non-discrimination, comprising both National Treatment and MFN, was introduced in the context of trade in goods as a follow-up to the previous chapter on tariffs and quotas. Both National Treatment and MFN re-appear in the context of trade in services, where, especially in the case of National Treatment, there is a wider range of derogation since services are less fully liberalized than trade in goods. At the core of both of these principles of non-discrimination is the "likeness" test, requiring some basic degree of similarity between the relevant goods in order for the obligation not to discriminate to be triggered. Various tests have arisen, mostly arising under GATT, the essence of which constitutes an analysis of the competitive conditions between the products being compared.

While GATT, dating from the mid-20th century has formed the backbone of the non-discrimination standard in world trade, preferential FTAs have embraced both National Treatment and MFN to varying degrees, often merely by incorporating GATT language. National Treatment penetrates deeply into a country's economic sovereignty by covering a broad swath of regulations, many of which apply long after the imported product has crossed the border. It is no surprise, then, that it is subject to numerous exceptions both in the GATT and in FTAs. These will be discussed in Chapter 6 on non-trade values.

While designed to foster deeper, more open trade beyond that achievable under GATT, FTAs are themselves in a sense antithetical to the MFN rule because they grant preferential treatment to the parties, going beyond what is available to the general membership of the WTO. This chapter outlined the requirements for FTAs to be GATT-compliant. The most important of these is the expectation that the FTA will indeed lower barriers to trade between the parties, not raise them. Other kinds of preferential trading arrangements, also seemingly transgressions of the GATT MFN principle, were touched upon. In an era where tariffs have been largely eliminated on most manufactured goods, these types of informal arrangements, like MOUs and MRAs, along with FTAs themselves, are becoming key instruments in trade liberalization for goods.

Discussion Questions

1. How is the "likeness" test conducted for National Treatment and Most Favoured Nation? What are some of the difficulties with this exercise?
2. What is the difference between *de jure* and *de facto* discrimination and why are both prohibited under GATT?
3. In what way does the National Treatment obligation represent a significant encroachment on regulatory autonomy?
4. How do preferential Free Trade Agreements fit into the WTO's framework?
5. Is bilateralism/regionalism better than multilateralism when it comes to trade? What are the advantages and drawbacks?

4 Dispute Settlement

4.1 Introduction

The previous chapters have already shown that on occasion conflict can arise in relation to the interpretation of the principles of world trade law. Specialized tribunals render rulings on these disputes that have legal consequences. These decisions in turn contribute to the body of law that governs world trade. Indeed, one of the central principles of world trade law is binding dispute settlement governed by the rule of law.

This chapter will look at the procedural rules governing world trade disputes. This will primarily consist of an examination of the rules and procedures of the highly successful WTO dispute settlement system – the jurisprudence of which has played a fundamental role in establishing world trade law as we understand it today. A discussion of the new Multi-Party Interim Appeal Arbitration Arrangement is now essential to understand the workings of the WTO dispute settlement system because of its broken appeals mechanism. From here the less structured dispute settlement procedures available in FTAs will be explored, noting the various approaches in some of the mega-regionals in particular. The importance of informal consultations as a means of resolving trade disputes before escalation into full-scale arbitration will be highlighted.

4.2 WTO Dispute Settlement

The WTO contains its own dispute settlement procedure to ensure that its obligations, contained in its various agreements, are enforceable. As seen in the previous chapter, the meaning of some concepts is not always clear and can be contested by members, particularly when the rules are applied in practice. The principle underlying the adjudication of these disputes is the perhaps obvious one that the WTO agreements have practical significance on the members and, by extension, on the producers and consumers who are the indirect beneficiaries of the world trading system. The WTO's dispute settlement system (DSS) also reiterates the organization's commitment to the rule of law. In some instances, this principle may compromise the relationship-building diplomatic function of the organization which seeks to achieve consensus in developing new trade rules. There is a strong argument

DOI: 10.4324/9781003465676-4

that the WTO's DSS is the most successful international tribunal in the world in an area, not just trade, having heard more cases than the United Nations' International Court of Justice and enjoying a high rate of compliance.

The WTO dispute settlement understanding (DSU) is a set of procedural rules for resolving trade disputes arising from the WTO agreements, including GATT. It was adopted in 1995 as a result of the Uruguay Round of negotiations at the same time the WTO itself was created. The previous system for dispute settlement under GATT was less legalistic and ultimately unsatisfying for signatories seeking proper legal redress. The modern DSU is contained in Annex 2 of the WTO Agreement. It is important to understand that there are no substantive obligations relating to trade in the DSU. The agreement concerns only the process of dispute settlement itself, meaning the juridical forum in which disputes regarding the main agreements which arise between WTO members are resolved. Its primary objective is to settle disputes through a multilateral process rather than unilateralism, as occurred in the past under the GATT. In an effort to preserve the peace between members in the spirit of its diplomatic function, the DSU requires consultations as a prelude to adjudication. There is also a provision for arbitration and mediation.

Article 3.2 of the DSU is a key provision which sets out the fundamental purpose of the WTO's DSS:

> The dispute settlement system of the WTO is a central element in providing security and predictability to the multilateral trading system. The Members recognize that it serves to preserve the rights and obligations of Members under the covered agreements, and to clarify the existing provisions of those agreements in accordance with customary rules of interpretation of public international law. Recommendations and rulings of the DSB [dispute settlement body] cannot add to or diminish the rights and obligations provided in the covered agreements.

It is worth drawing attention to several of the elements contained in this article. First, the DSS aims to provide "security and predictability." Second, its function is to "preserve the rights and obligations" of WTO members. The verb "clarify" is crucial. The DSS is designed only to make sense of the law as it was drafted in the WTO treaties, not to build upon it. Finally, and perhaps most importantly when considering the backlash against the Appellate Body, the DSB "cannot add to or diminish the rights and obligations" of the members. This is an exceedingly narrow mandate. It is a purely interpretive role, expressly designed to be restrained.

The WTO dispute settlement system, following the procedural rules of the DSU, has been used extensively by WTO members, in particular the developed countries. Since 1995 there have been over 600 disputes brought through its rules. There have been 238 panel reports issued, with 203 of these being adopted by the Dispute Settlement Body (DSB). Of the panel reports, 157 were appealed, resulting in 124 Appellate Body reports being adopted, with the last ones occurring in 2020. The two-stage process of WTO dispute settlement, consisting of a first-tier panel, followed by an appeal, will now be examined.

4.2.1 Adjudication Process – Panels

If there is an allegation of a WTO member's rights having been violated, disputing countries of the WTO must first attempt to achieve a diplomatic resolution. This process is known as "consultations" during which the complaining member submits a written request to the responding member and the WTO, outlining the issue and legal basis for the complaint. The responding member must reply within ten days and enter into consultations within 30 days of the request. The parties engage in confidential talks to exchange information, clarify facts, and attempt to resolve the dispute amicably. Consultations typically last up to 60 days but can be shortened or extended by mutual agreement. Other WTO members with substantial trade interests may request to join the consultation. If consultations fail to resolve the issue within 60 days, the complaining party may request the establishment of a dispute panel. The goal of consultations is to encourage dialogue and find a mutually acceptable solution without resorting to formal litigation.

If consultations fail, the Complainant may request the Dispute Settlement Body to establish a Panel. A Panel will be established unless there is a negative consensus not to do so (meaning that all WTO members object to it) which means that it is virtually automatic. The Panels are *ad hoc*, meaning that they are constituted for each dispute, after which point they return to their normal work – they are not employed by the WTO. Each Panel consists of three members who act as adjudicators. These people are not nationals of either party unless agreed by the parties. Article 7.1 of the DSU states that panels are empowered:

> To examine, in the light of the relevant provisions in (name of the covered agreement(s) cited by the parties to the dispute), the matter referred to the DSB by (name of party) in document . . . and to make such findings as will assist the DSB in making the recommendations or in giving the rulings provided for in that/those agreement(s).

Panels typically consist of three members, though parties can agree to a five-member panel within ten days of establishment. The WTO Secretariat proposes nominations for panellists to the parties. Panellists must be well-qualified individuals with expertise in international trade law or policy. They serve in their individual capacities, not as government representatives. Many WTO members nominate people to lists of indicative panellists from which parties can draw appointees. Parties can only oppose nominations for compelling reasons. If the parties cannot agree on panellists within 20 days, either party can request the WTO Director-General to appoint the panel.

After composition, the panel sets its own working procedures in consultation with the parties. The standard panel process involves two rounds of written submissions and two meetings with the parties. In the first round, the complaining party submits its arguments, followed by the responding party's rebuttal. A first substantive meeting is then held where parties present their cases orally. This is followed by a second round of written rebuttals and a second meeting with the panel.

Throughout this process, the panel may pose questions to the parties and request additional information. Third parties that have notified their interest in the dispute may also make submissions and be heard by the panel – these are known as *amicus curiae* briefs. To date, no panel has ever formally referred to an *amicus curiae* brief in rendering its decision. The panel may seek information and technical advice from experts if needed. Panel deliberations are confidential – taking place at the WTO headquarters in Geneva.

After considering the evidence and arguments, the panel issues an interim report to the parties for comment. The panel then issues its final report to the parties, which is circulated to all WTO members within three weeks. The DSB adopts the report within 60 days unless there is a consensus not to adopt or an appeal is filed (known as negative consensus). The entire panel process, from composition to issuance of the final report, should generally not exceed six months. In no case should it exceed nine months from panel establishment to circulation of the report to members. **[See Figure 4.1]**

This panel procedure aims to provide an efficient, rules-based mechanism for resolving trade disputes between WTO members. It balances the need for due process and thorough examination of the issues with the goal of prompt settlement of disputes. The procedure's structure, with opportunities for written submissions, oral hearings, and interim review, ensures that parties have the full opportunity to present their cases while allowing the panel to make an objective assessment of the matter.

4.2.2 Adjudication Process – Appeals

A panel decision may be appealed to the Appellate Body before it has been adopted by the Dispute Settlement Body. The Appellate Body process begins when a party to a dispute formally notifies the Dispute Settlement Body (DSB) of its decision to appeal a panel report. This notification must be made within 60 days of the circulation of the panel report to WTO members. Simultaneously, the appellant must file a Notice of Appeal with the Appellate Body Secretariat, which initiates the appellate proceedings.

The Appellate Body is supposed to consist of seven individuals who are standing members and who are not affiliated with any government. These people are exceptionally highly regarded experts in international trade law, drawn from the world's chief legal systems. Each member is elected for a four-year term which may be renewed once for a total of eight years' service. In the past, while the Appellate Body was still functioning, approximately 70 per cent of panel decisions were appealed. The reason for this high level of frequency is that appeals achieve delay and help domestic politicians "save face" by reporting to their constituents that they are doing everything in their power to maintain the measure, which is presumably of interest to their citizens, especially their well-organized suppliers.

The Appellate Body may uphold, modify, or reverse a panel decision. There is no remand power – the Appellate Body cannot send the matter back down to another panel to resolve questions of fact that were not addressed properly. Once an

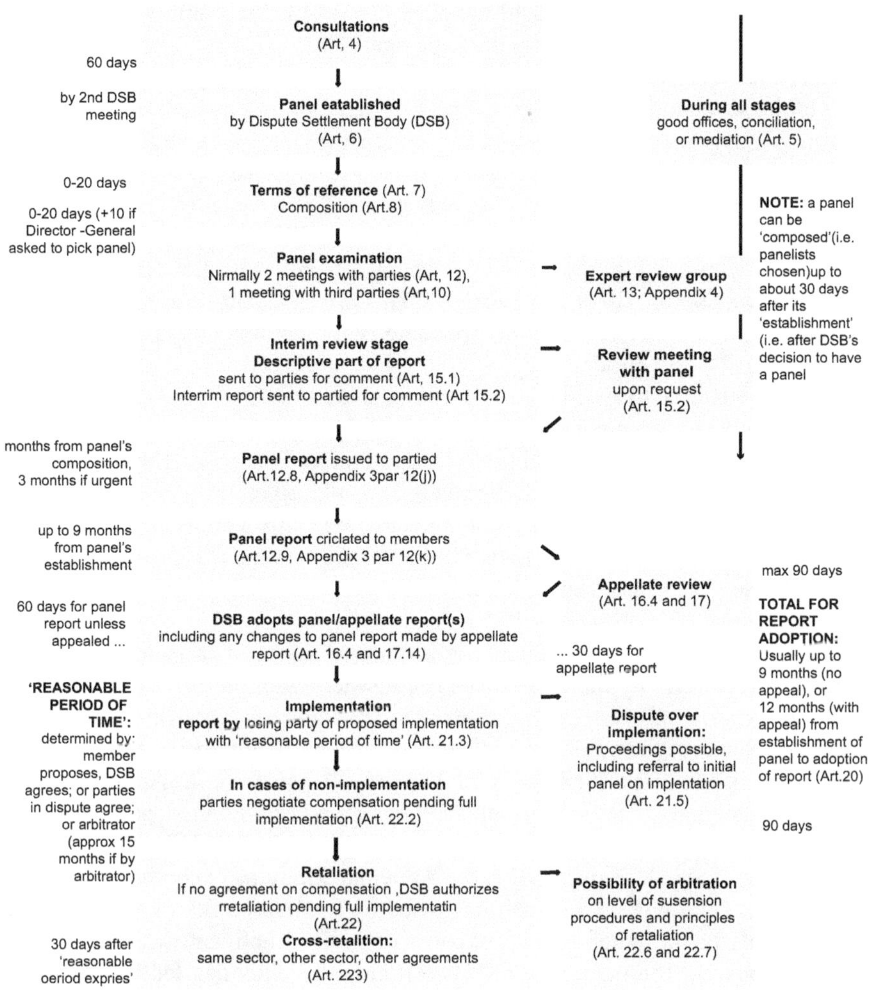

Figure 4.1 The World Trade Organization Dispute Settlement System

Source: The World Trade Organization (reproduced with permission)

appeal is filed, a division of three Appellate Body members is selected to hear the case. The selection process is designed to ensure randomness and unpredictability while also providing an opportunity for all Appellate Body members to serve regardless of their national origin. The division elects one of its members as the Presiding Member for the appeal.

The appellant must file a written submission within ten days of filing the Notice of Appeal. This submission outlines the alleged errors in the panel's legal interpretations and conclusions. Other parties to the dispute may file their own appeals (known as "other appeals") within 15 days of the initial Notice of Appeal. Within

25 days of the Notice of Appeal, the appellee(s) must file their written submissions responding to the claims raised by the appellant(s).

After the written submissions are filed, the Appellate Body division (usually three of the seven members) holds an oral hearing. During this hearing, the parties present their arguments and respond to questions from the division members. Third parties that have notified their interest in the dispute may also make oral statements and answer questions. Following the oral hearing, the Appellate Body division deliberates in private to reach its conclusions. To ensure consistency and coherence in decision-making, the division exchanges views with the other Appellate Body members before finalizing its report. This process, known as the "exchange of views," is a unique feature of the Appellate Body that helped maintain the consistency of WTO jurisprudence.

The Appellate Body is required to circulate its report within 60 days of the Notice of Appeal, with a maximum extension to 90 days in exceptional cases. The report addresses each of the legal issues and interpretations covered by the appeal. Once the Appellate Body report is circulated, it is placed on the agenda of the next DSB meeting, held typically every month. The DSB must adopt the report within 30 days of its circulation unless there is a consensus among WTO members not to do so. The negative consensus rule makes the adoption of Appellate Body reports virtually automatic.

The Appellate Body's jurisdiction is limited to issues of law and legal interpretations developed by the panel. This is consistent with the function of appeals courts in most countries. It cannot re-examine existing evidence or consider new evidence related to factual aspects of the dispute. As noted above, the Appellate Body's role is one of clarification of the law only. In so doing, the Appellate Body process is designed to provide a prompt and effective resolution to legal issues arising from panel reports.

However, since December 2019, the Appellate Body has been unable to hear new appeals due to a lack of quorum caused by the United States blocking new appointments to the body, citing concerns of judicial activism (essentially that it strayed beyond the mandate of DSU Article 3.2). This has led to a crisis in the WTO dispute settlement system, with some members exploring alternative arrangements such as the Multi-Party Interim Appeal Arbitration Arrangement (MPIA) to preserve appellate review in trade disputes. This will be explored further below.

4.2.3 WTO Dispute Settlement – Key Features

The WTO's dispute settlement system is exclusive – it is only available to WTO members. It is a state-to-state dispute settlement system, like the ICJ or the International Tribunal for the Law of the Sea. This means that only national (or the case of customs unions, supra-national) governments can bring or defend disputes. Sub-regional governments cannot nor can private individuals, corporations, or other organizations such as NGOs or trade unions. Some view this narrow set of participants as indicative of poor access, particularly for an organization that purports to serve the interests of global trade, and which seeks to raise standards of living worldwide.

There is arguably indirect access to WTO dispute settlement, as individuals or organizations can lobby their government to bring or defend claims. Moreover, panels and the Appellate Body *may* consider *amicus curiae* briefs and have done so on a few occasions, although, as mentioned earlier, there has yet to be a case in which either a panel or the Appellate Body has expressly referred to an *amicus* brief in rendering its decision. The Appellate Body set out the rules on the acceptance of *amicus curiae* briefs in a 1998 dispute brought against the European Union in relation to its ban on the material asbestos.[1] Canada had challenged the EU's law on the basis that it lacked scientific merit as a risk to health. There were a significant number of non-parties interested in taking part in the appeal (because of the health controversies surrounding various forms of asbestos). The Appellate Body established procedural requirements to be met by any person or entity wishing to file a written brief in the dispute. Individuals and groups do not have the right to submit documents to the panels or Appellate Body – the decision to accept them rests with the discretion of the tribunals. One of the key requirements stipulated by the Appellate Body was that there was a maximum page limit of 20 pages from each applicant or group.

Article 3.7 of the (DSU) states that before bringing a case, a member shall exercise their judgement as to whether action under these procedures would be fruitful. The aim of the dispute settlement mechanism is to secure a positive solution to a dispute. Article 6.2 establishes that the request for the establishment of a panel must identify the specific measures at issue and provide a brief summary of the legal basis of the complaint sufficient to present the problem clearly.

Article 23.1 establishes that the DSU is the proper venue for addressing violations of WTO obligations, nullification or impairment of benefits, or impediments to WTO objectives. These are the three 'causes of action' for WTO members seeking to use the dispute settlement system, meaning the legal basis for a member country to bring a complaint against another member. First, and most importantly is a violation complaint. In this type of complaint, the complaining member must demonstrate that a WTO obligation has been breached. These are the most common form of complaints. Nullification or impairment of WTO benefits are presumed from the existence of this breach. Secondly, there is a non-violation complaint. Here there may not be an actual breach of a WTO obligation, requiring the complainant to prove that there has been a nullification or impairment of their benefits as a WTO member. In this cause of action, a member may have followed the law strictly, but their actions may still have led to harm suffered by another member. Lastly, is there "any other situation." In this circumstance, for which there has not yet been an actual complaint, nullification or impairment must be proven. It is

1 European Communities – Measures Affecting Asbestos and Asbestos-Containing Products, WT/DS135/AB/R, adopted 5 April 2001

uncertain what the "any other situation" category was intended to address but it is often thought that it provides a degree of flexibility in terms of fulfilling the WTO's objectives on behalf of its members. The non-violation complaints have been considered as a way of addressing some of the issues in international trade which are not governed directly by WTO law, such as currency manipulation.[2]

Under Article 14.1 and 17.10 of the DSU, respectively, proceedings of the panel and Appellate Body are confidential. This has been thought to encourage frank and open communication between the parties and also to save time. The "secrecy" of WTO hearings has caused some consternation because the parties to WTO disputes are states which represent the interests of their citizens, not private companies which may have a more legitimate need for privacy. Over the years some of the WTO dispute settlement hearings have taken place in public. The first open hearing took place in the *EC-Hormones*[3] dispute in 2005 and since then there have been more than 20 disputes where at least some of the hearings were open to the public. This public viewing of hearings has typically been done through closed-circuit television broadcasts to a separate viewing room at the WTO's headquarters. It has required the agreement of the parties to the dispute, as the DSU does not explicitly provide for public hearings.

The move toward more open hearings has been welcomed by some as enhancing transparency and public understanding of the WTO system. Still, some developing countries have expressed concerns that open hearings may disadvantage them by increasing the costs and complexity of WTO litigation.[4]

4.2.4 Principles of Interpretation and Standards of Review

As mentioned above, Article 3(2) of the DSU states that recommendations and rulings of the DSB must "not add to or diminish Members' rights and obligations." This is often taken to indicate that WTO tribunals must not engage in judicial activism by adjudicating matters beyond that which were brought to their attention or making superfluous comments about what provisions mean which are not strictly necessary for resolving the dispute at hand. The alleged failure of the Appellate to exercise restraint in this regard is one of the reasons that the United States sought to debilitate it. Prevented from creating rights, the purpose of the panels and Appellate Body is therefore one of resolving ambiguities in the law. This means that much of what they do consists of interpretation.

The WTO dispute settlement system employs specific principles and methods for interpreting the WTO agreements, as mandated by Article 3.2 of the DSU. This article requires that WTO agreements be interpreted "in accordance

2 See, for example, United States – Measures on Steel and Aluminium (Mexico) (DS551) (5 June 2018) and United States – Measures on Steel and Aluminium (India) (18 May 2018) (DS547)

3 European Communities – Measures Concerning Meat and Meat Products (Hormones), WT/DS26/AB/R, WT/DS48/AB/R, adopted 13 February 1998

4 GV Puig and PJ Kuyper, "Transparency in WTO Dispute Settlement" in A Bianchi and A Peters (Eds.), *Transparency in International Law* (Cambridge University Press, 2013)

with customary rules of interpretation of public international law." The primary source for these customary rules is the Vienna Convention on the Law of Treaties (VCLT), particularly Articles 31–33. The Appellate Body has consistently referred to these provisions as reflecting customary international law on treaty interpretation.[5]

Several interpretive principles have been derived from the VCLT and applied by WTO panels and the Appellate Body. There is the good faith interpretation in accordance with the ordinary meaning of treaty terms in their context and in light of the treaty's object and purpose.[6] Furthermore, there has been consideration of context, including the treaty text, preamble, annexes, and related agreements.[7] Consideration of subsequent agreements, subsequent practice, and relevant rules of international law applicable between the parties.[8] Special meaning has been given to terms if it is established that the parties so intended.[9] The panels and Appellate Body have also made recourse to supplementary means of interpretation, including preparatory work and circumstances of conclusion, to confirm meaning or determine meaning when the primary means leave it ambiguous or lead to manifestly absurd results.[10]

The application of these principles has led to several notable approaches in WTO jurisprudence. The Appellate Body has emphasized a textual approach, focusing on the ordinary meaning of treaty terms. This is characterized by a strong emphasis on dictionary definitions as the starting point for establishing ordinary meaning.[11] The Appellate Body has also recognized that the meaning of treaty terms can evolve over time. For example, in *United States – Shrimp*, it stated that the term "exhaustible natural resources" in GATT Article XX(g) "must be read by a treaty interpreter in the light of contemporary concerns of the community of nations about the protection and conservation of the environment."[12] The principle of effectiveness in treaty interpretation has also been practiced by the WTO panels and Appellate Body. This requires giving effect to all terms of a treaty and avoiding interpretations that would render certain terms redundant.[13]

While Article 32 VCLT allows recourse to preparatory work as a supplementary means of interpretation, there has been debate about the appropriate weight to give to negotiating history. There is ongoing discussion about how to interpret WTO agreements in light of other international law norms, particularly in areas

5 United States – Standards for Reformulated and Conventional Gasoline, WT/DS2/AB/R, adopted 20 May 1996
6 Article 31(1) VCLT
7 Article 31(2) VCLT
8 Article 31(3) VCLT
9 Article 31(4) VCLT
10 Article 32 VCLT
11 I Van Damme, "Treaty Interpretation by the WTO Appellate Body" 21:3 European Journal of International Law 605 (2009)
12 WT/DS58/AB/R, at [129]
13 A Qureshi, *Interpreting WTO Agreements: Problems and Perspectives* (2nd ed. Cambridge University Press, 2015)

like human rights and environmental protection. Although the Appellate Body appears to favour a literal interpretation, some have argued for greater consideration of the object and purpose of WTO agreements as well as the broader context of the dispute.[14]

The applicable law to be examined by WTO panels and the Appellate Body consists of the covered WTO agreements, including the DSU itself, international agreements in place between the parties, and customary international law. The applicable law in a WTO dispute primarily consists of the WTO agreements and related legal instruments. Domestic legislation is also an element of applicable law – these are the "measures" which are being challenged.

Past panel and Appellate Body reports, while not binding precedent in the strict sense, are often considered and cited for consistency and coherence in interpretation. This contributes to a sense of consistency and predictability within the dispute settlement system, which is thought to be vital to its legitimacy among WTO members. It is sometimes thought that the lack of formal precedent prevents the development of jurisprudence upon which future decisions can be based, undermining the predictive capacity of the dispute settlement mechanism and, in so doing, preventing compliance and raising costs for its users. On the other hand, the freedom of panels and the Appellate Body to depart from previous tribunals' reasoning lends flexibility to the system. This can be important given the highly disparate economies of the WTO's members.

The onus of proof of a fact in WTO dispute settlement is on the party asserting it, just as the onus of demonstrating a breach of WTO law is on the complaining party. The onus shifts at various points, notably in relation to the articulation of a defence under GATT Article XX.

The standard of review adopted by the panels and Appellate Body is another important facet of the functioning of the WTO dispute settlement system. The standard of review adopted by panels of national laws requires them to make an "objective assessment of the matter" as specified in Article 11 of the DSU. As will be seen in Chapter 6, there are instances where a standard of "necessity" is applied for some of the general exceptions of GATT and GATS. The Anti-Dumping Agreement has a special standard of highly deferential review, described as a "one-of-a-kind treaty norm."[15] It requires panels to accept any "permissible" interpretation and has long been a point of criticism by the United States who feel that this has given too much latitude to the panels and the Appellate Body.

There is arguably some evidence of the use of a standard of "proportionality" or "balancing" of interests by panels, as well as the Appellate Body. Proportionality is a concept drawn from the jurisprudence of the European Court of Human Rights

14 H Horn and JH Weiler, "European Communities – Trade Description of Sardines: Textualism and its Discontents" in H Horn and PC Mavroidis (Eds.), *The WTO Case Law of 2002* (Cambridge University Press, 2005)

15 Y Rovnov, "Article 17.6(ii) of the WTO Anti-Dumping Agreement: Waiting for Chekhov's Gun to Go Off" 15:1 Journal of International Dispute Settlement 106 (2024)

and is often associated with impartial decision-making in international tribunals, notably investment arbitration.[16] As a term, it implies that there is a formulaic methodology for engaging in weighing and balancing divergent interests, such as those contained in the GATT general exceptions.

Under Article 17.6 of the DSU, appeals to the Appellate Body are limited to issues of law covered in the panel report and legal interpretations developed by the panel. The threshold for review of a panel's decision on these matters is thought to be a high one – the Appellate Body tends only to reverse or modify a panel's interpretation if the error is significant. Panels have the authority to seek information and technical advice from any individual or body.[17] The Appellate Body has the implied authority to consult experts. These powers are important given the volume of often highly technical information brought by the parties to the dispute settlement process, some of which include numeric data and economic or financial calculations.

4.2.5 Remedies in WTO Dispute Settlement

The panels and Appellate Body may issue recommendations or rulings. In terms of their legal effect, recommendations are not strictly binding but create strong expectations of compliance. Rulings, on the other hand, are considered legally binding on the parties to the dispute. Recommendations typically suggest ways for a member to bring a measure into conformity with WTO agreements. In contrast, rulings make definitive findings on whether a measure violates WTO rules. Recommendations are usually made by panels or the Appellate Body in their reports, somewhat resembling the concept of *obiter dicta* in the common law. Rulings are formally adopted by the DSB when it adopts panel or Appellate Body reports. There is some flexibility in how recommendations are implemented whereas rulings generally require specific actions to remove the violation found.

With regard to the consequences of non-compliance, failure to follow recommendations may lead to further dispute proceedings while non-compliance with rulings can potentially lead to authorized retaliation. It should be pointed out that in practice, the terms "recommendations" and "rulings" are often used together or interchangeably when referring to the outcomes of WTO disputes. The DSU refers to recommendations or rulings of the DSB as a single concept in many provisions. Once a panel or Appellate Body report is adopted by the DSB, its conclusions and recommendations become binding upon the parties, regardless of whether they are labelled as recommendations or rulings. The expectation is that the losing party will bring its measure into conformity with WTO rules as specified in the adopted report.

The primary remedy for breach of WTO law is withdrawal or amendment of the WTO-inconsistent measure – not damages as in many civil domestic systems or in

16 V Vadi, *Proportionality, Reasonableness and Standards of Review in International Investment Law and Arbitration* (Elgar, 2018)

17 Article 13 DSU

other aspects of international economic law. In one respect this could be viewed as a serious departure from a fundamental principle of customary international law – namely that parties which suffer harm as a consequence of the wrongdoing of states are entitled to full reparation.[18]

There are temporary remedies which may be applied by the winning member while the withdrawal or amendment is awaited. First, there is compensation, which means additional concessions granted by the losing member to the winning member, often in the form of tariff reductions. Secondly, there is retaliation (although that term is not used in the DSU) which means the suspension of concessions by the winning member against the losing member, typically in the form of tariff increases. Both of these alternative remedies must be authorized by the DSB. Retaliation in the form of a higher tariff is itself a barrier to trade. This approach can lead to an escalation of trade barriers, worsening trading relations rather than improving them. It is also often viewed as a kind of self-harm, especially for smaller countries which cannot absorb the economic damage caused by higher prices on imports from offending countries.

It is often claimed that there is no truly effective sanction for countries that do not comply with WTO dispute settlement rulings. Retaliation, it is sometimes argued, is only effective when it is used by a country of relatively equal economic power to the losing party; otherwise, it is an empty threat that is ultimately self-defeating for the winning country that imposes it. It is especially unhelpful for developing countries where the suspension of trade concessions would be barely noticed by a large, developed country.

Prompt compliance with WTO panel and Appellate Body recommendations is expected but not always possible. A reasonable time for implementation is allowed and while this is not specified in the text of the DSB, it is thought to be somewhere around six months. The implementation period addresses the reality that altering laws can be a time-consuming process in most democracies, in some cases requiring approval by more than one legislative body (e.g., the House of Representatives and the Senate of the United States Congress).

The overall compliance rate with WTO rulings is around 90 per cent. This suggests that the system has been largely effective in resolving disputes and inducing compliance. While the overall compliance rate is high, there are often delays in implementation. In some cases, countries implement only part of the ruling or take actions that do not fully address the concerns raised in the dispute. This can lead to further litigation through compliance proceedings. For instance, in the long-running dispute between the European Union and the United States over aircraft subsidies,[19] there have been multiple rounds of compliance proceedings due to disagreements over the adequacy of implementation measures. There have been

18 ARSIWA Article 42

19 European Communities and Certain Member States – Measures Affecting Trade in Large Civil Aircraft, WT/DS316/AB/R, adopted 1 June 2011; United States – Measures Affecting Trade in Large Civil Aircraft (Second Complaint), WT/DS353/AB/R, adopted 23 March 2012

some high-profile cases of non-compliance that have attracted significant attention. One example is the *United States – Gambling,*[20] explored in more depth in Chapter 8. Another notable case is *EC – Hormones,*[21] where the European Union maintained its ban on hormone-treated beef for many years despite adverse WTO rulings.

4.2.6 Reforms

A number of reforms to the WTO dispute settlement system have been proposed over the years to improve its effectiveness in terms of the implementation of the WTO-covered agreements. More recently these have dealt with the problem of Appellate Body member blockage by the United States (notably the MPIA, which will be explored further below). Access remains one of the WTO dispute settlement system's chief problems, particularly with respect to how it is perceived by the general public. The system's availability only to members may be seen to undermine its effectiveness as a world court of trade since it is often private traders (exporters and importers) who are most harmed by protectionist barriers. If the WTO panels and Appellate Body procedures were available to private parties, it would be a very different system, significantly removed from the domain of public international law, characterized by state-to-state dispute settlement. Even if WTO rules were directly enforceable in domestic courts, which they are not, this could cause problems of enforceability because of potential jurisdictional overlaps.

Tied to the problem of access (who can use the system) is the question of transparency, meaning who is able to witness the system in action. The confidentiality of WTO panel and Appellate Body hearings has been a vital feature of its efficiency. Rather than a public trial dealing with facts which may be readily understood by the public, the WTO courts deal heavily with economic data and the interpretation of legal provisions. Although these matters may be of limited interest to non-experts, the fact remains that courts which are not open to the public suffer from the perception of secretiveness. There is an adverse inference on the part of the public that such hearings are disregarding their concerns and that this is somehow undemocratic. Since WTO hearings involve the interaction of sovereign states, which represent the interests of their taxpaying citizens, this grievance is understandable to a degree. But opening up hearings to the public would almost certainly raise costs and lead to delays. Streaming on the Internet, as has been attempted in some investment cases, might be a sensible compromise.

Short timeframes were often viewed as one of the great strengths of the WTO dispute settlement system. Failure to adhere to the strict timeframes has also been cited with contempt by the United States. Yet some might contend that the timeframes are already too short and should be extended to reflect the increasing

20 United States – Measures Affecting the Cross-Border Supply of Gambling and Betting Services, WT/DS285/AB/R, adopted 20 April 2005

21 European Communities – Measures Concerning Meat and Meat Products (Hormones), WT/DS26/AB/R, WT/DS48/AB/R, adopted 13 February 1998

complexity of cases. There is not much point in having a hearing if there is no proper discussion of the legal issues.

Another commonly cited problem with the WTO dispute settlement system is the lack of participation by developing countries, rendered all the more frustrating given that two-thirds of WTO membership consists of this category of country. Developing countries may struggle to make use of the dispute settlement system because of its costs, in particular the cost of hiring skilled counsel. The Advisory Centre on WTO law, which is not affiliated with the WTO itself, has been able to offer legal assistance to developing countries on a pro bono basis. Additionally, there have also been historically few panel members from developing countries, although the Appellate Body has been reasonably well-represented by individuals with this background. It is an entirely legitimate criticism that without further involvement of developing countries, the WTO's dispute settlement system has dubious legitimacy as a genuine world court of international trade.

Remand powers for the panels and the Appellate Body may achieve some progress in addressing the charge that the Appellate Body engages in judicial activism by considering matters which were beyond its original mandate, notably matters of fact which might be more rightly considered by a newly constituted panel.

As noted earlier, compliance with panel and Appellate Body recommendations is generally quite good, although this too could be improved. Although losing parties occasionally criticized individual rulings, this has rarely reached the level of a challenge to the overall authority or legitimacy of the WTO dispute settlement system. Decisions are sometimes criticized for being too technical and, consequently, of limited value to non-expert readers. While this could be said of rulings of almost any domestic appellate courts throughout the world, there is an added problem with WTO cases that they are not only legally complex but often also economically so. Rulings have also been faulted for being too broad in their scope and addressing issues that were not strictly necessary to provide a resolution to the matter at hand.[22]

The WTO panels and Appellate Body arguably suffer from an excessively burdensome caseload, high even when the Appellate Body was properly constituted with its seven members. Recently a number of initiatives have been undertaken to simplify the content of Appellate Body reports. The section in each report on conclusions now summarizes the key points of the reasoning for those who do not wish to go through the entire text. Furthermore, except in some of the very large disputes such as the Large Civil Aircraft cases mentioned earlier, the length of reports has decreased, with few now exceeding 70 pages.

A series of informal discussions and consultations on reforming the WTO dispute settlement system took place at the WTO in 2023-2024. Led by Marco Molina, the Deputy Permanent Representative of Guatemala to the WTO, these reforms have been described as the "Molina Process."[23] The objective was to have

22 Comments from U S Bhatia, 11th Annual Update on WTO Dispute Settlement (3 May 2018)

23 See further P Van den Bossche, "The WTO Dispute Settlement Reform: A Critical Assessment of the February 2024 Consolidated Text of a Draft Ministerial Decision on Dispute Settlement" in V Vadi and D Collins (Eds.), *Handbook on International Economic Law* (Routledge, forthcoming)

substantive discussions to find practical solutions to the concerns identified with the dispute settlement system, with the aim of fulfilling the June 2022 ministerial mandate of having a fully and well-functioning dispute settlement system accessible to all members by 2024. The process culminated in February 2024, when Molina circulated a draft consolidated text for a Ministerial Decision on Dispute Settlement Reform. It included suggested changes regarding alternative dispute resolution, panel proceedings, compliance, guidelines for adjudicators, procedures to discuss legal interpretations, Secretariat support, transparency, accessibility, and technical assistance. The recommendations omitted some controversial issues, particularly regarding appeals, as "work in progress." This reflected the ongoing disagreements among members, especially between the United States and most other WTO members, on the future of the appellate mechanism.

While the Molina Process made significant strides in identifying areas of potential reform and consensus, it also highlighted the deep divisions that remain among WTO members on key issues, particularly regarding the appellate function. The process laid important groundwork for ongoing discussions, but achieving comprehensive reform of the WTO dispute settlement system remains a challenging task that will require continued negotiation and compromise among members.

4.3 The Multi-Party Interim Appeal Arbitration Arrangement (MPIA)

A minimum of three Appellate Body members are required to hear an appeal and, due to the United States blockage of new appointments, as of late 2019, there are none left. The Appellate Body no longer exists. Before exploring the innovative attempt at resolving this impasse, it is useful to briefly consider the essence of the United States' problem with the Appellate Body.

The United States blockage of the appointment of new Appellate Body members primarily relates to the Appellate Body's alleged overreach in its authority in interpreting WTO agreements as well as imposing obligations on the member states which were not agreed under WTO rules.[24] The United States asserted that, contrary to the Appellate Body's mandate under the DSU, the tribunal "added to or diminished rights or obligations" of the members under the covered agreements.[25] For example, in *United States – Continued Dumping and Subsidy Offset Act of 2000,*[26] the United States accused the Appellate Body of creating a new category of banned subsidies which was outside the scope of the Agreement on Subsidies and Countervailing Measures.[27] The United States insisted that the Appellate Body

24 WJ Davey, "WTO Dispute Settlement: Crown Jewel or Costume Jewellery?" 21 World Trade Review 291, 292 (2022)

25 USTR 2018 Report.

26 WTO, United States – Continued Dumping and Subsidy Offset Act of 2000 – Report of the Appellate Body (16 January 2003) WT/DS217/AB/R and WT/DS234/AB/R.

27 USTR 2018 Report, 22.

strictly follow WTO rules as written instead of applying "non-text-based interpretation," which in the United States' opinion could undermine members' rights to enact key measures such as safeguards.[28]

The United States has also been dissatisfied with the Appellate Body's statement that, absent "cogent reasons," the Appellate Body considers its reports (judgements) as precedents and therefore that the same legal issue should be resolved in the same manner.[29] The United States claimed that previous rulings adopted by the Appellate Body were therefore erroneously regarded by the Appellate Body as binding jurisprudence.[30] Rather than carrying precedential weight, as in the Anglo-American common law, the United States wanted previous Appellate Body rulings to be merely persuasive in establishing interpretations. This would ensure that the rule-making power of the WTO vests with its members rather than its judiciary.[31]

The United States also objected to non-compliance of the Appellate Body with the 90-day time limit for appeal (many have taken much longer than this, with the average over 140 days), as well as its issuance of "advisory opinions," essentially making legal statements which were not necessary for the resolution of the dispute at hand.[32]

There may be some merit in United States criticisms of the Appellate Body. Perhaps it did engage in judicial activism by overreaching in some of its interpretations of WTO law, going beyond what was required and arguably creating new law in the process – something the Appellate Body was never supposed to do. On the other hand, the inherent vagueness of certain aspects of WTO law, such as the understanding of a "public body" when considering the legality of subsidies, meant that some "gap-filling" was inevitable and in some respects desirable. By loose analogy, if legal principles are unclear then the Anglo-American common law has typically enabled judges to exercise discretion, as long as it is reasonable. Moreover, if interpreted literally, the constraint that the Appellate Body only "clarify" the meaning of WTO texts is arguably excessive. The act of clarification may require addition or subtraction of elements.

Lacking any members to adjudicate, appeals from panel rulings are now made "into the void" – meaning that they are stuck in limbo as to their legal significance, engendering uncertainty for governments, producers and consumers alike. Since the right of appeal is enshrined in the DSU, absence of the Appellate Body may cause the lower panel reports to be unable to be adopted. Indeed, it had been hoped that once the Appellate Body ceased to function WTO members would exercise

28 USTR 2018 Report, 24

29 Office of the United States Trade Representative, "2018 Trade Policy Agenda and 2017 Annual Report of the President of the United States on the Trade Agreements Program" (March 2018)

30 J Bacchus and S Lester, "The Rule of Precedent and the Role of the Appellate Body" 54:2 Journal of World Trade 183 (2020) at 185

31 Ibid., at 193

32 Ibid., at 193

restraint and avoid appealing decisions of the panels, essentially foregoing their right to appeal,[33] but this was not the case. At the time of writing, since the Appellate Body ceased to function, 20 cases have gone to appeal, including eight notified by the United States itself.

In 2020, a group of 16 WTO members led by the European Union established the Multi-Party Interim Appeal Arbitration Arrangement (MPIA). Constructed around the seldom-used arbitration provision of Article 25 of the DSU, the MPIA enables appeals from lower WTO panel decisions to a tribunal of three expert judges (selected at random from a roster of 10), much like an ordinary appeal to the old Appellate Body. The founders of MPIA emphasised the importance of preserving the two levels of adjudication and binding character in the WTO dispute settlement system,[34] which has been impaired due to the Appellate Body crisis. Crucially, the MPIA is not applicable to all members of WTO – only to participating members.[35] It is thus an example of plurilateralism – the advancement of new issues at the WTO through a smaller subset of its membership rather than the classic multilateral (every member) approach.

Article 15 of the Agreed Procedures for MPIA (Annex I to the MPIA statement) states that arbitral awards shall "only be notified" to the WTO DSB, but not formally accepted. Moreover, Article 25(3) of the Agreed Procedures explains that parties are bound by the terms of the award, which shall be final. In other words, their binding character does not hinge upon the DSB approval, but rather on the consensual agreement amongst the parties. While Article 3(2) of the DSU mentions the objective of "security and predictability" that dispute settlement will bring to the world trading system, paragraph 5 of the MPIA Agreement speaks instead of "*coherence* and predictability" [italics added]. This change in wording is telling. The emphasis on "coherence" appears to encourage consistent interpretations grounded in previous case law. It also suggests a principle of collegiality where conflicting views between arbitrators are less likely to transpire. This should foster legitimacy among MPIA rulings that should, in turn, enable trading countries to enact legislation which complies with a broadly accepted understanding of legal concepts, rather than ones which are perceived to be up for challenge. The three additional arbitrators (recall the original Appellate Body had seven standing adjudicators) are further believed to improve the efficiency of the MPIA in handling cases and also promote a more geographically diverse institution.[36] Despite these differences, the MPIA is similar to the Appellate Body in many respects. The scope of appeal is only limited to issues of law covered

33 See comments from J Hillman, "Restoring WTO Dispute Settlement: Lessons Learned" WTO Public Forum (2022) (video)

34 Statement on a Mechanism for Developing, Documenting and Sharing Practices and Procedures in the Conduct of WTO Disputes (30 April 2020) JOB/DSB/1/Add.12 (MPIA Statement)

35 Ibid., Annex 2 Article 9

36 D Sharma, "The Move Towards Multi-Party Interim Appeal Arbitration: How Efficacious?" 88 Arbitration: The International Journal of Arbitration, Mediation and Dispute Management 117 (2022)

by the panel report and legal interpretations developed by the panel. The MPIA arbitrators also have the authority to uphold, modify, or reverse the findings of the panel.

The MPIA was established as a temporary appeal arrangement and not intended to be a permanent solution to the Appellate Body crisis. The MPIA was only considered as a contingency in order to maintain basic procedural rights contained in the WTO DSU that had been jeopardized because of the non-functional Appellate Body. Although the creation of MPIA was seen by some as the best solution to bring back a central element of WTO dispute settlement,[37] there are some lingering questions about how the MPIA will work. First, the existence of the MPIA creates a gap between the participating and non-participating members. As noted above, unlike dispute settlement procedures under the DSU that are applicable to all WTO members, MPIA can only provide its services to countries that have given notification to the WTO that they intend to join. Instead of decreasing inequality between its members, the establishment of MPIA created an apparent disparity in the WTO. Second, it is not clear whether the MPIA is part of the WTO or is an extraneous mechanism.[38] Since the MPIA statement outlines that it is established in accordance with Article 25 of the DSU,[39] it might imply that MPIA is part of the WTO. On the other hand, funding for the MPIA comes only from its signatories, not from the WTO itself.

As outlined in Article 15 of the Procedures of MPIA, parties to the dispute must voluntarily accept that they will comply with the award as issued. This means that decisions issued by the MPIA do not bind other WTO members who are not participating in this body. In contrast, normal dispute settlement in WTO has an imperative nature where reports issued by the panels and Appellate Body will be considered "approved" by all WTO members unless there is a negative consensus. Unlike the real Appellate Body, arbitral awards issued under MPIA are only required to be notified to the DSB, but it is not mandatory that they are adopted.[40] Some believe that this arrangement undermines the legitimacy of the MPIA as a dispute settlement mechanism in WTO.[41] It is also not clear that the MPIA will address the criticisms levied by the United States concerning judicial overreach. Indeed, the United States remains sceptical towards MPIA, as does the United Kingdom. It could be argued that it would be difficult for the MPIA to function as a long-term solution if it is not supported by and applicable to all WTO members. This ignores the reality that it is exceedingly difficult to get multilateral consensus on any issues – suggesting that partial support will have to do.

37 'Multi-Party Interim Appeal Arbitration Arrangement (MPIA)' (WTO Plurilaterals)
38 H Gao, "Finding a Rule-Based Solution to the Appellate Body Crisis: Looking Beyond the Multiparty Interim Appeal Arbitration Arrangement" 24 Journal of International Economic Law 534 (2021) at 541
39 MPIA Statement, Annex 1
40 Ibid., Article 15
41 Gao, n 39 at 541–542

Colombia – Anti-Dumping Duties on Frozen Fries[42] was the first case to test the MPIA as an alternative to the Appellate Body. The case involved anti-dumping duties imposed by Colombia on frozen fries from Belgium, the Netherlands, and Germany. The Arbitrators upheld the Panel's finding that the European Union's claim regarding packaging cost-related adjustments fell within the Panel's terms of reference, rejecting Colombia's argument that part of this claim was not properly identified in the panel request. Procedurally, this case demonstrated several interesting aspects of how the MPIA functions. First, the Arbitrators issued their award only 74 days after the appeal was made, well within the 90-day timeframe regulated in Article 21.5 of the DSU. This was a notable departure from the practice of the WTO Appellate Body, which had often struggled to meet this deadline. Moreover, to expedite proceedings, the Arbitrators imposed strict word and time limits for oral hearings. They also suggested that the parties refrain from making any Article 11 DSU claims on appeal, to which the parties agreed. This approach highlights the MPIA's focus on streamlining the appeal process and addressing one of the main criticisms of the WTO Appellate Body system. Another procedural innovation was the increased transparency of the proceedings. With the permission of the parties, a video recording of the MPIA proceeding was made available, marking a departure from the traditionally closed nature of WTO dispute settlement proceedings. The MPIA's handling of this case demonstrated its potential as a viable alternative to the WTO Appellate Body. It showed that the MPIA can effectively resolve disputes while addressing some of the criticisms levelled at the previous system, particularly regarding the timeliness of decisions and procedural efficiency.

The MPIA has proven popular – it now has the support of 53 WTO member states including the European Union, Canada, Australia, China, and most recently Japan. Most observers appear to be generally impressed with the quality and timeliness of the *Colombia – Frozen Fries* ruling.[43] It leads one to wonder whether Appellate Body decisions have become longer and more complex than needed. At the time of writing, there are eight disputes currently before the MPIA and three more were finalized without appeal, withdrawn, or settled. Support for the MPIA has also been voiced by the business community. For example, Japan's (delayed) decision to sign onto the MPIA was motivated in part by Keidanren's (Japan's Federation of Business Organisations) recommendation that Japan take part for the sake of securing Japan's status as a safe trading nation.[44]

There are no feasible alternatives to the MPIA on the current horizon. Some have been suggested to overcome the Appellate Body crisis, but none offer realistic hope. Perhaps most obviously, the WTO could consider bringing back the Appellate Body into operation with some modifications in its role in line with

42 Colombia – Anti-Dumping Duties on Frozen Fries from Belgium, Germany and the Netherlands, WT/DS591/ARB25, Award of the Arbitrators, 21 December 2022.

43 A Yanovich, "WTO Issues First Award Under MPIA and Tackles Standard of Review in Anti-Dumping Disputes" Akin Gump (17 January 2023)

44 A Kuno, "Japan's Joining MPIA an Outside Chance to Boost Momentum for WTO Reform" East Asia Forum (1 May 2023)

the United States's requirements.[45] Another alternative would be a return to the panel-only system of the GATT before the WTO was established. However, considering the success of WTO dispute settlement in the last few decades, returning to the old regime would not be the best solution in this matter. Reforming the Appellate Body in step with the United States wishes, might seem advisable. Indeed, some changes, notably strict adherence to timeframes, could be applied immediately, should all members agree. But, it would seem that if the Appellate Body is to be revived with the support of the United States, the WTO would have to attempt to limit the body's authority so that it will not interpret the rules disproportionately, as the United States has alleged.

Under the general guidance of the WTO adjudicators, WTO members can decide to limit the role of the Appellate Body so that it will not overstep the boundaries as set out under the established rules. However, such fundamental changes would be very hard to implement in practice, even if new wording could be established in the DSU regarding the avoidance of "gap filling." United States Trade Representative Katherine Tai commented recently of the need for a "fundamental rethink of the dispute settlement system . . . to ensure that we end the practice of judicial rulemaking."[46]

It is difficult to envisage how the Appellate Body could be re-instigated with this sweeping restriction imposed upon it. The distinction between interpreting and making law, especially when principles were vaguely drafted, is often a fine one. One imagines that a new Appellate Body circumscribed in such a manner to suit the Americans would end up being effectively a remand court – merely re-hearing the initial dispute, rather than clarifying legal concepts in a meaningful manner. Over time it is likely that the Appellate Body would begin to drift towards "overreach" in seeking to clarify ambiguities naturally arising in the course of disputes. It is also quite likely that the United States would agitate once again were they to begin to lose cases.

4.4 Dispute Settlement Under FTAs

The WTO dispute settlement system is not the only recourse to resolving trade disputes between states, although it is unquestionably the most important and influential. As mentioned before, there are many thousands of preferential FTAs, most of which contain state-to-state dispute settlement chapters contemplating neutral arbitration panels composed of adjudicators drawn from both state parties.

4.4.1 Examples of Dispute Settlement Mechanisms Under FTAs

The RCEP agreement includes a comprehensive dispute settlement mechanism outlined in Chapter 19. The process begins with consultations between the parties to the dispute. The complaining party can request consultations with the responding

45 Davey, n 24 at 294
46 Comments from USTR Katherine Tai at the G20 Trade and Investment Ministers' Meeting (2023)

party regarding any matter covered by the agreement. The responding party must reply within seven days and enter into consultations within 30 days of receiving the request unless the parties agree otherwise. If consultations fail to resolve the dispute within 60 days (or 20 days for urgent matters), the complaining party may request the establishment of a panel. The panel request must identify the specific measures at issue and provide the legal basis for the complaint. The panel is to be composed of three members, with each party appointing one panellist and the parties agreeing on the chair. If they cannot agree, the RCEP Joint Committee will appoint the remaining panellists by lot from a roster of individuals.

The RCEP panel proceedings follow detailed rules of procedure. The panel is to issue an interim report to the parties within 150 days of its establishment. The parties have an opportunity to comment before the panel issues its final report within 30 days of the interim report. The panel's final report is binding on the parties. The responding party must bring the measure into conformity with the agreement within a reasonable period of time, to be determined by agreement or through arbitration if necessary. If the responding party fails to comply, the parties are to negotiate compensation. Failing that, the complaining party may suspend concessions or other obligations under the agreement, subject to certain conditions.

Importantly, the RCEP dispute settlement mechanism does not include an appellate review process. However, it does allow for alternative methods of dispute resolution, including good offices, conciliation, or mediation, which the parties can undertake at any time. A unique feature is that the RCEP panel can consider relevant interpretations in the WTO panel and Appellate Body reports when interpreting provisions of WTO agreements incorporated into RCEP. However, RCEP panel findings cannot add to or diminish rights and obligations under the agreement. Overall, the RCEP dispute settlement process aims to provide an effective, efficient, and transparent mechanism for resolving disputes between parties, while maintaining some flexibility through options for alternative resolution methods.

The CPTPP has its own dispute settlement process, outlined in Chapter 28 of the agreement. This process is designed to provide an effective, efficient, and transparent mechanism for resolving disputes between parties regarding the interpretation and application of the agreement. The dispute settlement process under the CPTPP begins with consultations between the parties. Any party can request consultations with another party regarding any matter covered by the agreement. The responding party must reply to the request within seven days and enter into consultations within 30 days of receiving the request (or 15 days for urgent matters, including those concerning perishable goods). The parties are required to engage in consultations in good faith and make every effort to reach a mutually agreed solution. If consultations fail to resolve the dispute within 60 days of the request (or 20 days for urgent matters), the complaining party may request the establishment of a dispute settlement panel. The panel request must be made in writing and identify the specific measures at issue and the legal basis for the complaint. The panel is to be composed of three members, with each party appointing one panellist and the parties agreeing on the chair. If they cannot agree, the remaining panellists will be appointed by lot from a roster of individuals.

The CPTPP panel proceedings follow detailed rules of procedure outlined in the agreement. The panel is required to issue an initial report to the parties within 150 days of its establishment (120 days for urgent matters). The parties then have an opportunity to comment before the panel issues its final report within 30 days of the interim report. The final report is to be released publicly within 15 days, subject to the protection of confidential information. If the panel finds that a party has failed to comply with its obligations under the agreement, the responding party must bring the measure into conformity within a reasonable period of time. This period is to be determined by agreement between the parties or through arbitration if necessary. If the responding party fails to comply, the parties are to negotiate compensation. Failing that, the complaining party may suspend benefits under the agreement, subject to certain conditions. The CPTPP dispute settlement process also allows for alternative methods of dispute resolution, including good offices, conciliation, or mediation, which the parties can undertake voluntarily at any time. Additionally, the agreement provides for the participation of interested third parties in the dispute proceedings. As with the RCEP procedure, the CPTPP dispute settlement mechanism does not include an appellate review process, which distinguishes it from some other trade agreements. The panel's final report is considered binding on the parties. This feature is intended to ensure the finality of decisions and promote efficient resolution of disputes.

The dispute settlement process under ASEAN agreements involves several steps and mechanisms. The primary dispute settlement mechanism for ASEAN economic agreements is outlined in the ASEAN Protocol on Enhanced Dispute Settlement Mechanism (EDSM), signed in 2004. This protocol establishes a formal process for resolving disputes between ASEAN member states regarding the interpretation or application of ASEAN economic agreements. The process begins with consultations between the disputing parties. Any member state can request consultations with another member regarding a dispute covered by ASEAN economic agreements. The responding party must reply to the request within ten days and enter into consultations within 30 days of receiving the request unless the parties agree otherwise.

If consultations fail to resolve the dispute within 60 days, the complaining party may request the establishment of a panel. The panel typically consists of three members selected from a roster maintained by the ASEAN Secretariat. The panel examines the matter and issues a report with its findings and recommendations, usually within 60–70 days of its establishment. Unusually for an FTA, either party may appeal the panel's report to the ASEAN Economic Ministers (AEM) within 30 days. The AEM then has 30 days to issue a decision on the appeal. The AEM's decision is final and binding on the parties. I apologize for the confusion in my previous response. The appeal to the AEM is more administrative in nature rather than a full legal appeal. It's not comparable to a typical judicial appellate process. The AEM can consider both legal and factual aspects of the panel report which is broader than the WTO Appellate Body. In practice, the AEM appeal mechanism has been rarely used, with ASEAN members often preferring diplomatic channels for dispute resolution.

If the losing party fails to comply with the panel or AEM ruling within a reasonable period of time, the winning party may request authorization to suspend concessions or other obligations against the non-complying party. The level of suspension is subject to arbitration if challenged. In addition to this formal process, ASEAN agreements emphasize the use of good offices, conciliation, and mediation to resolve disputes amicably. The ASEAN Secretary-General may offer these services to help parties reach a mutually agreed solution at any stage of a dispute. This appeal process reflects ASEAN's preference for consensus-based decision-making and diplomatic resolution of disputes, rather than a strictly legalistic approach.

The USMCA establishes a general dispute settlement procedure in Chapter 31 that aims to resolve disagreements between member countries regarding the interpretation or application of the agreement. This process begins with government-to-government consultations, where the parties attempt to resolve the issue through diplomatic means. If consultations fail to resolve the dispute within a specified timeframe, typically 30 to 75 days depending on the nature of the issue, the complaining party may request the establishment of a panel.

The USMCA panel formation process has been improved compared to its predecessor, NAFTA, to prevent potential blockages. Under the new system, panels are typically composed of five members, though the disputing parties may agree to a three-member panel. The selection process for panellists is designed to ensure that a panel can be formed even if one party refuses to participate, addressing a key weakness of the NAFTA system. Once established, the panel hears the case and is expected to issue its report within a specified timeframe, generally within nine months. The panel's report contains findings of fact, determinations on whether the measure in question is inconsistent with USMCA obligations, and the reasons for these findings and determinations. If the panel finds that a party has violated its USMCA obligations, the offending party is expected to bring itself into compliance with the agreement. Should the losing party fail to implement the panel's decision, the agreement provides for various enforcement mechanisms, including the possibility of compensation, suspension of benefits, or fines.

The USMCA also includes provisions for alternative dispute resolution methods, such as good offices, conciliation, or mediation, which parties can voluntarily undertake at any time. These proceedings are confidential and without prejudice to the rights of the parties in other proceedings. For disputes over obligations common to both the WTO and USMCA rules, a party can choose the dispute forum but can only bring the case to one forum. This provision helps prevent forum shopping and conflicting rulings on the same issue.

The aforementioned examples illustrate the powerful influence of the WTO's dispute settlement system, both in terms of the structure of the dispute settlement procedure as well as, perhaps more importantly, the remedies awarded to victorious parties (or more precisely, inflicted on losing parties). Losing parties in FTA trade disputes are not required to pay damages (as they are for example in investor-state dispute settlement) but to withdraw the unlawful measure. This approach reflects the disparate nature of harm caused by trade barriers which fall onto the shoulders of a wide variety of parties including exporters, importers, consumers, and employees. Payment directly to a sovereign government would not address these injuries and, therefore, fail to achieve full reparation, as required by Article 31 of the Articles on State Responsibility for Internationally Wrongful Acts.

4.4.2 Disputes Under FTAs

While there has been remarkably limited usage of these systems compared to that of the WTO,[47] some disputes have been brought under FTAs over the years. The settlement of disputes in the international trade arena is, therefore, sometimes characterized as fragmented, meaning that there are multiple fora in which aggrieved parties, usually states, may seek compensation or resolution. Distinct from trade, international investment law offers direct access by aggrieved businesses to arbitration against host states – known as investor-state dispute settlement (ISDS). Trade-oriented disputes have been framed as investment matters so that private companies can access the arbitration panels and the monetary compensation which they may offer, in contrast to WTO panels.

In 2018, the European Union initiated arbitration proceedings against South Korea, alleging that Korea had failed to comply with labour commitments outlined in the Trade and Sustainable Development chapter of their FTA. The European Union claimed that Korea had not made sufficient progress in ratifying and implementing fundamental International Labour Organization (ILO) conventions, particularly those related to freedom of association and the right to collective bargaining. This case was significant as it marked the first time the European Union had triggered the dispute settlement mechanism in the Trade and Sustainable Development chapter of any of its trade agreements. The arbitration panel was established in January 2021, following unsuccessful bilateral consultations between the parties. The European Union also invoked the dispute settlement provisions in its Association Agreement with Ukraine in 2020. The European Union requested consultations with Ukraine regarding a ban on exports of unprocessed timber. While this dispute did not proceed to full arbitration, it demonstrates the European Union's willingness to use dispute settlement mechanisms in its trade agreements.

Under NAFTA's general state-to-state dispute settlement mechanism, contained in Chapter 20, only three cases proceeded to the panel stage, with two resulting in final panel reports. The limited use of this mechanism was largely due to the ability of parties to block panel formation, which became evident after 1998 when the United States blocked a panel requested by Mexico in a sugar dispute. Several disputes that could have been brought under NAFTA's Chapter 20 were instead taken to the WTO's dispute settlement system. This trend was partly due to the difficulties in forming panels under NAFTA and the perceived advantages of the WTO system.

47 G Vidigal, "Why Is There So Little Litigation Under Free Trade Agreements? Retaliation and Adjudication in International Dispute Settlement" 20:4 Journal of International Economic Law 1 (2017)

The United States has been involved in several disputes under its FTAs. One notable case arose under the United States-Chile FTA in 2016 regarding Chile's price band system for agricultural products. The United States argued that Chile's system violated tariff commitments under the FTA, leading to consultations between the two countries. Another significant dispute occurred under the Dominican Republic-Central America-United States Free Trade Agreement (CAFTA-DR) in 2011. In this case, Guatemala was accused of failing to effectively enforce its labour laws, particularly in relation to the right of association, the right to organize and bargain collectively, and acceptable working conditions. This marked the first time the United States had brought a labour case under an FTA. The United States-Korea Free Trade Agreement (KORUS) has also seen disputes. In 2019, the United States requested consultations with South Korea regarding issues related to competition policy. The dispute centred on how Korea's competition authority conducted certain competition hearings.

FTA arbitration panels frequently refer to WTO jurisprudence in their decisions. This occurs because FTAs incorporate WTO principles and agreements by reference, making WTO interpretations relevant to FTA disputes. For example, in the NAFTA panel decision on *Broom Corn Brooms*,[48] the panel referred to WTO Appellate Body decisions in discussing the concept of "like products" under NAFTA Article 309. In the CAFTA-DR arbitration panel decision in *Costa Rica v El Salvador Tariffs on Goods*,[49] the panel cited several WTO Appellate Body reports when interpreting CAFTA-DR provisions on tariff classification. The NAFTA panel in *Cross-Border Trucking Services*[50] relied heavily on WTO jurisprudence in interpreting national treatment obligations under NAFTA. Turning to WTO case law for guidance, especially when interpreting provisions that are similar to or derived from WTO agreements, helps FTA panels promote consistency in the interpretation of international trade rules across different forums.

Jurisdictional conflicts between the WTO and FTAs may become more common in the future because of the proliferation of bilateral and regional trade treaties. One way to resolve such tensions might be through a forum of choice clauses in FTAs.[51] In a WTO case brought by the United States against Mexico as a consequence of the latter's tax regime on soft drinks,[52] Mexico based its defence on the "forum exclusion" clause in NAFTA, the precursor to the USMCA. Mexico argued that, since the case constituted part of a broader dispute that had previously been brought against the United States under NAFTA, the treaty's forum exclusion clause demanded that the NAFTA arbitration panel should be the only forum to resolve the dispute. The WTO panel disagreed, ruling that enabling a WTO panel

48 USA-97-2008-01

49 CAFTA-DR/ARB/2014/CR-ES/17

50 USA-MEX-98-2008-01

51 S Yang, "The Solution for Jurisdictional Conflicts Between the WTO and RTAs: The Forum Choice Clause" 23:1 Michigan State International Law Review 107

52 Mexico – Tax Measures on Soft Drinks and Other Beverages WT/DS308 (Panel Report, 7 October 2005)

to decide its own jurisdiction would diminish a complaining party's rights under the DSU. It appears that under WTO jurisprudence it will be difficult for forum exclusion clauses in FTAs to deny claimants access to the WTO dispute settlement system.

The overlapping of multiple dispute settlement procedures for the trade chapters of various FTAs entered into by the same states may lead to situations of so-called "forum shopping" where complainants choose the dispute settlement route which they feel gives them the best chance of success. Few FTAs offer a clear indication regarding their relationships to other agreements. Such matters may become even more problematic in an era of mega-regional multi-party trade agreements like the CPTPP and the RCEP.

The use of arbitration provisions in FTAs remains limited, with many disputes being resolved through diplomatic channels or consultations before reaching the arbitration stage. The European Union, for example, has also been working to strengthen and modernize the dispute settlement provisions in its newer trade agreements, such as those with Canada (CETA) and Japan, to make them more robust and effective. The relative scarcity of arbitration cases under EU FTAs can be attributed to several factors, including the preference for diplomatic solutions, the deterrent effect of having dispute settlement provisions, and the fact that many EU trade agreements are relatively recent, with dispute settlement mechanisms that have not yet been fully tested.

4.5 Conclusion

The interpretation and application of the principles of world trade law is an essential element of their effectiveness in maintaining the free flow of goods and services around the world. Binding dispute settlement is therefore a tremendously important principle of world trade law in its own right. The most significant of the mechanisms for dispute settlement in world trade is that of the WTO, among the most successful of all international tribunals. Its two-tier, highly structured format has enabled the functioning of much of the global economy for almost thirty years.

The WTO dispute settlement system has matured since its early days. The legal analysis conducted by panels and the Appellate Body is arguably more teleological than it was in the past. It is more aware of the ultimate purpose of clarifying members' rights and obligations with a view to maintaining the stability of the world trading system. Meanwhile, reliance on the WTO dispute settlement system has intensified in recent years as the negotiation forum of the WTO struggled to achieve progress in terms of improving market access. As the Appellate Body is currently embroiled in crisis it may be that in the coming years, WTO members may attempt to resolve their trade differences through the WTO's negotiating arm. It remains to be seen whether the MPIA will replace the Appellate Body on a permanent basis, or whether the Appellate Body will ultimately be revised, possibly in a modified form.

While nowhere near as heavily used as the WTO dispute settlement system, preferential FTAs often contain their own dispute mechanisms, in some cases modelled on that of the WTO but typically lacking an appeals route. Indeed, the omission of an appeals function from FTA arbitration could indicate that appeals are not needed, and, by extension, the WTO Appellate Body is not essential to the functioning of the WTO. The arbitration provisions of FTAs are poised to increase in significance commensurate with the growing scope and depth of these agreements. Emphasis on informal dispute settlement, in the form of negotiation and consultation, is likely to remain a central feature of both bilateral and regional dispute settlement, underscoring the historic importance of diplomacy within world trade as an adjunct to binding adjudication.

Discussion Questions

1. Is the WTO dispute settlement system sufficiently inclusive with regards to who/what it enables to participate in its proceedings as parties?
2. What is the purpose of an appeal under the WTO dispute settlement system? Is an appeal route necessary?
3. Why did the United States block the appointment of new Appellate Body members? Were they justified?
4. Is the Multi-Party Interim Appeal Arbitration Arrangement (MPIA) a good idea? What are its advantages and disadvantages?
5. How is trade dispute settlement under preferential Free Trade Agreements different than that of the WTO?

5 Trade Remedies

Subsidies, Anti-Dumping, and Safeguards

5.1 Introduction

GATT was quite successful in reducing tariffs and eliminating quotas throughout the 20th century. This left countries which were eager to continue protectionist policies, under the misguided belief that this would be economically beneficial, to seek alternative strategies. With limited means for making foreign products *less* attractive to consumers, politicians realized that the only way to improve the competitive standing of products from their own countries was by making them *more* attractive to consumers, chiefly by reducing their prices. This could be done through governmental assistance that would offset producers' costs. Later, especially as the heavily industrialized China joined the world trading community, another strategy occurred to the exporting firms themselves. Foreign markets could be vanquished by eliminating competition through price undercutting even if this resulted in short-term losses. A final strategy, and one which the GATT contemplated as a legitimate response to the sudden shock of opening borders to foreign goods, was to enable the imposition of temporary tariffs in order to offset the serious harms that could occur if an industry was not quite ready to deal with competition from abroad.

Collectively these three plans of action are labelled, somewhat confusingly, as "trade remedies" – essentially meaning the ways in which countries react to breaches of world trade principles by their trading neighbours. Trade remedies are today one of the most controversial, not to mention technical, aspects of world trade law. Domestic legislation empowering a country to impose retaliatory trade remedies in the form of tariffs on imports is among the chief weapons in today's "trade wars." Such tariffs, while arguably harmful in that they impose higher prices on domestic consumers, are designed to achieve deterrence. In theory, they prevent foreign countries from behaving unfairly when it comes to the level playing field which is achieved by world trade law's emphasis on free markets to be won by the best suppliers.

This chapter will illustrate the three concepts of subsidies, dumping, and safeguards alluded to previously. This will be done initially by reference to the relevant WTO disciplines but drawing also upon modifications of these rules seen in FTAs. The latter includes enhanced transparency and notification and specialized

DOI: 10.4324/9781003465676-5

procedures for non-market economies and state-owned enterprises. This chapter will also consider some examples of domestic trade remedies procedures, notably the United Kingdom's new "economic interest" test. This chapter will consider agricultural subsidies as well as new WTO disciplines on the restriction of fisheries subsidies. It should be noted that the WTO intended to establish trade remedies rules for services too, but this never occurred. Trade remedies are therefore primarily an element of industrial (as in manufacturing) policy as well as agricultural goods.

5.2 Subsidies

Subsidization is when a government intervenes directly in the market by assisting a particular industry or company, enabling it to lower its prices or improve its quality without bearing any of the costs. The logic behind the subsidy is that a benefit to your own manufacturers is just as good as a detriment to foreign ones, which is what tariffs achieved before they were largely eliminated.

Today subsidies remain one of the most popular forms of protectionism. Countries are increasingly willing to devote public resources towards the maintenance of private entities which would struggle to survive under normal market conditions. The renewed interest in industrial policy, which fell out of favour at the end of the 20th century, is driven by factors such as attempts to mitigate climate change, supply chain vulnerabilities exposed by the Covid-19 pandemic, and competition with China's state-led economic mode.

Subsidization tends to be associated with certain industries that are seen to play a pivotal role in a country's economic or social welfare. Subsidies also tend to be linked to countries where the state traditionally plays a larger role, such as in Asia as opposed to Europe and North America, although subsidization is by no means alien to these countries either. Indeed, one of the main problems with controlling subsidies through world trade law is the reality that governments always help their citizens, in fact, this is one of the roles that we expect governments to perform. The degree of support from the government will differ across societies, with those in the West, especially the United States, generally expecting a smaller role for government in favour of free markets, with countries like China and Russia having a much stronger tradition of state support in keeping with their communist past.

Even in countries characterized by free markets, the state tends to maintain a visible presence as a regulator or market mediator, ensuring that certain values like consumer safety and healthy competition are upheld. It is, therefore, difficult to establish a principle that subsidization is always wrong. The dilemma is establishing at what point does this support, or interference, reaches the level of an unfair or inefficient distortion of world trade.

5.2.1 The WTO Agreement on Subsidies and Countervailing Measures

One of the great achievements of the WTO was the Agreement on Subsidies and Countervailing Measures (SCM). This treaty among WTO members was the first and remains the only global agreement dealing directly with subsidies.

Perhaps most important of all, the SCM established a definition of subsidy – the first time ever in an international treaty. This is found in Article 1 of the SCM.

1.1 a subsidy shall be deemed to exist if:

(a)(1) there is a financial contribution by a government or any public body within the territory of a Member (referred to in this Agreement as "government"), i.e. where:

(i) a government practice involves a direct transfer of funds (e.g. grants, loans, and equity infusion), potential direct transfers of funds or liabilities (e.g. loan guarantees);
(ii) government revenue that is otherwise due is foregone or not collected (e.g. fiscal incentives such as tax credits);
(iii) a government provides goods or services other than general infrastructure, or purchases goods;
(iv) a government makes payments to a funding mechanism, or entrusts or directs a private body to carry out one or more of the type of functions illustrated in (i) to (iii) above which would normally be vested in the government and the practice, in no real sense, differs from practices normally followed by governments;

or

(a)(2) there is any form of income or price support in the sense of Article XVI of GATT 1994;

and

(b) a benefit is thereby conferred.

This section goes on to provide a list of examples of the types of governmental action which will indicate that a subsidy has taken place. These are a direct transfer of funds (e.g., cash grant); government revenue otherwise due is forgone (e.g., a tax credit); goods or services are made available by the government (e.g., a road link to a factory) or the government purchases goods (e.g., medical equipment for public hospitals). These examples cover a wide range of situations, encompassing a number of governmental initiatives which could operate to confer a benefit on the private sector, potentially distorting trade.

Importantly, though, in order for the measure to count as a subsidy it must be "specific." The principle of specificity is central to the notion of subsidization, injecting the necessary flexibility into the agreement in terms of what the WTO prohibits and what it does not. This enables governments to serve the interests of their citizens without falling foul of world trade rules. The concept of specificity illustrates that flexibility is a key principle of world trade law, allowing countries to fulfil their international trading obligations while retaining a degree of policy space.

Specificity, as the word suggests, contemplates assistance provided to a certain enterprise or group of enterprises, rather than generally to the economy as a whole. It usually means that a particular company has benefited, granting them a favourable position in world markets that they would not otherwise enjoy. Other aspects are relevant to the identification of the measure as specific. These are outlined in Article 2.2 of the SCM. First, where the government explicitly limits access to a subsidy to certain enterprises, this subsidy will be deemed specific. Second, if the government establishes objective criteria or conditions governing the eligibility for, and the amount of, a subsidy, then the subsidy will not be specific, meaning that they will not be unlawful under the SCM. It need not only be one company that benefits in order for the subsidy to count as specific. The use of a subsidy programme by a limited number of certain enterprises, predominant use by certain enterprises, the granting of disproportionately large amounts of subsidy to certain enterprises, and the manner in which discretion has been exercised by the granting authority in the decision to grant a subsidy can all fulfil the specificity requirement.

The purpose of the specificity principle can be discerned from these rules; in order for a measure to constitute a subsidy – only targeted assistance will fall within the discipline of the agreement. Generalized support or relief to large segments of society should not be construed as trade distortive. These kinds of government activity are merely the types of projects that governments should engage in for the wider economic welfare of their society.

In a dispute between the United States and China over alleged subsidies to steel and rubber industries, the Appellate Body clarified that the concept of specificity is also a flexible one and its determination will be done on a case-by-case basis (more discretion to the WTO courts) but that specificity will be established if there is a clear restriction on the particular enterprise or industry to which the contribution will apply.[1]

The concept of "benefit" is another crucial element in determining whether a government measure constitutes a subsidy under SCM. A benefit is considered to exist when the financial contribution provided by a government confers an advantage on the recipient compared to what would be available in the marketplace. These assessments will require a significant amount of evidence, much of which will be presented with the help of economists and other specialists. The Appellate Body in the *Canada – Aircraft*[2] dispute provided important clarification on the meaning of benefit. It stated that the existence of a benefit should be determined by comparing the terms of the financial contribution to those available in the market. A benefit exists when the recipient is better off than it would have been absent the government's financial contribution.

In practical terms, a benefit can take various forms. For instance, in the case of government loans, a benefit would exist if the interest rate charged by the government is lower than what the company could obtain from commercial banks. Similarly, for government equity infusions, a benefit occurs if the government provides capital on terms more favourable than those available from private investors. The

1 United States – Countervailing Duty Measures on Certain Products from China, WT/DS437/AB/R, adopted 16 January 2015

2 Canada – Measures Affecting the Export of Civilian Aircraft, WT/DS70/AB/R, adopted 20 August 1999

United States – Large Civil Aircraft (Second Complaint)[3] case further elaborated on the concept of benefit in relation to infrastructure provision. The Appellate Body ruled that the mere provision of infrastructure by the government does not automatically confer a benefit. Instead, it's necessary to examine whether the government has provided goods or services for less than adequate remuneration.

Another important aspect of benefit analysis is the selection of an appropriate benchmark for comparison. In *United States – Softwood Lumber IV,*[4] the Appellate Body addressed the issue of selecting a market benchmark when the government is the predominant supplier of goods. It ruled that investigating authorities may use alternative benchmarks, such as world market prices when domestic prices are distorted due to the government's predominant role in the market. The concept of benefit also extends to indirect subsidies – meaning those that are provided via an intermediary rather than from the government itself. In *United States – Tax Incentives,*[5] a WTO panel examined whether tax incentives provided by the United States state of Washington to the Boeing aircraft manufacturer conferred a benefit. The panel found that these measures did confer a benefit as they reduced Boeing's tax liability compared to what it would have been without the incentives.

The final element to evaluate when considering the definition of subsidy in Article I of the SCM is the concept of a "public body." The interpretation of what constitutes a public body has been the subject of significant debate and jurisprudence in WTO dispute settlement. The difficulty of defining "public body" was highlighted in a dispute between the United States and China regarding various attempts by the United States to counter Chinese subsidization in a number of industries including steel.[6] China had argued that contributions made by Chinese state-owned enterprises to private companies were not benefits and therefore not subsidies. The Appellate Body ultimately agreed with China and ruled that in order to be considered a public body and, therefore, capable of subsidizing, that entity must perform governmental functions and have the authority to give commands to a private body. This determination would need to be done on a case-by-case basis. On examination of the relevant companies providing the contribution, the Chinese state-owned enterprise did not have these powers, so the assistance that it offered could not be deemed a subsidy.

In *United States – Anti-Dumping and Countervailing Duties (China),*[7] the Appellate Body provided important clarification on this issue. It rejected the panel's

3 United States – Measures Affecting Trade in Large Civil Aircraft (Second Complaint), WT/DS353/AB/R, adopted 23 March 2012

4 United States – Final Countervailing Duty Determination with Respect to Certain Softwood Lumber from Canada, WT/DS257/AB/R, adopted 17 February 2004

5 United States – Conditional Tax Incentives for Large Civil Aircraft, WT/DS487/AB/R, adopted 22 September 2017

6 United States – Countervailing Duty Measures on Certain Products from China, WT/DS437/AB/R, adopted 16 January 2015

7 United States – Definitive Anti-Dumping and Countervailing Duties on Certain Products from China, WT/DS379/AB/R, adopted 25 March 2011

interpretation that any entity controlled by the government is a public body, instead ruling that a public body is an entity that possesses, exercises, or is vested with governmental authority. This ruling emphasized that the mere fact that a government is the majority shareholder of an entity does not automatically make it a public body. The Appellate Body stated that evidence of government ownership, while relevant, is not decisive in determining whether an entity is a public body. Instead, it's necessary to evaluate whether the entity in question is performing governmental functions.

The Appellate Body's interpretation was further refined in subsequent cases. In *United States – Carbon Steel (India),*[8] the Appellate Body elaborated that to qualify as a public body, an entity must not only possess governmental authority but must also exercise such authority by performing governmental functions. This case again highlighted the need for a case-by-case analysis, considering factors such as the entity's legal characteristics, the degree of government control, and the functions or conduct of the entity.

The *United States – Countervailing Measures (China)*[9] dispute provided additional guidance on identifying public bodies. The Appellate Body stressed that panels should examine whether the entity in question is vested with authority to exercise governmental functions, rather than focusing solely on whether the entity actually exercises such authority. This nuanced approach recognizes that an entity might possess governmental authority without necessarily exercising it in every instance. Clearly, the public body issue remains contentious, particularly in cases involving state-owned enterprises in countries with significant government involvement in the economy.

5.2.2 Categories of Subsidy Under the SCM

The SCM agreement establishes categories of subsidy further providing policy flexibility for WTO members in terms of the economic policies which they may choose to enact without breaching their international legal obligations.

The three categories of subsidy in the SCM are often depicted in the form of a "traffic light" using the colours red, yellow, and green. Red subsidies are those which are prohibited. Yellow (or amber) are only prohibited if they cause injury – much as drivers are only allowed to pass through a yellow light if it is unsafe to stop. Greenlight subsidies were created for subsidies serving research initiatives but these have all since expired so they no longer have any relevance (although they may have relevance for newly acceding WTO members).

Prohibited or "red light" subsidies, covered by Article 2 of the SCM, are those which are never allowed. These are deemed to be the worst form of governmental assistance, leading to benefits to certain enterprises which have a clear distortive effect on global trade. This type of assistance to the private sector was the precise

8 United States – Countervailing Measures on Certain Hot-Rolled Carbon Steel Flat Products from India, WT/DS436/AB/R, adopted 19 December 2014

9 United States – Countervailing Duty Measures on Certain Products from China, WT/DS437/AB/R, adopted 16 January 2015

reason that the SCM was created. The WTO community felt that the provision of support with a view to improving an entity's trade position constituted economically harmful protectionism.

Article 3 of the SCM states that prohibited subsidies are those which are contingent, in law or in fact, whether solely or as one of several other conditions, upon export performance. They are also subsidies which are contingent, whether solely or as one of several other conditions, upon the use of domestic over imported goods. An annex to the SCM outlines in greater detail the types of measures which may constitute prohibited export subsidies in the form of an illustrative list, meaning that it is only intended to help clarify the types of measures which will be covered, not to provide an exhaustive list. The annex includes currency retention schemes, favourable transportation charges for exports, exemptions from tax including special deductions for exports, and loans below commercial rates. All of these arrangements would place the relevant enterprise in an advantageous position relative to normal market conditions, allowing it to supply goods more effectively than its competitors in other countries.

The requirement of "specificity" does not need to be fulfilled for prohibited subsidies. All prohibited subsidies (meaning those which fit into the definition in Article 3) are deemed to be specific. Precluding the need to establish specificity makes it less difficult for complaining states to bring their case that an export subsidy should be prohibited. Economic programs aimed at supporting society at large should not have a focused export-oriented agenda. Perhaps more importantly from an evidentiary standpoint, the existence of a prohibited subsidy also precludes the need for the complainant WTO member to demonstrate that there has been an injury as a consequence of the subsidy. Injury is presumed if there is a prohibited, export subsidy or one which mandates the use of domestic over imported goods.

In *Australia – Automotive Leather*[10] dispute, Australia was found to have violated the SCM by subsidizing domestic companies that produced leather for car seats. The financial assistance offered by the government to the leather companies (low-interest loans as well as grants) fell into the prohibited category because it was clearly aimed at helping increase exports. The WTO panel inferred this from the fact that the Australian government was aware that its domestic market was too small to absorb all of the automotive leather being produced. Since there were not enough cars in Australia to justify the production of that many leather seats, the assistance must have been intended to encourage sales abroad.

The second category of subsidies under the SCM is actionable, or yellow light. These subsidies, outlined in Article 5 of the SCM, are permitted as long as they do not have adverse trade effects on other WTO members. As with the concept of specificity, the logic of this provision is that WTO members should retain the autonomy to craft policies which are in their own economic interests as long as this does not undermine other members.

10 Australia – Subsidies Provided to Producers and Exporters of Automotive Leather, WT/DS126/R, adopted 16 June 1999

In order for this kind of subsidy to be prohibited, the complainant member must demonstrate that its benefits as a member of the WTO are nullified, impaired or seriously prejudiced. This additional element renders the establishment of an actionable subsidy more challenging than that of prohibited subsidies. One of the most notable disputes in this area was *United States – Large Civil Aircraft (Second Complaint),*[11] also known as the Boeing-Airbus dispute. In this long-running case, the European Union challenged various United States federal, state, and local subsidies to Boeing as actionable subsidies. The WTO panel and Appellate Body found that certain NASA and Department of Defense research and development subsidies as well as tax breaks provided by the state of Washington, caused adverse effects in the form of serious prejudice to the European Union's interests. This case was significant because it dealt with complex issues of subsidy attribution and the assessment of adverse effects in a high-technology industry.

The most difficult aspect of the actionable subsidy is the concept of "serious prejudice" which is referenced in Article 6. Here the SCM lists the types of situations which are indicative of serious prejudice to the industry of a complaining member. This includes displacement or impediment of imports of a like product, severe price undercutting compared to a like product, and a large increase in the world market share of the subsidizing member. These are clearly highly fact-sensitive determinations which will require the submission of detailed evidence by the complainant. Alternative causes of any of these or other related harms to the complainant's industry must be discounted. For example, under Article 6.7(c) if the displacement or impediment of a like product was caused by a natural disaster, then serious prejudice will not be found and there will be no actionable subsidy. This rule illustrates the element of causality – the industry in the complaining member's territory has to have suffered as a consequence of the respondent WTO member's granting of a subsidy to the industry producing a like product.

In *Korea – Commercial Vessels,*[12] the European Communities challenged various Korean government measures supporting the shipbuilding industry as actionable subsidies. While the panel found that some of the measures constituted subsidies, it did not find sufficient evidence of adverse effects to conclude that they were actionable subsidies causing serious prejudice.

In a dispute regarding Korea's alleged subsidization of computer microchips, the WTO panel was required to assess whether the assistance granted by Korea to various companies which had not been clearly export-motivated had actually caused any injury to Japanese firms in the same industry.[13] The panel considered other possible causes of harm to the Japanese microchip industry, including reduced demand and changed habits of consumption for those products as well as developments in

11 United States – Measures Affecting Trade in Large Civil Aircraft (Second Complaint), WT/DS353/AB/R, adopted 23 March 2012

12 Korea – Measures Affecting Trade in Commercial Vessels, WT/DS273/R, adopted 11 April 2005

13 Japan – Measures Related to the Exportation of Products and Technology to Korea, WT/DS590, panel established 29 July 2020, proceedings terminated 23 March 2023.

technology, all of which had themselves, caused declining sales by Japanese firms. Establishing the so-called "counter-factual" in order to demonstrate the harmful effect of a subsidy relative to normal market conditions can be complicated.[14]

5.2.3 Remedies for Subsidies: Multilateral Countermeasures SCM Articles 4 and 7

The subsidies regime under WTO SCM is different from that of tariffs or quotas under the GATT because it has its own built-in system of remedies (hence the term "trade remedies"). First, members must withdraw a subsidy if there is determined to be a violation. Prohibited Subsidies must be withdrawn without delay. This normally means within about three months, with Actionable Subsidies having longer timeframes for withdrawal. If the subsidy is not withdrawn the Dispute Settlement Body may authorize "countermeasures." Countermeasures are the retaliatory suspension of concessions for related products, as envisioned by the normal regime for remedies under the DSU. The authorization from the DSB would arise following winning a dispute through the normal dispute settlement procedure.

There is also the potential to impose unilateral countervailing duties under Article X of the SCM. Unilateral here means that they can be applied without the permission of the WTO DSB. In other words, the injured member can apply them of their own accord, without having won or even initiated a formal dispute proceeding. A countervailing duty is a special fee, essentially a tariff, imposed by the injured state for the purpose of offsetting the effect of a subsidy. The advantage of pursuing the unilateral remedy, as opposed to the multilateral one is that it provides instant relief for a subsidy because it precludes the need to go through the dispute settlement process and to achieve a victory by a favourable panel recommendation. In order for a unilateral countervailing duty to be imposed lawfully there must be subsidized imports, injury to domestic industry, and a causal link. The SCM outlines detailed requirements for investigations to be conducted by the injured member before such duties can be imposed against the offending member. These investigations are resource-intensive and are typically carried out by a dedicated organization within each country.

Article 29 of the SCM granted members making the transition to market economy status the ability to support programmes and measures necessary to achieve this end. Such schemes will no longer be able to transgress the rules on prohibited subsidies – this leniency for transition economies is only relevant to actionable subsidies. China's Protocol of Accession to the WTO illustrates some of the controversies associated with the application of the concept of subsidy to a non-market economy where the state naturally has a larger role. Article 15(b) of the Protocol refers to "special difficulties" in applying the rules of the SCM agreement to

14 D Collins and TJ Park, "Deafening Silence or Noisy Whisper: Omission Bias and Foregone Revenue Under the WTO Agreement on Subsidies and Countervailing Measures" 51:6 Journal of World Trade 1069 (2017)

China in which case the importing WTO member "may then use methodologies for identifying and measuring the subsidy benefit which may take into account the possibility that prevailing terms and conditions in China may not always be the appropriate benchmarks." This means that the idea of governmental assistance as an unfair trade distortion does not translate very well to an environment where the state naturally maintains a strong influence.

An unusual remedy was implemented by the Appellate Body in the dispute relating to Australia's subsidy of automotive leather, previously mentioned. It was determined that simply requiring Australia to stop helping out its leather companies was not enough because these firms had already been given a significant advantage by virtue of the cheap government loans and grants. The Appellate Body therefore ordered the Australian government to take back the payments from the automotive leather companies. WTO remedies are normally forward-looking, so this retroactive monetary remedy was highly unorthodox. The Appellate Body justified this response by explaining that the money had already been used by the companies to produce new inventory, so although it was in a sense punishment for past behaviour, the effect, namely increased exports, was yet to take effect.

There has been much academic commentary on the appropriate scope and stringency of WTO disciplines on subsidies. Some argue that the SCM Agreement is overly restrictive and, therefore, fails to adequately account for legitimate policy objectives behind subsidies. The SCM Agreement's approach of treating all specific subsidies as potentially actionable, regardless of their purpose, may seem as misguided and could chill beneficial government interventions.[15] On the other hand, some hold that the WTO rules on subsidies are not stringent enough and allow too much policy space for trade-distorting subsidies.[16] Another key debate focuses on whether the WTO's subsidy rules should be reoriented to better support sustainable development goals. Some have advocated reforming WTO subsidy rules to create more policy space for environmental subsidies while tightening disciplines on environmentally harmful subsidies.[17] The treatment of state-owned enterprises (SOEs) and state capitalism under WTO subsidy rules is also hotly debated. Some believe that the current rules are inadequate to address the unique challenges posed by SOEs and state capitalist economies, arguing for new WTO disciplines in this area.[18] Finally, there remains a long-standing debate about the effectiveness and appropriateness of countervailing duties as a response to subsidies. It may be that the current

15 L Rubini, "The Wide and the Narrow Gate: Benchmarking in the SCM Agreement After the Canada–Renewable Energy/FIT Ruling" 16:2 World Trade Review 211 (2017)

16 AO Sykes, "The Questionable Case for Subsidies Regulation: A Comparative Perspective" 2:2 Journal of Legal Analysis 473 (2010)

17 I Espa and G Marín Durán, "Renewable Energy Subsidies and WTO Law: Time to Rethink the Case for Reform Beyond Canada–Renewable Energy/Fit Program" 21:3 Journal of International Economic Law 621 (2018)

18 M Wu, "The 'China, Inc.' Challenge to Global Trade Governance" 57:2 Harvard International Law Journal 261 (2016)

countervailing duty system is economically inefficient and should be eliminated entirely since subsidization is ultimately self-harming. Others defend the basic logic of countervailing duties while proposing refinements to their application.[19]

5.2.4 Agricultural Subsidies

Assistance provided to companies producing agricultural products is not covered by the SCM. These are handled by a separate WTO agreement called the Agreement on Agriculture (AoA). The AoA is a crucial component of the WTO's framework for regulating international trade in agricultural products. It was negotiated during the Uruguay Round and came into effect in 1995, with the aim of establishing a fairer and more market-oriented agricultural trading system.

Whereas the SCM had traffic lights, the AoA addresses agricultural subsidies through a system of coloured "boxes" that categorize different types of support based on their potential to distort trade. This system includes amber, blue, and green boxes. The amber box contains domestic support measures considered to be the most trade-distorting, such as price supports and production-linked subsidies. These subsidies are subject to reduction commitments, with developed countries agreeing to reduce their amber box support by 20 per cent over six years from a 1986–1988 base period.

The blue box covers subsidies that are linked to production-limiting programs. These are exempt from reduction commitments under certain conditions, as they are seen as less trade-distorting than amber box subsidies. The green box includes subsidies that are deemed to have minimal impact on trade, such as environmental protection programs and rural development initiatives. Green box subsidies are exempt from reduction commitments, provided they meet specific criteria outlined in Annex 2 of the AoA.

One of the key principles of the AoA is that all domestic support measures considered to distort production, and trade must be calculated into a Total Aggregate Measurement of Support (Total AMS). This Total AMS must then be reduced or maintained within defined limits. However, the agreement allows governments to support their rural economies through policies that cause minimal distortion to trade. The AoA also addresses export subsidies, which were prevalent in the agricultural sector prior to its implementation. The agreement required developed countries to reduce export subsidies by at least 36 per cent (by value) or by 21 per cent (by volume) over six years. For developing countries, the required cuts were 24 per cent (by value) and 14 per cent (by volume) over ten years.

In the *United States – Upland Cotton*[20] dispute, Brazil challenged various United States agricultural support programs for cotton as actionable subsidies under the SCM and also as breaches of the AoA. One of the key allegations in this dispute

19 PC Mavroidis and A Sapir, *China and the WTO: Why Multilateralism Still Matters* (Princeton University Press, 2021)

20 United States – Subsidies on Upland Cotton, WT/DS267/AB/R, adopted 21 March 2005

was that the United States had exceeded its commitments on domestic support under the AoA. Another significant claim related to export subsidies. Brazil alleged that United States payments to exporters and domestic users of United States cotton constituted an export subsidy inconsistent with Articles 3.3 and 8 of the AoA. These articles prohibit members from providing export subsidies for agricultural products in excess of their reduction commitment levels specified in their schedules. Brazil also challenged the United States export credit guarantee programs as violating export subsidy disciplines under the AoA. Brazil argued that these programs constituted export subsidies that were not scheduled under the AoA and therefore violated Articles 8 and 10.1 of the agreement. Article 10.1 requires members not to apply export subsidies in a manner that results in circumvention of export subsidy commitments.

The WTO panel and Appellate Body largely agreed with Brazil's claims. They found that certain United States domestic support measures for cotton were not protected by the peace clause and, therefore, subject to action under the SCM. The Appellate Body also upheld the panel's findings that the Step 2 payments to exporters were inconsistent with Articles 3.3 and 8 of the AoA, constituting prohibited export subsidies. Regarding the export credit guarantees, the Appellate Body found that these programs constituted export subsidies within the meaning of the AoA. As these subsidies were provided to upland cotton and other unscheduled products, they were found to be inconsistent with Article 10.1 of the AoA.

The AoA has been criticized for allowing developed countries, particularly the United States and European Union, to continue providing significant subsidies to their agricultural sectors. A large proportion of these subsidies go to a small number of large producers, potentially undermining farmers in developing countries. The Doha Round of trade negotiations, launched in 2001, aimed to build on the AoA by securing substantial improvements in market access and gradually withdrawing all forms of export subsidies. Negotiations were framed in terms of "modalities" which include formulas for lowering tariffs and cutting subsidies, along with a range of variations and flexibilities for some countries' specific circumstances.

A current proposal from Brazil envisages an agricultural subsidy package containing eight headings: domestic support, market access, new special safeguard mechanism for developing countries, export prohibitions and restrictions, export competition (subsidies), cotton, developmental assistance for cotton and lastly, over the limit subsidies in food stockpiling. Food security has emerged as one of the key issues in the tension between free trade and social stability. WTO rules do not prevent stockholding; they merely discipline subsidized procurement. Even subsidized procurement is allowed, provided that the developing country stays within its subsidy limit, usually 10 per cent of the value of production, although this can still be a substantial amount. Only India has exceeded its domestic support limit when using subsidies to buy into stocks and for only one product: rice. An interim 2013 WTO ministerial decision called a "peace clause" protected India from facing a legal challenge despite breaching its WTO commitment in this regard.

There is ongoing debate regarding the best way to address the special challenges of agricultural subsidies within the WTO framework. Some argue for more stringent disciplines on agricultural subsidies, contending that the current rules in the

AoA are too permissive.[21] Others emphasize the need to balance subsidy reduction with other objectives like food security, especially for developing countries.[22]

5.2.5 Fisheries Subsidies

Commercial fishing is a distinct industry of vital importance to many countries and one that has faced its own issues in relation to subsidization, particularly since many fish stocks around the world are facing severe depletion. The WTO Agreement on Fisheries Subsidies (AFS) was adopted at the WTO's Twelfth Ministerial Conference in 2022. It is the first WTO agreement to focus on sustainability and only the second multilateral agreement reached since the WTO was created, the other being the Trade Facilitation Agreement.

The AFS establishes a set of binding rules on the support governments are able to provide to their fishing sector. The provision of fisheries subsidies is prohibited in situations where concerns about the sustainability of fishing activities are the clearest. These are: first, when illegal, unreported, and unregulated fishing activities have been identified; second, when the health of fish stocks is assessed and their biomass is determined to be at alarmingly low levels; and third, when fishing occurs in unregulated high seas fisheries, meaning that no entity has competence for managing stocks sustainably.

The AFS is vital to prevent the most harmful effects of fisheries subsidies, not only for the marine environment but also for those who depend on healthy fish resources for their livelihoods and nutrition. The AFS will not enter into force until two-thirds of the WTO membership formally accept it. At the time of writing, 52 members have submitted their instrument of acceptance to the WTO.

5.3 Dumping

The second of the protectionist trade strategies to be explored in this chapter is dumping. Dumping is when a foreign company sells a product in a different country at a price that is lower than the price it sells the same product for in its home country. It can also refer to selling a product at a price that is lower than the cost of production.

For non-economists, dumping is one of the most difficult spheres of world trade law to comprehend because it seems counter-intuitive that a country should object to a supplier from another country selling products within its territory at artificially low prices. Surely consumers in the importing country should be pleased to be able to purchase goods cheaper than people in the country from which they originated, in some cases at prices below what the item cost to produce. While it may

21 D Orden, D Blandford and T Josling, *WTO Disciplines on Agricultural Support: Seeking a Fair Basis for Trade* (Cambridge University Press, 2011)

22 A Matthews, "Trade Rules, Food Security and the Multilateral Trade Negotiations" 41:3 European Review of Agricultural Economics 511 (2014)

benefit consumers, at least in the short term, it can be very harmful to producers. As the foreign firm eradicates competition through low prices, it can end up with a monopoly and thereafter charge artificially higher prices. Monopolies are inefficient because they tend to lead to unsatisfied consumer demand.

Dumping may be likened to the strategy of "predatory pricing" in which aggressive companies undercut their prices to out-compete their competitors with a view to putting them out of business, cornering the market, and then raising their prices to gouge consumers. Some sales below the cost price may be legitimate and not indicative of dumping. For example, there may be very intense competition in a market. There may be a decline in demand due to recession, with companies doing everything they can to survive during times of hardship. Prices may be drastically reduced to the point of being unprofitable in order to increase the volume of sales at an early stage in the product's lifecycle. This kind of strategy is sometimes adopted by companies introducing a new product which is unfamiliar to customers in order to get them to buy. Once there is a loyal customer base the price normalizes.

Much like subsidies, dumping rose to prominence as a protectionist strategy in the late 20th century as tariffs began to disappear across the industrialized world. Dumping is often linked to subsidies because in order for a company to be able to offer goods for sale at unrealistically low prices in other countries they may be receiving illegal assistance from their home government.

5.3.1 The WTO Anti-Dumping Agreement

The WTO does not prohibit dumping itself. It could not do so even if it wanted to because dumping is a commercial strategy employed by private firms over which the WTO has no authority. This captures the essence of the public element of world trade law as a branch of public international law. Since it does not discipline the practice of dumping, the WTO instead controls its members' response to it, meaning how and when they impose anti-dumping duties. Such duties can be levied against products in response to dumping only in certain narrow circumstances and must be proportionate to the extent of the dumping. Anti-dumping duties cannot punish the dumping nation (or more accurately, its suppliers). They are intended to normalize the price charged in the importing state to eliminate market distortions from artificially low prices. Anti-dumping duties are by far the most common of the three trade remedies in terms of investigations, measures imposed, and disputes.

Article VI of GATT contained some limited rules on dumping but, lacking in detail, these were enlarged upon by the Anti-Dumping Agreement (ADA). Article 2.1 defines dumping in the following way:

> a product is to be considered as being dumped, i.e. introduced into the commerce of another country at less than its normal value, if the export price of the product exported from one country to another is less than the comparable price, in the ordinary course of trade, for the like product when destined for consumption in the exporting country.

Article 2.2 goes on to outline the way to determine whether dumping has occurred through price comparison of the like products. If the market situation is such that there are no like products which can be compared (e.g., because of an insufficient volume of transactions), a comparison can be made with a like product in a third country (sometimes described as a surrogate). A third option for ascertaining whether dumping has occurred and at what degree (the margin of dumping), is a calculation of the costs of production plus reasonable administrative costs (sometimes described as a constructed cost).

Before an anti-dumping duty can be imposed, the national anti-dumping authority must determine whether there is a difference between the export price and normal value. This exercise can be quite fact-intensive. The difference in price must not be small. The price comparison must be at the same point in the transaction. Differences that would naturally affect prices should be disregarded. Such differences could include bulk sales where there are discounts or sales between affiliated companies where special prices are offered.

Article 3 of the ADA concerns the determination of injury for the purposes of levying appropriate anti-dumping duties. The term "material injury" is not defined but the standard is lower than the "serious injury" standard for safeguards, to be discussed further below. This determination is based on evidence regarding the quantity of the dumped product and its effect on producers of such domestic products.

There must be a significant increase in the quantity of dumped products. The economic factors to be considered include sales, profits, outputs, market share, productivity, returns on investment, cash flow, inventories, employment, and wages. These matters are readily quantifiable and therefore open to objective assessment by dispute settlement panels should the anti-dumping duty be challenged by the home country of the company that has allegedly been dumping. There must be a causal link. The deleterious effects of dumping must be distinguished from effects from other factors, such as the fact that the company is making a product which consumers do not want at the prices offered, or perhaps that the company is poorly managed.

Several significant anti-dumping disputes have been brought through the WTO dispute settlement system. *United States – Hot-Rolled Steel,*[23] brought by Japan against the United States, addressed key issues in anti-dumping investigations. The Appellate Body ruled on important aspects of fair comparison in dumping margin calculations, including the use of "zeroing" and the treatment of affiliated parties. Zeroing was a controversial dumping margin calculation method that involved setting a value of zero for instances where the export price of a product is higher than the home market price, essentially ignoring a valid data point. Hot Rolled Steel established that investigating authorities must make allowances for differences affecting price comparability and that the arm's length test used by the United States for affiliated party transactions was inconsistent with WTO rules because of the

23 United States – Anti-Dumping Measures on Certain Hot-Rolled Steel Products from Japan, WT/DS184/AB/R, adopted 23 August 2001

Appellate Body's interpretation of the phrase "sales in the ordinary course of trade" which appears in the ADA.

In *EC – Bed Linen,*[24] India challenged the European Communities' anti-dumping measures on cotton-type bed linen. This case was significant for its rulings on zeroing practices in anti-dumping calculations. The Appellate Body found that zeroing, as applied by the European Communities in this case, was inconsistent with the Anti-Dumping Agreement, as it did not take into account the full universe of export transactions. *United States – Continued Zeroing*[25] addressed the ongoing use of zeroing in various United States anti-dumping proceedings. The Appellate Body confirmed that zeroing is prohibited in all contexts of anti-dumping proceedings, including original investigations, administrative reviews, and sunset reviews. This ruling significantly impacted United States anti-dumping practices.

In *EU – Biodiesel,*[26] Argentina challenged the EU's anti-dumping measures on biodiesel fuel. This case addressed the issue of adjusting costs in anti-dumping investigations when domestic prices are considered to be distorted. The Appellate Body found that the European Union had acted inconsistently with the ADA by failing to calculate the cost of production on the basis of records kept by the producers.

Chinese companies have been the main targets of anti-dumping duties because of China's massive industrialization and export-oriented economy. China has also been challenged for its imposition of anti-dumping duties on other countries. For example, the United States challenged China's anti-dumping and countervailing duties on grain-oriented flat-rolled electrical steel in 2010.[27] The case addressed important issues regarding the transparency and procedural fairness of anti-dumping investigations. The Appellate Body found that China had acted inconsistently with the ADA by failing to disclose essential facts and provide adequate explanations for its determinations.

China's Accession Protocol to the WTO featured prominently in anti-dumping disputes at the WTO. Accession protocols for new members (who joined the WTO after its creation in 1995) typically contain additional special rules for each new member, accommodating their particular concerns usually through phase-in periods during which time-strict rules of membership may not apply. China's Accession Protocol provided for a specialized procedure for the assessment of dumping because of China's non-market economy status, allowing a looser methodology for price comparison based on a surrogate price from a third country. This effectively made a determination of dumping an easier exercise against Chinese companies.[28]

24 European Communities – Anti-Dumping Duties on Imports of Cotton-Type Bed Linen from India, WT/DS141/AB/R, adopted 12 March 2001

25 United States – Continued Existence and Application of Zeroing Methodology, WT/DS350/AB/R, adopted 19 February 2009

26 European Union – Anti-Dumping Measures on Biodiesel from Argentina, WT/DS473/AB/R, adopted 26 October 2016

27 United States – Countervailing and Anti-Dumping Measures on Grain-Oriented Flat-Rolled Electrical Steel from the United States, WT/DS414/AB/R, adopted 16 November 2012

28 Article 15 Accession of the People's Republic of China, WT/L/432 (23 November 2001)

The logic behind this procedure is that it is very difficult to ascertain a normal price for any commodity where prices are not set by market forces but by governmental policy. This provision was set to expire in late 2016, at which point China was deemed to be a market economy entitled to the normal (stricter) method of determination of dumping. Some members, such as the United States, have argued that the special non-market procedure should still apply.

If a WTO member imposes anti-dumping duties without proper justification this can amount to a breach of WTO law and entitle the injured member to retaliate in the manner that it would do were the losing member imposing unlawful tariffs. Like GATT, the ADA is enforceable through the WTO Dispute Settlement procedures. The manner in which panels should interpret the provisions of the ADA and by extension, how they should review the factual determinations made by domestic anti-dumping authorities has been the subject of some controversy. It is outlined in Article 17.6(ii) which reads:

> the panel shall interpret the relevant provisions of the Agreement in accordance with customary rules of interpretation of public international law. Where the panel finds that a relevant provision of the Agreement admits of more than one permissible interpretation, the panel shall find the authorities' measure to be in conformity with the Agreement if it rests upon one of those permissible interpretations.

The concept of "permissible interpretation" suggests that broad discretion to national anti-dumping authorities should be accorded by the panel where possible. Although this may be seen to confer much autonomy to WTO members, essentially allowing them to use their own judgement when levying anti-dumping duties against other members, it risks injecting uncertainty into the process. It may also undermine one of the central interpretive principles of the Vienna Convention on the Law of Treaties, namely that words be given an ordinary meaning which conforms to the objective of the agreement in which they are situated.[29] Countries like the United States, which currently exhibit much *animus* towards the WTO may rightly view this aspect of the ADA to justify their expectation that they will be granted deference by panels.

It is possible to apply anti-dumping duties on products where there is a threat of material injury to the domestic industry, without actual damage yet being demonstrated. In the softwood lumber dispute between the United States and Canada (which was both a dumping case as well as a subsidy case – subsidies often enable companies to charge lower prices abroad) it was determined by a WTO panel that further dumped imports are imminent and that unless protective action is taken, a material injury will occur in the near future. The panels and Appellate Body will accordingly consider whether imports are entering the country that will

29 Article 31

significantly depress prices in that particular industry. They will also look at existing inventories of the allegedly dumped goods.

Several key debates have emerged regarding the anti-dumping rules under the WTO framework. One major debate concerns the economic justification and effects of anti-dumping measures. Anti-dumping duties may be characterized as a form of protectionism rather than a means of addressing genuine unfair trade practices. The current rules allow for much discretion in determining dumping and injury, leading to the overuse of anti-dumping measures. Others defend the basic rationale of anti-dumping rules as a necessary tool to address predatory pricing and maintain fair competition in international trade.[30]

The issue of zeroing in dumping margin calculations remains contentious. The continued use of zeroing by some WTO members, despite repeated Appellate Body rulings against it, arguably undermines the effectiveness of the dispute settlement system. As with subsidies, another significant debate revolves around the treatment of non-market economies in anti-dumping investigations. The concept of "particular market situation" in Article 2.2 of the ADA has become increasingly important as a potential alternative to non-market economy methodologies, especially in the context of China's changing status in the WTO system. A more nuanced approach to assessing market distortions that focuses on price comparability rather than broad categorizations of economies may be appropriate.[31] The procedural aspects of anti-dumping investigations have also been subject to criticism as lacking in fairness and transparency.[32]

5.4 Safeguards

The last of the three trade remedies issues is safeguards. This principle of world trade law acknowledges that liberalizing trade, for example by lowering tariffs, can sometimes lead to economic harm, especially when the importing country or its producers are not ready to face global competition. Safeguards, as the name implies, are designed to allow countries to change their minds, by temporarily imposing tariffs while their economies adapt to the new situation with a view to mitigating any socially harmful effects in the short term. This is why safeguards have also earned the nickname "safety valves" – they relieve some of the pressures associated with free trade. Without them, many countries would have been unwilling to lower their tariffs at all. As such, the notion of safeguards reflects a principle of pragmatism that runs throughout world trade law. It is a system of law that is rooted in the realities of politics and the frailties of domestic economies.

30 PC Mavroidis, PA Messerlin, and JM Wauters, *The Law and Economics of Contingent Protection in the WTO* (Elgar, 2008)

31 W Zhou and A Percival, "Debunking the Myth of 'Particular Market Situation' in WTO Antidumping Law" 19:4 Journal of International Economic Law 863 (2016)

32 E Vermulst, *The WTO Anti-Dumping Agreement: A Commentary* (Oxford University Press, 2005)

5.4.1 GATT Article XIX and the Agreement on Safeguards

Building upon Article XIX of GATT, the Agreement on Safeguards sets out when and how WTO members are allowed to transgress their obligations to observe tariff commitments and not to impose quotas. These "Safeguards" are authorized protectionism against goods that have been traded fairly. They are therefore distinct from retaliatory measures against the unfair trade practices of subsidies and dumping. Article XIX of GATT became known as the "escape clause" because it allows WTO members to escape from their obligations when it is vital for them to do so.

The essential principles of safeguards are best understood from a reading of the original GATT. Article XIX.1 of GATT reads as follows:

(a) If, as a result of unforeseen developments and of the effect of the obligations incurred by a contracting party under this Agreement, including tariff concessions, any product is being imported into the territory of that contracting party in such increased quantities and under such conditions as to cause or threaten serious injury to domestic producers in that territory of like or directly competitive products, the contracting party shall be free, in respect of such product, and to the extent and for such time as may be necessary to prevent or remedy such injury, to suspend the obligation in whole or in part or to withdraw or modify the concession.
(b) If any product, which is the subject of a concession with respect to a preference, is being imported into the territory of a contracting party in the circumstances set forth in sub-paragraph (a) of this paragraph, so as to cause or threaten serious injury to domestic producers of like or directly competitive products in the territory of a contracting party which receives or received such preference, the importing contracting party shall be free, if that other contracting party so requests, to suspend the relevant obligation in whole or in part or to withdraw or modify the concession in respect of the product, to the extent and for such time as may be necessary to prevent or remedy such injury.

There are, therefore, three conditions that must be fulfilled for safeguards to be applied by WTO members. First, there must be an increase in imports of the product in question; second, the increase must be caused by developments that were unforeseen; and third, the increase of imports must cause or threaten to cause serious injury to a domestic industry producing a like or directly competitive product. Serious injury will not be an easy test to satisfy. It is stricter than that of material injury associated with subsidies and dumping.

A WTO member may restrict imports of products temporarily if its domestic industry is injured or threatened with injury that has been caused by a "surge" in imports. An import surge may be a real or absolute increase in imports of a particular product, or it can be relative – meaning an increase in the imports' share of a shrinking market, even if the import quantity has not increased.

Individual firms can make a request to their governments to initiate safeguard actions in response to these situations. As with countervailing measures for subsidies and anti-dumping duties for dumping, safeguard actions require investigations by national authorities. These procedures, many of the rules of which are set out in the Agreement on Safeguards, must be transparent and non-arbitrary. The investigating authorities in the country intending to impose the safeguards must announce publicly when any hearings are going to take place and provide an opportunity for interested parties, like the exporters from other countries as well as companies in the importing country, to present evidence about how harmful their imports are. This should include evidence relating to whether the safeguard measure is in the public interest as a restriction on free trade.

The Agreement of Safeguards sets out criteria for determining whether a serious injury is being caused or is threatened to be caused, including the factors that must be considered in assessing the impact of imports on the domestic industry in question. This could be demonstrated by increases in unemployment, declining profitability, share value or bankruptcies. There is also a causation requirement. It is not enough that the domestic industry is suffering; the suffering must be the result of the import surge. A causal link must be established between the increase in imports and the injury sustained by the industry. Other factors that could have contributed must be discounted, such as poor-quality products, high prices, or excessive wages.

In *United States – Wheat Gluten,*[33] a dispute initiated by the European Communities against the United States for its safeguard measures imposed on imports of wheat gluten, the Appellate Body ruled on the causation analysis required under the AS emphasizing that investigating authorities must separate and distinguish the injurious effects of increased imports from those of other factors. In *United States – Lamb,*[34] brought by Australia and New Zealand, the Appellate Body provided guidance on the definition of "domestic industry" for safeguards purposes, ruling that the United States had defined the industry too broadly by including lamb growers and feeders along with packers and breakers.

Once permitted, a safeguard measure must only be applied to the extent necessary to prevent or remedy the serious injury and to allow the industry to adjust to the increase in imports. The safeguard tariff or quota should not reduce the quantity of imports below the annual average for the last three years for which import statistics are available unless a higher reduction can be clearly justified because of the severity of injury sought to be avoided. In order for safeguards to be lawful, the increase in imports must be recent, sudden, and sharp. If these criteria are not satisfied, then there will be no economic emergency, which is the essential principle of the safeguard regime. This also requires that the import surge must be unforeseen. If the domestic industry had known about the harm done by the surge in advance, they likely would have been able to deal with it by restructuring their commercial activities.

33 United States – Definitive Safeguard Measures on Imports of Wheat Gluten from the European Communities, WT/DS166/AB/R, adopted 19 January 2001

34 United States – Safeguard Measures on Imports of Fresh, Chilled or Frozen Lamb Meat from New Zealand and Australia, WT/DS177/AB/R, WT/DS178/AB/R, adopted 16 May 2001

Argentina imposed safeguard measures in the form of increased duties on shoes from various countries beyond the levels they had committed under their GATT-bound tariffs. Argentina believed that it needed to impose these emergency measures because it had liberalized some sectors of its economy to international trade under the regional MERCOSUR agreement with other South American countries too rapidly. But, MERCOSUR had no safeguard regime, so Argentina attempted to justify its imposition of emergency tariffs under the WTO instead. The European Union complained, arguing that under WTO law Argentina's safeguards had to be imposed evenly against injury-causing imports from all countries, including other South American ones within MERCOSUR.[35] The Appellate Body agreed, ruling that Argentina's safeguard regime on European shoes was illegal because it discriminated against European shoes without justification; the European imports of shoes were no more damaging than those from other South American countries. This case was crucial in establishing that safeguard measures can only be imposed when imports increase as a result of unforeseen developments.

A series of high-profile disputes relating to safeguards imposed by the United States on steel,[36] resulted in the Appellate Body to further stress the need for a reasoned and adequate explanation of how the facts support the determination made, particularly regarding the existence of "unforeseen developments."

Much as with countervailing duties and anti-dumping duties, trade remedies must not be applied where there are other explanations for the observed harms suffered by the domestic industry. This is known as the "non-attribution requirement." Domestic investigating authorities must not attribute injuries to the domestic industry to other factors that are also causing injury at the same time as increased imports. *United States – Line Pipe,*[37] brought by Korea against the United States, concerned the non-attribution rule. Here the Appellate Body emphasized that under Article 4.2(b) of the Agreement on Safeguards, investigating authorities must establish explicitly that injury caused by factors other than increased imports is not attributed to increased imports. This requires a reasoned and adequate explanation of how the facts support their determination. The Appellate Body clarified that while the Agreement on Safeguards does not prescribe a specific methodology for separating and distinguishing the injurious effects of different factors, the method chosen must ensure that injurious effects of other factors are not attributed to increased imports.

Importantly, the Appellate Body stated that the non-attribution requirement does not necessarily imply that increased imports alone must be capable of causing serious injury, nor that injury caused by other factors must be excluded from the determination of serious injury. Rather, it requires that the injurious effects

35 Argentina – Safeguard Measures on Imports of Footwear, WT/DS121/AB/R, adopted 12 January 2000

36 United States – Steel Safeguards (DS248, DS249, DS251, DS252, DS253, DS254, DS258, DS259)

37 United States – Definitive Safeguard Measures on Imports of Circular Welded Carbon Quality Line Pipe from Korea, WT/DS202/AB/R, adopted 8 March 2002

caused by increased imports be distinguished and separated from the injurious effects caused by other factors. The Appellate Body also noted that the competent authorities must provide a reasoned and adequate explanation of how they ensured that injury caused by factors other than increased imports was not attributed to increased imports.

When a WTO member restricts the imports from another WTO country in order to safeguard the producers in one of its domestic industries, it should give something back in compensation. This is because safeguards are meant to counter fair trade, not unfair trade as in the case of subsidies or dumping. The importing country should enter into consultations with the exporting country to come up with an appropriate arrangement. If no agreement is reached, then the exporting country can retaliate by taking an equivalent action, such as raising the tariffs on exports from the country that is imposing the safeguard measure. The retaliating country often has to wait several years before it is allowed to do this with the WTO's support. This process is overseen by the WTO's Committee on Safeguards. As of the end of 2023, more than 424 safeguard measure investigations were reported to the WTO. Just over half of these resulted in the actual imposition of safeguard measures. India has been the most frequent user of safeguards, followed closely by Indonesia.

If safeguards are imposed without the relevant procedure, outlined in the Agreement on Safeguards, complaints can be brought through the WTO's dispute settlement system. Given the danger that China posed with respect to import surges in WTO countries because of its manufacturing capacity, a special Safeguard procedure was established for Chinese exports as part of China's terms of accession to the WTO. This special mechanism, which expired in 2013, established a lower threshold for the application of safeguards, including a lower standard of injury, against Chinese imports than against those from all other countries.

5.5 Trade Remedies in FTAs

Few FTAs exceed the provisions contained in the relevant WTO agreements with regard to subsidies, dumping or safeguards. The CPTPP, for example, makes the statement that each party "retains its rights and obligations under Article VI of GATT 1994, the AD Agreement and the SCM Agreement."[38] The CPTPP does elaborate somewhat on transparency requirements in trade remedies investigations including enhanced notification requirements. The USCMA contains additional material regarding cooperation between the parties to combatting duty evasion which means the evasion of anti-dumping, countervailing (anti-subsidy) or safeguard duties through the use of false customs documentation. The USMCA further establishes specialized dispute settlement procedures for the review of trade remedies via binational panels.[39]

38 Article 6.8.1
39 Chapter 10, Sections C and D, respectively

The USMCA procedure is based upon that of its predecessor NAFTA. Under NAFTA, the trade remedies rules had some key differences compared to WTO rules, particularly in the areas of anti-dumping and countervailing duties. NAFTA Chapter 19 established a unique binational panel review system for anti-dumping and countervailing duty determinations. This allowed parties to request review by binational panels instead of domestic courts, which was not available under the WTO system. NAFTA panels were required to apply the domestic law of the importing country, including its standard of review. This differed from WTO panels, which apply WTO agreements and international law principles. There was no standing appellate body under NAFTA. Instead, there was a limited extraordinary challenge procedure for procedural irregularities. NAFTA panel reviews were generally faster than WTO dispute settlement, with strict deadlines for panel formation and decisions. NAFTA panels consisted of five members, with each involved country selecting two panellists and the fifth chosen by agreement.

Replacing NAFTA, USMCA largely maintained the Chapter 19 binational panel system for anti-dumping and countervailing duty disputes. The USMCA has enhanced transparency, requiring parties to establish and maintain electronic filing systems for trade remedy investigations, and improving access to information. There are new provisions to strengthen cooperation between parties to address potential evasion of trade remedy duties. The USMCA allows for the sharing of information on trade remedy investigations between parties' investigating authorities.

There have been relatively few disputes brought under the trade remedies provisions of FTAs compared to the numerous cases brought through the WTO system. One significant case arose under NAFTA when Canada challenged the United States' use of zeroing in anti-dumping investigations involving Canadian softwood lumber.[40] The NAFTA panel found that the use of zeroing was inconsistent with United States law and ordered the United States Department of Commerce to recalculate dumping margins without using this methodology. Another case under NAFTA involved Mexico's challenge of United States anti-dumping duties on cement.[41] Mexico argued that the United States had improperly calculated dumping margins and failed to consider all relevant economic factors in its injury determination. The dispute was ultimately resolved through a negotiated agreement rather than a panel ruling, highlighting the potential for diplomatic solutions within the FTA framework. Another NAFTA/USMCA case examined the requirement of serious injuries for safeguards, determining that the relevant imports of photovoltaic cells from Canada were insufficient to constitute a substantial share of total imports into the United States, particularly since there was a decline in imports over the course of the period of investigation.[42]

40 United States – Final Dumping Determination on Softwood Lumber from Canada, NAFTA Panel No. USA-CDA-2002-1904-02, Decision of the Panel on Remand (9 June 2005)

41 Re: Matter of Gray Portland Cement and Clinker from Mexico, NAFTA Secretariat File No. USA-MEX-2000-1904-10, Decision of the Panel (14 December 2006)

42 Crystalline Silicon Photovoltaic Cells Safeguard Measure, Final Report (USA-CDA-2021-31-01)

The Dominican Republic-Central America-United States Free Trade Agreement (CAFTA-DR) has also seen disputes related to trade remedies. For example, Costa Rica recently initiated a case against El Salvador regarding safeguard measures imposed on imports of flat-rolled products of iron or non-alloy steel. This case is noteworthy as it involves a dispute between two developing countries within the agreement, rather than a challenge to actions taken by the United States. Under the United States-Korea Free Trade Agreement (KORUS), there have been consultations regarding trade remedy measures, though these have not progressed to formal dispute settlement. For instance, Korea raised concerns about United States anti-dumping duties on oil country tubular goods, leading to bilateral discussions but not a full panel proceeding.

5.5.1 Bilateral Safeguards

One key difference between the WTO and preferential FTAs when it comes to trade remedies concerns bilateral safeguards. Given the extent of FTAs, there is increasing concern regarding the use of bilateral safeguards as opposed to global ones to be imposed at the WTO level. These are safeguard duties imposed against products originating from an FTA partner, the need for which has arisen because the FTA granted greater access (reduced tariffs) for those products than were available under the WTO via the MFN principle.

To date, there have only been a small number of bilateral safeguard disputes. One such dispute occurred when the South African Customs Union (SACU) imposed a safeguard duty on frozen chicken from the European Union under the provisions of the EU-SACU Economic Partnership Agreement (EPA). An arbitration panel under that treaty held that the safeguard duty was legitimate in order to protect the industry in Africa from injury.[43]

The India-Malaysia Comprehensive Economic Cooperation Agreement (CECA) saw the use of bilateral safeguards when India imposed provisional safeguard duties on imports of refined palm oil from Malaysia in 2019. India cited a surge in imports causing injury to its domestic industry as justification under the agreement's bilateral safeguard clause. Under the Korea-India Comprehensive Economic Partnership Agreement (CEPA), India initiated bilateral safeguard investigations on imports of phthalic anhydride and polybutadiene rubber from Korea in 2019.

The proliferation of bilateral safeguard provisions in FTAs has raised concerns about their potential discriminatory effects. The selective nature of these measures could lead to more frequent actions against non-FTA members, potentially diverting trade away from efficient producers not covered by the agreements. It is unclear whether bilateral safeguards in FTAs make it easier or harder to impose protective measures compared to WTO rules. While it could be argued that FTAs

43 SACU Safeguard Measure on Frozen Chicken from the EU, Final Report of the Arbitration Panel (3 August 2022)

should facilitate the use of safeguards to enable deeper liberalization commitments, some evidence suggests many FTAs actually impose stricter disciplines on safeguard use between members. There is also a controversy about whether invoking an FTA-specific safeguard precludes the simultaneous use of WTO safeguards, and how to reconcile potentially conflicting obligations under different agreements. As preferential trade agreements have expanded to cover more trade and include deeper commitments, the role of bilateral safeguards has evolved. Many recent FTAs include more sophisticated safeguard provisions with detailed procedural requirements, limitations on duration, and frequency of use, and in some cases, complete prohibition of safeguards after a transition period. Commentators note that bilateral safeguard provisions in FTAs are more trade-friendly than those of the WTO since they primarily limit the form of safeguard measures to tariffs (rather than quotas) and the duration is significantly shorter. On the other hand, they tend not to address special and differential treatment for developing countries in FTAs.[44]

5.5.2 Domestic Trade Remedies Investigations Bodies

Every country maintains an agency within their government responsible for implementing trade remedies, including those issued under WTO rules or under those of preferential FTAs. These agencies conduct the investigations required for the imposition of countervailing (anti-subsidy) anti-dumping duties and safeguards. In the European Union this task is performed by the European Commission and in the United States, it is the International Trade Commission within the Department of Commerce. In the United Kingdom, this is the Trade Remedies Authority, created in the years following the United Kingdom's departure from the European Union. While all domestic trade remedies investigation bodies, must conduct their investigations in line with WTO rules, there is some latitude for each country to design its own procedures. One unique element of the TRA's approach to the imposition of trade remedies is the Economic Interest Test (EIT).

The EIT considers the expected impact on the United Kingdom of imposing a new measure (e.g., a countervailing duty in response to a foreign subsidy), compared to the impact of not imposing that measure. The aim of the process is to determine whether the implementation of a proposed trade remedies measure is in the wider economic interest of the United Kingdom. The test considers the following factors: the extent of the injury caused to United Kingdom industry by the imports being investigated and the benefits to that industry of removing the injury; the economic significance of affected United Kingdom industries and consumers; the likely impact on wider United Kingdom industries and on consumers; the likely impact on particular geographic areas or groups within the United Kingdom; the likely consequences for the competitive environment and the structure of United Kingdom markets for these goods, and other matters that considered relevant. In

44 J Xu, "One Step Forward and Two Steps Back? Evolution of Bilateral Safeguard Provisions in Preferential Trade Agreements" 55:3 Journal of World Trade 433 (2021)

anti-dumping and countervailing duty investigations where the presence of dumped or subsidized imports are causing injury has been established, the economic interest test is presumed to be met unless the TRA is satisfied that the application of the measures is not in the economic interest of the United Kingdom. In safeguard investigations, there is no such presumption.

In conducting the EIT analysis, some of the factors the TRA may look at include the value added, meaning the contribution that United Kingdom industries make to the value of the United Kingdom-produced goods at different stages of the supply chain; employment, such as how many people are employed within the industry on work that is directly related to the product in question at each United Kingdom location; market share of United Kingdom producers, as a proportion of total sales of this type of goods in the United Kingdom; market structure, including the size distribution of United Kingdom producers and what proportion of the market is accounted for by small- and medium-sized enterprises; the upstream and downstream industries within the United Kingdom and how they are related to the industry that applied to us to investigate the case for a new measure; and finally, consumers, in terms of how the product used and by whom.

5.6 Conclusion

This chapter explored the controversial subject of trade remedies – particular categories of trade policy which are perceived to be so potentially harmful that they entitle countries to take unilateral action to redress them. The WTO, as the origin of most of the key principles in world trade law, has set out detailed rules regarding when and how these actions can be taken but leaves much discretion to each country. As bilateralism has proliferated, refinements to trade remedies rules have taken effect, especially in relation to enhanced transparency. The particular issue of bilateral safeguards resulting from deeper liberalization in FTAs promises to be a source of controversy in the future. Yet perennial issues concerning the appropriateness and design of trade remedies remain the most pressing challenges in this field of world trade law.

Subsidization strikes at the heart of trade policy and actions taken against it, in the form of countervailing tariffs, could operate to undermine a country's economic sovereignty as it seeks to sustain vital industries that cannot withstand competition. Agriculture and fisheries are among the most important of these, deserving their own disciplines. Likewise, the illogic of anti-dumping duties which raise prices for domestic consumers, seems to ignore the reality that some countries have achieved industrial capacity that enables them to achieve competitive dominance, perhaps deservedly so.

Enabling safeguard tariffs to protect vulnerable industries from import surges acknowledges the fundamental weakness underlying much of world trade law and the rationale of economic efficiency which underpins it. Many economies are simply unable to participate in globalization because they are inadequate or underdeveloped, with adverse social consequences that should not be minimized. Without the safety valve of safeguards, it would be impossible for these places to participate in a world trading community unshielded by tariffs or quotas. The danger for the world trading system is that, with the principles of trade remedies available and governed by arguably imprecise if not ill-conceived rules, the strategies of countervailing and anti-dumping duties as well as safeguards could be abused as disguised protectionism. These are difficult lines to be drawn, requiring ongoing vigilance as well as enhanced clarity through adjudication.

Discussion Questions

1. Why does the Agreement on Subsidies and Countervailing Measures (SCM) create different categories of subsidies?
2. What is meant by the requirement of "specificity" under the SCM? Why does this concept exist?
3. What is wrong with dumping? Does the WTO framework respond to it adequately/appropriately?
4. Under what circumstances are safeguards allowed? How have these been affected by bilateralism/regionalism?
5. Is there a difficulty with integrating non-market economies into the rules governing trade remedies?

6 Public Interest and Non-Trade Values

6.1 Introduction

Governments have responsibilities beyond the economic prosperity that is induced by lowering barriers to trade. This chapter will examine the key public interest issues which have traditionally operated as justifications for breach of trade commitments. These came into the lexicon of world trade law originally through GATT Article XX and its very basic principles in relation to health and what would now be called "the environment." In addition to outlining how GATT Article XX has worked in practice, this chapter will consider the expansion of these concepts by reference to modern issues such as environmental protection/climate change (including carbon board adjustments), sustainability, national security (manifest commonly as sanctions), food security, and labour issues. Many of these non-trade values have received greater attention in FTAs such as the USMCA, the FTAs of the European Union, and the CPTPP, notably through the use of non-regression clauses which prevent regulatory backsliding in order to attract trade. Entirely new fields, such as gender and indigenous rights will be examined in the context of specialized chapters in FTAs.

While non-trade values have always been a significant point of controversy, even for those who normally espouse free trade, these issues have become particularly salient in recent years. This is likely due to at least three factors. The first of these is the fervour with which global leaders have responded to concerns relating to human-induced climate change, reflected most notably by the pursuit of "net zero" carbon dioxide emission policies in some cases to the point of wilful reduction in living standards. This is environmentalism of a kind far beyond what was envisaged when politicians first became aware of the harms of pollution in the 20th century. The second contribution to the rise of anti-trade sentiment relates to where free trade has been perceived to adversely affect public health. There has been a growing sense of the need to protect consumers from unhealthy products for some time (a phenomenon that will be discussed in more depth in the next chapter) but it was the hysteria with which many nations responded to the Covid-19 pandemic, notably in relation to export bans of vaccines, that most clearly revealed that trade, and, with it, economic prosperity, was not a top priority. Lastly, recent wars, especially Russia's invasion of Ukraine, have spawned a series of economic sanctions

DOI: 10.4324/9781003465676-6

including trade embargoes. The suspension of MFN trading status for Russia by several WTO members is a strong indication that countries are quite willing to abandon the principles of free trade when there are geopolitical concerns at play.

6.2 WTO General Exceptions GATT Article XX

The WTO's primary objective is the liberalization of trade for the purpose of economic advancement and increased prosperity across the globe. Yet economic matters are not the organization's only concern. This was evident even in the original GATT when many issues, especially the environment, had not yet grasped the public's attention.

GATT drafters included exceptions which would allow contracting parties to deviate from their commitments where there were sufficiently strong non-economic concerns in play in order to preserve global wellbeing in a more holistic manner. These matters are sometimes described as negative externalities, meaning unintended adverse consequences. Some have argued that the justifications listed in GATT Article XX allow insufficient regulatory space for members to address important social concerns, particularly given that they were written during a very different era.[1] This issue is exacerbated by the fact that practice has shown that it is exceedingly difficult for a WTO member to use one of the Article XX exceptions to defend itself against the accusation of breach of WTO obligations by another member.

It is difficult to overstate the impact of general exceptions of GATT Article XX as they have not only formed the basis of many disputes; their language has reappeared in hundreds of bilateral and regional FTAs, often with minimal changes.

6.2.1 The Enumerated Exceptions

In the interests of brevity, the most important of the enumerated exceptions of Article XX are as follows:

> nothing in this Agreement shall be construed to prevent the adoption or enforcement by a contracting party of measures:
>
> (*a*) necessary to protect public morals;
> (*b*) necessary to protect human, animal or plant life or health;
> (*g*) relating to the conservation of exhaustible natural resources if such measures are made effective in conjunction with restrictions on domestic production or consumption;

Public morals are an important non-trade principle because it is an indistinct concept with the potential to cover a wide range of policy measures including issues

1 For example, S Cho, *The Social Foundations of World Trade* (Cambridge University Press, 2015)

relating to cultural values. In *EC – Seal Products*[2] a dispute brought by Canada and Norway originated from the European Communities implementation of regulations that prohibited the importation and marketing of seal products within the European Union. The European Union justified the ban on the grounds of public moral concerns over animal welfare, particularly the methods used in seal hunting. Canada and Norway, both with significant sealing industries, argued that this ban violated WTO rules and unfairly discriminated against their products. The dispute centred on the interpretation and application of Article XX(a) which allows for trade restrictions necessary to protect public morals. In its ruling, the WTO Appellate Body upheld the European Communities' right to ban seal products on moral grounds, recognizing animal welfare as a legitimate moral concern. *EC-Seal Products* affirmed that WTO members have the right to determine their own public moral standards and to implement trade measures to uphold these standards. The ruling also provided important guidance on how the public morals exception should be interpreted and applied in the context of international trade disputes.

Human, animal or plant life or health is a somewhat more concrete category exception, although health itself can mean various things including quality of life and longevity, even emotional states such as happiness. The *Thailand – Importation of and Internal Taxes on Cigarettes*[3] dispute was one of the first to provide a comprehensive interpretation of Article XX(b). The dispute arose when the United States challenged Thailand's import restrictions and internal taxes on cigarettes. Thailand had effectively banned the importation of foreign cigarettes while allowing the sale of domestic cigarettes. Thailand justified its measures under Article XX(b), arguing that they were necessary to protect human health from the harmful effects of cigarette consumption. The GATT panel acknowledged that smoking constituted a serious risk to human health and that measures designed to reduce cigarette consumption fell within the scope of Article XX(b). However, the panel found that Thailand's import restrictions were not "necessary" within the meaning of Article XX(b). The panel reasoned that there were less trade-restrictive alternatives available to Thailand to achieve its health objectives, such as implementing strict, non-discriminatory labelling and ingredient disclosure regulations, or banning cigarette advertisements for both domestic and imported cigarettes. This dispute confirmed that health protection measures could indeed fall under the exception. Second, it introduced the concept of "necessity" in relation to health measures, establishing that a measure must not only be aimed at protecting health but must also be necessary to achieve that objective. In so doing it emphasized the importance of considering less trade-restrictive alternatives when evaluating the necessity of a measure.

The conservation of natural resources is often viewed as synonymous with environmental protection, although this issue is arguably covered by b). These concepts

2 European Communities – Measures Prohibiting the Importation and Marketing of Seal Products, WT/DS400/AB/R, WT/DS401/AB/R, adopted 18 June 2014

3 Thailand – Restrictions on Importation of and Internal Taxes on Cigarettes, DS10/R, adopted 7 November 1990

are reasonably straightforward, although the precise understanding of a resource is debatable. The leading case under GATT Article XX(g) on the conservation of exhaustible natural resources is *United States – Import Prohibition of Certain Shrimp.*[4] The dispute arose when India and various other Asian countries challenged a United States law that prohibited the importation of shrimp and shrimp products from countries that did not use turtle excluder devices in their shrimp trawling operations. The United States justified this import ban under GATT Article XX(g), arguing that it was a measure relating to the conservation of sea turtles, which it considered an exhaustible natural resource. In its ruling, the Appellate Body interpreted the term "exhaustible natural resources" to include both non-living and living resources, including endangered species like sea turtles.

This rather expansive interpretation was significant as it allowed for the application of Article XX(g) to a wider range of environmental concerns. Secondly, the Appellate Body elaborated on the meaning of the phrase "relating to" in Article XX(g). It held that there must be a close and genuine relationship between the measure and the conservation of exhaustible natural resources. In this case, the Appellate Body found that the United States measure was indeed related to the conservation of sea turtles. The *United States – Shrimp Turtle* dispute established that WTO members have the right to take trade measures to protect the environment, including in relation to resources outside their jurisdiction. The case has been frequently cited in subsequent disputes involving environmental measures and has influenced national policies on trade and environmental protection.

In *United States – Gasoline,*[5] the Appellate Body confirmed that clean air could be considered an "exhaustible natural resource" under Article XX(g). This interpretation was further expanded in the *United States – Shrimp* case, where the Appellate Body held that "exhaustible natural resources" include not only mineral or non-living resources but also living species that may be susceptible to depletion. This broad interpretation potentially allows for climate change mitigation measures to fall under the scope of Article XX(g).

Recent developments suggest a potential broadening of WTO exceptions that could apply to climate change measures. Given the worldwide alarm over climate change, often sensationally described as a "climate crisis" to engender panicked support, along with the inescapable difficulties in establishing precisely what mechanisms drive it, it is likely that environmental-oriented policies will be used as justifications for a greater number of trade-related restrictions in the future. It will be interesting to see how the WTO, as a member-driven organization lacking any express competence in environmental or even scientific matters, will deal with these issues.

The relationship between WTO rules and climate change policies extends beyond Article XX. The Agreement on Subsidies and Countervailing Measures (SCM Agreement) may be relevant, as many climate change policies involve

4 United States – Import Prohibition of Certain Shrimp and Shrimp Products, WT/DS58/AB/R, adopted 6 November 1998

5 United States – Standards for Reformulated and Conventional Gasoline, WT/DS2/AB/R, adopted 20 May 1996

subsidies or other forms of government support. Currently, the SCM Agreement does not have a general exception for environmental measures, which creates legal uncertainty for certain types of climate subsidies. Some scholars have proposed extending the Article XX exceptions to the SCM Agreement to provide more legal certainty for climate change subsidies or by creating a specific environmental exception in the SCM Agreement itself.[6]

6.2.2 The Chapeau

The specific policy issues previously noted are preceded by what is known as the "chapeau" to Article XX. This is the most challenging aspect of the WTO's General Exceptions, covering the way in which they are used less so than their content. The chapeau specifies that the enumerated justifications must be:

> Subject to the requirement that such measures are not applied in a manner which would constitute a means of arbitrary or unjustifiable discrimination between countries where the same conditions prevail, or a disguised restriction on international trade.

The chapeau appears to embody a principle of good faith – openness and honesty in trade dealings between states. It implies that WTO members must honour the spirit of the law, not just the letter of it. Put another way, it is designed to ensure that exceptions are not abused. The enumerated exception must be applied even-handedly with a view to minimizing its intrusion into the trading affairs of members of the WTO community. Case law has shown that satisfying the chapeau is exceedingly difficult – there are very few cases where members have succeeded in defending trade-restrictive measures through Article XX because of this screen.

The procedure for evaluating a measure under the GATT's General Exceptions must begin with the panel considering whether the measure fits into one of the enumerated exceptions. Secondly, the availability of the general exception is limited by the requirement that the exception not be either arbitrary or unjustified discrimination or a disguised restriction on international trade, which the panel must also investigate.

The functionality of the chapeau is well illustrated by the aforementioned *United States – Shrimp Turtle* case. The United States tried to use the conservation of natural resources exception of GATT Article XX(g) this exception to justify the ban and, as noted above, the panel (and the Appellate Body) agreed that this enumerated justification fit. But, when implementing the second stage of the test via the chapeau, the Appellate Body found that the application of the measure constituted arbitrary and unjustifiable discrimination between countries where the same conditions prevail. The United States provided countries in the Western Hemisphere (mainly in the

6 R Howse, "Climate Mitigation Subsidies and the WTO Legal Framework: A Policy Analysis" International Institute for Sustainable Development (May 2010)

Caribbean) with technical and financial assistance and longer transition periods to adopt turtle exclusion devices. The four Asian countries that filed the complaint were not given the same advantages as the Western Hemisphere countries. Moreover, rather than impose an outright ban, the Appellate Body ruled that the United States should have worked towards the negotiation of a global treaty on sea turtle preservation.

The effect of the chapeau element of the General Exceptions is further reflected in the *China – Rare Earths*[7] dispute. Here China attempted to use Article XX(b) and (g) as a justification for various export restrictions on rare earths like tungsten and molybdenum. It argued that its export restrictions on these valuable substances, which are critical components of electronic equipment like mobile phones and batteries, were essential because of environmental pollution associated with the mining of these metals that are a natural resource. The pollution had to be prevented, so the Chinese said because it was harmful to human health. The WTO panel ruled against China, siding with the United States and European Union who had complained about the ban as a violation of Article XI of GATT which prohibits export quotas. The export restrictions were not viewed as necessary to fulfil these non-trade objectives, in large part because China continued extracting the metals from the ground on an industrial scale for use (or storage) domestically, which made their environmental claims look empty.

6.2.3 Carbon Border Adjustment Mechanisms (CBAMs)

There is one specific policy aimed at supporting a non-trade value that is worthy of special analysis. Carbon border adjustment mechanisms (CBAMs) are tariffs imposed on imports based on the type of production process (high carbon intensity, which is allegedly contributing to accelerated climate change). CBAMs are supposedly designed to address carbon "leakage" meaning the emission of carbon at the place of production of a product before it is imported. The rationale behind them is that it is not fair for places like the European Union to control carbon emissions when producing goods, only to import them from countries which pay no heed to carbon reduction and, therefore, contribute to harmful climate change. The failure to control carbon emissions is also a kind of domestic subsidy. Firms that do not need to make these adjustments may be in a superior position competitively. By imposing a tariff on imports that are produced through high carbon emissions, a CBAM addresses one of the alleged causes of climate change and also levels the playing field competitively between producers that were required by their home state to lower their emissions and those that were not.

The EU's CBAM[8] works by requiring importers of certain carbon-intensive goods to purchase certificates corresponding to the carbon emissions embedded in

7 China – Measures Related to the Exportation of Rare Earths, Tungsten, and Molybdenum, WT/DS431/AB/R, WT/DS432/AB/R, WT/DS433/AB/R, adopted 29 August 2014

8 Established by Regulation (EU) 2023/956 of the European Parliament and of the Council, which was adopted on 10 May 2023.

those products. The price of these certificates is linked to the price of carbon allowances in the EU's Emissions Trading System (ETS). This approach aims to level the playing field between EU producers, who are subject to the ETS, and foreign producers who may not face equivalent carbon pricing in their home countries. Initially, the EU's CBAM applies to a limited range of goods that are particularly carbon-intensive and at high risk of carbon leakage. These include cement, iron and steel, aluminium, fertilizers, electricity, and hydrogen. Importers are required to register with national authorities and report detailed information about the embedded emissions in their imported goods. The regulation also establishes procedures for calculating embedded emissions, verifying declarations, and managing the issuance and surrender of CBAM certificates. The products affected by CBAMs will no doubt become more expensive, acting as a distortion of international trade in favour of EU products. Indeed, CBAMs are regarded by some as disguising a protectionist aim.[9]

Although the EU's CBAM is designed to be compliant with WTO rules, since the requirement to purchase certificates will be imposed on imported products and not domestic ones, it arguably violates GATT's National Treatment obligation. As noted in Chapter 2, discrimination would necessitate that the products in question are "like." The fact that products are made at different levels of carbon intensity is likely to be insufficient to preclude a finding of likeness based on existing case law regarding consumer taste and products' end usage. A CBAM might also be viewed as a quantitative restriction on imports, violating Articles XI and XIII of GATT.

GATT Article II:2(a) permits the imposition of "internal taxes" (taxes on products rather than on income) as long as it is done consistently with regards to the like domestic product, and does not breach National Treatment. But, it is far from clear that the CBAM would be considered an internal tax. It may be viewed as an internal regulatory charge on goods produced with high carbon emissions. Indeed, some hold that the EU's CBAM probably would not qualify as a border tax adjustment under WTO law because it is part of the European Union's carbon emission trading scheme rather than a charge on goods. Whether the United Kingdom's proposed CBAM would satisfy this definition remains to be seen.

In the event that a CBAM such as the European Union's was viewed as GATT non-compliant, it might be justified via GATT's general exceptions, designed to integrate non-trade policy concerns. As noted above, GATT Article XX(g) allows otherwise trade-restrictive measures that relate to the conservation of natural resources, provided that they are applied in a manner which is not arbitrary or discriminatory. Article XX(b) permits trade restrictions undertaken which are necessary for the protection of human, animal or plant life, or health. Regulating imports on this basis is generally allowed under WTO law, seen, for example, in the *United States – Shrimp* case regarding efforts to save sea turtles through restrictions on shrimp imports. The necessity test will apply to Article XX(b) justifications. It is

9 S Singham, "The Impact of Carbon Leakage Mechanisms on Growth" The Growth Commission (United Kingdom) (October 2024)

unclear that the CBAM is the least-trade restrictive way of controlling harmful carbon emissions, which arguably have an impact on human health although this is debatable since carbon dioxide itself is not toxic to human life.

CBAMs may also raise issues in relation to subsidization which could transgress WTO law. In other words, a border tax based on carbon emission in production may be justified on the basis that the failure to tax properly in the originating country amounts to a subsidy, granting that product the upper hand in markets where environmental regulations are more strict. The CBAM would therefore effectively function as a countervailing (anti-subsidy) duty. But, under the WTO's Agreement on Subsidies and Countervailing Measures, finding subsidization is not easy because the relevant benefit (soft-touch environmental regulations) would need to be "specific" – meaning applied to certain companies or groups of companies. While this might also be demonstrable, the application of countervailing duties requires a product-specific finding of injury to the domestic industry in the importing country, unless it could be proven that the benefit of the lower regulation was expressly tied to export, which would be difficult for the government to prove.

6.2.4 General Agreement on Trade in Services (GATS) General Exceptions

Something should be said also of the General Exceptions which appear under the WTO's services agreement, the General Agreement on Trade in Services (GATS). Services, including the GATS, will be the subject of Chapter 8. For now, it is useful to draw attention to the key elements of the General Exceptions contained in Article XIV of GATS:

> Nothing in this Agreement shall be construed to prevent the adoption or enforcement by any Member of measures:
>
> (a) necessary to protect public morals or to maintain public order;
> (b) necessary to protect human, animal or plant life or health;
> (c) necessary to secure compliance with laws or regulations which are not inconsistent with the provisions of this Agreement including those relating to:
>
>   (i) the prevention of deceptive and fraudulent practices or to deal with the effects of a default on services contracts;
>   (ii) the protection of the privacy of individuals in relation to the processing and dissemination of personal data and the protection of confidentiality of individual records and accounts;
>   (iii) safety;
>
> (d) inconsistent with Article XVII [National Treatment], provided that the difference in treatment is aimed at ensuring the equitable or effective imposition or collection of direct taxes in respect of services or service suppliers of other Members;

Article XIV also includes a chapeau which is almost identical to that of Article XX of the GATT. The obvious differences between GATS' General Exceptions and those of GATT include the addition of new categories, including "public order" as a component of the public order exception as well as entirely new exceptions relating to fraud, privacy, and safety. There is also an exception relating to direct taxes which will be examined further in Chapter 10 in relation to digital services taxes. Of these, the exceptions for privacy and safety are particularly important. They also show that the drafters of GATS were prescient regarding the importance of online commerce that would explode in the 21st century. We would now recognize these concepts as underpinning laws in relation to data protection and cybercrime. It is worth noting also that the connectors of GATS XIV all require that the measure is "necessary" – there is no reference to the softer "related to" test of GATT Article XX(g).

The precise functionality of GATS will be explored in the next chapter, however for now it is appropriate to evaluate how GATS General Exceptions work as, to a degree they build upon the framework contained in Article XX of GATT. The public morals/public order enumerated exception has been the subject of most disputes. As suggested in the context of GATT, this exception is clearly quite broad, however, it is restricted by an interpretive footnote which adds that the public order exception may be invoked only where a genuine and sufficiently serious threat is posed to one of the fundamental interests of society. This is evidently a very high standard.

United States – Gambling[10] involved an attempted justification on the basis of upholding public morality. Antigua challenged United States laws which prohibit the remote supply of gambling and betting services, including those offered on the Internet. While this violated commitments that the United States had undertaken under the GATS, the United States claimed that these domestic laws were nevertheless justified because they were necessary to protect public morals and to maintain public order. The panel stated that the notion of public morals and public order can vary in time and space and depend on a range of factors, including prevailing social, cultural, ethical, and religious values. The panel resorted to an ordinary dictionary as a means of interpretation, concluding that the two concepts (morality and order) overlapped and taken together, intended to capture genuine threats to the fundamental interests of society.

The United States claimed that Internet gambling could lead to organized crime, money laundering, as well as fraud. It also represented a serious risk to children as well as human health because of the greater risk it posed of addiction. These concerns were accepted as legitimate by the panel and upheld by the Appellate Body, which also ruled that the United States ban was necessary to address these harms. The United States lost the case regardless because of the

10 United States – Measures Affecting the Cross-Border Supply of Gambling and Betting Services, WT/DS285/AB/R, adopted 20 April 2005

chapeau to GATS XIV. The United States applied the ban on online gambling unevenly while the United States prohibited online card games from Antigua, they allowed online betting on domestic horseracing, suggesting a hidden protectionist aim.

In *China – Audiovisuals,*[11] China attempted to rely on the public moral defence found in both GATS to support its restrictions on imported films, DVDs, and various publications including magazines and books. The United States initiated a complaint against China, arguing that China's laws unfairly discriminated against United States movies and publications because China required that importation and distribution of these products must be done in conjunction with a registered Chinese entity. China held the view that only such an organization would be able to identify whether foreign entertainment could undermine Chinese cultural identity. The Appellate Body ruled that the public morals defence could have been used in this way, but that China had failed to demonstrate that the import and distribution controls were necessary for fulfilling the goal of upholding public morals. This was because a less trade restrictive way of protecting Chinese culture may plausibly have been available. The Appellate Body further clarified that the protection of public morals and public order requires some explanation – it cannot simply be asserted. If China had believed that foreign films, music, and magazines represented a threat to its cultural identity, then this would have had to be shown convincingly, which had not been done in this instance. The Appellate Body clarified that " 'public morals' denotes standards of right and wrong conduct maintained by or on behalf of a community or nation."[12] It would seem that the government has the right to determine, in specific circumstances, what the scope of public morals is, according to their own values. It may be that even outward-facing restrictions on the basis of public morals, meaning those which are relevant to the behaviour of people in other countries (e.g., economic sanctions) can be covered by the general exceptions clause.[13]

The *Argentina – Financial Services*[14] dispute between Panama and Argentina, initiated in 2012, also involved the invocation of GATS Article XIV. Argentina sought to justify certain measures affecting the supply of financial services under Article XIV(c), claiming they were necessary to secure compliance with Argentine tax laws and regulations. The panel found that Argentina's measures were indeed designed to secure compliance with relevant laws and regulations. However, the panel concluded that Argentina had not demonstrated that its measures were "necessary" within the meaning of Article XIV(c). The Appellate Body largely upheld

11 China – Measures Affecting Trading Rights and Distribution Services for Certain Publications and Audiovisual Entertainment Products, Appellate Body Report, WT/DS363/AB/R, adopted 19 January 2010

12 Ibid., at [6.465]

13 I Bogdanova, "Targeted Economic Sanctions and WTO Law: Examining the Adequacy of the National Security Exception" 48:2 Legal Issues of Economic Integration 171 (2021) at 249

14 Argentina – Measures Relating to Trade in Goods and Services, Appellate Body Report, WT/DS453/AB/R, adopted 9 May 2016

the panel's findings, resulting in Argentina's failure to successfully invoke Article XIV(c) as a complete defence.

While the WTO dispute settlement bodies have recognized the legitimacy of various public policy objectives under GATS Article XIV, they have set a high bar for demonstrating the necessity of trade-restrictive measures and their compliance with the chapeau requirements, as under GATT Article XX. This approach reflects the WTO's attempt to balance the right of members to pursue legitimate policy objectives with the need to prevent abuse of the general exceptions clause.

The General Exceptions under Article XX of the GATT and Article XIV of the GATS have been subjects of extensive academic commentary and debate regarding the way that WTO members must balance between trade liberalization and regulatory autonomy as manifest in the recognition of non-trade values. Some argue that the interpretation of Article XX has evolved to provide greater deference to domestic regulatory choices. This evolution represents a shift towards recognizing the legitimacy of diverse domestic policy objectives within the framework of international trade rules.[15]

Others express concern that an overly broad interpretation of the General Exceptions could undermine the fundamental principles of the WTO system. This view calls for a more stringent application of the necessity test and the chapeau requirements to ensure that the exceptions do not end up facilitating protectionist measures.[16] The interpretation and application of the "necessity" test under both GATT Article XX and GATS Article XIV have been particularly contentious. Some have argued against the notion that the necessity test involves a balancing of the measure's trade restrictiveness against its contribution to the stated objective. Instead, the test should focus solely on whether the measure is the least trade-restrictive option reasonably available to achieve the desired level of protection.[17] Another point of contention concerns the application of the chapeau of Article XX and Article XIV.

The current approach to the chapeau, focusing on the manner of application of measures, is thought by some to be inconsistent with its text and context. It may be more appropriate to reconstruct the chapeau concentrating on the substantive content of measures rather than their application. The role of the General Exceptions in addressing contemporary global challenges, such as climate change and public health crises, has also been a topic of academic discussion. Some believe that while Article XX provides some flexibility, there is a need for amendment of WTO rules to adequately address climate-related trade measures.[18]

15 R Howse and E Tuerk, "The WTO Impact on Internal Regulations – A Case Study of the Canada-EC Asbestos Dispute" The EU and the WTO: Legal and Constitutional Issues 283 (2001).

16 PC Mavroidis, *The General Agreement on Tariffs and Trade: A Commentary* (Oxford University Press, 2005)

17 D Regan, "The Meaning of "Necessary" in GATT Article XX and GATS Article XIV: The Myth of Cost-Benefit Balancing" 6:3 World Trade Review 347 (2007)

18 BJ Condon, "Climate Change and Unresolved Issues in WTO Law" 12:4 Journal of International Economic Law 895 (2009)

6.3 Essential Security

In what has surely become among the most controversial aspects of world trade law, a country's essential security may be asserted as a justification for breaching the principles of world trade law. The ability of a state to safeguard its national security is a vital safety valve. It recognizes that a state's capacity to protect itself from an external threat is fundamental to statehood. Of all the issues that are more important than free trade, the safety of a state's citizens is surely the greatest. In an era of heightened geopolitical conflict, the essential security exceptions have grown in importance and this is only likely to continue. The capacity to abandon one's trade obligations in order to safeguard national security carries with it the risk of abuse, such that it threatens to undermine the sanctity of the world trading system.

In WTO law, the essential security exception is found in GATT Article XX, GATS Article XIV, and the Trade Related Aspects of Intellectual Property Agreement (TRIPS) Article 73. The TRIPS Agreement will be examined directly in Chapter 9 on intellectual property. Since the essential security provisions of these three WTO agreements are broadly similar, only GATT Article XX will be quoted directly:

> Nothing in this Agreement shall be construed:
>
> (a) to require any contracting party to furnish any information the disclosure of which it considers contrary to its essential security interests; or
> (b) to prevent any contracting party from taking any action which it considers necessary for the protection of its essential security interests
>
> (i) relating to fissionable materials or the materials from which they are derived;
> (ii) relating to the traffic in arms, ammunition and implements of war and to such traffic in other goods and materials as is carried on directly or indirectly for the purpose of supplying a military establishment;
> (iii) taken in time of war or other emergency in international relations; or
>
> (c) to prevent any contracting party from taking any action in pursuance of its obligations under the United Nations Charter for the maintenance of international peace and security.

Article XX(b) is probably the most important provision as it contains the primary essential security obligation, clearly elevating it above all other principles in world trade law. The severity of the essential security exemption is demonstrated by the fact that it is phrased in "self-judging" language. WTO members are able to assert that their essential security is under threat ("which it considers necessary"). This would suggest that once asserted, an essential security justification for a trade barrier cannot be challenged through the WTO dispute settlement procedures. It is now clear that this is not true, however, a very high standard of deference will be employed by panels that have been tasked with assessing the validity of such measures. The language of Article XXI contemplates the existence of an extreme circumstance, mirroring the customary international law principle of necessity and force majeure.[19]

One early case dealing with the essential security provision of GATT is the *United States – Trade Measures Affecting Nicaragua*,[20] which occurred under the GATT system before the establishment of the WTO. This case involved a United States embargo on all trade with Nicaragua, which the United States justified under GATT Article XXI. The United States argued that the security exception was self-judging, meaning that each contracting party had the right to determine for itself what actions were necessary for the protection of its essential security interests. Nicaragua contested this interpretation, arguing that the invocation of Article XXI should be subject to review. The GATT Council established a panel to examine the matter, but the United States blocked the adoption of the panel's terms of reference that would have allowed the examination of the justification of the measures under Article XXI. As a result, the panel was limited to examining the trade effects of the measures without considering their justification under the security exception. This case highlighted the contentious nature of the essential security provision and the challenges in its interpretation and application.

The *Sweden – Import Restrictions on Certain Footwear*[21] case is another example, albeit from the pre-WTO era, where the essential security exception was invoked. Sweden imposed global quotas on certain footwear, citing GATT Article XXI. Sweden argued that the decline of its domestic footwear production threatened its economic security and its planning for self-sufficiency in vital products in times of war. While many contracting parties expressed doubts about the justification, the measure was not formally challenged through the dispute settlement process. This case demonstrates an early attempt to broaden the concept of essential security to include economic security considerations.

The most significant dispute dealing with the Essential Security provision of GATT Article XXI was ironically brought by Ukraine against Russia in 2019. In *Russia – Measures Concerning Traffic in Transit,*[22] the annexation of Crimea by Russia in 2014 led to the imposition of economic sanctions by various countries against Russian entities. In response, Russia imposed transit bans and other restrictions preventing the transit of goods from Ukraine to Kazakhstan and other bordering countries. Ukraine brought a dispute to the WTO claiming this was a breach of the GATT. Russia asserted that the measures were necessary for the protection of

19 Articles on State Responsibility, Articles 25 and 23.

20 United States – Trade Measures Affecting Nicaragua, GATT Panel Report, L/6053, 13 October 1986 (unadopted)

21 Sweden – Import Restrictions on Certain Footwear, GATT Panel Report, L/4250, adopted 11 November 1975

22 Russia – Measures Concerning Traffic in Transit, Panel Report, WT/DS512/R, adopted 26 April 2019

its essential security interests under Article XXI. Russia further argued the WTO panel lacked jurisdiction to evaluate its measures. The United States aligned with Russia's interpretation of the purely self-judging nature of Article XXI of the GATT in the dispute. But, the United States aided Ukraine by imposing economic sanctions on Russia at the time of the invasion. Russia refused to provide any factual evidence or legal arguments in the dispute, forcing the panel to consider only publicly available information. Still, the panel came up with a standard of "not implausible" in the lawful application of the security justification – a fairly low bar. It ruled in favour of Russia holding it was acceptable for them to use the Essential Security provision to enforce the transit restrictions on Ukrainian goods.

The *Russia – Traffic in Transit* panel was very careful to tread lightly on WTO members' sovereignty in terms of its characterization of the Crimean annexation under international law. The panel ruled that it was "not relevant" to its determination whether Russia bears "any international responsibility for the existence of this situation to which Russia refers." Despite winning the case, Russia objected to the panel's reference to the "international community's" condemnation of the annexation of Crimea. The panel ended up replacing the phrase "international community" with "the UN Resolution" – narrowing the language somewhat in the final report. Although the panel's decision to subject Article XXI to some level of review, in this case, is a significant development, it raises new questions about the standard of review and the extent of deference to be accorded to members invoking the exception.[23]

The WTO panel's legal reasoning in *Saudi Arabia – Measures Concerning the Protection of Intellectual Property Rights*[24] regarding the essential security provision built upon the precedent set in the *Russia – Traffic in Transit* case. The panel rejected Saudi Arabia's argument that the dispute was not justiciable due to national security concerns, affirming its jurisdiction to review the invocation of the security exception under Article 73(b)(iii) of the TRIPS Agreement. The panel first assessed whether the measures in question fell within the scope of the relevant subparagraph of Article 73(b). The panel determined that there was indeed a "situation of heightened tension or crisis" between Saudi Arabia and Qatar that constituted an "emergency in international relations" as required by Article 73(b)(iii). The panel noted that when a group of states repeatedly accuses another of supporting terrorism and extremism, this, in itself, reflects and contributes to a situation of heightened tension relating to their security interests. The panel then examined whether the measures were taken for the protection of Saudi Arabia's essential security interests and whether there was a plausible connection between the measures and those interests. The panel applied a "minimum requirement of plausibility" test, which was less stringent than a full necessity analysis. It found

23 G Vidigal, "WTO Adjudication and the Security Exception: Something Old, Something New, Something Borrowed – Something Blue?" 46:3 Legal Issues of Economic Integration 927 (2019)

24 Saudi Arabia – Measures Concerning the Protection of Intellectual Property Rights, Panel Report, WT/DS567/R, adopted 16 June 2020.

that Saudi Arabia's articulation of its essential security interests was "minimally satisfactory" in the circumstances of the case. The panel found that the measures preventing Qatari nationals from obtaining legal representation in Saudi Arabia to enforce intellectual property rights were plausibly connected to Saudi Arabia's essential security interests and thus justified under Article 73(b)(iii). However, the panel concluded that Saudi Arabia's failure to apply criminal procedures against an alleged Saudi-based broadcast pirate was not sufficiently connected to its essential security interest.

Another significant dispute relating to essential security is *European Union – Certain Measures Concerning Palm Oil and Oil Palm Crop-Based Biofuels,*[25] initiated by Malaysia against the European Union in 2021. While this case is still ongoing, it involves the invocation of the essential security exception under GATT Article XXI by the European Union. The European Union has argued that its measures regarding palm oil-based biofuels are necessary for the protection of its essential security interests, particularly in relation to climate change and energy security. This case is noteworthy because it expands the traditional understanding of "essential security interests" to include environmental and climate-related concerns. The European Union's argument suggests that climate change mitigation and adaptation measures could potentially fall under the scope of essential security. As this case progresses, it may provide important insights into how the WTO dispute settlement system evaluates the essential security exception in the context of environmental and climate policies.

The principle of essential security is the foundation of economic sanctions, such as trade embargoes, which would otherwise operate as violations of the prohibition on quotas contained in Article XI of GATT. The use of economic sanctions has expanded in recent years due to rising geopolitical conflicts, notably Russia's invasion of Ukraine. Not long after Russia's invasion of Ukraine, several nations, led by Canada and Ukraine, suspended the application of MFN treatment to Russian goods on the basis of GATT Article XXI. Russia responded to this with an official statement of concern that the essential security provisions of WTO law were being unduly politicized, potentially leading to a fragmentation of the multilateral trading system and a loss of credibility of the WTO.

On the other hand, it would appear that the invasion of Ukraine by Russia is a "war or other emergency in international relations," as specified in Article XXI. Moreover, "essential" is different from "national." It does not need to be a direct threat to Canadian or United States national security in order for the provision to be triggered. There may be an indirect threat due to the emergency in international relations. A WTO member's essential security interests probably also include the respect for all internationally recognized borders and the prohibition of territorial acquisition by military force. Under Essential Security, WTO members can therefore adopt

25 European Union – Certain Measures Concerning Palm Oil and Oil Palm Crop-Based Biofuels, WT/DS593/1, Request for Consultations received on 9 December 2019

whatever measures they consider necessary; actions are not restricted to war-related products such as arms. They can include tariffs on all products or other sanctions.

The broadly worded nature of Article XXI was designed to enable members to interpret it as they wish, affording them the ability to strike an appropriate balance between trade and security. Countries imposing the tariffs in response to security emergencies recognize that state practice helps establish the legitimacy of state action in the future. This is why it is important that members explain as precisely as possible why they are invoking Article XXI. Otherwise, it is indeed open for abuse. For example, the allegation by the United States that tariffs needed to be imposed on steel in order to protect the domestic steel industry (which could become vital in the event of war) seems far-fetched. Such tariffs would probably have been better characterized as safeguard measures.

Much as the revocation of MFN status unfolding today in the context of the ongoing invasion of Ukraine, the *Russia – Transit* and *Saudi Arabia – Intellectual Property* disputes demonstrate the highly problematic nature of incorporating essential security into international trade law. Permitting its use indiscriminately undermines the benefits of WTO membership and invites protectionist abuse. Disallowing it could sideline the WTO as an economic body, detaching from the most important aspects of international law, such as territorial integrity. In order to strike an appropriate balance, WTO members relying on the essential security provisions should clarify precisely how and why they are using them and suspend WTO benefits only to the extent that they are strictly necessary. Although WTO panels will not review the existence of the security interests and the necessity of the measure, they will still evaluate whether the state has properly articulated its security interests. This makes it possible to identify whether the measure was invoked in good faith.[26]

The essential security exceptions under WTO law have been a subject of significant academic debate and analysis. One of the primary controversies concerns the self-judging nature of the security exception. Some hold that the exception is inherently self-judging, meaning that each member state has the right to determine for itself what constitutes its essential security interests. This interpretation is thought to be consistent with the text, context, and negotiating history of Article XXI.[27] Others argue for a more nuanced approach, urging that states have considerable discretion in invoking the security exception, this discretion is not absolute and should be subject to some form of review by WTO panels or the Appellate Body.[28] The scope and limits of the essential security exception have also been extensively debated. The potential for abuse of the exception has been highlighted leading some to advocate for a balanced approach that respects both national security concerns and the integrity of the international trading system. It is felt that there is a

26 A Ventouratou, "Litigating Economic Sanctions" 21 The Law and Practice of International Courts and Tribunals 633 (2022)

27 R Alford, "The Self-Judging WTO Security Exception" 2011 Utah Law Review 697 (2011)

28 D Akande and S Williams, "International Adjudication on National Security Issues: What Role for the WTO?" 43 Virginia Journal of International Law 365 (2003)

need for good faith application of the exception with the panels having the authority to review whether a measure falls within the scope of Article XXI.[29]

Others hold that the interpretation of the security exception is not expansive enough. The traditional understanding of security threats may need to be expanded to encompass new forms of threats in the digital age while cautioning against an overly broad interpretation that could undermine the WTO system.[30] Climate change mitigation measures may even be justified under the security exception as some might consider this to be a different kind of security threat. A rebalancing mechanism has been proposed that would allow affected countries to impose proportionate countermeasures in response to security-based trade restrictions, arguing that this approach could help preserve the stability of the trading system.[31]

6.4 Non-Trade Values in FTAs

Given that they contain extensive obligations relating to the promotion of trade between treaty partners, FTAs also tend to include references to non-trade values as a means of striking a balance between economic and social goals. Much as FTAs typically exceed the WTO in terms of trade liberalization, these agreements often provide for non-trade values in a more comprehensive manner than seen at the WTO. This is one of the advantages of being able to negotiate the text of an FTA among a smaller number of treaty partners where agreement on contentious issues is more likely.

6.4.1 General Exceptions

The legacy of the WTO's General Exceptions is reflected in the fact that many if not most FTAs incorporate GATT XX-style language, in some cases verbatim. The general exceptions may appear in a chapter specifically designed for that purpose.[32] Some FTAs contain general exceptions which go beyond those contained in the GATT/GATS. For example, some EU FTAs, which use the GATT general exceptions as a baseline, also contain exceptions for "public security."[33]

One significant variation can be found in the CPTPP. Article 29.1 of the CPTPP includes language that explicitly mentions the protection of Indigenous rights. This addition is not present in GATT Article XX and reflects the evolving nature of international trade agreements to address a broader range of social and cultural concerns. The EU-Canada Comprehensive Economic and Trade Agreement

29 T Voon, "The Security Exception in WTO Law: Entering a New Era" American Journal of International Law Unbound (2019)
30 S Peng, "Cybersecurity Threats and the WTO National Security Exceptions" 18:2 Journal of International Economic Law 449 (2015)
31 S Lester and H Zhu, "A Proposal for 'Rebalancing' to Deal with 'National Security' Trade Restrictions" 42 Fordham International Law Journal 1451 (2019)
32 For example, Chapter 32 of USMCA
33 For example, CETA Article 28.3(2)a

(CETA) offers another example of an expanded general exceptions clause. Article 28.3 of CETA not only incorporates the GATT Article XX and GATS Article XIV exceptions by reference but also explicitly, and arguably redundantly, includes measures necessary to protect public security or public morals. This addition provides clearer justification for measures that might be taken for reasons of national security or ethical concerns, which are not as explicitly covered in the WTO agreements. The USMCA takes a different approach by including chapter-specific exception clauses. For instance, Article 32.1 provides general exceptions for the trade-in goods chapters, closely mirroring GATT Article XX, while Article 15.10 provides exceptions specific to cross-border trade-in services. This structure allows for more tailored exceptions that consider the unique aspects of different types of trade and economic activities.

Some FTAs have also clarified the application of General Exceptions to environmental measures. The EU-South Korea Free Trade Agreement, in its Article 2.15, explicitly states that the general exceptions include environmental measures necessary to protect human, animal, or plant life or health. This clarification removes any ambiguity about whether environmental protection falls within the scope of the exceptions, which has been a subject of interpretation in WTO jurisprudence.

Some FTAs have altered the connecting words found in GATT Article XX, attempting to provide more clarity or flexibility in the application of general exceptions. This modification of language is an effort to address some of the interpretive challenges that have arisen in WTO jurisprudence. For example, in Article 28.3, CETA uses the phrase "adopted and applied to protect" instead of "necessary to protect" for some of its exceptions. This change in language could be interpreted as lowering the threshold for justifying measures under the exceptions, as "adopted and applied to protect" may be seen as a less stringent requirement than "necessary to protect." The EU-Singapore Free Trade Agreement provides another example of modified language in its general exceptions. Article 11.1 of the agreement uses the phrase "designed and applied" instead of "necessary" or "relating to" for some of its exceptions. This wording could potentially provide more flexibility in justifying measures, as it focuses on the Intent and application of the measure rather than its necessity or relationship to the objective.

The chapeau of GATT Article XX/GATS Article XIV is common to many general exception clauses in FTAs. One noteworthy, if small, change can be found in the ASEAN-Australia-New Zealand Free Trade Agreement (AANZFTA). In Chapter 15, Article 1, paragraph 3, the agreement states that "such measures are not applied in a manner which would constitute a means of arbitrary or unjustifiable discrimination between the Parties where *like* [emphasis added] conditions prevail, or a disguised restriction on trade in goods or services or investment." The use of "like conditions" instead of "same conditions" potentially provides more flexibility in the application of the exceptions.

While many FTAs use the WTO agreements as a template for their general exceptions, there is a trend towards expanding and clarifying these provisions to provide greater policy space and address specific concerns of the parties involved. These variations can have significant implications for how trade rules are balanced against other public policy objectives in the context of bilateral or regional trade agreements. It should be noted that it can be difficult to make comparisons across various treaties regarding the scope of their general exceptions given that the positive commitments from which they derogate may themselves be different.

Trade disputes involving general exceptions under FTAs have occurred in several instances. One notable case arose under NAFTA regarding sugar trade. Mexico imposed an anti-dumping duty on imports of high fructose corn syrup from the United States.[34] The United States challenged this measure under NAFTA Chapter 19, arguing it violated Mexico's obligations. Mexico defended its action by invoking NAFTA's general exception provisions,[35] claiming the measure was necessary to protect its domestic sugar industry, which it considered vital to its economic interests and rural development. This dispute highlighted the tension between trade liberalization commitments and the desire to protect sensitive domestic industries.

Another significant case involved Canada and Costa Rica under their bilateral FTA. Costa Rica imposed restrictions on imports of Canadian potatoes, citing phytosanitary concerns. Canada contested these measures, arguing they were not scientifically justified and constituted a disguised restriction on trade. Costa Rica invoked the agreement's general exceptions clause,[36] claiming the measures were necessary to protect plant life and health. This case underscored the challenges in balancing legitimate regulatory objectives with trade commitments, particularly in the context of agricultural trade and food safety.

The Australia-United States Free Trade Agreement (AUSFTA) has also seen disputes involving general exceptions. Australia implemented plain packaging requirements for tobacco products, which the United States tobacco industry argued violated intellectual property protections under AUSFTA. Australia defended its policy by invoking the agreement's General Exceptions,[37] asserting that the measure was necessary to protect public health. This case highlighted the intersection of trade, intellectual property, and public health policies within the framework of FTA obligations and exceptions.

In the context of the EU-South Korea FTA, a dispute arose when South Korea imposed restrictions on certain European Union food products, citing food safety concerns. The European Union challenged these measures, arguing they were disproportionate and not based on scientific evidence. South Korea invoked the agreement's General Exceptions clause to justify its actions as necessary for the protection of human health.[38] This case demonstrated the ongoing challenges in reconciling food safety regulations with trade liberalization commitments.

34 United States – Anti-Dumping Investigation of High Fructose Corn Syrup (HFCS) from the United States, NAFTA Chapter 19 Panel, MEX-USA-98-1904-01, Final Decision of the Panel (3 August 2001)

35 Article 2101

36 Article XII.1

37 Article 22.1

38 Article 2.15

6.4.2 Sustainability Chapters

Some preferential FTAs have dedicated chapters to sustainability issues, including the environment and labour. Such chapters often do not create substantive obligations, but rather create committees to promote dialogue and regulatory contribution. For example, UMSCA has an independent labour expert board to oversee the implementation of specific aspects of the agreement. Sustainability is further thought to be an integrative concept, covering a range of topics. In that sense, these non-trade values are not true exceptions but rather substantive legal principles in their own right.

The environmental chapter of USMCA is Chapter 24, which contains several key provisions aimed at environmental protection and sustainable development. This chapter represents a significant expansion of environmental commitments compared to NAFTA. One of the central provisions is Article 24.3, which recognizes each party's "sovereign right" to establish its own levels of domestic environmental protection while also calling on parties to "strive to ensure" that their laws provide for "high levels of environmental protection." This language balances national sovereignty with a commitment to environmental stewardship. Article 24.8 incorporates seven multilateral environmental agreements (MEAs) into the USMCA, making them enforceable through the agreement's dispute settlement mechanism. These MEAs include the Montreal Protocol on ozone-depleting substances and the Convention on International Trade in Endangered Species of Wild Fauna and Flora. This provision strengthens the link between trade and environmental obligations.

The USMCA introduces new obligations regarding marine environmental protection in Article 24.12, which requires parties to take action to prevent and reduce marine litter. This includes addressing land and sea-based pollution and promoting waste management infrastructure. Article 24.7 requires parties to conduct environmental impact assessments for central government projects that may have significant environmental effects. This provision aims to ensure that environmental considerations are integrated into decision-making processes for major projects. Article 24.4 allows environmental disputes to be brought to the same dispute settlement system as other USMCA commitments. However, it specifies that such disputes can only be brought if the lowering of environmental standards creates a trade or investment advantage and affects trade. This provision sets a threshold for when environmental measures can be challenged under the agreement.

The CPTPP has been noted for its inclusion of non-trade elements, particularly in relation to Indigenous and gender rights. Indeed, this is reflected in the treaty's title "comprehensive and progressive." These provisions represent an evolution in how trade agreements address social and environmental concerns alongside economic objectives. With respect to gender rights, the CPTPP includes language recognizing the importance of women's economic empowerment. Article 23.4 of the Development chapter states that parties "recognise that enhancing opportunities in their territories for women, including workers and business owners, to participate in the domestic and global economy contributes to economic development." While this language is largely aspirational, it signals an acknowledgment of gender issues in trade policy that was largely absent from previous agreements. The agreement also includes a commitment for parties to "consider undertaking cooperative activities" to enhance women's ability to access and benefit from CPTPP opportunities. These activities could include providing advice, training, and enhancing access to markets.

Regarding indigenous rights, the CPTPP preamble recognizes "the importance of traditional knowledge, as well as practices and traditional lifestyles that contribute to the conservation and sustainable use of biological diversity." This acknowledgement is innovative in its explicit recognition of indigenous knowledge systems in a major trade agreement. The inclusion of these provisions represents progress in making trade agreements more inclusive and responsive to social concerns.

Another innovative aspect of the CPTPP is its attempt to balance trade liberalization with the right of governments to regulate in the public interest. The agreement includes language affirming "the inherent right of each Party to regulate within its territory to achieve legitimate public policy objectives." This provision is seen as an attempt to address concerns about trade agreements constraining domestic policy space, including in areas related to gender and Indigenous rights.

While it does contain general exceptions modelled on GATT Article XX,[39] unusually, for a modern agreement, the RCEP does not contain dedicated chapters or extensive provisions on environment, labour, human rights, indigenous rights, or gender rights. The RCEP does establish a Committee on Sustainable Growth under Article 18.6, which is tasked with work on SMEs, economic and technical cooperation, and "emerging issues." Addressing sustainable development could potentially fit under "emerging issues" for this committee although this appears to be a relatively limited institutional mechanism rather than substantive provisions on environmental or social issues.

The African Continental Free Trade Agreement (AfCFTA) addresses non-trade values to an extent, though its primary focus is on economic integration and trade facilitation across the African continent. The agreement includes provisions related to the environment, human rights, labour, and culture, but these are not as comprehensive as its trade-related clauses. Regarding environmental sustainability, the AfCFTA acknowledges the importance of environmental protection in its preamble. Article 3(g) of the agreement lists among its general objectives to "promote and attain sustainable and inclusive socio-economic development, gender equality and structural transformation of the State Parties." This broad objective can be interpreted to include environmental considerations, although it does not explicitly mention them.

AfCFTA also touches on environmental issues in Article 26, which deals with technical barriers to trade. It states that member countries have the right to adopt standards necessary for environmental protection, provided these measures do not create unnecessary obstacles to trade. However, AfCFTA does not contain specific provisions or dedicated articles addressing environmental protection or climate change mitigation. Concerning human rights and labour issues, AfCFTA makes some reference to these topics, albeit in a limited manner. Article 3(e) includes

39 Article 17.12

among its objectives the promotion of "social and economic development and human rights." Additionally, Article 27(2)(d) mentions the protection of human, animal, or plant life or health as a legitimate reason for adopting or enforcing measures that might otherwise be inconsistent with the agreement's provisions on trade in services. Labour rights are not extensively addressed in the AfCFTA. However, the agreement does recognize the importance of labour mobility in achieving its goals. Article 3(d) aims to "promote and attain sustainable and inclusive socio-economic development, gender equality and structural transformation of the State Parties," which can be interpreted to include labour considerations.

Cultural aspects are mentioned in the context of trade in services. Article 18(2) of the AfCFTA Protocol on Trade in Services recognizes the right of member states to regulate and introduce new regulations to meet national policy objectives, including the protection of cultural heritage and cultural diversity. This provision allows countries to maintain some control over cultural industries and services within the framework of the free trade agreement.

6.4.3 Non-Regression Clauses

Non-regression clauses in FTAs are provisions that commit parties to maintain or improve their existing levels of regulatory standards, particularly in areas such as labour rights and environmental protection. These clauses serve as a safeguard against the lowering of standards that could potentially give one party an unfair competitive advantage. The primary purpose of non-regression clauses is to prevent a "race to the bottom" in regulatory standards. They aim to ensure that trade liberalization does not come at the cost of weakening important protections for workers, the environment, or other areas of public interest. By including these clauses, parties to an FTA signal their commitment to maintaining high standards and preventing regulatory backsliding.

Non-regression clauses typically require that neither party weaken or reduce the protections afforded in their environmental or labour laws in a manner that would affect trade or investment between the parties. For example, the United Kingdom-EU Trade and Cooperation Agreement (TCA) includes commitments to non-regression in areas such as environmental protection and workers' rights. The TCA contains the following statement:

> The Parties affirm their common understanding that their economic relationship can only deliver benefits in a mutually satisfactory way if the commitments relating to a level playing field for open and fair competition stand the test of time, by preventing distortions of trade or investment, and by contributing to sustainable development. However, the Parties recognise that the purpose of this Title is not to harmonise the standards of the Parties. The Parties are determined to maintain and improve their respective high standards in the areas covered by this Title.[40]

40 Article 355.4

This approach is elaborated in Article 387.2 which states that parties shall not weaken or reduce their social or labour protections in a manner affecting trade (or investment) between the parties. This requirement applies also to environmental protection under Article 391.2. Chapter 8 of the TCA sets out the minimum international standards in areas such as labour and the environment to which the parties are committed, giving some shape to the substantive nature of the non-regression norms.

There is an additional specialized "rebalancing" section in the TCA designed to respond to significant divergences between the parties in labour, the environment and subsidy policy via unilateral retaliation by the other party. The essence is contained in paragraph 411.2:

> If material impacts on trade or investment between the Parties are arising as a result of significant divergences between the Parties in [labour and social, environmental or climate protection, or with respect to subsidy control], either Party may take appropriate rebalancing measures to address the situation. Such measures shall be restricted with respect to their scope and duration to what is strictly necessary and proportionate in order to remedy the situation. Priority shall be given to such measures as will least disturb the functioning of this Agreement. A Party's assessment of these impacts shall be based on reliable evidence and not merely on conjecture or remote possibility.

Such non-regression clauses (also known as "standstill" or "ratchet" clauses) are common in modern FTAs, having first appeared in NAFTA. They are seen as a key part of the movement towards the recognition of the role of states in ensuring the observation by investors of corporate social responsibility principles, such as they relate to the environment as well as human rights.[41] An example of such a provision can be found in the Canada-EU Comprehensive Economic and Trade Agreement (CETA):

> The Parties recognise that it is inappropriate to encourage trade or investment by weakening or reducing the levels of protection afforded in their labour/environment law and standards.
>
> 2. A Party shall not waive or otherwise derogate from, or offer to waive or otherwise derogate from, its labour/environment law and standards, to encourage trade or the establishment, acquisition, expansion or retention of an investment in its territory.
> 3. A Party shall not, through a sustained or recurring course of action or inaction, fail to effectively enforce its labour/environment law and standards to encourage trade or investment.[42]

41 See M Footer, "Bits and Pieces: Social and Environmental Protection in the Regulation of Foreign Investment" 18:1 Michigan State International Law Review 33 (2009)

42 Article 23.4 (labour) and Article 24.5 (environment)

Non-regression clauses are thought to have had provided rather limited protection, at least in the case of the environment.[43]

There have been very few disputes arising under FTAs for breach of non-regression provisions. One such claim was brought under the Dominican Republic-Central America United States Free Trade Agreement (CAFTA-DR). The United States argued that Guatemala had failed to enforce its own labour laws in part by preventing workers from forming unions, allegedly resulting in their competitive advantage over United States workers. The tribunal was unable to find that any weakening took place in a manner affecting trade, ruling that "attempting to establish that an effect on prices is due to a failure to enforce and not to . . . other factors would often be so fraught with difficulty as to make proof of trade effects impossible."[44] This assessment was despite the fact that the CAFTA tribunal articulated a relatively weak trade effects test; the United States had needed to demonstrate merely that Guatemala's disputed practices had conferred "some competitive advantage on an employer or employers engaged in trade with the United States."[45]

Commentators have noted that this appears to be a fairly low threshold, compared, for example, to the injury test in safeguard proceedings, which requires substantial industry-wide effects.[46] Yet the CAFTA tribunal still found no evidence that any cost savings that might have accrued to Guatemalan exporters as a result of the alleged enforcement failures provided a competitive advantage. The USMCA non-regression model subsequently reversed the logic of the Guatemala ruling by placing the onus on the state enacting the regressive measure to justify that its non-fulfilment of a labour or environment standard does not affect trade or investment between the parties, which is otherwise presumed from the derogation.[47] This wording is not seen in the TCA. The threshold for harm in the TCA is high, as evident in the adjective "material" in the phrase "material impact."

The interpretation of non-regression clauses can be complex. While they generally prohibit the lowering of standards, they do not necessarily prevent all changes to regulations. Parties may still have the flexibility to adjust their regulatory approaches, as long as the overall level of protection is not reduced. This allows for some regulatory innovation and adaptation to new circumstances while still maintaining the spirit of the non-regression commitment. Non-regression clauses also serve a political purpose. They can help allay concerns from domestic constituencies who fear that trade agreements might lead to a deterioration of

43 A Jordan, V Gravey, B Moore, and C Reid, "EU-UK Trade Relations: Why Environmental Policy Regression will Undermine the Level Playing Field and What the United Kingdom Can Do to Limit It" Brexit and the Environment, Friends of the Earth (undated) at 8

44 Dominical Republic – Central America – United States of America, In the Matter of Guatemala – Issues Relating to the Obligations Under Article 16.2.1(a) of the CAFTA-DR, Final Report of the Panel, circulated 14 June 2017, para 58–60.

45 Ibid., at [190]

46 M Bronckers and G Gruni, "Retooling the Sustainability Standards in EU Free Trade Agreements" 24:1 Journal of International Economic Law 110 (2021)

47 Article 23.4 footnote 9

important social and environmental standards. By explicitly committing to maintain or improve these standards, governments can demonstrate that trade liberalization and high regulatory standards are not mutually exclusive.

In practice, the effectiveness of non-regression clauses depends on various factors, including the specific wording of the clause, the willingness of parties to enforce them, and the robustness of the agreement's dispute settlement mechanisms. Some critics argue that these clauses may not be sufficient to prevent regulatory backsliding, especially if the economic incentives to lower standards are strong.

6.4.4 Essential Security Clauses

Essential security provisions modelled on GATT Article XXI are commonly included in FTAs, though they often feature some modifications in language and scope. The appearance of essential security provisions in FTAs reflects the critical importance of these provisions as an aspect of state sovereignty. The non-trade value of security is clearly an element of statehood that supersedes the principles of world trade law.

The CPTPP includes an essential security provision in Article 29.2. It states:

> Nothing in this Agreement shall be construed to . . . prevent a Party from applying measures that it considers necessary for the fulfilment of its obligations with respect to the maintenance or restoration of international peace or security, or the protection of its own essential security interests.

This language is similar to GATT Article XXI, but it explicitly mentions "maintenance or restoration of international peace or security" alongside the protection of essential security interests. "Restoration" is the additional work here – cultivating the idea of bringing back something that has already been lost.

USMCA contains a security exception in Article 32.2 that closely mirrors GATT Article XXI. However, it adds a unique provision in paragraph 3: "For greater certainty, if a Party invokes Article 32.2 in an arbitral proceeding initiated under Chapter 14 (Investment) or Chapter 31 (Dispute Settlement), the tribunal or panel hearing the matter shall find that the exception applies." This addition appears to limit the ability of dispute settlement bodies to review the invocation of the security exception.

RCEP includes a security exception in Article 17.13 that is quite similar to GATT Article XXI. It states:

> Nothing in this Agreement shall be construed: (a) to require a Party to furnish or allow access to any information the disclosure of which it determines to be contrary to its essential security interests; or (b) to preclude a Party from applying measures that it considers necessary for the fulfilment of its obligations with respect to the maintenance or restoration of international peace or security, or the protection of its own essential security interests.

The main difference here is the use of "determines" instead of "considers" in Part (a), and the combination of elements from GATT Article XXI(b) and (c) in RCEP's Part (b). The word "determines" arguably conveys a deeper, perhaps more objective or empirical investigation than "considers."

The EU-Japan Economic Partnership Agreement (EPA) includes a security exception in Article 1.5 that states: "Nothing in this Agreement shall be construed . . . to prevent either Party from taking any action which it considers necessary for the protection of its essential security interests." This provision is more concise than GATT Article XXI, omitting the specific circumstances listed in GATT Article XXI(b)(i–iii).

Article XIV of the MERCOSUR Services Protocol contains a security exception that closely mirrors the language of GATT Article XXI. This provision closely follows the structure and language of GATT Article XXI, including the self-judging phrase "it considers necessary" when referring to measures taken to protect essential security interests. It also includes similar specific circumstances under which the exception can be invoked, such as measures relating to fissionable materials or taken in time of war. The main difference appears to be in the wording of Part (b) (i), which in MERCOSUR refers to "the provision of services directly or indirectly to ensure the supply of armed forces" rather than GATT's broader language about traffic in arms and other goods for supplying military establishments. However, the overall scope and intent of the provision remain very similar to GATT Article XXI.

6.5 Conclusion

World trade law is primarily focused on economic matters – trade is fundamentally an economic concern, designed to maximize the standard of living of parties who engage in the exchange of goods and services. But, world trade law is not immune to the social dimension of trade or to the reality that unbridled trade has the potential to inflict harm on society in the form of environmental or cultural erosion. In recent years the dangers imposed on national security from free trade as well as the potential for trade barriers to be used as instruments of geopolitics have grown. The original GATT evinced sensitivity to these issues in its General Exceptions. Drafted in the language of the 1940s before the era of climate change and cybercrime, these provisions, while robust in spirit, seem pragmatically outdated. Preferential FTAs have modified GATT Article XX in some instances providing greater precision as well as deference to a wider range of non-trade values, in some cases with dedicated chapters. Sustainability in its various forms, is thus a principle of world trade law.

When evaluating a public policy-based exception for a violation of world trade law, it is not enough to identify a particular non-trade concern that matters to the country enacting the offending law. The country must show that the law was not applied in a discriminatory or uneven fashion, meaning that it was applied in the same way to imports from all countries. For public morals and animal health, the country applying the illegal measure also has to demonstrate that there was not a less trade-restrictive method that could have fulfilled the same objective – the difficult test of necessity. This exercise will involve a weighing and balancing of various different regulatory actions that the government could have taken and the effects that these may or may not have had on international trade in affected products. Outside the General Exceptions, the essential security provision of WTO law and preferential FTAs is approached entirely differently – it is constructed in self-judging language which, while not removing from the scrutiny of international tribunals, grants broad deference to the country enacting the measure. From this, we can conclude that proportionality may be regarded as a principle of world trade law.

It is crucial that when relying upon an exception in any instrument of world trade law, the member country must do so in a manner that is honest and forthright. The exceptions should not be abused. This is often described as a principle of "good faith," a term which lawyers love because it covers all sorts of underhanded behaviour. Good faith, reflected previously in the notion of transparency, is very much an integral principle of world trade law.

It is clear that a compromise must be struck between the right of a country to invoke an exception and the rights guaranteed in the rest of the world trade law – like tariff bindings and non-discrimination. The WTO panels and Appellate Body as well as arbitration tribunals constituted under FTAs are tasked with maintaining this delicate balance. In many ways, this exercise encapsulates the essential conflict that exists at the heart of the relationship between world trade law and the sovereign rights of the countries which adhere to it. In performing this role international tribunals are able to guard against the exploitation of alleged policy goals as tools of protectionism. In an era characterized by the deep penetration of issues like climate change, health, and the importance of cultural identity, this is certain to become increasingly difficult.

Discussion Questions

1. Are the GATT General Exceptions sufficiently mindful of non-trade/public policy concerns?
2. What function is served by the Chapeau of GATT Article XX and GATS Article XIV?
3. Could the Essential Security exception of GATT be exploited/abused? What could guard against this?
4. What are non-regression clauses in preferential FTAs and how are they assessed by tribunals?
5. What is meant by the concept of sustainability and how is it integrated into world trade law?

7 Health and Safety

Sanitary and Phytosanitary and Technical Barriers to Trade

7.1 Introduction

Non-tariff barriers in the form of health and safety regulations on goods as they cross international borders have become far more significant than simple tariffs, which were the dominant form of protectionism throughout most of the 20th century. The view that certain products may be unsafe for certain markets means that some products will be prohibited entirely from import whereas many others will only be permitted to cross international borders following costly and time-consuming inspection and testing. These are sometimes referred to as conformity assessment procedures and are often expensive and time-consuming. While libertarians might view this as the intrusion of the state into our lives – adults are perfectly capable of deciding for themselves what products they wish to use – others would see safeguarding the interests of citizens as an essential duty for the government.

In many countries, there are thousands of health and safety regulations in place. Exporting into these countries can be problematic. World trade law aims to minimize such barriers where they are unnecessary, meaning where risk is minimal, or where different regulations in two countries cover the same risk and are therefore redundant. There is no need for a product to be tested twice – once in its home market, then again at its destination. Weak regulations, meaning those which do not address a product's capacity to harm people or animals/plants, can give an advantage to those products with regard to those from other countries where regulations are strict. On the other hand, disproportionate health and safety regulations can be seen as a form of protectionism. This is often the case when they are excessive relative to the risks which they purport to address or when they are applied on top of a foreign regulation that is able to cover the same risk, effectively doubling the administrative burden involved in international trade.

This chapter will discuss the principles behind the leading non-tariff barriers to trade in goods, increasing in tandem with the growth of the regulatory state. Reflecting on the WTO's Sanitary and Phytosanitary (SPS) and Technical Barriers to Trade (TBT) Agreements, the chapter will consider mutual recognition and conformity assessment agreements contained in preferential FTAs. The chapter will underscore the importance of harmonizing standards as well as regulatory cooperation, often reflected in the work of specialized committees at the multilateral and

DOI: 10.4324/9781003465676-7

bilateral levels. It will also consider the role of science in identifying and managing risk where it represents a barrier to trade.

7.2 Health and Safety Rules as Trade Barriers

The balance between health and safety concerns and the desire for free trade and low-priced, high-quality goods from other countries is a contentious aspect of world trade law. Part of the problem is that even as people enjoy low-cost products from around the world, many tend to prioritize health and safety over purely economic considerations. This preference for health and safety over free trade is often driven by a perception of risk. Consumers tend to be more averse to risks that are perceived as involuntary, uncontrollable, or catastrophic in nature. The potential health and safety risks associated with imported goods, such as contaminated food or unsafe products, can be seen as fitting this profile, leading to greater public concern.

Basing product health and safety standards on the social aspect of risks rather than their scientific realities is fraught with problems as these elements of harm mitigation are difficult to quantify and, therefore, apply with consistency and predictability. Stakeholder engagement, popular in other spheres of trade law, may be particularly unhelpful in the context of standard-setting for precisely this reason. People are always free not to purchase products if they feel they are unsafe, even if scientific evidence informs us otherwise. Moreover, research has shown that people are more likely to support trade policies that are perceived as fair and equitable, rather than purely focused on economic efficiency.[1] Concerns about worker exploitation, environmental degradation, or the erosion of domestic industries in the name of free trade can lead to public opposition, even if such policies may result in lower prices.

In some cases, protectionist measures ostensibly aimed at protecting public health and the safety of citizens may be used as a pretext for shielding domestic industries from foreign competition. Additionally, the costs of overly restrictive health and safety regulations can be passed on to consumers in the form of higher prices, potentially offsetting the benefits of free trade. Ultimately, the relative importance of health/safety and free trade is likely to vary depending on the specific context, the perceived risks and benefits, and the political and cultural values of the population. Policymakers must carefully navigate this balance, taking into account both economic and non-economic considerations to ensure the best outcomes for their constituents.

One of the difficulties in dealing with health and safety regulations as barriers to trade is the reality that the perception of risk, particularly regarding food safety, is significantly influenced by cultural factors. Risk perception is thought to be fundamentally a social process, with cultural values and beliefs playing a crucial role in

1 AM Mayda and D Rodrik, "Why Are Some People (and Countries) More Protectionist Than Others?" 49:6 European Economic Review 1393 (2005)

determining which risks societies choose to emphasize or downplay. They contend that different cultural worldviews lead to varying interpretations of the same risks.[2] Although experts often assess risk based on statistical probabilities, the public's perception of risk is more complex and influenced by various psychological and cultural factors.[3] There are significant variations in how different cultures perceive and prioritize risks. They observed that cultural factors could lead to divergent risk perceptions even when presented with the same scientific information. The role of cultural narratives and social constructions is key in shaping risk perceptions related to food. He argues that cultural contexts provide the frameworks through which individuals interpret and respond to potential food hazards.[4] The idiosyncratic nature of approaches to certain risks must therefore inform the deference with which world trade law responds to these issues as trade barriers.

7.3 Health and Safety Regulations as Non-Tariff Barriers at the WTO

The GATT drafters were aware of the importance of the health and safety of people when they established the Article XX General Exceptions. But, as noted in the previous chapter, the General Exceptions of GATT are limited in scope even though they refer to broad concepts like health. When the WTO was created some 45 years later, it was felt that the regulatory complexity of modern non-tariff barriers concerning health and safety product requirements called for more comprehensive treatment under WTO law. Two special agreements were created: the Agreement on Sanitary and Phytosanitary Measures (SPS Agreement) and the Agreement on Technical Barriers to Trade (TBT Agreement). Together these instruments capture another key principle of world trade law: harmonization. Harmonization essentially embodies the notion of achieving the same ends via different regulatory means.

7.3.1 The Sanitary and Phytosanitary (SPS) Agreement

Safety standards for food are uniquely important to the health of society. A special agreement covering measures related to food safety and animal and plant health standards was, therefore, created: the Sanitary and Phytosanitary Measures (SPS) Agreement. Phytosanitary simply means relating to the health of plants.

Article 1 of the SPS outlines its scope of application. The agreement applies to all sanitary and phytosanitary measures which may, directly or indirectly, affect international trade which effectively means food and food-related products. The risks intended to be addressed by such measures are those relating to diseases in organic material which may be harmful to human, animal or plant life, or health.

2 M Douglas and A Wildavsky, *Risk and Culture: An Essay on the Selection of Technological and Environmental Dangers* (University of California Press, 1982)

3 P Slovic, "Perception of Risk" 236:4799 Science 280 (1987)

4 J Zinn, *Social Theories of Risk and Uncertainty: An Introduction* (Wiley-Blackwell, 2008)

The central obligation of the agreement is found in Article 2.2 which reads:

> Members shall ensure that any sanitary or phytosanitary measure is applied only to the extent necessary to protect human, animal or plant life or health, is based on scientific principles and is not maintained without sufficient scientific evidence.

Members may depart from scientific evidence when setting their regulations if scientific evidence is insufficient on the basis of "available pertinent information."[5] The SPS goes on to state:

2. Sanitary or phytosanitary measures which conform to international standards, guidelines or recommendations shall be deemed to be necessary to protect human, animal or plant life or health.
3. Members may introduce or maintain sanitary or phytosanitary measures which result in a higher level of sanitary or phytosanitary protection than would be achieved by measures based on the relevant international standards, guidelines or recommendations, if there is a scientific justification.

The SPS agreement allows WTO members to set their own standards in relation to food, animal, and plant health. This is a recognition of the important aspect of sovereignty which is the regulation of health and safety of citizens. However, in order for such rules to be viewed as legitimate by the WTO from the standpoint of their effect on international trade, they must be justified either by scientific evidence or through deference to a recognized international standard-setting body. The SPS lists three such organizations, each of which has its own internal decision-making procedures which are susceptible to political influence.[6] This is precisely why the SPS encourages all WTO members to participate in the setting of international standards through these kinds of organizations.

WTO members are therefore encouraged to implement international standards, guidelines and recommendations on food safety, where they exist. Rules which conform to international standards are presumed to conform to the SPS. If these guidelines do exist and the WTO member follows them, then it is unlikely that such a regulation would ever lead to a dispute because of the built-in assumption that they are valid.

One of the key principles of the SPS is that WTO members are permitted to enact the food safety laws that they wish. In particular, they can do this even if they result in higher standards than those indicated by international bodies, but only if there is scientific justification. Such higher standards could impose trade barriers as imports would, therefore, be required to satisfy them. There is, therefore,

5 Article 5.7

6 E Vos and S Röttger-Wirtz, "EU Food Law and the WTO: Trade, Science and Politics" in D Prévost, I Alexovicova, and JH Pohl (Eds.), *Restoring Trust in Trade* (Hart, 2018)

a high degree of deference accorded to WTO members. This is the essence of harmonization.

This means that there must be adequate risk assessment of the risks to human, animal or plant life or health. Adequate risk assessment will include having scientists examine the relevant products for various diseases and organisms, testing the likelihood of exposure to citizens under different conditions and what the actual dangers are. If there is insufficient scientific evidence to demonstrate that a particular health regulation is needed, WTO countries may provisionally adopt the law anyway on the basis of the available pertinent information. This kind of risk-adverse approach does require that the country make an effort to seek additional information in order to get a more complete picture at a later date.

Article 2.3 proceeds to state "Members shall ensure that their sanitary and phytosanitary measures do not arbitrarily or unjustifiably discriminate between Members where identical or similar conditions prevail" and that "sanitary and phytosanitary measures shall not be applied in a manner which would constitute a disguised restriction on international trade." This recalls the language of GATT Article XX's chapeau.

WTO members are encouraged to base their SPS regulations on international standards where possible in order to prevent needless duplication with such standards presumptively legitimate from the perspective of health protection.[7] In this way, regulatory approaches among WTO members are "harmonized." Furthermore, the SPS Agreement obliges WTO members to recognize each other's standards as equivalent, even where the regulations differ, if the exporting member can objectively demonstrate to the importing member that its measures achieve the importing member's appropriate level of protection.[8]

The SPS Agreement strongly emphasizes the process behind risk assessment, essentially deferring to each member state to set its own level of risk provided that it was ascertained on the basis of reasonable evidence. This is seen in Article 5:

1. Members shall ensure that their sanitary or phytosanitary measures are based on an assessment, as appropriate to the circumstances, of the risks to human, animal or plant life or health, taking into account risk assessment techniques developed by the relevant international organizations.

The SPS adds: "Members should, when determining the appropriate level of sanitary or phytosanitary protection, take into account the objective of minimizing negative trade effects."[9] In other words, health measures on food must not be used as a cloak to grant favourable treatment to domestic goods or to goods from certain countries because this would operate as an economically harmful market distortion.

7 Articles 3.1 and 3.2
8 Article 4.1
9 Article 5.4

In keeping with the principle of transparency, the SPS further mandates that members must share information and respond to requests regarding food sanitation regulations including an explanation for their imposition in various circumstances.

There are two approaches to SPS measures by WTO members. One which is characteristic of the United States is to focus on the text of the agreement and to enact measures which aim to address only those risks for which there is a genuine scientifically demonstrable risk. The other approach is that of the European Union, which espouses the "precautionary principle" in which even small risks where there is limited scientific evidence of danger should be eliminated where possible.

The precautionary principle is a policy approach that suggests taking protective measures against potential risks even in the absence of full scientific proof of harm. In other words, it advocates erring on the side of caution when scientific evidence about an environmental or health risk is uncertain.[10] The precautionary principle can lead to overly restrictive regulations that impose significant economic costs without clear benefits. The principle is also vague and can be used to justify banning any new technology or product.[11] The precautionary principle shifts the burden of proof to those introducing a new technology or product to demonstrate it is safe, rather than requiring proof of harm. This can stifle innovation and make it harder to bring beneficial new products to market. It may also be viewed as anti-science and prevents the development of solutions to pressing problems. The precautionary principle can be applied inconsistently. Precaution is often invoked for new technologies like genetically modified foods, but not for older, potentially hazardous practices. This selective application undermines the principle's credibility. There are also challenges in determining what level of precaution is appropriate and who should bear the costs. On the other hand, in the face of potentially catastrophic threats like climate change or pandemics, precaution may be essential.

One of the early disputes brought under the SPS was the *Australia – Salmon*[12] dispute which dealt with Australia's ban on the importation of fresh, chilled, and frozen salmon from Canada. Canada argued that Australia's ban violated several provisions of the SPS. First, there was the question of whether Australia's import ban was based on a proper risk assessment, as required by Articles 5.1 and 2.2 of the SPS Agreement. The WTO panel initially found that Australia had not based its measure on a risk assessment, thus violating these articles. Another significant issue concerned whether Australia's measures were consistent with Article 5.5 of the SPS, which prohibits arbitrary or unjustifiable distinctions in levels of protection if such distinctions result in discrimination or a disguised restriction on international trade.

The panel and later the Appellate Body found that Australia had indeed violated this provision by applying different levels of protection to salmon compared to other fish products like herring and finfish, without justification. The dispute also

10 CR Sunstein, *Laws of Fear: Beyond the Precautionary Principle* (Cambridge University Press, 2005)
11 J Morris, *Rethinking Risk and the Precautionary Principle* (Butterworth-Heinemann, 2000)
12 Australia – Measures Affecting Importation of Salmon, WT/DS18/AB/R, adopted 6 November 1998

raised questions about Article 5.6 of the SPS Agreement, which requires that SPS measures not be more trade-restrictive than necessary to achieve the appropriate level of protection. Initially, the panel found that Australia had violated this provision, but the Appellate Body reversed this finding due to insufficient factual findings. The WTO Appellate Body, while modifying some of the panel's reasoning, ultimately upheld the core findings against Australia. It concluded that Australia had acted inconsistently with Articles 5.1, 2.2, 5.5, and 2.3 of the SPS Agreement.

In *Japan – Agricultural Products II,*[13] the United States challenged Japan's restrictions on the import of various agricultural products, such as apples, cherries, and nectarines, based on the potential presence of codling moths. Japan argued that its measures were necessary to prevent the introduction and spread of this pest, which could harm its domestic agricultural industry. The Appellate Body ruled that Japan's measures were inconsistent with the SPS Agreement, as they were not based on a proper risk assessment. The Appellate Body found that Japan had failed to consider relevant scientific evidence and had not adequately explained how its measures achieved the appropriate level of protection. This case highlighted the need for SPS measures to be based on a thorough and objective assessment of risks, taking into account available scientific evidence and the specific circumstances of the importing country. It also emphasized the importance of transparency and non-discrimination in the application of such measures.

The United States challenged India's import restrictions on various agricultural products, such as poultry meat and eggs, based on concerns about avian influenza.[14] India argued that its measures were necessary to protect against the introduction and spread of this disease, which could harm its domestic poultry industry. The panel and Appellate Body ruled that India's measures were inconsistent with the SPS Agreement, as they were not based on a proper risk assessment. The panel noted that India had failed to consider relevant scientific evidence and had not adequately explained how its measures achieved the appropriate level of protection. The case underscored the need for SPS measures to be based on a thorough and objective assessment of risks, taking into account available scientific evidence and the specific circumstances of the importing country. It also emphasized the importance of transparency and non-discrimination in the application of such measures.

A conflict arises between the "science-based" approach and the "hazard-based" one, as seen most notably in the hormone-treated beef dispute.[15] The dispute originated when the European Union banned the import of meat containing artificial beef growth hormones, despite their approval for use in the United States. The European Union has maintained a ban on hormone-treated beef since 1989, which applies to all EU member states. The ban was initially implemented as a temporary

13 Japan – Measures Affecting Agricultural Products, WT/DS76/AB/R, adopted 19 March 1999

14 India – Measures Concerning the Importation of Certain Agricultural Products, WT/DS430/AB/R, adopted 19 June 2015

15 European Communities – Measures Concerning Meat and Meat Products (Hormones), WT/DS26/AB/R, WT/DS48/AB/R, adopted 13 February 1998

measure and was made permanent in 2003. The trade consequences of this prohibition have been significant, particularly affecting beef exports from the United States and Canada to the European Union. Prior to the ban, the United States exported about $100 million worth of beef annually to the European Union, but this dropped to nearly zero after the ban was implemented. This led to a long-standing trade dispute between the European Union and these countries.

In the *EU – Beef Hormones*[16] dispute, the United States and Canada challenged the European Union's ban, arguing that it violated several provisions of the SPS Agreement. One aspect related to whether the European Union had conducted an adequate risk assessment to support its ban, as required by Articles 5.1 and 5.2. The United States contended that the European Union failed to provide scientific evidence justifying the ban and that there was a clear worldwide scientific consensus supporting the safety of hormone-treated beef for consumers. Another issue related to the interpretation of Article 3.1 of the SPS which requires that sanitary measures be "based on" international standards, guidelines, or recommendations. The Appellate Body clarified that this does not mean SPS measures must "conform to" such standards, rejecting the panel's initial interpretation. The Appellate Body ultimately ruled against the European Union, finding that its ban was not based on a proper risk assessment as required by the SPS Agreement. Despite this ruling, the European Union maintained its ban, citing ongoing scientific reviews and opinions suggesting potential health risks associated with hormone-treated beef. Hormone-treated beef remains controversial, as many people are worried about ingesting animal products that have been treated with any kind of chemicals, especially growth hormones.

In reaching this conclusion, the Appellate Body clarified that there were no minimum procedural requirements for domestic risk assessment in order to satisfy a country's non-compliance with an international standard. This means that it is not necessary for a member who enacts an SPS-oriented measure to conduct an investigation, engage in some kind of formal fact-finding mission or to publish a report in which the law is justified scientifically. In that sense, the WTO does accord members significant freedom to enact the food health laws that they want for the reasons that they want, as long as there is some indication of integrity in the process. The Appellate Body went even further in allowing discretion to members in relation to their SPS rules when it said that the presence of a "scientific controversy" or disagreement about a particular health danger does not prevent a country from relying upon minority scientific opinion, as opposed to the mainstream. Assessing the specific risks in relation to certain products is particularly problematic for the WTO dispute settlement where much of the evidence upon which risk assessment is based is in the hands of the private producers of dangerous products, not the governments themselves which come before the WTO as negotiators and litigators.

16 European Communities – Measures Concerning Meat and Meat Products (Hormones), WT/DS26/AB/R, WT/DS48/AB/R, adopted 13 February 1998

The SPS was litigated again through the WTO dispute settlement system in another very controversial dispute relating to genetically modified organisms (GMOs). GMOs are organic products created through gene manipulation by companies to be superior to naturally occurring equivalents, often because they are resistant to insects or can grow larger or in less hospitable environments. GMOs are seen by many as a vital tool in the eradication of world hunger. Others view them as a dangerous interference with natural processes leading to disastrous consequences to human, animal, and plant ecosystems as well as the private property of more traditional farmers.

The *EC – Biotech*[17] case involved the United States, Canada, and Argentina as complainants against the European Communities (EC) regarding the EC's regulatory regime for GMOs. The complainants argued that the EC's moratorium and product-specific measures on GMOs violated Article 8 and Annex C(1)(a) of the SPS Agreement, which requires members to complete approval procedures without undue delay. They contended that the EC had failed to process applications for GMO approvals within a reasonable time frame, effectively creating a barrier to trade. The complainants further claimed that the EC's measures were inconsistent with Article 5.1 of the SPS Agreement, which requires that SPS measures be based on appropriate risk assessments. They argued that the EC had not conducted proper risk assessments to justify its restrictive measures on GMOs. They also asserted that the EC's measures violated Article 2.2 of the SPS Agreement, which stipulates that SPS measures should be applied only to the extent necessary to protect human, animal, or plant life or health, and should be based on scientific principles. The complainants contended that the EC's measures were not scientifically justified and were therefore inconsistent with Article 5.5 of the SPS Agreement. They argued that the EC was treating GMOs differently from similar non-GMO products without justification.

The panel found that the EC's *de facto* moratorium and product-specific measures resulted in "undue delay" in the approval process, violating Article 8 of the SPS. This was a significant victory for the complainants, as it confirmed that the EC's regulatory regime had created unjustified barriers to trade in GMOs. Regarding the claims under Articles 5.1 and 2.2, the panel chose not to rule on these issues for the general moratorium. However, for the product-specific measures and member state safeguard measures, the panel found that these were not based on risk assessments as required by Article 5.1 and were therefore inconsistent with this provision and, by extension, Article 2.2. The panel did not make a finding on the alleged violation of Article 5.5, as it considered that the complainants had not presented sufficient evidence to support this claim.

It must be recognized that, while the panel ruled against many of the EC's measures, it did not challenge the EC's right to maintain a regulatory system for GMO approval or to conduct rigorous safety assessments. The ruling primarily focused

17 European Communities – Measures Affecting the Approval and Marketing of Biotech Products, WT/DS291/R, WT/DS292/R, WT/DS293/R, adopted 21 November 2006

on the procedural aspects and the scientific basis of the EC's measures. The EC Biotech case again illustrates the WTO dispute settlement system's emphasis on process rather than on results as a way of resolving an incredibly sensitive debate between two superpowers. Put another way, the WTO is not the final arbiter of scientific truth in tightly contested disputes but rather is a body that scrutinizes the way in which any governmental decisions that have effects on trade are reached. It seems that the highly complex way in which the European Union makes these types of decisions may be at the core of the GMO debate rather than anything fundamental about the relative safety of GMO and natural foods.

These cases demonstrate the ongoing tensions between science-based decision-making and other considerations, such as consumer preferences, environmental concerns, and the protection of domestic industries. While the WTO panels and Appellate Body have emphasized the importance of basing SPS measures on scientific evidence, it has also recognized the need for flexibility in addressing legitimate public policy objectives, such as protecting human, animal, or plant health. As the global trading system continues to evolve and new challenges emerge, such as the increasing prevalence of zoonotic diseases and the growing importance of sustainability in agricultural production, the role of the WTO's SPS will likely continue to be a subject of debate and discussion among member countries and stakeholders.

One of the key debates regarding the SPS Agreement surrounds its purpose, with some believing that the agreement serves primarily to preserve market access commitments and prevent disguised protectionism. In this way, the agreement is not aimed at establishing a post-non-discrimination/non-protectionism trade regime, but rather its various provisions can be traced back to a single economic rationale: preserving market access commitments.[18] Others have argued that the SPS Agreement goes beyond simply preserving market access and introduces new constraints on domestic regulatory autonomy. It has been suggested that the agreement has altered the WTO legal order from a regime focused on non-discrimination to one that interdicts unnecessary obstacles to trade, even if enacted for non-protectionist purposes.[19]

The science-based obligations in the SPS Agreement have been a particular focus of academic scrutiny. Some take issue with the SPS Agreement's science-based obligations because they result in the second-guessing of national regulatory choices by international adjudicators, whose legitimacy to do so is at least questionable.[20] The precise meaning of "science" itself is now heavily contested – with some governments and organizations appearing to be unwilling to countenance dissent, which is an essential element of the scientific method. This was seen especially

18 R Howse, "Democracy, Science, and Free Trade: Risk Regulation on Trial at the World Trade Organization" 98:7 Michigan Law Review 2329 (2000)

19 D Neven and J Weiler, "Japan: Measures Affecting the Importation of Apples (AB-2003-4): One Bad Apple? (DS245/AB/R): A Comment" 5:2 World Trade Review 159 (2006)

20 JL Dunoff, "The Death of the Trade Regime" 10:4 European Journal of International Law 733 (1999)

during the Covid-19 era. It is also believed that the SPS Agreement's emphasis on international standards and scientific justification places a disproportionate burden on developing countries with limited scientific and regulatory capacity.[21] Some have expressed concern that the SPS Agreement could conflict with other regulatory regimes in the food safety arena, raising questions about the hierarchy between SPS obligations and other international commitments.[22]

7.3.2 The Agreement on Technical Barriers to Trade (TBT)

Like health, regulations relating to product safety and other technical requirements like those dealing with environmental protection and consumer welfare laws can be as important for safeguarding the citizens of WTO member countries. Problems arise when there are too many different standards across the world. This is because it is difficult for the producers and exporters of goods not only to comply with these rules but sometimes even to know what they are in the first place.

Technical regulations are designed to enhance trade by informing consumers precisely where products originate from and what they contain. As with health-related rules, technical regulations of all sorts can become instruments of protectionism – they can be used as obstacles to international trade by imposing entirely unnecessary or overly complicated procedures on exporters. The objective of the WTO is to ensure that technical regulations are genuine and not illegitimate trade barriers.

The Technical Barriers to Trade (TBT) Agreement attempts to ensure that regulations, standards, as well as testing, and certification procedures do not create illegitimate barriers to international trade under the guise of safety or consumer protection. It obliges that WTO members must not enact technical regulations that are more trade-restrictive than necessary in order to fulfil whatever the legitimate objective is.

When making this, assessment the member country must consider the risks that non-fulfilment of the goal would impose. This essentially means that the efforts undertaken by each country in achieving a particular product safety or consumer awareness objective must be done in a manner that does not restrict international trade. So, any such laws must be clearly connected to the risk that is being controlled. The more serious the risk, the greater an imposition on international trade permissible.

The TBT applies to all technical regulations (that are mandatory) and standards (which are optional) not covered by SPS. In that sense, the TBT is sometimes described as a "carve-out" from the SPS. The TBT deals with matters such as product characteristics, labels, packaging, testing, and certification. There are

21 S Zarrilli, "The SPS Agreement and the Developing Countries" 22:9 The World Economy, 1191 (1999)

22 L Gruszczynski, *Regulating Health and Environmental Risks Under WTO Law: A Critical Analysis of the SPS Agreement* (Oxford University Press, 2010)

non-discrimination requirements for all relevant regulations, which must not create unnecessary barriers to trade. Justifications for TBTs include scientific evidence, as with the SPS, but also consumer preference. Recalling that the WTO has no authority directly over the private sector, WTO members should endeavour to get non-governmental organizations to apply standards in an even-handed, non-trade restrictive way. As with all WTO agreements, there are also transparency and notification obligations.

An example of a product standard that could potentially operate as a trade barrier is the European Union's standard for power, control, and communication cables used in construction works.[23] This standard, while voluntary, has become *de facto* mandatory for many manufacturers seeking to sell their products in the EU market. For non-EU manufacturers, especially those from developing countries, complying with this standard can present significant challenges. The standard requires extensive testing and certification procedures, which can be costly and time-consuming.

At the core of the TBT Agreement is Article 2 which outlines the primary obligations regarding technical regulations. Article 2.1 establishes the fundamental principle of non-discrimination, requiring that imported products be accorded treatment no less favourable than that accorded to like products of national origin and to "like" products originating in any other country. This ensures a level playing field for all trading partners. Under TBT "likeness" extends to products that serve the same purpose.

Article 2.2 introduces the concept of necessity, stipulating that technical regulations shall not be more trade-restrictive than necessary to fulfil a legitimate objective. This article also provides a non-exhaustive list of legitimate objectives, including national security requirements, prevention of deceptive practices, and protection of human health or safety, animal or plant life or health, or the environment. The necessity test in Article 2.2 requires WTO members to carefully consider the trade impacts of their regulations and explore less trade-restrictive alternatives where possible.

It is useful to contrast the TBT's necessity test with that of GATT Article XX(a) and (b) since, in some respects, the TBT is an enlargement of GATT's General Exceptions. Necessity under the TBT agreement applies specifically to technical regulations, while GATT Article XX applies to a broader range of measures that may violate other GATT obligations. In TBT disputes, the complainant bears the burden of proving that a measure is more trade-restrictive than necessary whereas in GATT Article XX cases, the respondent bears the burden of proving the measure is necessary to achieve the stated objective. The TBT necessity test explicitly requires consideration of the risks non-fulfilment would create, which is not a formal requirement in the GATT Article XX analysis, although it may be considered implicitly. The TBT necessity test involves a more explicit relational analysis between the measure's trade restrictiveness and its contribution to the objective whereas the GATT Article XX analysis focuses more on the necessity

23 EN 50575

of the measure to achieve the objective. Both tests consider the availability of less trade-restrictive alternatives but the TBT analysis focuses on "reasonably available" alternatives while the GATT analysis considers whether alternatives are "reasonably available" and provides an "equivalent contribution" to the objective.

Transparency obligations form another critical aspect of the TBT, primarily addressed in Article 2.9. This article requires members to notify other WTO members through the Secretariat of proposed technical regulations that may have a significant effect on trade. It also mandates that members allow reasonable time for other members to make comments in writing, discuss these comments upon request, and take these comments and discussions into account.

Article 2.4 promotes the use of international standards (although none are specified), requiring members to use them as a basis for their technical regulations where they exist or their completion is imminent, except when such international standards would be ineffective or inappropriate for the fulfilment of legitimate objectives pursued.

The agreement extends similar obligations to standards and conformity assessment procedures. Article 4 requires members to ensure that their central government standardizing bodies accept and comply with the Code of Good Practice for the Preparation, Adoption and Application of Standards in Annex 3 of the agreement. Articles 5 through 9 deal with conformity assessment procedures, applying principles similar to those for technical regulations, including non-discrimination, necessity, and transparency.

Article 13 establishes the Committee on Technical Barriers to Trade, which provides a forum for consultations on matters pertaining to the operation of the agreement and the furtherance of its objectives. This committee plays a crucial role in monitoring the implementation of the agreement and facilitating dialogue between members on TBT-related issues.

There have been a number of disputes between WTO members on the basis of the TBT Agreement, although still somewhat less than under the SPS. In recent years the TBT Agreement has become more widely used by WTO members, in part because of the expansion of safety rules for all sorts of products many of which could be exploited as potential barriers to trade in an era of declining tariffs.

In a critical dispute brought under the TBT, Peru challenged a regulation adopted by European Communities that provided that only food products that were prepared from a certain sub-species of sardines found around the coasts of the eastern North Atlantic Ocean, as well as the Mediterranean and Black Seas could be marketed and preserved as "sardines."[24] Only products of this species could be sold on the shelves of European stores with the word "sardines" on the tin. Peru argued that the EC regulation violated the TBT because it did not adhere to international standards set by the Codex Alimentarius Commission, a well-recognized international food standards agency. The Commission said that the label "sardines"

24 European Communities – Trade Description of Sardines, WT/DS231/AB/R, adopted 23 October 2002

was not restricted to species of fish found in the North Atlantic, Mediterranean and Black Seas. The panel and later Appellate Body agreed with Peru, ruling that the international standard limited the sardines to various species (which included those kinds found in the waters around Peru) and that this international standard was effective in accomplishing all three of the EC's objectives in their tighter regulation: market transparency, consumer protection, and fair competition. Europe's attempt to restrict the definition of sardines was nothing more than an attempt to promote the sale of European fish.

The TBT was the source of a dispute in relation to the French prohibition on the importation or sale of asbestos products.[25] This law was challenged by Canada which has a major asbestos production industry. Asbestos is a material composed of thin fibrous crystals that was widely used throughout the 19th and 20th centuries because of its resistance to heat as well as its affordability. The prolonged inhalation of asbestos fibres can cause lung damage and even cancer. In the dispute brought by Canada against the European Union, the challenged law was both the ban on Canadian asbestos as well as exceptions to it for certain types of cellulose and glass fibres. The panel and the Appellate Body both agreed that the French measure was a discriminatory trade barrier because it treated Canadian asbestos differently than French asbestos. But, the WTO panel allowed the European law on the basis that it was justified under the GATT's exceptions for human health.

The panel and Appellate Body clarified what will constitute a technical regulation such that it is captured by the TBT. Technical regulations will consist of mandatory requirements relating to a product's characteristics, which can be physical descriptions as well as functionality. This definition, which the Appellate Body thought applied to the European Union's asbestos ban, is regularly cited in WTO disputes relating to technical regulations. It means that the TBT agreement is often engaged whenever the GATT's general exceptions relating to health are used as a justification for an otherwise trade-restrictive regime.

Indonesia brought a complaint under the TBT Agreement against the United States because of its prohibition on clove-flavoured cigarettes.[26] The United States domestic law banned the production or sale of cigarettes containing the additive clove (as well as other flavourings like cherry, vanilla, and coconut) but expressly allowed the production and sale of cigarettes containing other additives, such as the popular flavouring menthol, almost all of which were produced in the United States. The reason for the restriction on these varieties of flavoured cigarettes was to ensure that young people, who were seen as being more likely to be attracted by the same types of flavouring found in candy, would not become hooked on cigarettes to become lifetime smokers.

25 European Communities – Measures Affecting Asbestos and Asbestos-Containing Products, WT/DS135/AB/R, adopted 5 April 2001

26 United States – Measures Affecting the Production and Sale of Clove Cigarettes, WT/DS406/AB/R, adopted 24 April 2012

Indonesia, which is the world's leading producer of clove cigarettes, argued that this law violated national treatment under the GATT as well as the TBT and the SPS Agreements. The WTO panel found that the ban was a technical regulation, as per the definition established in the asbestos case. It went on to rule that the United States ban was also discriminatory, violating the TBT's national treatment guarantee. This was based on their finding that clove cigarettes are "like" menthol cigarettes because they appeal to young smokers. When the United States appealed the decision, the Appellate Body agreed with most of these conclusions adding that the United States law had a severe detrimental impact on the competitive opportunities of Indonesia's clove cigarettes, which was a critical component of the non-discrimination guarantee in the TBT. Interestingly, the United States never complied with this ruling. Instead, the United States indicated that intends to pursue further studies in relation to menthol and may ultimately impose restrictions on this type of flavouring in tobacco products.

The dispute between Indonesia and Australia regarding Australia's plain packaging cigarettes legislation,[27] was part of a broader challenge against Australia's tobacco plain packaging measures, with several other countries also filing complaints. The dispute centred on Australia's Tobacco Plain Packaging Act 2011 and related regulations, which mandated standardized packaging for all tobacco products sold in Australia. These measures required cigarette packs to be sold in a uniform dark brown colour, with no logos or brand imagery, and with health warnings covering a significant portion of the packaging. Indonesia argued that Australia's plain packaging measures violated Article 2.2 of the TBT Agreement which stipulates that technical regulations should not be more trade-restrictive than necessary to fulfil a legitimate objective. Indonesia contended that Australia's measures were overly restrictive and that there were less trade-restrictive alternatives available to achieve Australia's public health objectives. They argued that the plain packaging requirements went beyond what was necessary to inform consumers about the health risks of smoking and to prevent deceptive practices. Indonesia further claimed that the measures were inconsistent with the National Treatment provision of Article 2.1 of the TBT.

Indonesia argued that the plain packaging requirements had a detrimental impact on the competitive opportunities for imported tobacco products in the Australian market, particularly affecting premium brands which relied heavily on brand recognition and distinctive packaging. Indonesia also asserted that Australia's measures violated Article 2.5 of the TBT Agreement. This article relates to the preparation, adoption, and application of technical regulations. Indonesia argued that Australia had failed to adequately explain the justification for its measures in terms of the objectives referred to in Article 2.2. Indonesia also claimed that the measures were inconsistent with Article 2.9 of the TBT Agreement, which outlines

27 Australia – Certain Measures Concerning Trademarks, Geographical Indications and Other Plain Packaging Requirements Applicable to Tobacco Products and Packaging, WT/DS435/AB/R, WT/DS441/AB/R, adopted 29 June 2020

notification and consultation requirements for WTO members when introducing new technical regulations. Indonesia contended that Australia had not followed proper procedures in notifying other WTO members about the proposed measures and allowing for comments before their implementation.

Regarding the claim under Article 2.2, the panel found that while the plain packaging measures did restrict trade, they were not more trade-restrictive than necessary to fulfil a legitimate objective. The panel accepted Australia's argument that the measures were designed to improve public health by reducing the use of tobacco products. It concluded that Indonesia had not demonstrated that alternative measures would be equally effective in achieving Australia's health objectives. On the Article 2.1 claim, the panel rejected Indonesia's argument. It found that any detrimental impact on competitive opportunities for imported tobacco products stemmed from legitimate regulatory distinctions, rather than discrimination against imports. The panel noted that the measures applied equally to all tobacco products, regardless of their origin. Concerning Article 2.5, the panel found that Indonesia had not established that Australia failed to explain the justification for its measures upon request. The panel noted that Australia had provided extensive explanations of its plain packaging measures in various forums, including in response to questions in the TBT Committee. As for the claim under Article 2.9, the panel found that Australia had not acted inconsistently with its obligations. It concluded that Australia had notified other WTO members of the proposed measures, provided information upon request, and allowed reasonable time for other members to make comments.

Some other disputes arising under the TBT should be mentioned. Mexico challenged the United States' dolphin-safe labelling requirements for tuna products, arguing that they violated the TBT Agreement by discriminating against Mexican tuna products and creating unnecessary obstacles to trade.[28] The WTO panel and Appellate Body found that the United States' measures were inconsistent with Article 2.1 of the TBT Agreement because they accorded less favourable treatment to Mexican tuna products compared to like products of national origin and from other countries.

Canada and Mexico challenged the United States' mandatory country-of-origin labelling (COOL) requirements for beef and pork products, arguing that they violated the TBT Agreement by discriminating against imported livestock and creating unnecessary obstacles to trade.[29] The WTO panel and Appellate Body found that the COOL measures were inconsistent with Article 2.1 of the TBT Agreement because they accorded less favourable treatment to imported livestock compared to like domestic livestock.

The European Union challenged Brazil's tax measures on imported information and communication technology (ICT) products, arguing that they violated the TBT

28 United States – Measures Concerning the Importation, Marketing and Sale of Tuna and Tuna Products, WT/DS381/AB/R, adopted 13 June 2012

29 United States – Certain Country of Origin Labelling (COOL) Requirements, WT/DS384/AB/R, WT/DS386/AB/R, adopted 23 July 2012

Agreement by discriminating against imported products and creating unnecessary obstacles to trade.[30] The WTO panel found that certain Brazilian tax measures were inconsistent with Article 2.1 of the TBT because they accorded less favourable treatment to imported ICT products compared to like domestic products.

The United States, New Zealand, and Australia challenged Indonesia's import licensing regimes for horticultural products, animals, and animal products, arguing that they violated the TBT by creating unnecessary obstacles to trade.[31] The WTO panel found that certain Indonesian measures were inconsistent with Article 2.2 of the TBT Agreement because they were more trade-restrictive than necessary to achieve their stated objectives.

These cases demonstrate the WTO's efforts to ensure that technical regulations and standards adopted by member countries do not create unnecessary obstacles to international trade, as required by the TBT. The rulings have helped to clarify the obligations of WTO members and the standards they must meet when implementing technical measures that affect trade. The outcomes of these disputes have had significant implications for the affected countries and industries, as they have required the revision or removal of technical measures that were found to be inconsistent with WTO rules. The cases also illustrate the challenges in balancing the legitimate objectives of technical regulations, such as protecting human health and safety or the environment, with the need to avoid creating unnecessary barriers to trade. The WTO has recognized the right of members to adopt technical measures to achieve these objectives, provided that they are not applied in a manner that discriminates against imported products or creates unnecessary obstacles to trade.

Like the SPS Agreement, the TBT Agreement has been the subject of significant academic debate regarding its purpose, scope, and implications for domestic regulation and international trade. One key area of discussion concerns the agreement's objectives and approach to balancing trade facilitation with regulatory autonomy. Some argue that the TBT Agreement aims to strike a balance between members' right to regulate and the desire to avoid unnecessary obstacles to international trade. The agreement allegedly does this by imposing disciplines on the preparation, adoption, and application of mandatory technical regulations and voluntary standards.[32]

The interpretation of key TBT provisions has also generated substantial academic analysis. examine the Appellate Body's approach to interpreting the TBT Agreement in the EC-Sardines case. In particular, some commentators have claimed that the Appellate Body has adopted an overly textualist approach that failed to

30 Brazil – Certain Measures Concerning Taxation and Charges, WT/DS472/AB/R, WT/DS497/AB/R, adopted 11 January 2019

31 Indonesia – Importation of Horticultural Products, Animals and Animal Products, WT/DS477/AB/R, WT/DS478/AB/R, adopted 22 November 2017

32 G Marceau and JP Trachtman, "The Technical Barriers to Trade Agreement, the Sanitary and Phytosanitary Measures Agreement, and the General Agreement on Tariffs and Trade: A Map of the World Trade Organization Law of Domestic Regulation of Goods" 36:5 Journal of World Trade 811 (2002)

adequately consider the object and purpose of the agreement.[33] The implications of the TBT Agreement's emphasis on international standards have also been a point of contention. Some hold that this focus raises important questions about legitimacy and democratic accountability in global governance.[34] The open-endedness of the TBT Agreement's reference to international standards could exacerbate these tensions.

While both the SPS and the TBT agreements emphasize the use of scientific evidence, the TBT Agreement provides more flexibility for members to consider non-scientific factors in their regulatory decisions.[35] This has positive and negative elements – while flexibility in theory grants greater autonomy to national governments, including the accommodation of cultural attitudes towards risk, there is a corresponding lack of certainty, potentially raising the costs of compliance for traders.

7.4 Health and Safety Under and Free Trade Agreements

The growing importance of health and safety regulations as non-tariff barriers to trade has led them to feature prominently in FTAs as trading parties seek to clarify the scope of their obligations in these fields and perhaps most importantly, work to achieve harmonization in approach to the mitigation of risks with a view to minimizing trade friction.

7.4.1 SPS and TBT Measures in FTAs

Generally, FTAs tend not to go far beyond what is contained in the SPS. In its SPS chapter, the CPTPP speaks "reinforc[ing] and build[ing] on the SPS Agreement."[36] Parties also reaffirm their rights and obligations under the SPS Agreement.[37] FTAs sometimes exceed the requirements of WTO SPS and TBT agreements. FTAs may allow party countries to impose stricter SPS measures than what is required under the WTO SPS Agreement. For instance, Article 7.2 of the CPTPP allows parties to "adopt or maintain SPS measures necessary for the protection of human, animal or plant life or health, provided that such measures are not inconsistent with the provisions of this Agreement." This appears to give countries more flexibility to set their own SPS standards, even if they are more stringent than international norms.

Some FTAs go further than that of the WTO by expressly requiring the harmonization of SPS measures among the participating countries. Article 9.4 of the USMCA states that the parties "shall work jointly to enhance the compatibility

33 H Horn and J Weiler, "European Communities – Trade Description of Sardines: Textualism and its Discontents" in *The WTO Case Law of 2002* (Cambridge University Press, 2005)

34 S Bernstein and E Hannah, "Non-State Global Standard Setting and the WTO: Legitimacy and the Need for Regulatory Space" 11:3 Journal of International Economic Law 575 (2008)

35 J Peel, *Science and Risk Regulation in International Law* (Cambridge University Press, 2010)

36 Article 7.2 (b)

37 Article 7.4.1

of their respective sanitary and phytosanitary measures." This goes beyond the WTO SPS Agreement, which only encourages the use of international standards as a basis for national SPS measures. The principle of harmonization is furthered by provisions on regulatory cooperation in the establishment of SPS regulations. For example, the EU-Canada Comprehensive Economic and Trade Agreement (CETA) establishes a Regulatory Cooperation Forum to "facilitate and promote regulatory cooperation" between the parties.[38] This allows for closer coordination and information-sharing on SPS regulations, going beyond the WTO's focus on transparency and non-discrimination.

While Article 5.1 of the WTO SPS Agreement requires risk assessments to be based on scientific principles, some FTAs allow for a broader consideration of factors. The EU-Vietnam Free Trade Agreement, for example, states that risk assessment can take into account "relevant scientific evidence, relevant processes and production methods, relevant inspection, sampling and testing methods, prevalence of specific diseases or pests, existence of pest- or disease-free areas, relevant ecological and environmental conditions, and quarantine or other treatment."[39] This expands the scope of what can be considered in the risk assessment process.

It is noteworthy that some FTAs, particularly those of the European Union, may also incorporate the precautionary principle, which, as noted earlier, allows countries to take SPS measures even in the absence of full scientific evidence. For instance, the EU-Japan Economic Partnership Agreement states that "where there are threats of serious or irreversible damage, the lack of full scientific certainty shall not be used as a reason for postponing cost-effective measures to prevent environmental degradation."[40] This goes beyond the WTO SPS Agreement, which only allows precautionary measures to be temporary.

Turning to TBT measures, FTAs in some instances go beyond the requirements of the WTO TBT Agreement. Most notably, while the TBT Agreement encourages the use of international standards, FTAs often go further by requiring the harmonization of technical regulations and standards among the participating countries. The USMCA, for instance, mandates that the parties work jointly to enhance the compatibility of their respective technical regulations.[41]

FTAs often impose more stringent transparency and notification requirements than the TBT Agreement. The Korea-United States Free Trade Agreement (KORUS FTA), for instance, requires the parties to notify each other of any proposed technical regulation or conformity assessment procedure, even if it is based on an international standard.[42] While the TBT Agreement recognizes the needs of developing countries, FTAs involving developing countries may provide more tailored provisions for technical assistance, capacity building, and transitional

38 Article 21.6
39 Article 6.4
40 Article 16.9
41 Article 11.4
42 Article 9.6

periods. The EU-Vietnam Free Trade Agreement, for example, includes a chapter on Trade and Sustainable Development that addresses the development challenges faced by Vietnam.

Many modern FTAs include regulatory cooperation chapters which work towards eliminating frictions that arise as a consequence of differing approaches to the mitigation of risks such as those affecting health and safety. To take a leading example, the Regulatory Cooperation chapter of the RCEP aims to facilitate trade and investment among member countries by promoting good regulatory practices and reducing unnecessary regulatory burdens. It recognizes the sovereign right of each party to identify its regulatory priorities and establish its levels of regulatory protection while seeking to enhance the compatibility and interoperability of regulatory measures across the region.

One of the key provisions in this chapter is Article 14.3, which outlines the general principles for regulatory cooperation. These principles include transparency, public consultation, and the use of regulatory impact assessments. The article emphasizes the importance of basing regulations on sound scientific and technical information as well as considering the impact of regulations on SMEs. Article 14.4 of the chapter focuses on the implementation of good regulatory practices. It encourages RCEP members to establish and maintain processes or mechanisms to facilitate effective interagency coordination and review of proposed regulatory measures. This provision aims to improve the quality and efficiency of regulatory decision-making within each member country. The chapter also addresses the issue of regulatory coherence in Article 14.5. This article encourages parties to promote regulatory compatibility and convergence by implementing common principles in their regulatory processes and exploring the recognition of equivalent regulatory measures.

The language used in this article is largely non-binding, using terms like "endeavour to" and "may include," which provides flexibility for member countries in implementation. Article 14.6 of the Regulatory Cooperation chapter deals with enhancing regulatory cooperation and compatibility. It encourages parties to cooperate in various ways, including through information exchange, dialogues, and joint activities. This article also promotes the use of regulatory harmonization and mutual recognition agreements where appropriate, which can significantly reduce trade barriers by allowing products approved in one country to be sold in another without additional regulatory hurdles. The chapter includes provisions for transparency and public consultation in Article 14.7. This article encourages parties to publish proposed regulations in advance and provides opportunities for public comment. It also promotes the consideration of comments received from other parties, which can help prevent the creation of unnecessary trade barriers.

An innovative aspect of the RCEP's Regulatory Cooperation chapter is found in Article 14.8, which establishes a Committee on Regulatory Cooperation. This committee is tasked with overseeing the implementation of the chapter, facilitating information exchange, and identifying areas for future cooperation. The establishment of this committee provides a formal mechanism for ongoing dialogue and collaboration on regulatory issues among RCEP members. Article 14.9 addresses the important issue of contact points. Each party is required to designate and notify a contact point to facilitate communication on matters arising under this chapter. This provision ensures that there are clear channels for communication and coordination on regulatory matters among RCEP members.

The UK-EU TCA includes several provisions aimed at promoting regulatory cooperation between SPS and TBT measures. Regarding SPS measures, the TCA establishes a framework for ongoing cooperation and dialogue between the United Kingdom and the European Union to manage risks related to human, animal, and plant health. The agreement requires both sides to ensure that any SPS border controls are proportionate to the identified risks. To facilitate this, a new Trade Specialised Committee on Sanitary and Phytosanitary Measures has been established to regularly review these controls and explore potential facilitation without compromising biosecurity. The TCA also incorporates the concept of "zoning" for SPS measures, which allows imports from pest and disease-free areas of the United Kingdom or the European Union to continue even if there are geographically concentrated outbreaks elsewhere. This provision aims to minimize unnecessary trade disruptions in the event of localized health issues. Furthermore, the agreement commits both parties to ongoing cooperation on important issues such as animal welfare, antimicrobial resistance, and sustainable food systems. This demonstrates a shared commitment to addressing broader concerns beyond mere trade facilitation. In terms of TBT regulations, the TCA establishes sector-specific annexes and working groups for industries such as automotive, chemicals, pharmaceuticals, organic products, and wine. These mechanisms are designed to promote ongoing dialogue and cooperation in these key sectors.

7.4.2 Conformity Assessment and Mutual Recognition in Free Trade Agreements

Conformity assessment is a crucial aspect of FTAs, ensuring that goods traded between countries meet the necessary technical regulations and standards. By granting mutual recognition for conformity assessment FTAs can facilitate deeper economic integration and reduce regulatory divergence among the participating countries. For example, the CPTPP requires each party to accept the results of conformity assessment procedures conducted by bodies located in the territory of another party, provided that the procedures meet certain criteria. Similarly, the EU-Canada CETA establishes a framework for the mutual recognition of conformity assessment results for specific product sectors.

FTAs sometimes recognize the conformity assessment procedures of partner countries as equivalent to those of one's own country, precluding redundant checks at borders. Mutual recognition of SPS measures is one of the ways in which preferential FTAs improve upon the SPS Agreement, and which merely encourages this behaviour among WTO members. Sometimes mutual recognition is contained in separate Mutual Recognition Agreements.

Articles 5.6 and 5.7 of the Canada-EU CETA set out how equivalence is granted for SPS measures. It is worth quoting this provision in full to give a sense of the complexity of these issues from a technical standpoint.

Article 5.6 – Equivalent

1. The importing Party shall accept the SPS measure of the exporting Party as equivalent to its own if the exporting Party objectively demonstrates to the importing Party that its measure achieves the importing Party's appropriate level of SPS protection.

Article 5.7 – Trade conditions

1. The importing Party shall make available its general SPS import requirements for all commodities. If the Parties jointly identify a commodity as a priority, the importing Party shall establish specific SPS import requirements for that commodity, unless the Parties decide otherwise. In identifying which commodities are priorities, the Parties shall cooperate to ensure the efficient management of their available resources. The specific import requirements should be applicable to the total territory of the exporting Party.
2. Pursuant to paragraph 1, the importing Party shall undertake, without undue delay, the necessary process to establish specific SPS import requirements for the commodity that is identified as a priority. Once these specific import requirements are established, the importing Party shall take the necessary steps, without undue delay, to allow trade on the basis of these import requirements.
3. For the purpose of establishing the specific SPS import requirements, the exporting Party shall, at the request of the importing Party:

    a. provide all relevant information required by the importing Party; and
    b. give reasonable access to the importing Party to inspect, test, audit and perform other relevant procedures.

One of the main difficulties in conformity assessment under FTAs is ensuring the equivalence of technical regulations and standards between the participating countries. Even when standards are harmonized, differences in testing methods, certification procedures, and accreditation systems can still create barriers to trade. Negotiating mutual recognition for specific product sectors can be a complex and time-consuming process, often requiring extensive technical cooperation and trust between the parties involved.

Another challenge is the potential for regulatory divergence over time. As countries update their technical regulations and standards to address new challenges or technological developments, the equivalence of conformity assessment procedures may be disrupted. FTAs often include provisions for regulatory cooperation and information-sharing to mitigate this risk, (sometimes called "dynamic alignment") but maintaining harmonization can be an ongoing challenge.

The capacity of conformity assessment bodies in developing countries can also be a concern. Many FTAs include technical assistance and capacity-building measures to help developing countries strengthen their conformity assessment infrastructure. However, disparities in technical expertise, laboratory facilities, and accreditation systems can still create barriers to trade, particularly for small- and medium-sized enterprises. Furthermore, the costs and delays associated with conformity assessment procedures can be a significant burden for businesses, especially for small-scale producers and exporters. FTAs often aim to streamline conformity assessment requirements and reduce unnecessary duplication, but the complexity of navigating different regulatory systems can still be a challenge. Despite these difficulties, conformity assessment remains an essential component of FTAs, ensuring that traded goods meet the necessary safety, quality, and environmental standards. By harmonizing technical regulations and facilitating mutual recognition of conformity assessment results, FTAs can help to reduce technical barriers to trade and promote greater economic integration between participating countries.

FTAs frequently include provisions for the mutual recognition of conformity assessment procedures and test results with TBT measures. For example, the EU-Japan Economic Partnership Agreement, for example, establishes a framework for the mutual recognition of conformity assessment results for specific product sectors.[43] Many FTAs establish institutional mechanisms for regulatory cooperation on TBT issues, such as technical working groups or committees. These bodies facilitate the exchange of information, the alignment of regulations, and the resolution of TBT-related disputes. The Canada-EU CETA creates a Committee on Trade in Goods to oversee the implementation of the TBT chapter.[44]

As with SPS measures, TBT measures can be minimized through mutual recognition agreements (MRAs) between countries, with or without an FTA. For example, the United Kingdom and Australia already had an MRA in place for various products including automotive parts, medical devices and low-voltage equipment which predated the United Kingdom-Australia FTA. These goods can be sold in each country without additional testing in the importing country. MRAs play a crucial role in facilitating international trade by reducing technical barriers related to goods and health and safety regulations. These agreements allow trading partners to recognize each other's conformity assessment procedures, thereby streamlining the process of certifying products for market access.

Traditional MRAs focus on mutual recognition of conformity assessment procedures, while enhanced MRAs go further by recognizing the equivalence of regulatory standards between partners. One of the most comprehensive examples of mutual recognition is the EU's internal market. Products lawfully sold in one EU member state can be sold in any other, even if they don't fully comply with the technical rules of the importing country. This principle has significantly reduced trade barriers within the European Union, although exceptions may apply for public safety, health, or environmental concerns.

Various MRAs have been established between countries and trading blocs. For instance, the EU-US MRA on marine equipment, signed in 2004, is an example

43 Article 4.10
44 Article 21.1

of an enhanced MRA based on international maritime standards. This agreement allows for mutual recognition of rules, not just testing procedures, in the specific sector of marine equipment. Another notable example is the Trans-Tasman Mutual Recognition Arrangement (TTMRA) between Australia and New Zealand, established in 1998. This comprehensive agreement covers a wide range of goods and occupations, allowing products that meet regulatory standards in one country to be legally sold in the other without additional requirements.

MRAs can play a significant role in the pharmaceutical and medical device sectors. For example, the EU-Switzerland MRA includes provisions for Good Manufacturing Practice (GMP) of pharmaceuticals. This allows for mutual recognition of GMP inspections, reducing duplicative efforts and facilitating trade in pharmaceutical products. Following its exit from the European Union, the United Kingdom has been actively pursuing MRAs with various partners. The United Kingdom-Switzerland MRA, for instance, covers sectors such as motor vehicles, GMP of pharmaceuticals, and Good Laboratory Practice of chemicals.

Despite the presence of conformity assessment recognition for SPS or TBT matters, there is a potential for regulatory divergence over time. As partners may update their regulations independently, maintaining equivalence can become increasingly difficult. This concern has been particularly prominent in discussions about the United Kingdom's future regulatory alignment with the European Union post-Brexit. Another challenge lies in the limited scope of many MRAs. Traditional MRAs often cover only specific sectors or types of products, leaving significant areas of trade subject to duplicative testing and certification requirements. Expanding the scope of MRAs can be a complex and time-consuming process, requiring extensive negotiations and trust-building between regulatory authorities.

There are also concerns about the potential for MRAs to lead to a race to the bottom in terms of regulatory standards. Some believe that mutual recognition of health and safety regulations could pressure countries to lower their standards to remain competitive, potentially compromising consumer safety or environmental protections. On the other hand, MRAs typically include safeguards to maintain high standards and allow for exceptions in cases of legitimate public interest concerns. The implementation of MRAs can also face practical challenges. Ensuring consistent interpretation and application of the agreement across different regulatory bodies and jurisdictions can be complex. Training and capacity building for conformity assessment bodies and regulators are often necessary to ensure smooth implementation.

Failure to recognize another country's health and safety regulations on food and other products can act as an obstacle to trade agreement negotiations. To take a recent example, Canadian farmers are disappointed with the fact that the United Kingdom's food inspection standards do not recognize Canadian food safety rules as equivalent to the United Kingdom. Canadian beef and pork exports were entitled to access the European Union (and United Kingdom) markets under CETA but these imports have largely failed to materialize because meat processing methods which are considered normal in North America are not approved by the United Kingdom. Likely influenced by the European Union's approach to GMOs, the United

Kingdom will not permit hormone-treated beef into its market. This impasse has prevented the finalization of an upgrade to the United Kingdom-Canada FTA.

Committees created under FTAs are often responsible for rendering "equivalence" decisions regarding the compliance of imports with health and safety requirements. This leads to questions as to the nature of the evidence reviewed by these committees as well as their composition and their openness to scrutiny as well as to public input. Some agricultural committees may even have sub-units such as animal welfare. There can be linkages between these issues as sustainability principles.

MRAs are seen as effective tools for reducing regulatory barriers to trade generally. They are thought to help address the trade-impeding effects of different conformity assessment procedures without requiring full harmonization of standards.[45] Some commentators have been more critical of MRAs, pointing out that the implementation of mutual recognition can be challenging due to differences in regulatory cultures and institutional frameworks across countries.[46]

It has been argued that although FTAs often contain provisions for regulatory cooperation, including conformity assessment, the actual impact on reducing technical barriers to trade has been limited.[47] While mutual recognition can theoretically reduce trade barriers, in practice it often faces implementation difficulties due to regulatory divergences and trust issues between trading partners.[48] Overly prescriptive conformity assessment requirements in trade agreements can potentially infringe on domestic regulatory space and policy-making autonomy.[49] There must be careful design and implementation of conformity assessment and mutual recognition provisions with a view to balancing trade facilitation with regulatory autonomy and effectiveness.

7.5 Conclusion

The extent to which countries are able to safeguard the health and safety of their citizens is perhaps the most significant obligation that a state owes to its citizens. The Covid-19 era demonstrated the extent to which many people were prepared to surrender their freedom in exchange for their governments' assurance that they would be to the extent possible, protected from danger. Improvements in science and technology, while enhancing medical care and prolonging lives, have also

45 B Hoekman and PC Mavroidis, "Regulatory Spillovers and the Trading System: From Coherence to Cooperation" 6:S3 Global Policy 44 (2015)

46 K Nicolaïdis and M Egan, "Transnational Market Governance and Regional Policy Externality: Why Recognize Foreign Standards?" 8:3 Journal of European Public Policy 454 (2001)

47 AR Young, "Liberalizing Trade, Not Exporting Rules: The Limits to Regulatory Co-Ordination in the EU's 'New Generation' Preferential Trade Agreements" 22:9 Journal of European Public Policy 1253 (2015)

48 J Pelkmans, "Mutual Recognition: Economic and Regulatory Logic in Goods and Services" Bruges European Economic Research Papers, No. 24, 2012

49 DP Steger, "The Culture of the WTO: Why It Needs to Change" 10:3 Journal of International Economic Law 483 (2007)

uncovered many dangers in the form of toxins to which previous generations were never exposed. Enacting laws to prohibit dangerous elements from traded goods is, therefore, an important role for our governments. But, it is also one that can be exploited, masking economic protectionism with the cover of protecting the vulnerable.

SPS and TBT measures, disciplined variously by the WTO and FTAs are at the front line of this debate. Former WTO Director-General Pascal Lamy warned about what he called "precautionism" as a new challenge to global trade, especially in the wake of the Covid-19 pandemic. He defined "precautionism" as those measures designed to protect people from risks as opposed to traditional protectionism which aims to protect producers from foreign competition. He explained that governments, anxious and scarred by the pandemic, would likely impose more rules and regulations on imports, often driven by health and safety concerns. This increased focus on risk and safety could create new barriers to trade that are more complex to resolve than traditional tariffs or quotas. Lamy noted that with precautionism, the highest standard becomes the benchmark, making harmonization challenging.[50]

The European Union is perhaps most emblematic of this approach, enacting health and safety regulations which are generally considered to be among the most comprehensive in the world. These regulations aim to ensure a high level of protection for consumers across the EU member states. This approach may not fit with more individualistic places like the United States, where people are more inclined to make their own personal decisions about health and safety risks rather than seek their governments to make them on their behalf. Yet the European Union exports its product health and safety regulations through its network of FTAs, using its market size to require partner countries to adopt standards which are at least equivalent to its own.

The stringency of EU regulations has led to debates about their impact on trade and business competitiveness as well as their legitimacy. Some believe that EU health and safety regulations can indeed act as non-tariff barriers to trade, particularly for non-EU countries seeking to export to the EU market. The costs associated with complying with these regulations can be significant, especially for small- and medium-sized enterprises (SMEs). On the other hand, proponents of EU regulations argue that they create a level playing field within the single market and can actually facilitate trade by harmonizing standards across member states. High standards can drive innovation and improve product quality, potentially enhancing competitiveness in the long run.[51]

This chapter has explored the functionality of the WTO's SPS and TBT agreements, noting their preference for international standards and scientific evidence but also stressing the importance of risk management as a process rather than as a point of fact. The contribution of FTAs in this regard exemplifies the world trade

50 See P Lamy, *The Geneva Consensus* (Cambridge University Press, 2013)
51 AR Young, "The European Union as a Global Regulator? Context and Comparison" 22:9 Journal of European Public Policy 1233 (2015)

principle of harmonization – seeking to recognize another country's regulatory risk mitigation strategies as equal to one's own, where possible. An emphasis on regulatory cooperation and dialogue among FTA partners has provided a pathway towards improvements in this exercise. As ever, transparency and communication of concerns relating to trade may be one of the best ways of promoting deeper liberalization.

Discussion Questions

1. Are the SPS and TBT Agreements sufficiently sensitive to the sovereignty of WTO members?
2. What is meant by the concept of scientific evidence and how could this be problematic?
3. Are risks to health too subjective to be controlled as barriers to trade?
4. What is the difference between a regulation and a standard and how does the TBT Agreement address both?
5. How do bilateral/regional Free Trade Agreements address SPS and TBT issues and how is this different from the approach at the WTO?

8 Trade in Services

8.1 Introduction

Much of the economic growth, especially in the developed world, is in the area of services. Often under-emphasized by politicians who regularly appeal to manufacturing, especially as a source of employment, services have also become a vital contributor to globalization. In 2022, services contributed more than 63 per cent of global GDP. For some countries which lack natural resources and large-scale manufacturing, like the United Kingdom and Singapore, the services sector is the largest contributor to GDP, accounting for 72 per cent and 70 per cent of the total in 2022, respectively. Despite the enormous significance of services in the world economy, they are poorly liberalized relative to goods which are often traded at zero or near-zero tariffs. Indeed, it is a distinct failing in the world trading system that services comprise 60 per cent of world GDP but only 20 per cent of trade. This paradox remains concerning as many expect that trade in services will expand in the coming decades due to advances in technology, especially in telecommunications. The separate, but related phenomenon of digital trade will be discussed in Chapter 10.

This chapter will explore the legal principles governing trade in services – now a cornerstone of the global economy, especially in developed countries. It will emphasize comparatively poor levels of liberalization of trade in services relative to that of goods, in part due to the lack of commitments undertaken by WTO members through the General Agreement on Trade in Services (GATS), rectified somewhat by expanded provisions on services in FTAs. One of the central principles of world trade law in relation to the liberalization of services is once again the notion of mutual recognition – the willingness of countries to acknowledge that the standards they place on the delivery of services are deemed to be equivalent to those of trading partners. The piecemeal liberalization of services also discloses another principle of world trade law – regulatory flexibility in the face of highly complex and dynamic economic sectors.

8.2 The General Agreement on Trade in Services (GATS)

The WTO's GATS, dating from the organization's inception in the mid-1990s, remains the key source of legal principles for trade and services. In addition to the

DOI: 10.4324/9781003465676-8

fact that they are heavily regulated at the domestic level, another one of the reasons that trade services have not been as fully liberalized as goods is because it is difficult to define services – by their nature, they are intangible, consisting of actions rather than things. When the GATS was drafted, members of the nascent WTO knew that in order to open up the delivery of services across borders, they would have to pinpoint precisely what was meant by "service." They also recognized that the definition would need to be open-ended and promote flexibility so that members do not feel compelled to over-commit beyond their willingness because of the expansive nature of the concept itself.

8.2.1 Scope of GATS

Article I of the GATS categorizes "services" with reference to four modes of supply.

For the purposes of this Agreement, trade in services is defined as the supply of a service:

(a) from the territory of one Member into the territory of any other Member;
(b) in the territory of one Member to the service consumer of any other Member;
(c) by a service supplier of one Member, through commercial presence in the territory of any other Member;
(d) by a service supplier of one Member, through presence of natural persons of a Member in the territory of any other Member.

These categories, or more precisely "modes," are (a) cross-border, (b) consumption abroad, (c) commercial presence, and (d) presence of natural persons. Cross-border covers services which may be supplied across international borders, such as a lawyer in one WTO member providing advice over the telephone to a client in the territory of another WTO member. Consumption abroad refers to situations where the consumer travels across international borders to consume a service, such as a patient going overseas to receive medical treatment. Commercial presence is a wide category of service delivery where a commercial entity from one WTO member establishes itself in another WTO member's territory for the purposes of delivering services. This could be seen for example when a United Kingdom bank opens a branch in Tokyo. Commercial presence is also known as foreign direct investment, which is a distinct category of commercial activity from trade. Finally, the presence of natural persons is when the individual supplier moves to another country to supply a service on a temporary basis, as when a software engineer from India goes to work in Australia on a project before returning home. Importantly though, this does not cover immigration (permanent moving).

The omission of so-called Mode 5 supply of services is thought to be a weakness of GATS. Mode 5 refers to services that are incorporated into or embedded in goods which are then traded across international borders. Examples include software, design, and engineering services that are incorporated into manufactured products – sometimes known as the Internet of Things. For many countries, Mode 5 services represent a significant portion of their exports and imports. Mode 5 services face tariffs when incorporated into goods, unlike other services. Essentially, an economically significant and growing segment of services trade is not properly addressed by the existing GATS framework, potentially limiting liberalization and creating policy/regulatory challenges as the nature of trade evolves.

Arriving upon this almost-definition was itself an achievement of GATS, despite the fact that the definition is not as clear-cut as one might wish. Perhaps better than a precise definition, the advantage of the categories of services supply is not merely that they addressed the amorphous nature of services, but that they enable WTO members to tailor their obligations, undertaking commitments to liberalize services in some sectors, but not others. Mode 3 (commercial presence) is generally considered the most liberalized mode, accounting for around 60 per cent of services trade. Mode 3 is also known as foreign direct investment – effectively when a company locates to another territory. Modes 1 (cross-border) and 2 (consumption abroad) are also relatively liberalized, accounting for over 25 per cent and around 15 per cent of services trade, respectively. Mode 4 (Presence of natural persons) is by far the least liberalized, accounting for only about 1 per cent of services trade. Mode 4 is probably also the most controversial since it encompasses foreign individuals entering a country to work; in what is sometimes viewed as taking jobs away from locals.

Common restrictions on Mode 1 include requirements for a local presence, such as a branch or office within the relevant country. Restrictions on cross-border data flows can also restrict the cross-border delivery of services. Consumption abroad could be restricted by limits on foreign exchange availability for consumers who need to pay for the service they receive in local money. Many controls are in place on Mode 3, including limitations on foreign equity participation, requirements for joint ventures with local firms or restrictions on types of legal entities. On presence of natural persons, some countries impose quotas on the number of foreign service suppliers, economic needs tests for new workers, residency requirements, limitations on duration of stay or restrictions to certain categories of workers such as high-skilled.

Underscoring a vital legal principle in trade in services, the definition of services in Article I does not include services "normally supplied in the exercise of governmental authority." This carves out from the scope of GATS commitments a broad range of services including things like security, medical services, educational services, and some utilities. The breadth of this exception will vary from country, being larger in countries which have a larger public sector. For example, most medical services would not be covered by the definition of services in the GATS in the United Kingdom because the National Health Service is effectively a branch of the United Kingdom government. Some hold that the terms "commercial basis" and "in competition" are not clearly defined, leading to uncertainty about the scope of the exclusion.[1] Others suggest that the exclusion may be interpreted narrowly, potentially covering only a limited range of core government functions.[2]

1 M Krajewski, "Public Services and Trade Liberalization: Mapping the Legal Framework" 6:2 Journal of International Economic Law 341 (2003)

2 R Adlung, "Public Services and the GATS" 9:2 Journal of International Economic Law 455 (2006)

8.2.2 General Obligations

The first part of the GATS consists of General Obligations, meaning those which apply to all WTO members and which are not optional (although members are allowed to maintain some agreed exemptions). Foremost of the General Obligations is Most Favoured Nation (MFN) provision which was seen in Article I of the GATT. In Article II of GATS, the MFN provision prohibits discrimination between "like" services or service providers from different countries. Since the case law for "likeness" under the GATS is much less developed than it is under the GATT, GATT "likeness" case law may be helpful to panels or the Appellate Body interpreting this provision. "Likeness" applies both to the service itself and the service suppliers and in that sense, it is a wider concept than that found in GATT. Under GATS MFN, "no less favourable" modifies conditions of competition in a manner that is discriminatory on the basis of national origin. It also applies both to *de jure* as well as *de facto* discrimination.

Under GATS, the "likeness" test applies to both services and service suppliers, whereas GATT only considers the likeness of products. This adds complexity to the GATS analysis, as it requires considering the characteristics of both the service and the provider. Comparing suppliers, usually companies, is a different exercise than comparing the service itself. While the fact that they provide the same service will be useful in establishing likeness between two providers, it is not determinative. As with the GATT, whether or not either of these comparisons is satisfied will be decided on a case-by-case basis that will turn on facts, often backed up by numerical data (e.g., changes in sales figures). In looking at the suppliers themselves, WTO panels and the Appellate Body have demonstrated that this will also involve a consideration of whether or not the suppliers are in a competitive relationship with each other, although this is not always sufficient to establish likeness.

"Likeness" was evaluated in the *China – Electronic Payments*[3] dispute that dealt with China's regulation of electronic payment services for card-based transactions. The panel had to determine whether the electronic payment services provided by foreign suppliers were "like" those provided by China UnionPay (CUP), the domestic supplier. The panel reaffirmed the criteria established in previous WTO jurisprudence for assessing likeness in the context of services. These criteria include the nature and characteristics of the services, their end-uses, consumer preferences, and the services' classification. In applying these criteria, the panel found that the electronic payment services provided by foreign suppliers and those provided by CUP were indeed "like" services. The panel noted that both foreign and domestic suppliers provided services that facilitated transactions between cardholders, merchants, and banks and that these services shared similar characteristics and end-uses. Moreover, the panel considered that consumers generally viewed these services as substitutable.

3 China – Certain Measures Affecting Electronic Payment Services, WT/DS413/R, adopted 31 August 2012

The panel observed that China's regulations treated the services of CUP and those of potential foreign suppliers similarly, which supported the conclusion that these services were "like" for the purposes of GATS Article XVII. The panel also addressed the issue of whether foreign and domestic suppliers of electronic payment services were "like" service suppliers. In this regard, the panel considered factors such as the nature of the services provided, the regulatory framework applicable to the suppliers, and the characteristics of the suppliers themselves. The panel concluded that foreign suppliers of electronic payment services were indeed "like" CUP for the purposes of the national treatment obligation. One notable aspect of the panel's approach was its rejection of China's argument that differences in the scale of operations between CUP and potential foreign entrants should be considered in the likeness analysis. The panel stated that such differences in scale or market position did not necessarily render the services or service suppliers "unlike" for the purposes of GATS Article XVII.

The likeness analysis may vary depending on which mode is being considered. For example, likeness in Mode 3 (commercial presence) may involve comparing characteristics of established businesses. As referenced earlier, services are often intangible, making direct comparisons more challenging than for physical goods. The criteria used for goods (e.g., physical characteristics, end-uses) may not be directly applicable to services. The regulatory environment plays a more significant role in determining likeness for services. Differences in regulation between service sectors may be relevant to assessing likeness.

For example, in financial services, retail banking, and investment banking services may not be considered "like" despite both being banking services, due to differences in regulation and consumer protection concerns. For professional services, the qualifications and licensing of service providers (e.g., lawyers, doctors) may be crucial in determining likeness, whereas such factors would not be relevant for goods. In telecommunications, fixed-line and mobile services might be assessed differently in terms of likeness depending on the specific market and regulatory context. For tourism services, online booking platforms and traditional travel agencies might require careful analysis to determine if they are "like" service suppliers, considering factors such as business models and consumer interaction. The GATS likeness test thus requires a more nuanced and context-specific analysis compared to GATT, reflecting the complex nature of services trade.

There have been other WTO dispute settlement cases that have addressed the "likeness" test for services under GATS non-discrimination provisions, though the jurisprudence is still limited compared to GATT. In *Argentina – Financial Services*[4] the Appellate Body found that the likeness of services and service suppliers may be established based on criteria relating to the competitive relationship between them. Alternatively, likeness may be presumed where a measure provides for differential treatment based exclusively on origin. The Appellate Body further

4 Argentina – Measures Relating to Trade in Goods and Services, WT/DS453/AB/R, adopted 9 May 2016

emphasized the need to assess various criteria relevant to the competitive relationship when origin is not the sole basis for differential treatment.

Article III of the GATS is the transparency provision. Here members are required to publish all measures which pertain to services and inform other members of changes. The transparency obligations in relation to services can be onerous since services tend to be more heavily regulated than goods. Consider, for example, the degree of training and qualification that doctors are required to undergo. This is another reason that trade in services suffers many impediments relative to that of goods – there is simply more regulatory burden facing services and their suppliers in most countries, even at the domestic level.

The General Exceptions of the GATS of Article XIV are broadly similar to those of the GATT, with some minor differences, notably the addition of "public morals" as a ground of justification. General exceptions were discussed in Chapter 6 on non-trade values.

8.2.3 Specific Obligations

The second part of the GATS consists of specific obligations, where its structure differs most significantly from that of the GATT. The Specific Obligations are not mandatory – they are only assumed by WTO members to the extent that they wish to do so. This means that GATS is a much more flexible agreement than its goods counterpart. This underscores a mindset among the global community, represented by the membership of the WTO, that barriers to trade in services are more acceptable than those placed on goods.

Article XVII contains the GATS' national treatment commitment. Under this provision, to the extent that countries choose to make this commitment, they must accord to services and suppliers of any other member treatment that is no less favourable than it accords to its own "like" services or suppliers. National treatment commitments are made via each member's Schedule of Specific Commitments which is arranged via the four modes of supply – members can commit by services sector (e.g., transportation, tourism) and via mode of supply; a process which is roughly analogous to the tariff scheduling for goods. This grants the member wide latitude to craft their international trade policy with regard to services. More cautious countries will commit fewer sectors and modes, and more open ones, like the United Kingdom, will commit more.

Since the application of a commitment within a schedule is complicated, based on terminology that was used, in some cases countries can disagree as to whether they have or have not made a national treatment commitment in their GATS schedule. This issue arose in the *United States – Gambling*[5] case. Antigua argued that the United States had made specific commitments to provide market access for "recreational services" under its GATS Schedule, which should be interpreted to

5 United States – Measures Affecting the Cross-Border Supply of Gambling and Betting Services, WT/DS285/AB/R, adopted 20 April 2005

include gambling and betting services. The United States contended that it had not made any such commitments for gambling services. The panel and subsequently the Appellate Body had to interpret the United States Schedule of Commitments using the rules of treaty interpretation under the Vienna Convention on the Law of Treaties. They concluded that the United States commitments did indeed cover gambling and betting services, based on the ordinary meaning of the terms used in the United States Schedule, considered in their context and in light of the object and purpose of the GATS.

In *China – Audiovisuals,*[6] China had argued that "sound recording distribution services" did not extend to sound recordings that were distributed by electronic means but only distribution in physical form, as in CDs. The Appellate Body ruled against China, determining that a reasonable understanding of the phrase "sound recording distribution services" contemplates electronic as well as physical forms of delivery. In rendering this decision, the Appellate Body relied on the way this phrase had been used by other WTO members in making their service commitments, as well as the fact that the words were sufficiently generic in that what they apply to may change over time. "Distribution" could evolve to mean something different in line with the rise of the Internet and the popularity of music downloading/streaming.

In *China – Electronic Payment Services,*[7] the United States challenged China's restrictions on foreign suppliers of electronic payment services. The panel found that China had made specific commitments for these services and that its requirements for service suppliers to have local currency business licenses violated its national treatment obligations.

The other specific commitment in the GATS is market access. Market access contemplates the degree to which a WTO member's internal market is open to services suppliers, or consumers, from other members. The Market access rules in Article XVI penetrate deeply into each member state's capacity for self-government in services, but only to the extent that each member has made commitments in this area. The Market Access provision is framed in quantitative terms. Under Article XVI of GATS, WTO members who have committed the relevant service and mode of supply must not place numeric restrictions on the entry of foreign service suppliers. This applies whether or not there is a discriminatory element in the restriction based on nationality. In other words, the rules apply even with respect to entirely domestically produced services. Article XVI states:

1. With respect to market access through the modes of supply identified in Article I, each Member shall accord services and service suppliers of any other Member treatment no less favourable than that provided for under the terms, limitations and conditions agreed and specified in its Schedule.(8)

6 China – Measures Affecting Trading Rights and Distribution Services for Certain Publications and Audiovisual Entertainment Products, WT/DS363/AB/R, adopted 19 January 2010

7 China – Certain Measures Affecting Electronic Payment Services, WT/DS413/R, adopted 31 August 2012

2. In sectors where market-access commitments are undertaken, the measures which a Member shall not maintain or adopt either on the basis of a regional subdivision or on the basis of its entire territory, unless otherwise specified in its Schedule, are defined as:

   (a) limitations on the number of service suppliers whether in the form of numerical quotas, monopolies, exclusive service suppliers or the requirements of an economic needs test;
   (b) limitations on the total value of service transactions or assets in the form of numerical quotas or the requirement of an economic needs test;
   (c) limitations on the total number of service operations or on the total quantity of service output expressed in terms of designated numerical units in the form of quotas or the requirement of an economic needs test;*(9)*
   (d) limitations on the total number of natural persons that may be employed in a particular service sector or that a service supplier may employ and who are necessary for, and directly related to, the supply of a specific service in the form of numerical quotas or the requirement of an economic needs test;
   (e) measures which restrict or require specific types of legal entity or joint venture through which a service supplier may supply a service; and
   (f) limitations on the participation of foreign capital in terms of maximum percentage limit on foreign shareholding or the total value of individual or aggregate foreign investment.

Market access restrictions consist primarily of quantitative limits on the provision of services. These include caps, the number of service providers in a particular industry, the value of the service transactions they can participate in, the number of people they can employ, or the amount of foreign capital invested in the service supplier. Since they are measurable, they bear a resemblance to tariffs for goods, except, unlike tariffs, market access limits are prohibited outright (again, only if a commitment has been made in the members' GATS schedule of commitments).

The prohibition on imposing these kinds of limits on services applies regardless of whether the restriction is discriminatory (meaning that it only applies to foreign service providers) or non-discriminatory (applies equally to foreign and local service providers). This latter aspect of market access has a profound impact on the country's services economy. Indeed, the elimination of market access restrictions was designed as a tool of services liberalization generally, in addition to facilitating trade via non-discrimination between domestic and foreign services. For example, a restriction on the number of foreign banks allowed to set up branches is clearly a discriminatory market access barrier that will impact trade in services, whereas a license issued by the government for *all* new banks based on the minimum amount of capitalization required would be a non-discriminatory market access barrier that would affect competition in the banking sector of that country.

The *United States – Gambling* dispute, noted previously, examined the meaning of market access commitments. The panel assessed whether the United States' measures prohibiting the remote supply of gambling services were inconsistent with its market access obligations under GATS Article XVI:2. This article prohibits members from maintaining certain types of quantitative restrictions in sectors where they have made specific commitments. The panel and Appellate Body found that the United States' measures amounted to a "zero quota" on the cross-border supply of gambling services, which was deemed to be a quantitative restriction prohibited under Article XVI:2(a) and (c). This interpretation was significant as it clarified that outright prohibitions could be considered quantitative restrictions under GATS.

Expanding access to markets in more service industries is intended to increase competition either from local suppliers or suppliers from other WTO members. Enhanced competition should lead to superior services at lower prices. It may also improve employment opportunities and spur innovation. On the other hand, intensifying competition in services can also lead to some suppliers going out of business because they cannot withstand new market entrants, just as it can lead to a loss of jobs for service suppliers who are not as skilled or who are overpriced. This is a perennial tension in international trade law – both in services and goods. Some services are believed to operate better when there is no competition. These are the so-called natural monopolies, such as utilities, rail networks or postal services. A single provider may be more efficient in these situations because capital costs of entry are so high (e.g., each railway company having its own set of railway lines). Other services, like banking and telecommunications also raise security risks when they are operated by foreigners, so they have to be more carefully monitored by governments. These issues were explored in the chapter on non-trade values.

WTO members list their specific commitments (National Treatment and Market Access) in a Schedule of Specific Commitments and may specify certain limitations on these commitments. This is known as a Positive List approach which may be contrasted with a Negative List, in which all sectors are committed and only the derogations are listed. The Positive List format is less conducive to liberalization and therefore has been rejected in favour of Negative List by a number of FTAs.

Although GATS ensures that foreign suppliers of services in listed sectors do not suffer discrimination and that the sectors in which they operate are not subject to restrictions on market access, it is not intended to compensate companies from other countries for any difficulties they might face because they are foreign, such as lack of familiarity with consumer preferences or the regulatory environment. The requirement of transparency in GATS Article III could help resolve some of these difficulties.

The optional nature of much of the legal obligations within GATS (via the Specific Obligations of National Treatment and Market Access) has meant that GATS has not achieved significant liberalization of services trade, although this may be more of an intended feature of GATS than a problem in its functionality. GATS is associated with complexity and lack of transparency. The structure and language of the GATS have been criticized for being overly complex and opaque. This complexity can make it difficult for developing countries to fully engage in negotiations and understand their commitments. Some have argued that the GATS disproportionately benefits developed countries and large multinational corporations. This asymmetry is partly due to the greater capacity of developed countries to negotiate favourable terms and the dominance of their service firms in global markets. There are also concerns that the GATS may constrain governments' ability to regulate in the public interest, creating a so-called "regulatory chill" as countries may be hesitant to introduce new regulations that could be challenged under GATS rules.[8] Some contend that the GATS creates pressure for privatization of public services, putting pressure on governments to commercialize public services which could potentially undermine access to essential services in developing countries.[9]

8.2.4 Domestic Regulation and Mutual Recognition

The sections in GATS on Domestic Regulation and Mutual Recognition are critical because they facilitate market access in sectors where GATS commitments have been made. Put more plainly, these provisions help smooth access which might be practically more difficult even if a sector is notionally open but in practice, the supply of services will face barriers with respect to the qualifications of the service provider.

The key provision here is Article VI.1 on Domestic Regulation which reads: "In sectors where specific commitments are undertaken, each member shall ensure that all measures of general application affecting trade in services are administered in a reasonable, objective and impartial manner." Reasonable, objective, and impartial are clearly highly discretionary concepts – but they underscore the values that are inherent in GATS (and the WTO generally). Members should endeavour to enable service suppliers to enter each other markets where possible, meaning where the skills and abilities of that person are likely to be such that consumers will not be harmed.

A subset of mostly developed WTO members adopted a Joint Initiative on Services Domestic Regulation aimed at increasing transparency, predictability, and efficiency of procedures for authorization of service providers. Seventy-two WTO members agreed to implement the new disciplines although they apply on an MFN basis to all WTO members – benefiting everyone. The Joint Initiative on Services Domestic Regulation is a plurilateral negotiation effort under the World Trade Organization (WTO) aimed at developing new rules on domestic regulation of services.

One of the key features of the initiative is its focus on transparency, predictability, and efficiency of procedures for authorization of service providers. The disciplines developed through this initiative cover licensing requirements and procedures, qualification requirements and procedures, and technical standards. These are areas where opaque or overly burdensome regulations can create significant barriers to trade in services, particularly for small- and medium-sized enterprises. These disciplines are designed to be applied on an MFN basis, meaning they will benefit all WTO members, not just the participants in the initiative. They

8 Krajewski, n 1

9 S Sinclair and J Grieshaber-Otto, "Facing the Facts: A Guide to the GATS Debate" Canadian Centre for Policy Alternatives (2002)

aim to reinforce good regulatory practices without prescribing specific regulatory approaches. They provide built-in flexibilities for implementation, allowing participants to preserve space for differences in regulatory capacity and approaches. For example, some obligations can be implemented "to the extent practicable," giving members some leeway in application. Provisions for special and differential treatment are included, allowing developing economies to delay the application of specific provisions in sectors where they face implementation difficulties for up to seven years. This approach recognizes the challenges that developing countries may face in implementing new regulatory disciplines.

The initiative also marks a significant milestone in promoting gender equality in trade. For the first time in a WTO-negotiated text, the disciplines include a provision on non-discrimination between men and women in authorization procedures for service suppliers. This reflects a growing recognition of the importance of women's economic empowerment in international trade. Participating members have agreed to incorporate these disciplines into their respective GATS schedules as "additional commitments" under GATS Article XVIII. This means the disciplines will complement existing specific commitments undertaken by participating members in their GATS schedules, without affecting any existing rights and obligations under the GATS or other WTO agreements.

Recognition is an essential feature of modern trade relations both for goods (as discussed in the previous chapter in relation to health and safety rules) and with regard to services. Even if a market access commitment is made, it will be of no use to a service supplier if their qualifications to supply the service are not recognized in the receiving state and they cannot practice their trade. Article VII of GATS reads as follows:

1. For the purposes of the fulfilment, in whole or in part, of its standards or criteria for the authorization, licensing or certification of services suppliers, and subject to the requirements of paragraph 3, a Member may recognize the education or experience obtained, requirements met, or licenses or certifications granted in a particular country. Such recognition, which may be achieved through harmonization or otherwise, may be based upon an agreement or arrangement with the country concerned or may be accorded autonomously.
2. A Member that is a party to an agreement or arrangement of the type referred to in paragraph 1, whether existing or future, shall afford adequate opportunity for other interested Members to negotiate their accession to such an agreement or arrangement or to negotiate comparable ones with it. Where a Member accords recognition autonomously, it shall afford adequate opportunity for any other Member to demonstrate that education, experience, licenses, or certifications obtained or requirements met in that other Member's territory should be recognized.
3. A Member shall not accord recognition in a manner which would constitute a means of discrimination between countries in the application of its standards or criteria for the authorization, licensing or certification of services suppliers, or a disguised restriction on trade in services.

This provision of GATS contemplates special arrangements between two or more WTO members through which recognition is granted on a preferential basis. These will be explored in greater detail under the section on services in FTAs.

Article VI:4 calls for the development of disciplines to ensure that qualification requirements, technical standards, and licensing requirements do not constitute unnecessary barriers to trade in services. In keeping with the understanding of necessity developed in General Exceptions jurisprudence, the necessity test should be interpreted in a way that preserves regulatory autonomy while preventing disguised restrictions on trade. Some contend that the necessity test could be construed too strictly, and potentially be used to challenge a wide range of domestic regulations, potentially undermining regulatory sovereignty.[10] Overly stringent disciplines could disproportionately affect developing countries with limited regulatory capacity.

Article VII arguably creates tension between encouraging preferential arrangements with a view to facilitating service delivery and the MFN principle. While Article VII:3 allows for recognition arrangements between certain members, it also requires that adequate opportunity be afforded to other interested members to negotiate their accession to such agreements or to negotiate comparable ones. This provision creates a complex balancing act between promoting deeper integration through MRAs and maintaining non-discrimination through the MFN principle. It has been argued that the provision does not go far enough in encouraging recognition and that more proactive measures are needed to facilitate the movement of professionals across borders.[11] The flexible nature of Article VII allows for a gradual and context-specific approach to recognition that respects regulatory diversity. Together Articles VI and VII of GATS create a framework for regulatory cooperation which, while effective, creates challenges in implementing this framework, particularly given the diversity of regulatory approaches across WTO members.[12]

8.2.5 GATS Annexes

The GATS Annexes on Telecommunications and Financial Services contain important provisions that extend and clarify the application of GATS rules to these specific sectors. First, the Annex on Telecommunications specifically addresses the telecommunications sector, recognizing its dual role as both a distinct sector of economic activity and as an underlying transport means for other economic activities. It applies to all measures of a WTO member that affect access to and

10 P Delimatsis, "Due Process and 'Good' Regulation Embedded in the GATS – Disciplining Regulatory Behaviour in Services Through Article VI of the GATS" 10:1 Journal of International Economic Law 13 (2007)

11 K Nicolaïdis and JP Trachtman, "From Policed Regulation to Managed Recognition in GATS" in P Sauvé and R Stern (Eds.), *GATS 2000: New Directions in Services Trade Liberalization* (Brookings Institution, 2010)

12 JA Marchetti and PC Mavroidis, "The Genesis of the GATS (General Agreement on Trade in Services)" 22:3 European Journal of International Law 689 (2011)

use of public telecommunications transport networks and services. It explicitly excludes measures affecting cable or broadcast distribution of radio or television programming. This distinction is important as it delineates the boundary between telecommunications services and broadcasting services, which are often regulated differently. A key feature of the Annex on Telecommunications is its focus on ensuring access to and use of public telecommunications transport networks and services. It requires WTO members to ensure that service suppliers of any other member are accorded access to and use of public telecommunications transport networks and services on reasonable and non-discriminatory terms and conditions. This provision is crucial for enabling cross-border trade in services that rely on telecommunications infrastructure.

The Annex also addresses the issue of transparency. It requires WTO members to make publicly available all relevant information on conditions affecting access to and use of public telecommunications transport networks and services. This includes information on tariffs, technical interfaces, bodies responsible for standards, and any licensing or registration requirements. The transparency provisions are designed to reduce information asymmetries and facilitate market entry for foreign service providers. Another important aspect of the Annex is its treatment of technical cooperation. It encourages and supports telecommunications cooperation among developing countries at the international, regional, and sub-regional levels. This provision recognizes the importance of telecommunications infrastructure for economic development and aims to promote capacity building in developing countries. The Annex also addresses the issue of relation to international organizations and agreements. It recognizes the importance of international standards for global compatibility and interoperability of telecommunication networks and services. It encourages cooperation with relevant international organizations and the use of international standards where appropriate.

A significant feature of the Annex is its provisions on access to and use of public telecommunications transport networks and services. It specifies that such access should be granted on reasonable and non-discriminatory terms and conditions. This includes the right to purchase or lease equipment that interfaces with the network, to interconnect private leased or owned circuits with public networks, and to use operating protocols of the service supplier's choice in the supply of any service. The Annex also recognizes the right of WTO members to take necessary measures to ensure the security and confidentiality of messages, subject to the requirement that such measures are not applied in a manner that would constitute a means of arbitrary or unjustifiable discrimination or a disguised restriction on trade in services.

The *Mexico – Telecommunications*[13] dispute involved the interpretation and application of the GATS Annex on Telecommunications which Mexico had incorporated into its GATS schedule of commitments. The United States argued that Mexico had failed to ensure that the company Telmex provided interconnection to

13 Mexico – Measures Affecting Telecommunications Services, WT/DS204/R, adopted 1 June 2004.

United States carriers on reasonable rates, terms, and conditions, as required by these commitments. One issue that arose related to the interpretation of the term "reasonable rates" used in the Annex. The panel had to determine what constituted "reasonable" in the context of international interconnection rates. In doing so, it considered various benchmarks, including cost-oriented pricing principles. The panel ultimately concluded that the rates charged by Telmex were not "reasonable" as they significantly exceeded cost-based rates. The case also raised important questions about the concept of "anti-competitive practices" as referenced in the Annex. The United States argued that Mexico had failed to maintain appropriate measures to prevent Telmex from engaging in anti-competitive practices. The panel had to interpret this provision and determine whether Mexico's regulatory framework was sufficient to meet its obligations. In its analysis, the panel found that Mexico's measures actually required Telmex to engage in practices that limited competition, such as fixing uniform settlement rates in agreements with foreign carriers. The panel also adopted a broad interpretation of the term "cost-oriented," suggesting that rates should be brought into a reasonable relationship with the cost of providing the service.

The GATS Annex on Financial Services specifically addresses the financial services sector, of vital importance to many countries, such as the United Kingdom and Switzerland. This annex clarifies that the supply of a financial service refers to the definition provided in paragraph 2 of Article I of the GATS Agreement. This scope is broad, encompassing a wide range of financial activities. One of the key features of the Annex is its definition of financial services. It provides a comprehensive list of activities that fall under this category, divided into two main groups: insurance and insurance-related services and banking and other financial services. The insurance category includes activities such as direct life and non-life insurance, reinsurance, insurance intermediation, and auxiliary services. The banking and other financial services category is even more extensive, covering activities like deposit-taking, lending, financial leasing, payment services, trading in various financial instruments, asset management, and advisory services, among others.

The Annex also addresses the important concept of "services supplied in the exercise of governmental authority" in the context of financial services. It specifies that this includes activities conducted by central banks or monetary authorities in pursuit of monetary or exchange rate policies, activities that are part of statutory social security or public retirement plans, and other activities conducted by public entities using government financial resources or guarantees. This clarification is crucial for delineating the boundary between public and private sector activities in financial services.

A significant provision of the Annex is the "prudential carve-out" clause. This clause recognizes the right of members to take measures for prudential reasons, such as protecting investors, depositors, or policyholders, or ensuring the integrity and stability of the financial system. However, it also stipulates that such measures should not be used as a means of avoiding commitments or obligations under the agreement. This provision aims to strike a balance between allowing necessary regulatory oversight and preventing unjustified trade barriers. The Annex on

Financial Services also encourages members to recognize the prudential measures of other countries, either through harmonization or otherwise. This can be done through agreements or autonomously. The Annex provides guidelines for such recognition arrangements, emphasizing transparency and the opportunity for interested members to join or negotiate comparable arrangements.

It is unclear whether the prudential carve out of the Financial Services Annex provides a broad exemption for financial regulations or if it should be interpreted more narrowly. Some argue that it should be interpreted broadly to give WTO members sufficient regulatory space to address financial stability concerns.[14] Others contend that a broad interpretation could potentially undermine the liberalization commitments made under the GATS.[15] It has been suggested the Annex's prudential carve-out provides a more flexible exception than the General Exceptions of GATS Article XIV, as it does not require the same level of necessity testing.[16] It may make more sense for the prudential carve-out to be subject to similar disciplines as other GATS exceptions to prevent abuse.[17]

In *Argentina – Financial Services,*[18] the panel and Appellate Body had to interpret the prudential carve-out in the context of Argentina's tax measures affecting financial services. The Appellate Body emphasized that the prudential carve-out is not a typical exception provision like GATS Article XIV. Instead, it found that the provision allows measures to be taken for prudential reasons, subject to the requirement that such measures are not used as a means of avoiding GATS commitments or obligations. This interpretation suggests a more flexible approach to the prudential carve-out compared to other GATS exceptions. However, the Appellate Body also noted that measures taken under the prudential carve-out must have a rational relationship of cause and effect between the measure and the prudential reason. This introduces an element of scrutiny into the application of the provision, potentially limiting its scope.

8.3 Services in FTAs

The relatively weak liberalization of trade in legal services achieved multilaterally by GATS – in large part due to WTO members' unwillingness to open their borders to services delivery, probably due to concerns with the competitive strength of their own suppliers as well as concerns relating to quality – has shifted strategies of

14 B De Meester, "Testing European Prudential Conditions for Banking Mergers in the Light of Most Favoured Nation in the GATS" 11:3 Journal of International Economic Law 609 (2008)

15 CM Cantore, "Shelter from the Storm: Exploring the Scope of Application and Legal Function of the GATS Prudential Carve-Out" 48:4 Journal of World Trade 1223 (2014)

16 M Yokoi-Arai, "GATS' Prudential Carve Out in Financial Services and Its Relation with Prudential Regulation" 57 International and Comparative Law Quarterly 613 (2008)

17 A Mitchell, J Hawkins, and N Mishra, "Dear Prudence: Allowances Under International Trade and Investment Law for Prudential Regulation in the Financial Services Sector" 19:4 Journal of International Economic Law 787 (2016)

18 Argentina – Measures Relating to Trade in Goods and Services, WT/DS453/AB/R, adopted 9 May 2016

liberalization to the bilateral and regional level. In such situations, treaty partners are able to selectively open service sectors and to recognize qualifications of those service providers without doing so for the entirety of the WTO's global membership.

Article V of GATS deals with economic integration agreements in services trade. This article allows WTO members to enter into economic integration agreements that liberalize trade in services among parties, without having to extend the same treatment to all other WTO members under the MFN principle. To qualify for this exception, such agreements must: (a) have "substantial sectoral coverage" in terms of number of sectors, volume of trade affected, and modes of supply; and (b) provide for the elimination of substantially all discrimination between parties in the covered sectors, either immediately or within a reasonable timeframe.

8.3.1 Services Chapters in FTAs

The services chapters of preferential FTAs tend to be structured along similar lines to GATS, setting out the scope in terms of coverage than the core obligations of non-discrimination, market access, and domestic regulation. Financial services are often excluded from the services chapters of FTAs, in some cases getting their own dedicated chapters, as in the case of the CPTPP. Generally speaking, the trend appears to be towards more comprehensive services chapters in FTAs, reflecting the growing importance of services in international trade.

One additional feature found in some service chapters of FTAs is the prohibition of a local presence requirement. For example, Article 10.6 of the CPTPP specifies: "No Party shall require a service supplier of another Party to establish or maintain a representative office or any form of enterprise, or to be resident, in its territory as a condition for the cross-border supply of a service." This facilitates the market entry of foreign services suppliers – precluding the need to maintain an office or facility in the target country, which could be discouraging.

As noted earlier, many FTAs use a Negative List approach for services, unlike GATS which uses a Positive List approach. With a negative list, all service sectors are liberalized by default except those specifically listed as exceptions. FTAs like the CPTPP prohibit certain types of market access restrictions that are still permitted under GATS, including limitations on the number of service suppliers, restrictions on the total value of service transactions or assets, and limits on the total number of service operations or quantity of service output. Under GATS these commitments are optional.

FTAs often include stronger commitments on regulatory transparency compared to GATS, particularly in the financial services sector. For example, the CPTPP requires members to publish proposed financial sector regulations in advance and allow stakeholders to comment on proposed regulations. Many modern FTAs, like the USMCA or the UK-EU TCA, contain digital trade chapters which can enhance the delivery of services. These issues will be explored in greater detail in Chapter 10.

Some FTAs include a ratchet mechanism, which means that any future liberalization of a service sector automatically becomes part of the agreement's commitments. This approach achieves progressively greater liberalization and prevents backsliding, meaning a situation in which a party were to impose new restrictions that it had not done in the past.

Some FTAs have demonstrated particularly significant commitments in their negative lists of specific commitments for market access and national treatment. For example, the EU-Japan Economic Partnership Agreement includes significant service commitments, particularly from Japan. Japan made commitments to open its legal services market, allowing EU lawyers to advise on third-country law and international law. In financial services, Japan committed to allowing EU firms to engage in the cross-border transfer of financial information for data processing. In telecommunications, Japan committed to allowing 100 per cent foreign ownership of telecommunications companies. The agreement includes strong provisions on domestic regulation of services, aiming to ensure licensing and qualification procedures are not unnecessarily burdensome.

Another EU agreement, CETA, includes notable service commitments. For example, Canada made significant commitments to professional services, including allowing temporary entry for EU professionals in fields like engineering and architecture. In financial services, Canada committed to allowing EU firms to provide portfolio management services to Canadian collective investment schemes. The agreement includes a framework for mutual recognition of professional qualifications, which could further facilitate services trade.

The USMCA expanded services commitments in several areas including enhanced market access in financial services, including allowing United States firms to provide portfolio management services to Mexican pension funds. There were also improved commitments for cross-border services in areas like express delivery and telecommunications.

The China-Australia Free Trade Agreement (ChAFTA) included some notable commitments from China in relation to services. In financial services, China committed to allowing Australian financial institutions to establish subsidiaries for futures trading. In education services, China committed to allowing Australian providers to establish wholly owned international schools in certain free trade zones. In tourism services, China committed to allowing Australian travel agencies to provide certain services in China.

MERCOSUR has made significant strides in liberalizing trade in services among its member countries, which include Argentina, Brazil, Paraguay, and Uruguay. The MERCOSUR Protocol on Trade in Services, signed in 1997, establishes a framework specifically aimed at promoting the free trade of services within the bloc. This protocol is designed to facilitate regional integration by creating a more cohesive market for services, which is a more ambitious approach compared to GATS. MERCOSUR adopts a negative list approach for some commitments under its Protocol on Trade in Services. This means that all sectors are considered open unless explicitly excluded from liberalization efforts. This approach can potentially lead to broader market access compared to the positive list approach used by GATS, where only specified sectors are committed to liberalization. The negative list method encourages member states to be more proactive about liberalizing their service sectors. The MERCOSUR Protocol also sets specific timelines for progressive liberalization of services trade among its members. It aimed for substantial liberalization within ten years of its entry into force, providing a clear roadmap for members to follow. This contrasts with the open-ended nature of GATS commitments, which do not impose specific deadlines for achieving liberalization goals.

AfCFTA's Protocol on Trade in Services is a comprehensive framework aimed at liberalizing and promoting intra-African trade in services. The Protocol builds upon the provisions in GATS but includes additional material, notably Article 8 which emphasizes the right to regulate services within their territories to meet national policy objectives, as long as this does not impair the rights and obligations arising from the Protocol. Article 10 of the Protocol addresses domestic regulation, requiring State Parties to maintain or institute judicial, arbitral, or administrative tribunals or procedures that provide for the prompt review of administrative decisions affecting trade in services. This provision aims to ensure transparency and fairness in the regulatory process, going beyond the requirements of GATS in terms of specificity. Another unique feature of the AfCFTA Protocol is its emphasis on capacity building, as outlined in Article 27. This article recognizes the importance of technical assistance and cooperation to support parties' efforts to strengthen their capacities in the supply of services. It requires parties to mobilize resources and implement measures to enhance service sector development, a provision that goes beyond what is included in GATS. Article 18 of the Protocol requires State Parties to consider progressively liberalizing service sectors' commitments and modes of supply to promote critical sectors of growth as well as social and sustainable development. This approach is more prescriptive than the general commitment to progressive liberalization in GATS.

There have been very few disputes brought under the services chapters of FTAs using the arbitration mechanisms in those agreements. Many comprehensive FTAs with robust services chapters are relatively recent, giving less time for disputes to arise and be adjudicated. Services barriers tend to be "behind the border" regulatory measures that are more complex to challenge than traditional goods barriers like tariffs. Many service issues are resolved through bilateral consultations rather than formal dispute settlement. For overlapping issues, parties may prefer to use the WTO dispute settlement system given its more established jurisprudence.

Many disputes may be resolved through consultations or the threat of formal proceedings, without reaching the arbitration stage. The existence of these mechanisms can serve as a deterrent to non-compliance and provide a framework for resolving disagreements. As global trade in services continues to grow and digital trade becomes increasingly important, it is possible that there may be more use of FTA dispute settlement mechanisms for services-related issues in the future. Areas such as e-commerce, data localization, and cross-border data flows are likely to be potential sources of disagreement as countries navigate the complex regulatory landscape of the digital economy. These issues will be explored further in Chapter 10.

The evolution of dispute settlement in recent FTAs also suggests a trend towards more specialized procedures for services and investment-related disputes. For example, the CPTPP and the TCA include detailed provisions for financial services disputes, recognizing the unique regulatory considerations in this sector and the need for specialized expertise among adjudicators.

8.3.2 Mutual Recognition Agreements (MRAs)

Recognition of qualifications of service providers is often enshrined formally in Mutual Recognition Agreements (MRAs) which are separate agreements between countries, or in some cases between professional bodies in different countries. They are not part of a formal FTA itself. Such arrangements are alluded to in Article VII of GATS, discussed above. The advantage of MRAs is that they are settled and predictable, rather than flexible and prone to change without notice. This allows service suppliers to establish a client base in a target country, secure in the knowledge that their capacity to deliver that service will remain lawful without additional requirements, such as certificates or training periods. MRAs typically also provide for ongoing cooperation and dialogue between the relevant regulatory bodies in the signatory countries. This enables the MRA to achieve dynamic recognition – meaning one that adapts to changes in the provision of services over time. This gives greater assurance to service suppliers (and to their clients) that there will not be disruptions in service delivery across international borders due to any changes in regulations over time.

To take one notable example, the United Kingdom and Switzerland signed an MRA for financial services in 2024 (known as the Berne Financial Services Agreement). The core of the agreement is found in Article 8 which states as follows:

> In respect of the Covered Sectors, each Party considers that the domestic regulatory and supervisory frameworks of the other Party achieve equivalent outcomes with regard to financial stability, market integrity and the protection of investors and consumers within the scope of the Agreement and its Sectoral Annexes.

One of the most comprehensive MRAs for services is the Trans-Tasman Mutual Recognition Arrangement (TTMRA) between Australia and New Zealand. Implemented in 1998, the TTMRA covers a wide range of regulated occupations and allows professionals registered to practice in one country to be recognized and work in the other without the need for further testing or qualification. Using a negative list approach, the agreement provides for automatic recognition of qualifications for most regulated occupations including doctors, nurses, teachers, lawyers, and engineers. There is also ongoing cooperation between regulatory bodies to maintain alignment of standards and a dedicated dispute resolution mechanism.

Within the European Union, the Professional Qualifications Directive[19] establishes a system of mutual recognition for regulated professions across EU member

19 Directive 2005/36/EC, as amended

states. While not technically an MRA, it functions in a similar manner and is one of the most extensive systems of professional recognition globally. This agreement sets out automatic recognition for seven sectoral professions (doctors, nurses, midwives, pharmacists, architects, veterinary surgeons, and dental practitioners). There is also a general system for other regulated professions based on comparing qualifications and mechanisms for ongoing regulatory cooperation and information exchange. The EU system has greatly facilitated professional mobility within the single market, though challenges remain in implementation for some professions and member states.

The USMCA includes provisions for developing MRAs for professional services. While not as comprehensive as the TTMRA or EU system, several profession-specific MRAs have been developed under this framework. One notable example is the Tri-National Mutual Recognition Agreement for International Practice in Architecture, which facilitates the recognition of architects between Canada, the United States, and Mexico. This includes standardized requirements for education, experience, and examination as well as a common application process for recognition and ongoing cooperation between national regulatory bodies.

MERCOSUR's Services Protocol contains provisions for mutual recognition of qualifications, licenses, and certifications among member countries. Article XI of the Protocol encourages member states to develop mutually acceptable standards for professional services. Likewise, ASEAN has developed MRAs for several professional services as part of its efforts to create an ASEAN Economic Community. These include MRAs for engineering services, nursing services, architectural services, medical practitioners, dental practitioners, accountancy services, and tourism professionals. The ASEAN MRA on Engineering Services, implemented in 2005, serves as a good example. This agreement establishes standardized requirements for education, experience, and professional development along with a central coordinating committee to oversee implementation.

The Asia-Pacific Economic Cooperation (APEC) forum has also made efforts to facilitate services MRAs among its members. The APEC Engineer Agreement, while not a formal MRA, establishes a framework for recognizing substantial equivalence of professional competence in engineering. It includes agreed standards for education, professional development, and ethical conduct. It also establishes a system of national monitoring committees, regular peer review of member jurisdictions, and the facilitation of temporary mobility, with permanent registration still subject to local requirements.

In the financial services sector, the Asia Region Funds Passport (ARFP) is a notable initiative that, while not strictly an MRA, functions similarly by allowing cross-border marketing of managed funds. Launched in 2019 with Australia, Japan, Korea, New Zealand, and Thailand as initial participants, the ARFP contains harmonized standards for fund operators and products, a common application process for passport registration and provision for ongoing regulatory cooperation and information sharing. While still in its early stages, the ARFP has the potential to significantly boost cross-border investment in the Asia-Pacific region.

Many services MRAs are profession-specific rather than comprehensive agreements covering multiple sectors. This reflects the complexity of regulating professional services and the need for detailed understanding of qualification requirements and professional standards in each field. In the legal services sector, the International Bar Association (IBA) has developed guidelines for MRAs, though implementation remains limited. The EU-Canada CETA includes provisions for negotiating an MRA for legal services, demonstrating ongoing interest in this lucrative sector.

The CPTPP includes an annex on professional services that encourages members to work towards mutual recognition of professional qualifications and develop mutually acceptable standards for licensing and certification of professional service suppliers. One noteworthy example here relates to the legal profession, which tends to face significant barriers due to its jurisdiction-specific nature.[20] The CPTPP's Annex on Professional Services recognizes the unique nature of legal services and the importance of regulatory autonomy in this field. The annex acknowledges that the practice of law requires in-depth knowledge of domestic legal systems, which can vary significantly between jurisdictions. As such, it does not attempt to harmonize legal qualifications or standards across member countries but rather focuses on encouraging cooperation and mutual recognition where possible.

The CPTPP Annex on professional services encourages CPTPP members to engage in dialogue and cooperation to facilitate the provision of legal services within the free trade area. Parties should seek to allow foreign lawyers to provide legal services on a temporary basis, particularly in relation to international law and the law of the jurisdiction in which they are licensed. This provision aims to facilitate cross-border legal services while respecting domestic regulatory requirements. The annex also addresses the issue of foreign legal consultants. CPTPP parties should aim to permit foreign lawyers to practice as foreign legal consultants in their jurisdiction, providing advice on the law of the country where they are licensed, on international law, and on international commercial transactions. However, it recognizes that members may impose certain requirements, such as registration or obtaining a license, to practice as a foreign legal consultant.

Emphasizing transparency in the regulation of legal services, the Annex calls for members to make publicly available information regarding the requirements and procedures for obtaining licenses or registrations to practice law. This includes information on educational requirements, examinations, experience requirements, conduct and ethics, professional development and re-certification, scope of practice, and local knowledge requirements. The Annex also addresses the issue of partnerships and associations between local and foreign lawyers. CPTPP members should endeavour to allow foreign lawyers to enter into partnerships or associations with local lawyers, subject to domestic regulatory requirements. This provision aims to

20 See D Collins, *The Public International Law of Trade in Legal Services* (Cambridge University Press, 2018)

facilitate collaboration between legal professionals from different jurisdictions and enhance the provision of cross-border legal services.

CPTPP members should also try to develop mutually acceptable standards and criteria for the licensing and certification of lawyers. It suggests that these standards could include considerations such as education, examinations, experience, conduct and ethics, professional development and re-certification, scope of practice, and local knowledge. The Annex also encourages CPTPP members to work towards allowing lawyers licensed in one member country to obtain qualifications in the law of another member country through clear, well-defined, and transparent processes. This could involve, for example, allowing foreign lawyers to sit for limited licensing examinations or complete adaptation periods to gain admission to the host country's bar.

Generally, MRAs stress the importance of ongoing regulatory cooperation and information exchange to maintain trust and alignment of standards. They also emphasize the need for balance between facilitating mobility and maintaining appropriate regulatory oversight to protect consumers and maintain professional standards. It can be challenging to implement MRAs in federal systems where professional regulation may be a state/provincial responsibility, as in the United States. There is an important role for professional bodies and industry associations in developing and implementing MRAs, often in cooperation with government regulators.

8.4 Plurilateral Initiatives for Trade in Services

There have been some plurilateral initiatives regarding trade in services is recent years. Plurilateral agreements are multi-party and open to accession by any country. They typically also deal with a specific sector or issue, rather than in the case of a conventional FTA which tend to be comprehensive. Services may be particularly well suited to plurilateralism since they require greater flexibility than trade in goods, with numerous contingencies across different modes of supply. They also tend to be of greater interest to a smaller subset of countries at a more advanced stage of economic development.

8.4.1 The Trade in Services Agreement (TiSA)

TiSA was an ambitious attempt to liberalize and expand global trade in services beyond the existing framework of the GATS. TiSA aimed to update and expand on GATS by using a negative list approach for services liberalization, meaning all sectors would be opened by default unless explicitly excluded. It also included new rules on e-commerce, data flows, and regulatory cooperation. TiSA intended to cover sectors like financial services, telecommunications, transportation, and professional services. It was also going to enhance regulatory transparency, especially for financial services. The agreement was designed to be compatible with WTO rules and potentially multilateralized in the future to include more WTO members, a so-called "open plurilateral." Negotiations on TiSA began in 2013 but stalled in 2016 without reaching a final agreement.

Although TiSA negotiations involved 23 WTO members accounting for about 70 per cent of global services trade, it notably excluded major emerging markets like China, India, and Brazil. This limited its potential scope and impact. TiSA negotiations touched on sensitive topics like data flows, financial services regulation, and temporary movement of workers, which proved difficult to resolve. The 2016 United States presidential election and subsequent change in administration led to a shift in United States trade policy priorities away from international trade, removing a key driving force behind TiSA. Concerns had been expressed about potential pressure for privatization of public services. There were also worries about constraining governments' regulatory space, especially in developing countries. There was perceived to be a lack of transparency in negotiations, with limited public access to negotiating texts. Lastly, there were also fears that it could undermine efforts to strengthen multilateral trade rules through the WTO.

While TiSA negotiations did not reach a conclusion, they highlighted the growing importance of services trade in the global economy and the need for updated international rules in this area. Many of the issues addressed in TiSA, such as digital trade and regulatory cooperation, have since been taken up in other trade agreements and forums. The experience of TiSA also underscores the challenges of negotiating complex plurilateral agreements outside the WTO framework and the importance of inclusivity in global trade talks.

8.4.2 The Indo-Pacific Economic Framework (IPEF)

IPEF is an economic initiative launched by the United States in 2022 with 13 partner countries in the Indo-Pacific region. It is not designed as a traditional comprehensive FTA but rather aims to establish high-standard commitments in four pillars: Connected Economy (covering selected trade issues), Resilient Economy (focusing on supply chains), Clean Economy (addressing clean energy, decarbonization, and infrastructure), and Fair Economy (dealing with tax and anti-corruption issues). Unlike the WTO, IPEF does not involve a single undertaking, allowing partners to conclude agreements separately rather than waiting to finalize all elements of a comprehensive deal. The framework is designed to be flexible, with partners not required to join all four pillars, though most have opted to participate in all except for India, which has opted out of the trade pillar.

IPEF addresses trade in services, though again in a more limited way compared to traditional FTAs. The IPEF's approach to services trade is primarily focused on digital trade and emerging technologies rather than comprehensive services liberalization across all sectors. Within the Connected Economy pillar of IPEF, which is led by the United States Trade Representative, there are provisions related to digital trade and the digital economy. These aim to establish rules and standards for cross-border data flows, data localization, and other aspects of the digital services trade.

The IPEF does not include traditional market access commitments for services, such as those typically found in free trade agreements. There are no schedules of specific commitments for services sectors or modes of supply as would be seen in agreements modelled after the GATS. Instead, the IPEF takes a more targeted approach, focusing on areas like digital trade, supply chain resilience, and clean energy. For example, the supply chain agreement signed by IPEF partners aims to enhance collaboration and resilience in critical sectors, which could indirectly affect trade in related services. However, this agreement does not contain specific commitments to liberalize trade in services.

The IPEF is still evolving, and, as of the time of writing, not all components have been finalized. The trade pillar, which would likely contain the most relevant provisions for services trade, is still under negotiation. The lack of traditional market access commitments, including in services, has been a point of criticism from some stakeholders who argue that this limits the IPEF's potential to deepen economic linkages among partners. The IPEF's approach to services trade reflects a shift in United States trade policy, moving away from comprehensive free trade agreements towards more targeted, flexible arrangements. This new model focuses on specific issues and sectors deemed critical for the 21st century economy, rather than broad-based liberalization across all services sectors.

8.5 Conclusion

Services are among the most important sectors of economic activities in many countries around the world. Trade in services has been bolstered by the age of telecommunications following the establishment and rise of the Internet at the turn of the 21st century. Yet trade in services remains poorly liberalized, both in proportion to its economic significance and in relation to trade in goods. This is largely due to the complexity of regulation covering services as well as sensitivities concerning not just competitive vulnerabilities but also competence and consumer safety.

The WTO's GATS broke new ground in the 1990s by conceiving categories of service delivery which enabled WTO members to selectively open up their services to foreign supply at their own pace. While the results may not have been as extensive as were wished, GATS has been credited with creating a more secure environment for trade in services through the progressive removal of barriers to trade. Since many of the elements of GATS are optional, its success in liberalizing services depends on the will of WTO members to make commitments. Unfortunately, many members maintain broad restrictions on services. As the global economy becomes increasingly service-oriented and digitally driven, the importance of GATS disciplines and their interpretation through the WTO dispute settlement system is likely to grow.

Meanwhile, services have continued to feature prominently in preferential FTAs, with parties provided greater detail and deeper commitments, often by precluding the need for a local presence. Even as FTAs have exhibited less coverage for services than many would have wished, MRAs have helped fill the void by addressing pragmatic barriers to trade in services in the form of accepting foreign qualifications or by reducing the steps necessary to achieve this. Piece by piece, profession by profession, mutual recognition arrangements have begun to chip away at some of the major obstacles to services trade, unlocking much economic potential and value to consumers.

Discussion Questions

1. How does the GATS address trade in services differently than the GATT addresses trade in goods?
2. What is meant by exclusion of services "supplied in the exercise of governmental authority?" Why does GATS have this restriction?
3. What is meant by market access and how is it covered in GATS?
4. What is mutual recognition and why is it important to trade in services?
5. How do preferential/regional free trade agreements attempt to liberalize services beyond that of GATS?

9 Intellectual Property Rights and Trade

9.1 Introduction

Intellectual property protection is crucial for the global economy, especially in high-tech industries like pharmaceuticals and digital media, where the Internet has facilitated easy copying. The international trade in counterfeit goods and services is estimated to exceed $250 billion annually. Intellectual property is among the most valuable assets to many trading companies and counterfeit goods cost the global economy billions of dollars per year.

In the early 1990s, as the WTO was being established, developed nations grew increasingly concerned about losing valuable exports to newly industrializing markets due to weak or non-existent intellectual property laws. These countries feared losing their competitive edge in producing high-value goods and services to poorer nations that could replicate them cheaply. Consequently, incorporating intellectual property protection into the new WTO became a top priority, heavily lobbied for by multinational corporations from the United States, Japan, and Europe.

This chapter will consider the way in which trade agreements have attempted to protect intellectual property rights with a view to liberalizing trade in goods and services. While the principles of intellectual property have been developed in national legal systems, especially those of the United States, the main agreement governing trade in intellectual property is the WTO TRIPS Agreement. This chapter will examine it as well as deeper commitments made in the context of FTAs such as the USMCA (in relation to patent and copyright protection) and the CPTPP (concerning geographical indicators). Issues in relation to pharmaceuticals will be explored including the TRIPs waiver for vaccines, arising from the Covid-19 pandemic.

The justification for intellectual property protection is both ethical and economic. It is considered fair to reward creative individuals for their efforts, particularly when their work benefits others. Economically, the argument is that without such protection, innovation incentives decrease, potentially reducing global welfare by limiting new products and ideas. Intellectual property rights can facilitate technology transfer by providing legal certainty for innovators and creators operating in global markets. Strong intellectual property protection can encourage innovation and creativity, potentially leading to the development of new products

DOI: 10.4324/9781003465676-9

and services for international trade. On the other hand, strong intellectual property rights can also act as a form of trade barrier, granting temporary monopolies that may restrict competition and affect market access.[1]

Weak intellectual property protection in developing countries may not significantly impact innovation incentives, since these markets lack substantial disposable income for intellectual property products. Moreover, many developing nations lack the technological capacity to reproduce advanced forms of intellectual property, such as patented innovations. These arguments have led some to question whether intellectual property protection should have been included in the WTO's mandate at all.

9.2 Trade Related Intellectual Property Rights (TRIPS) Agreement

The TRIPS Agreement is the WTO's intellectual property agreement and is probably the most important intellectual property treaty in the world. It was created along with the WTO itself in 1995.

9.2.1 Objective and Scope

The objective of TRIPS, outlined in the preamble, is to reduce distortions in international trade while protecting intellectual property rights. It aims to ensure that intellectual property rights do not become impediments to trade. This goal is premised on the notion that failure to protect intellectual property is a *de facto* restriction on market access. Few companies would be prepared to trade with countries where intellectual property protections are weak out of fear that the products they send there will be copied and undersold, harming their profits. It recognizes that intellectual property rights are private rights and acknowledges the underlying public policy objectives of national systems for the protection of intellectual property, including developmental and technological objectives.[2] More generally, the TRIPS seeks to reward creators of intellectual property, encouraging others to do so in the future. At the same time, it aims to serve the public interest by enabling the dissemination of knowledge which is of value to people around the world.

TRIPS is another manifestation of the principle of harmonization that features prominently in world trade law; the agreement focuses on achieving alignment between WTO member states in terms of their approach to the recognition of intellectual property rights. It does this by establishing minimum levels of protection of seven categories of intellectual property both substantively and procedurally. It also subjects these rights, as protected by domestic legal systems of the WTO members, to WTO dispute settlement. As with all WTO agreements, the rights and obligations of TRIPS are between member nations, not private individuals or firms.

1 JE Stiglitz, "Economic Foundations of Intellectual Property Rights" 57:6 Duke Law Journal 1693 (2008)
2 Article 7

A significant portion of TRIPS is dedicated to enforcement measures. It requires members to ensure that enforcement procedures are available under their national laws to permit effective action against any act of infringement of intellectual property rights.[3] The agreement specifies civil and administrative procedures and remedies that must be available, including injunctive relief, damages, and the disposal of infringing goods.[4] TRIPS also mandates that members provide for criminal procedures and penalties at least in cases of wilful trademark counterfeiting or copyright piracy on a commercial scale.[5] Additionally, it requires members to adopt procedures to enable right holders to obtain the cooperation of customs authorities to prevent the importation of counterfeit trademark or pirated copyright goods.[6] The agreement includes transitional arrangements that provide developing countries with additional time to implement the provisions.[7] It also established the Council for TRIPS to monitor the operation of the agreement and members' compliance with their obligations.[8]

In keeping with the principle of world trade law that recognizes the importance of non-trade values, TRIPS allows members to adopt measures necessary to protect public health and nutrition, and to promote the public interest in sectors of vital importance to their socio-economic and technological development, provided such measures are consistent with the provisions of TRIPS.[9] It also recognizes the need to prevent the abuse of intellectual property rights or practices that unreasonably restrain trade or adversely affect the international transfer of technology.[10]

Non-discrimination is a foundational principle of TRIPS, as it is with other aspects of trade law (seen already in the GATT, for example). Article 3 of TRIPs contains a National Treatment obligation. Under this provision, each member must accord nationals of other member states treatment that is no less favourable than it accords its own nationals with regard to IP protection. The MFN, found in Article 4, states that any advantage granted by a member to the nationals of any other member must be granted unconditionally to all members. National Treatment and MFN apply to both *de jure* and *de facto* discrimination. It is also noteworthy that National Treatment and MFN are subject to exceptions granted in international IP treaties. It is important to draw attention to the fact that protection for "nationals" refers to the origin of the rights holder, not the thing itself. This is consistent with intellectual property principles contained in legal systems around the world.

3 Article 41
4 Articles 42–49
5 Article 61
6 Articles 51–60
7 Articles 65–66
8 Article 68
9 Article 8.1
10 Article 8.2

9.2.2 Substantive Obligations

TRIPS covers seven categories of IP rights: copyright, trademark, patents, geographical indicators, undisclosed information, industrial designs, and integrated circuits. Of these, the first four are the most important both economically and in the context of trade.

First, copyright protects the expression of an idea, not the idea itself. Under the TRIPS copyright protection must be extended for at least fifty years after the death of the author. Each year, new works "fall into the public domain" because this fifty-year period following the death of the author expires. Some recent examples of such works include: WH Auden, British American poet; Pablo Neruda, Chilean poet and diplomat; JRR Tolkien, British author of *The Lord of the Rings*. TRIPS requires members to comply with the substantive provisions of the Berne Convention, with the exception of moral rights, and additional rights held by authors of creative works.[11] It explicitly extends copyright protection to computer programs and compilations of data.[12]

It is important to note that while these works may be entering the public domain in countries with life plus fifty years terms, many countries (including the United States and EU member states) have extended copyright terms to life plus seventy years or even longer. In these countries, works by authors who died fifty years ago would still be under copyright protection. There are various exceptions to copyright such as fair use (copying portions of a work for an educational purpose).

TRIPS provisions on the limits of copyright came under investigation of the WTO dispute settlement system in a complaint brought by the European Union against the United States relating to the playing of music in public places.[13] Under United States domestic copyright law, as in many countries, use of music in stores and restaurants was exempt from the requirement to obtain the rights holder's permission and pay a royalty fee under what was known as the "business exemption" category. In order to qualify for this exemption, the size of the premises in which the music was played was limited to a certain area by square footage.

The United States claimed that this limitation on copyright protection fell within the TRIPS special case exemption which captures the normal exploitation of the work and does not prejudice the legitimate interests of the rights holder. Ruling in favour of the European Union, the WTO panel noted that the size specified under the United States exemption was quite large, meaning that a substantial majority of premises were covered by it. This included places which would have the commercial ability to pay royalty fees to the rights holders of the music. The United States law was simply not sufficiently protective of music rights holders.

Second, trademarks are signs that distinguish goods based on their source and distinctiveness. Under TRIPS, trademark protection must be extended for

11 Article 9

12 Article 10

13 European Communities – Section 110(5) of the United States Copyright Act, WT/DS160/R, adopted 27 July 2000

seven years and are renewable indefinitely. Trademarks require commercial use and registration. TRIPS defines what types of signs must be eligible for protection and sets out the minimum rights conferred on their owners.[14] It also provides special protection for well-known marks.[15]

Some of the most valuable trademarks in the world today include Apple, the Apple logo and name are among the most recognizable and valuable trademarks globally; Google, both the name and the multicoloured logo are highly valuable trademarks; Microsoft, the name and the four-square window logo are significant assets; Amazon, the name and the "smile" arrow logo are extremely valuable trademarks; Coca-Cola, the distinctive script and red colour are iconic trademarks; McDonald's, the golden arches logo is one of the most recognized trademarks worldwide; Nike, the "swoosh" symbol is a highly valuable trademark. It is noteworthy that these leading trademarks are associated with both goods and services and are internationally known, denoting significant value in terms of trade. The value of trademarks arises not just from their recognition but also from their ability to command premium pricing, customer loyalty, and market share in their respective industries.

Under TRIPS, trademarks that have been registered in any member country grant the owner the exclusive right to prevent all third parties not having the owner's consent from using in the course of business identical or similar signs for goods or services which are identical or similar to those for which the trademark was registered. The purpose of this guarantee is to prevent confusion among consumers in the marketplace, a situation which tends to be presumed when there is a sufficient degree of similarity. Precisely how the notion of similarity will be determined is up to the domestic legal system of each WTO member state.

Unlike copyright, once registered, trademarks can be protected for an unlimited period. This reflects the essential commercial purpose of the trademark as distinct from copyrighted works of art which have cultural value independent of their economic worth. Members may, and many do, require that trademark registrations be renewed, but this may not be more than once every seven years. Members are free to determine any conditions attached to the licensing and assigning of trademarks under their national laws, although TRIPS maintains a prohibition on the compulsory licensing of trademarks.

Australia – Tobacco[16] was one of the key trademark disputes dealt with through the WTO dispute settlement system. This high-profile dispute, initiated by several countries against Australia's plain packaging laws for tobacco products, had significant implications for public health policies and trademark rights. In 2018, the WTO panel ruled largely in favour of Australia, finding that the measures were not more trade-restrictive than necessary to fulfil a legitimate objective.

14 Articles 15–21

15 Article 16.2–16.3

16 Australia – Certain Measures Concerning Trademarks, Geographical Indications and Other Plain Packaging Requirements Applicable to Tobacco Products and Packaging, WT/DS435/AB/R, WT/DS441/AB/R, adopted 29 June 2020

An earlier dispute, *United States – Section 211 Omnibus Appropriations Act of 1998*[17] was instigated by the European Communities against the United States in 1999, challenging a United States law that prevented Cuban nationals from renewing certain trademarks. The Appellate Body found that aspects of the United States law violated national treatment and most-favoured-nation obligations under TRIPS, highlighting the intersection of IP rights and political considerations.

Third, TRIPS introduces provisions on geographical indications (GIs), requiring members to provide legal means to prevent the use of misleading geographical indications and prohibiting the registration of geographical indications for wines and spirits that are not originating in the place indicated.[18] GIs are a form of intellectual property protected under the TRIPS. They identify goods as originating in a particular territory, region, or locality where a given quality, reputation, or other characteristic of the good is essentially attributable to its geographical origin. GIs therefore resemble trademarks, except that they are always related to a particular geographical point of origin. Some of the most well-known geographical indications include Champagne from France, Scotch Whisky from Scotland, Parmigiano Reggiano from specific provinces in Italy, Darjeeling Tea from India, and Roquefort cheese from France.

TRIPS provides that WTO members must make sure that they prevent the misuse of place names by competitors seeking to take unfair advantage of the goodwill associated with products from particular locations by misleading consumers. In order to qualify for GI status under any member's national laws it is not necessary to show that the product from that geographical area is, in fact, better or different from a similar product that comes from somewhere else. All that must be shown is that a particular reputation or goodwill has been established in that location with respect to that product, meaning that consumers are choosing to buy that particular variety of goods because of its association with that place and its distinctive tradition or culture. To avoid the use of a geographical indicator that misleads the public in this respect, producers may use qualifying words like "imitation" or "like," such as "Basmati-style" rice or "Roquefort-style" cheese.

The makers of alcoholic beverages tend to be concerned about geographical indications because this is a vital component of their distinctiveness and therefore their competitive advantage. TRIPS consequently grants higher levels of protection for geographical indicators for wines and spirits. Competitors may not use the geographical name to link with their product even where there is no danger of the public being misled and there is no provision to qualify the product's origin using "imitation" or "like." A special additional agreement on geographical indications for wines was negotiated as part of the Doha Round agenda. The extra protection for wine and spirits is viewed by some as a legitimate way of protecting hard-won reputational advantages, whereas others see the tougher rules as an unnecessary restriction on marketing that is ultimately against consumer interests.

17 United States – Section 211 Omnibus Appropriations Act of 1998, WT/DS176/AB/R, adopted 1 February 2002
18 Articles 22–24

Some exceptions for protected geographical indication status are allowed under TRIPS, such as if the name has already become a generic term and it is now too late to restrict the association to a particular location. For example, cheddar now refers to a particular type of medium-hard yellowish cheese but it does not have to come from Cheddar, England, where it was originally made centuries ago. Parmesan cheese as it is now known in most English-speaking countries outside of Europe (originally Parmigiano-Reggiano cheese from Italy) also falls within this exception.

EC – Protection of Trademarks and Geographical Indications for Agricultural Products and Foodstuffs[19] was a key geographical indicator case initiated by the United States and Australia against the European Union in 2003. It addressed the EU's system for protecting GIs. The complainants argued that the EU system discriminated against non-EU GIs and failed to protect trademarks adequately. The panel found that certain aspects of the EU's geographical indicators regulation were inconsistent with TRIPS, leading to changes in EU law and influencing global GI protection standards.

The protection of GIs has been a source of controversy and debate in international trade negotiations. One key issue is the scope of protection. The European Union advocates for a high level of protection for all products, while countries like the United States prefer a more limited approach, primarily focused on wines and spirits. This disagreement reflects fundamental differences in how various nations view the relationship between geographical origin and product quality.

Another contentious issue in relation to GIs is the treatment of generic terms. Some names that are protected GIs in one country may be considered generic terms in another. For example, "feta" is a protected GI in the European Union but is considered a generic cheese type in many other countries. This discrepancy has led to trade disputes and complicated negotiations in international forums. Conflicts between GIs and existing trademarks have also emerged as a significant challenge. The resolution of these conflicts varies by jurisdiction and has been a point of contention in trade negotiations. This issue highlights the complex interaction between different forms of intellectual property protection in a globalized economy.

Proponents argue that GIs protect traditional knowledge and support rural development. Critics, however, contend that they can create barriers to trade and limit competition. This disagreement reflects broader tensions between the protection of local traditions and the promotion of free trade. Implementation challenges present another set of issues, particularly for developing countries. Many nations face difficulties in establishing and enforcing GI protection systems due to limited resources and institutional capacity. This situation has led to calls for increased technical assistance and capacity building in the realm of intellectual property protection.[20] These controversies have played out in various international

19 European Communities – Protection of Trademarks and Geographical Indications for Agricultural Products and Foodstuffs, WT/DS290/R, adopted 20 April 2005

20 D Gangjee, *Relocating the Law of Geographical Indications* (Cambridge University Press, 2012)

forums, including WTO negotiations and bilateral trade agreements. The European Union has been pushing for stronger GI protections in its trade agreements, while the United States has generally resisted these efforts. This ongoing debate reflects the complex intersection of intellectual property rights, trade policy, and cultural heritage in the global economy.[21]

Fourth and finally, TRIPS requires member countries to make patents available for any inventions in all fields of technology, provided they are new, involve an inventive step, and are capable of industrial application.[22] Patents cover new inventions that have industrial applications, meaning that they have a practical, commercial use. TRIPS allows requirements on patentability and ensures that protection must be granted for at least twenty years, after which point the invention can be reproduced commercially. Exceptions for patentability exist to protect the public interest – this will be examined further in relation to compulsory licensing.

Typically, some of the most valuable patents tend to belong to major technology, pharmaceutical, and engineering companies. Patents related to key technologies in areas like telecommunications, artificial intelligence, biotechnology, and renewable energy are often considered highly valuable. For example, patents related to 5G technology, gene editing, electric vehicle batteries, or key smartphone features have become very valuable in recent years. The exact value of individual patents is often not publicly disclosed and can change over time based on technological developments and market conditions.

It is important to understand that, after the patent lapses, the underlying inventions may be reproduced lawfully without any payment or royalties or permission from the original patent holder. The twenty-year minimum time frame is intended to balance the incentives needed to encourage innovation and creativity while ensuring that useful inventions may be widely disseminated to maximize their value to society, once the original inventor has been sufficiently rewarded for their work. TRIPS requires that patents must confer exclusive rights on the patent holder to sell the relevant product or process and to assign or license it to third parties.

Patents must be available under the national laws of member states for both products as well as processes and are extended in almost all fields of technology. Governments may refuse to issue a patent if its commercial exploitation is disallowed for reasons of public order or morality. TRIPS permits governments to decline to register patents for plants and animals or for surgical or diagnostic methods. The rationale for these latter exceptions is that it is in the public interest to have useful medical procedures made as widely available as possible.

WTO members may exclude from patentability inventions which deserve to be protected from commercial exploitation because they are necessary in order to safeguard public order, public morality and the need to protect human, animal or plant life, or health as well as to avoid serious prejudice to the environment. These exceptions must not be abused – if the member country is willing to allow the

21 M Blakeney, *The Protection of Geographical Indications: Law and Practice* (Elgar, 2014)
22 Article 27.1

commercial exploitation of an invention that was created by one of its own nationals but attempts to restrict its patentability by a foreigner, then it will not be able to take advantage of this provision.

In *Indonesia – Autos,*[23] the panel examined the United States complaint against Indonesia regarding its national car program, which required participating vehicles to bear a unique, domestically owned Indonesian trademark. The United States argued that the Indonesian law discriminated against nationals of other WTO members with respect to the "acquisition" and "maintenance" of trademark rights as specified in footnote 3 to Article 3. This provision defines the type of "protection" embraced by TRIPS to include matters affecting the availability, acquisition, scope, maintenance and enforcement of intellectual property rights as well as those matters affecting the use of intellectual property rights, including trademarks. The panel rejected the United States claim regarding an impairment to the acquisition of trademarks, reasoning that the program merely stipulated that only certain signs could be used as trademarks, and there was no evidence that the right to trademarks excluded from the program could not be obtained in a non-discriminatory manner under Indonesian law.

Despite the fact that they strongly incentivized firms to undertake expensive foreign registration activities (registering trademarks in Indonesia rather than in their home state), the measure was not genuinely discriminatory based on national origin. Furthermore, as to the maintenance of trademarks, in *Indonesia – Autos* the United States had argued that partners in the national car program would be unlikely to use their global trademarks in Indonesia out of fear of confusing consumers. It would be more likely, they asserted, that the global trademark would be cancelled for non-use in Indonesia. There is nothing obviously unfair in requiring a firm to register its intellectual property domestically since this type of system subjects foreign firms to precisely the same rules as it does domestic firms. Full National Treatment would allow every firm to seek intellectual property protection in its home country rather than require it to establish such rights over the host state in which it invests, effectively establishing local brands as well as bringing intellectual property-based claims in the courts of the host state rather than in its own.

TRIPS' patent rules came under scrutiny by a WTO panel in the *Canada – Pharmaceuticals*[24] dispute. This dispute involved a complaint brought by the European Communities against Canada's regulatory patent review provisions which permitted the general manufacturers of pharmaceuticals to produce samples of the patented product for use during the regulatory review process. The European Communities had argued that this law was discriminatory because it was aimed at pharmaceutical products which, in practice, only foreign firms created. Holding that the European Communities did not demonstrate that the regulatory review provision was discriminatory either *de jure* or *de facto*, the panel elaborated that

23 Indonesia – Certain Measures Affecting the Automobile Industry, WT/DS54/R, WT/DS55/R, WT/DS59/R, WT/DS64/R, adopted 23 July 1998

24 Canada – Patent Protection of Pharmaceutical Products, WT/DS114/R, adopted 7 April 2000

the term "discrimination" potentially encompasses a wide range of meanings and should be construed on a case-by-case basis within the precise context of the issue at hand. The panel did not explain how the phrase "whether products are imported or locally produced" should be interpreted. It may require WTO members to apply exceptions in a non-discriminatory manner in order to ensure that governments do not engage in protectionism where intellectual property rights holders tend to be foreign firms. The provision could also be seen to impose a duty on member states not to deny patents on the basis of the field of technology or the location of the firm that develops it.

India – Patent Protection for Pharmaceuticals[25] was another important patent dispute, initiated by the United States against India in 1996. The United States claimed that India had failed to establish a mechanism for filing patent applications for pharmaceutical and agricultural chemical products, as required by TRIPS Article 70.8. The panel ruled in favour of the United States, leading to changes in India's patent laws and significantly impacting the global generic drug industry. In *India – Patent Protection for Pharmaceutical and Agricultural Chemical Products,*[26] which was similar to the previous case against Canada but brought against India, further reinforced the need for India to implement a "mailbox" system for patent applications as required by TRIPS Article 70.8. A mailbox patent system is a requirement for developing countries to receive and file patent applications from countries that are delaying the implementation of domestic patent laws. The term comes from the metaphorical "mailbox" that stores and receives the applications. In another patent case, *Canada – Term of Patent Protection,*[27] the United States argued that Canada's patent term for patents filed before 1989 violated TRIPS Article 33, which requires a minimum patent term of 20 years from the filing date. The Appellate Body ruled in favour of the United States, leading Canada to amend its Patent Act.

9.2.3 Compulsory Licensing

The compulsory licensing provisions of the TRIPS Agreement, found in Article 31, have been a source of significant controversy and debate since the agreement's inception. These provisions allow governments to authorize the use of a patented invention without the consent of the patent holder under certain circumstances, which has led to tensions between developed and developing countries as well as between the pharmaceutical industry and public health advocates.

The scope of the license is limited to the purpose for which it was authorized. Remuneration will be paid to the rights holder. This highly controversial mechanism generally operates during a national health emergency when members are

25 India – Patent Protection for Pharmaceutical and Agricultural Chemical Products, WT/DS50/AB/R, adopted 16 January 1998

26 Ibid., WT/DS79/R, adopted 22 September 1998

27 Canada – Term of Patent Protection, WT/DS170/AB/R, adopted 12 October 2000

unable to afford patented drugs in needed quantities. Most of the countries that might wish to take advantage of the compulsory licensing provision in order to combat the spread of deadly diseases like AIDS and malaria are the very ones that lack the technological ability to duplicate pharmaceuticals cheaply. In order to deal with this problem, the WTO decided in 2001 to allow generic copies of drugs that were made under compulsory licenses to be exported to specific countries that lack production capacity. In other words, developed countries are allowed under WTO law to manufacture generic medications on behalf of the listed poor countries that need them in emergency circumstances, provided that some compensation is paid to the patent holder.

Emergency and adequate compensation are not defined under TRIPS. Norway, Canada, India, the European Union, and China have indicated their openness to such regimes as exporters of generic medicines to developing countries. Thus far only Canada has actually used the compulsory licensing scheme to supply medicine to a developing country, allowing the pharmaceutical company Apotex to export a generic AIDS medication to Rwanda.

During the Covid-19 pandemic, most of the approved vaccines were developed by firms in developed countries (as well as China and Russia) but the Western-made mRNA vaccines were thought to be the most effective and therefore the most in-demand. Low-income countries consequently had a much lower vaccination rate. This imbalance led the WTO, in 2022, to approve a waiver of protections for Covid-19 vaccine patents, previously secured under TRIPS. High-income countries were initially opposed to the waiver on the grounds that it would have an adverse effect on innovation, as well as pharmaceutical quality and safety. These countries ultimately eased their objections once they were sufficiently supplied with vaccines.

One of the primary controversies surrounding compulsory licensing is the balance between protecting intellectual property rights and ensuring access to essential medicines, particularly in developing countries. TRIPS was negotiated with substantial input from the multinational pharmaceutical industry, which sought to establish strong patent protection on a global basis. This tension became particularly apparent during the HIV/AIDS crisis in the late 1990s and early 2000s when developing countries sought to use compulsory licensing to produce or import generic versions of patented antiretroviral drugs.[28]

The interpretation and implementation of Article 31 have been contentious. Developed countries and pharmaceutical companies have often argued for a narrow interpretation of the circumstances under which compulsory licenses can be issued. In contrast, developing countries and public health advocates have pushed for a broader interpretation to address public health crises. This debate led to the adoption of the Doha Declaration on the TRIPS Agreement and Public Health in 2001, which affirmed that the TRIPS Agreement does not and should not prevent members from taking measures to protect public health.

28 FM Abbott, "The TRIPS Agreement, Access to Medicines, and the WTO Doha Ministerial Conference" 5:1 Journal of World Intellectual Property 15 (2002)

Another significant controversy in relation to compulsory licensing relates to countries lacking manufacturing capacity in the pharmaceutical sector. Article 31(f) of TRIPS originally limited compulsory licensing predominantly to supply the domestic market, which posed a problem for countries unable to manufacture medicines domestically. This provision effectively precluded the possibility for developing countries without manufacturing capacities to make effective use of compulsory licensing.[29] This issue was partially addressed by the 2003 WTO decision to waive Article 31(f) under certain conditions, later formalized as Article 31bis of the TRIPS.

The effectiveness of the compulsory licensing system has also been debated. While some argue that the mere threat of compulsory licensing can lead to price reductions and improved access to medicines, others contend that the system is too cumbersome and politically fraught to be widely used. The administrative and procedural requirements for compulsory licensing under Article 31 of the TRIPS Agreement make it difficult for developing countries to make expeditious use of this flexibility.[30] The use of compulsory licensing has often led to diplomatic tensions and trade pressures. Developed countries, particularly the United States, have been accused of using bilateral and regional trade agreements to impose "TRIPS-plus" provisions that limit the use of compulsory licensing.

The Covid-19 pandemic reignited debates over compulsory licensing and intellectual property rights more broadly. The proposal for a TRIPS waiver for Covid-19 vaccines and treatments, initially put forward by India and South Africa in October 2020, highlighted ongoing disagreements about the appropriate balance between innovation incentives and global public health needs. The waiver debate reflects longstanding tensions between the Global North and South over the role of intellectual property rights in promoting innovation and ensuring equitable access to medicines.[31]

Critics of the current compulsory licensing system argue that it does not adequately address the needs of developing countries, particularly in emergency situations. They contend that the process is too slow, complex, and subject to political pressures. To some, the compulsory licensing system under TRIPS has proven to be an insufficient and inappropriate mechanism to address public health needs, especially in the context of a global pandemic. Proponents of strong intellectual property protection, on the other hand, argue that compulsory licensing, if overused, could undermine incentives for pharmaceutical innovation. They contend that the existing flexibilities in TRIPS are sufficient to address public health concerns when properly implemented. A balance must be struck between providing access to existing medicines and maintaining incentives for the development of new ones.

29 H Hestermeyer, *Human Rights and the WTO: The Case of Patents and Access to Medicines* (Oxford University Press, 2007)

30 JH Reichman, "Compulsory Licensing of Patented Pharmaceutical Inventions: Evaluating the Options" 37:2 Journal of Law, Medicine & Ethics 247 (2009)

31 B Mercurio, "WTO Waiver from Intellectual Property Protection for COVID-19 Vaccines and Treatments: A Critical Review" 62:1 Virginia Journal of International Law 9 (2021)

9.2.4 TRIPS and Developing Countries

The question of whether the interests of developing countries are adequately addressed by the WTO TRIPS Agreement is a subject of much debate. In one sense, TRIPS does provide a framework for intellectual property protection that can stimulate innovation and foreign direct investment in developing countries. TRIPS contains provisions aimed at supporting developing countries, such as Article 66.2, which requires developed country members to provide incentives for technology transfer to least-developed countries. Additionally, the Doha Declaration on TRIPS and Public Health in 2001 reaffirmed flexibility for developing countries to protect public health, particularly regarding access to medicines.

However, critics argue that TRIPS primarily serves the interests of developed countries and multinational enterprises, potentially hindering development and access to knowledge in the Global South. The TRIPS Agreement was designed primarily by developed countries for the benefit of their industries. The agreement has been criticized for imposing one-size-fits-all standards that may not be appropriate for countries at different stages of development.[32]

One major concern is the impact of TRIPS on access to medicines in developing countries. While the Doha Declaration provided some flexibility, implementation has been challenging. Developing countries have faced persistent pressure from developed countries and their pharmaceutical industries when seeking to implement TRIPS obligations. Furthermore, some argue that TRIPS limits policy space for developing countries to tailor intellectual property regimes to their specific needs and development goals. Some countries may not be ready for these obligations. TRIPS prematurely requires developing and least-developed countries to adhere to relatively high standards of intellectual property protection before their national innovation systems have sufficiently matured. Accepting the strict requirements of TRIPS is one of the reasons that has led to delays to WTO accession, notably in the case of China and Russia. Since TRIPS appears to provide a necessary legal framework for protecting intellectual property, this could encourage innovation and foreign investment in developing countries. Stronger IPRs may well expand the flow of technology to developing countries under the right circumstances.

Intellectual property is often viewed as the product of advanced economies where there are resources available to support research and innovation and where large, competitive markets encourage companies to improve their products and services. In that sense, the protection of intellectual property through TRIPS and other instruments may foreclose developing countries from participating more fully in trade. Mandatory technology transfer obligations in trade agreements may be one way to rectify this imbalance.

The technology transfer provisions in the TRIPS Agreement, particularly Article 66.2, require developed country members to provide incentives to enterprises

32 PK Yu, "The Objectives and Principles of the TRIPS Agreement" 46 Houston Law Review 979 (2009)

and institutions in their territories to promote and encourage technology transfer to least-developed country (LDC) members. This provision aims to enable LDCs to create a sound and viable technological base. However, the effectiveness of Article 66.2 has been criticized on several grounds. The provision lacks specificity, as it does not clearly define what constitutes adequate "incentives" or "technology transfer," making it difficult to enforce or measure compliance. Moreover, the obligation only applies to transfers to LDCs, excluding other developing countries that may also benefit from technology transfer. Critics also argue that developed countries have not provided sufficient or effective incentives to meaningfully increase technology transfer to LDCs. Many developed nations often report on general development assistance programs rather than specific technology transfer incentives, leading to questions about whether they are truly meeting their obligations under Article 66.2.

The enforcement of this provision of TRIPS has proven challenging, partly because intellectual property rights are recognized as private rights under TRIPS, making it difficult for governments to compel the transfer of technologies they may not directly control. Additionally, some observers have noted that many LDCs lack the absorptive capacity to effectively utilize transferred technologies, limiting the impact of the provision even when implemented.[33] It may be necessary to strengthen the implementation and monitoring of Article 66.2 as well as explore alternative mechanisms to promote technology transfer to developing countries.

9.2.5 Intellectual Property and Trade Retaliation

Under Article 22.3 of the WTO Dispute Settlement Understanding, a country that has been harmed by a violation of a WTO agreement may – in certain circumstances – retaliate against the other country by withholding benefits under a different WTO agreement. The use of intellectual property protection under the TRIPS agreement as a form of retaliation for breaching other WTO rules is a controversial issue. While the WTO dispute settlement system allows for cross-retaliation in certain circumstances, using TRIPS obligations as leverage raises significant legal and practical concerns.

The WTO's dispute settlement system generally requires that retaliation be taken in the same sector as the violation. However, in some cases, the Dispute Settlement Body (DSB) has authorized cross-retaliation, allowing a complaining party to suspend concessions in a different sector or agreement. This is particularly relevant for developing countries that may lack the economic leverage to effectively retaliate in the same sector.

The small Caribbean country Antigua applied for permission to cross-retaliate under Article 22 when the United States failed to uphold its obligations, having

33 CM Correa, "Can the TRIPS Agreement Foster Technology Transfer to Developing Countries?" in KE Maskus and JH Reichman (Eds.), *International Public Goods and Transfer of Technology Under a Globalized Intellectual Property Regime* (Cambridge University Press, 2005)

lost the *United States – Gambling* dispute (in which it applied unlawful restrictions on Antiguan online gambling services). A WTO arbitrator found that Antigua could seek to suspend obligations under the TRIPS Agreement. Antigua's determination that it was not practicable or effective to suspend concessions or other obligations with respect to the same sector as that in which a violation was found (online gambling) was seen as consistent with the requirements of Article 22.3. Permitting this has arguably set a precedent. Antigua is a small country and thus has limited ability to effect significant economic damage by suspending intellectual property protections. Countries with larger economies could do the same, this could be quite problematic for intellectual property rights holders – potentially leading to damages in the billions of dollars.

Issues of cross-retaliation in intellectual property arose in other disputes. When the United States failed to comply with a WTO ruling on cotton subsidies,[34] Brazil sought authorization to cross-retaliate by suspending TRIPS. In that case, Brazil never acted on its authorization to suspend TRIPS obligations. Cross-retaliation may be viewed as a way that developing countries can use their rights within the WTO system to encourage more economically dominant countries to abide by the agreements that make up the WTO system. But, it may be politically dangerous for developing countries to do so. The main barrier facing the less powerful WTO members in seeking to implement cross-retaliation in TRIPS is likely to be political in nature, in the form of pressures from industry groups and governments of more powerful members.

The suspension of TRIPS obligations may prove to be the most effective form of cross-retaliation for developing WTO members. Suspending patent protection for pharmaceuticals or copyright for software could create significant pressure on developed countries to comply with WTO rulings. Using the non-protection of intellectual property as a retaliatory tool could undermine the global intellectual property system and potentially harm innovation and technology transfer. The use of TRIPS retaliation could create an atmosphere of uncertainty in the international intellectual property system and may reduce incentives for research and development in critical areas.

The legality of using TRIPS obligations as retaliation is also debatable. The phrase "cross-retaliation" does not appear in the WTO Dispute Settlement Understanding but is shorthand to describe a situation where the complaining country retaliates (i.e., suspends concessions or other obligations) under a sector or an agreement which has not been violated by the defending country. While "cross-retaliation" is permitted under WTO rules, it must still meet certain criteria, including proportionality and effectiveness. The suspension of TRIPS obligations must therefore be carefully calibrated to ensure it does not exceed the level of nullification or impairment caused by the original violation.[35] Furthermore, the practical implementation of TRIPS-based retaliation could be challenging. Developing countries may lack the institutional capacity to effectively suspend IP

34 United States – Subsidies on Upland Cotton, WT/DS267/AB/R, adopted 21 March 2005

35 J Pauwelyn, "The Calculation and Design of Trade Retaliation in Context: What Is the Goal of Suspending WTO Obligations?" in C Brown and J Pauwelyn (Eds.), *The Law, Economics and Politics of Retaliation in WTO Dispute Settlement* (Cambridge University Press, 2010)

protections without causing unintended harm to their own economies. Additionally, such actions could potentially violate other international agreements or bilateral treaties. It is also important to consider the broader implications for the multilateral trading system. Some believe that using intellectual property as a retaliatory tool could lead to a fragmentation of the international intellectual property system and could undermine the WTO's role in global governance.[36]

9.3 Intellectual Property and FTAs

TRIPS has been the most important intellectual property agreement in the world with regard to its impact on trade. But, as with many spheres of law, preferential FTAs have gone further than TRIPS in some respects. Most intellectual property chapters of FTAs tend to reiterate the principles found in TRIPS, but some go further.

Many FTAs exceed the TRIPS in terms of intellectual property protection through provisions often referred to as "TRIPS-plus," as mentioned earlier. Unsurprisingly, United States FTAs are notable for this, given that the United States is home to many of the world's most innovative companies. For example, with respect to copyright term extension, the United States-Singapore FTA requires protection for the life of the author plus 70 years (Article 16.4.4). This is also found in the EU-South Korea FTA's Article 10.6.

While the TRIPS has no specific provision for data exclusivity, the period during which the medicine marketing authorization holder enjoys exclusive rights to the data obtained from preclinical and clinical trials, the United States-Korea FTA specifies five years for new chemical entities, three years for new clinical information (Article 18.9.1). The EU-Canada CETA grants this protection for six to eight years (Article 20.29).

Article 17.9.8 of the United States-Australia FTA provides for patent term extension to compensate for unreasonable delays in patent examination or marketing approval – a feature which does not appear in TRIPS. Moreover, there are no specific provisions on Digital Rights Management in the TRIPS. In contrast, the United States-Chile FTA prohibits circumvention of technological measures that control access to copyrighted works (Article 17.7.5). Similarly and controversially, there are no specific provisions on Internet Service Provider liability for intellectual property breaches in the TRIPs. The United States-Colombia FTA includes detailed provisions on ISP liability and safe harbours (Article 16.11.29).

The TRIPS Agreement offers quite basic protection for GIs via Articles 22–24. The EU-Japan Economic Partnership Agreement sets out a list of specific GIs to be protected, going beyond TRIPS (Chapter 14, Annex 14-B). While TRIPS has general provisions on enforcement, found in Part III, the EU-Vietnam FTA establishes more detailed provisions on border measures, including ex officio action by customs authorities (Article 12.43).

36 H Grosse Ruse-Khan, "A Pirate of the Caribbean? The Attractions of Suspending TRIPS Obligations" 11:2 Journal of International Economic Law 313 (2008)

Interestingly, TRIPS does not require accession to additional intellectual property treaties whereas article 15.1.2 of the United States-Morocco FTA requires parties to ratify or accede to several WIPO treaties. Finally, traditional knowledge and genetic resources are addressed through very basic provisions in TRIPS; the 2001 Doha Declaration mandates that the TRIPS Council considers the protection of traditional knowledge and folklore. The Peru-China FTA includes specific binding provisions on protecting traditional knowledge and genetic resources (Article 145).

The CPTPP includes a chapter on intellectual property rights that aims to establish consistent standards for intellectual property protection and enforcement across party countries. The CPTPP's intellectual property protections include patent protection found in Article 18.37. This requires member countries to make patents available for inventions in all fields of technology, provided they are new, involve an inventive step, and are capable of industrial application. The CPTPP's trademark protection is contained in Article 18.18 which specifies that parties must provide trademark protection, including for collective and certification marks. Article 18.78 obliges parties to ensure legal means to prevent misappropriation of trade secrets. Articles 18.30 to 18.36 establish procedures for the protection and recognition of geographical indications.

Article 18.63 of the TPP which would have required extending copyright protection to the life of the author plus 70 years, was suspended when the agreement became the CPTPP (after the United States departure). This means that CPTPP countries are not obligated to extend their copyright terms beyond their current domestic laws. For example, New Zealand will maintain its existing copyright term of 50 years after the end of the calendar year in which the author died for books, screenplays, music, lyrics, and artistic works. For films and sound recordings, the term expires 50 years after the end of the calendar year in which they were made or published. This change reflects a more balanced approach to intellectual property rights in the CPTPP, taking into account the diverse interests of the remaining parties after the United States withdrew from the agreement. It is also, of course, consistent with the protections required under TRIPS.

Enforcement measures for these rights are found in articles 18.71 to 18.77 of the CPTPP. These outline civil and administrative procedures and remedies for IP infringement, including provisions for damages and injunctive relief, much as contained in TRIPS. The IP chapter of the CPTPP further establishes that customs authorities have the power to suspend the release of suspected counterfeit or pirated goods.[37] Some argue that the patent protections in Article 18.37 could delay the entry of generic drugs into the market, potentially affecting access to affordable medicines. Moreover, the digital rights management provision,[38] which provides legal protections against the circumvention of technological protection measures, may be viewed as potentially limiting fair use and innovation. Additionally, the CPTPP's robust enforcement measures have raised concerns about potential

37 Article 18.76
38 Article 18.68

overreach and impact on Internet freedom. A party's failure to fulfil its intellectual property obligations under the CPTPP could be resolved via arbitration under the agreement's dispute settlement provisions.

Regarding patent term extensions, the CPTPP requires member countries to provide these extensions to compensate for unreasonable delays in patent examination or regulatory approval processes, as stipulated in Article 18.46. In contrast, RCEP does not mandate patent term extensions instead leaving this decision to individual member countries, as outlined in RCEP Chapter 11, Section C.

Data exclusivity is another area of divergence between the CPTPP and RCEP two mega-regional agreements. The CPTPP provides for at least five years of data exclusivity for new pharmaceutical products and three years for new clinical information, as stated in Article 18.50. RCEP, however, does not include specific provisions on data exclusivity, again leaving this matter to national legislation, as per RCEP Chapter 11.

Both RCEP and CPTPP include provisions on Technological Protection Measures (TPMs), but the CPTPP's provisions are more detailed and stringent. TPMs refer to legal provisions that prohibit the circumvention of technological measures used to protect copyrighted work. The CPTPP requires criminal penalties for circumvention of TPMs, as per Article 18.68, while RCEP only requires "effective legal remedies," as stated in Article 11.15. Internet Service Provider (ISP) liability is another area where the agreements diverge. The CPTPP includes detailed provisions on ISP liability and safe harbours in Article 18.82 while RCEP only includes a general provision encouraging cooperation between ISPs and right holders, as outlined in RCEP Article 11.13.

The enforcement provisions in the two agreements also differ significantly. The CPTPP includes more detailed and stringent enforcement provisions, including requirements for pre-established damages and criminal procedures for commercial-scale trademark counterfeiting and copyright piracy, as stipulated in CPTPP Articles 18.74 and 18.77. RCEP's enforcement provisions, found in Section J, are less prescriptive. Finally, RCEP includes provisions on genetic resources, traditional knowledge, and folklore in Article 11.53, which are not present in the CPTPP. This reflects the diverse membership of RCEP, which includes countries with varying approaches to these issues.

Some mention should be made of the plurilateral Digital Economy Partnership Agreement (DEPA) which will be explored further in the next chapter on Digital Trade. While DEPA does not deal with intellectual property directly, some of its provisions have relevance to intellectual property. Article 1.4: states that DEPA shall not apply to the extent of any inconsistency with a Party's rights and obligations concerning intellectual property contained in another international agreement a Party is party to. Moreover, in Module 9 (Innovation and the Digital Economy), Article 9.3 on Public Domain specifies that parties "recognise the importance of a rich and accessible public domain" and that they "acknowledge the importance of informational materials, such as publicly accessible databases of registered intellectual property rights that assist in the identification of subject matter that has fallen into the public domain." Unlike some other digital trade agreements, like the digital trade chapter of the USMCA, DEPA does not include provisions prohibiting forced disclosure of source code or protecting intellectual property rights in the digital realm. The lack of robust intellectual property provisions may be viewed as a potential shortcoming of the DEPA.

There have been few trade disputes under the arbitration provisions of FTAs relating to intellectual property rights as they often take the form of investment disputes.[39] Moreover, many intellectual property-related disputes under FTAs are resolved through consultations or other non-litigious means, which may not be publicly reported. The relative lack of formal disputes does not necessarily indicate a lack of conflict over the implementation of FTA obligations relating to intellectual property.[40]

Technology transfer features in TRIPS and is dealt with in various FTAs. For example, the EU-Vietnam Free Trade Agreement (EVFTA) which entered into force in 2020, includes specific provisions on technology transfer. Article 12.3 of the agreement states that "the Parties shall facilitate access to and use of technology and promote, facilitate and, where appropriate, finance projects relating to transfer of technology." While not explicitly labelled as technology transfer, Chapter 18 of the CPTPP on Intellectual Property contains provisions that can facilitate technology transfer. For example, Article 18.16 addresses cooperation in patent processing, which can indirectly promote technology transfer. The USMCA includes provisions related to technology transfer in its Chapter 19 on Digital Trade. Article 19.18 specifically addresses government information and access to software source code, which can impact technology transfer. Although not yet ratified, the EU-MERCOSUR agreement includes a chapter on Technology Transfer (Chapter XX). It emphasizes the importance of technology transfer for sustainable development and includes provisions for cooperation in this area.

The China-ASEAN Free Trade Agreement includes provisions for technology cooperation and transfer, particularly in areas such as agriculture, information technology, and environmental protection. The Japan-India Economic Partnership Agreement contains a dedicated chapter (Chapter 8) on Technical Cooperation and Capacity Building which includes provisions related to technology transfer. Finally, AfCFTA includes provisions for technology transfer, particularly in the context of sustainable development and industrialization.

9.4 Indigenous and Traditional Knowledge

In some respects, Indigenous traditional knowledge conflicts with Western concepts of intellectual property, such as those referenced in TRIPS and in FTAs. One fundamental difference lies in the concept of ownership. Indigenous knowledge is typically held collectively by communities and passed down through generations,

39 For example, *Eli Lilly and Company v The Government of Canada*, UNCITRAL, ICSID Case No. UNCT/14/2, Award, 16 March 2017

40 B Mercurio, "Awakening the Sleeping Giant: Intellectual Property Rights in International Investment Agreements" 15:3 Journal of International Economic Law 871 (2012)

rather than owned by individuals. Western intellectual property systems, in contrast, focus on individual creators and time-limited rights. This fundamental difference in ownership concepts makes it challenging to fit traditional knowledge into existing intellectual property frameworks.[41] Another significant disparity is the mode of knowledge transmission. Much Indigenous knowledge is preserved orally rather than in written form. Western intellectual property systems generally require written documentation, making it difficult to establish prior art or prove ownership of traditional knowledge. This reliance on written records can disadvantage Indigenous communities whose knowledge is primarily oral.[42]

The holistic nature of indigenous knowledge also poses challenges when interfacing with Western intellectual property systems. Indigenous knowledge often integrates spiritual, cultural, and practical elements holistically. Western IP, on the other hand, tends to compartmentalize knowledge into discrete, protectable units. This reductionist approach can fail to capture the interconnected nature of traditional knowledge systems.

The concept of time in relation to knowledge protection is another area of conflict. Indigenous communities view their traditional knowledge as a perpetual heritage to be preserved indefinitely. Most Western intellectual property rights, however, expire after a set time period, which is incompatible with Indigenous notions of intergenerational knowledge.[43] Furthermore, there is a fundamental difference in how the value of knowledge is perceived. Western intellectual property systems are primarily designed to provide economic incentives and commercial exploitation rights. Indigenous peoples often prioritize the cultural, spiritual, and community value of their knowledge over its commercial potential.[44]

These fundamental differences have led to numerous cases of exploitation of traditional knowledge by Western companies, often termed "biopiracy." One notable example is the case of the neem tree. In 1994, the European Patent Office granted a patent to W.R. Grace Company for a fungicide derived from the neem tree, despite its long history of use in Indian traditional medicine. After a decade-long legal battle, the patent was revoked in 2005 due to lack of novelty.[45] Another instance of biopiracy involves ayahuasca, a traditional Amazonian plant preparation. In 1986, American scientist Loren Miller patented a variety of the Amazonian plant *Banisteriopsis caapi*, used in traditional ayahuasca ceremonies. The patent was initially revoked after protests from Indigenous groups but later reinstated. This case

41 C Oguamanam, "Localizing Intellectual Property in the Globalization Epoch: The Integration of Indigenous Knowledge" 11:2 Indiana Journal of Global Legal Studies 135 (2004)

42 I Mgbeoji, "Patents and Traditional Knowledge of the Uses of Plants: Is a Communal Patent Regime Part of the Solution to the Scourge of Bio Piracy?" 9:1 Indiana Journal of Global Legal Studies 163 (2001)

43 P Drahos, "Indigenous Knowledge, Intellectual Property and Biopiracy: Is a Global Bio-Collecting Society the Answer?" 22:6 European Intellectual Property Review 245–250 at 243 (2000)

44 G Dutfield, *Intellectual Property, Biogenetic Resources and Traditional Knowledge* (Earthscan, 2004)

45 V Shiva, "Biodiversity, Intellectual Property Rights, and Globalization" in B de Sousa Santos (Ed.), *Another Knowledge Is Possible: Beyond Northern Epistemologies* (Verso, 2007)

highlighted the difficulties in proving prior art for orally transmitted knowledge.[46] The case of hoodia, a plant traditionally used by the San people of southern Africa as an appetite suppressant, provides another example. In 1995, the South African Council for Scientific and Industrial Research patented hoodia's active compound without the San's knowledge. After negotiations, a benefit-sharing agreement was reached, but the case underscored the need for prior informed consent in the use of traditional knowledge.[47]

In 1997, the Texas-based RiceTec Inc. was granted a patent for "Basmati rice lines and grains," despite basmati being a traditional variety cultivated for centuries in India and Pakistan. After legal challenges, some of the patent's claims were withdrawn.[48] The case of the herb turmeric demonstrates how Western intellectual property systems can be used to appropriate traditional knowledge. In 1995, two Indian-born researchers at the University of Mississippi were granted a United States patent for the use of turmeric in wound healing. This patent was successfully challenged by India's Council of Scientific and Industrial Research, as the use of turmeric for this purpose had been documented in ancient Sanskrit texts.[49]

As a final example, the Maasai, a pastoralist ethnic group inhabiting parts of Kenya and Tanzania, have faced numerous instances of their cultural elements being commercialized without their consent or benefit. Italian company Masai Barefoot Technology (MBT) trademarked the name "Masai" in various jurisdictions for their shoe technology. This appropriation of the Maasai name for commercial purposes occurred without consultation with or compensation to the Maasai people, despite the company drawing on the tribe's reputation for their athletic prowess and distinctive walking style.

These examples demonstrate how Western intellectual property systems can be used to appropriate and monopolize traditional knowledge, often without recognition or compensation to the Indigenous communities who developed and preserved this knowledge over generations. They highlight the urgent need for legal frameworks that can adequately protect traditional knowledge while respecting indigenous cultural values and practices. The ongoing efforts at the World Intellectual Property Organization (WIPO) to develop an international legal instrument for the protection of traditional knowledge aim to address these issues. However, bridging the conceptual gaps between indigenous knowledge systems and Western intellectual property frameworks remains a significant challenge.

46 LM Fecteau, "The Ayahuasca Patent Revocation: Raising Questions About Current U.S. Patent Policy" 21:1 Boston College Third World Law Journal 69 (2001)

47 R Wynberg, "Rhetoric, Realism and Benefit-Sharing: Use of Traditional Knowledge of Hoodia Species in the Development of an Appetite Suppressant" 7:6 Journal of World Intellectual Property 851 (2004)

48 D Rangnekar, "The Basmati Patent: The Rise of the 'Sui Generis' Protection" 36:47 Economic and Political Weekly 4353 (2001)

49 A Agrawal, "Indigenous Knowledge and the Politics of Classification" 54:173 International Social Science Journal 287 (2002)

TRIPS does not reference Indigenous or traditional knowledge. However, the 2001 Doha Declaration broadened the TRIPS Council's mandate to examine "the relationship between the TRIPS Agreement and the Convention on Biological Diversity, the protection of traditional knowledge and folklore." Some developing countries have proposed amending TRIPS to require disclosure of the origin of genetic resources and associated traditional knowledge in patent applications. However, this has not been agreed upon. The lack of specific protection for traditional knowledge in TRIPS has been a point of contention, with some arguing it leaves traditional knowledge vulnerable to misappropriation. Discussions continue in the TRIPS Council on how to address traditional knowledge issues, but there is no consensus on whether or how to modify TRIPS to explicitly protect traditional knowledge.

In contrast with the WTO, FTAs have increasingly incorporated provisions related to Indigenous or traditional forms of intellectual property, though the extent and nature of protection varies across agreements. The most comprehensive protections are generally found in agreements involving countries with significant indigenous populations.

The CPTPP includes some provisions related to traditional knowledge and genetic resources. Article 18.16 of the CPTPP recognizes the relevance of traditional knowledge associated with genetic resources to intellectual property systems. It also affirms that quality patent examination can include consideration of traditional knowledge in determining prior eligibility.[50] However, critics have argued these provisions are relatively limited compared to more robust protections advocated by Indigenous groups.

The USMCA goes further in explicitly recognizing Indigenous rights related to intellectual property. Article 20.B.14 requires parties to endeavour to promote Indigenous innovation through their intellectual property systems. It also calls for cooperation between parties on issues related to traditional knowledge, traditional cultural expressions, and genetic resources. The Peru-Australia Free Trade Agreement includes provisions requiring informed consent and benefit sharing for the use of genetic resources and associated traditional knowledge.[51] Similarly, New Zealand has advocated for including protections for Māori traditional knowledge in its trade negotiations.

Many Indigenous advocates argue that existing intellectual property frameworks in free trade agreements remain inadequate for protecting traditional forms of knowledge. They contend that Western concepts of individual ownership and time-limited protection are often incompatible with indigenous understandings of collective, intergenerational knowledge.[52] Although there is a trend towards greater recognition of Indigenous intellectual property in trade agreements, the extent of

50 Article 18.16

51 Article 17.16

52 P Drahos, *Intellectual Property, Indigenous People and Their Knowledge* (Cambridge University Press, 2014)

protection remains limited and contentious. Most agreements focus on cooperation and recognition rather than creating new enforceable rights. Significant gaps remain between the protections advocated by many Indigenous groups and those typically included in FTAs.

9.5 Intellectual Property and Trade With China

Tensions between China and Western countries, particularly the United States, over intellectual property rights and compliance with WTO rules have been a significant source of trade friction in recent years. These difficulties stem from several interrelated factors and have complex implications for global trade and innovation. One issue has been that, historically, China did not have the same understanding of intellectual property rights that the West has done. China has a long tradition of valuing the collective over individual rights, which contrasts with Western notions of individual property rights.[53] While Western countries have had established intellectual property regimes for centuries, China only began seriously developing its IP laws in the 1980s. China's intellectual property laws have undergone significant developments over the past few decades, aligning them more closely with established standards.

Despite intellectual property laws becoming similar to Western countries, enforcement remains a significant issue in China. Violations of China's own intellectual property are still common and, in many ways, normalized in China.[54] China has often prioritized rapid economic development over strict intellectual property protection. Moreover, the Chinese public's understanding and acceptance of intellectual property rights is still evolving. In terms of trade agreements, China advocates for maintaining TRIPS standards in international forums, sometimes aligning with other developing countries, rather than pushing for stronger protections like many Western nations.

China – Measures Affecting the Protection and Enforcement of Intellectual Property Rights (DS362) was a key intellectual property dispute brought under the TRIPS agreement by the United States against China in 2007, challenging various aspects of China's intellectual property regime. The dispute covered issues such as the disposal of counterfeit goods, copyright protection for works not authorized for publication in China, and criminal thresholds for trademark and copyright infringements. The panel's mixed ruling led to some changes in Chinese intellectual property laws and highlighted the challenges of enforcing IP rights in large markets.

China's Accession Protocol to the WTO contains several provisions related to intellectual property obligations. China agreed to fully comply with the TRIPS Agreement immediately upon accession, without any transition period that was available to other developing country members. This meant China had to implement all TRIPS provisions from day one of its WTO membership. The protocol

53 J Longo, *A Brief Analysis of the Chinese Intellectual Property Regime* (Michigan State University, 2019)

54 Ibid

required China to enforce its laws related to intellectual property rights protection, including measures against copyright piracy and trademark counterfeiting. China committed to protecting undisclosed information and trade secrets which were an area of particular concern for foreign businesses operating in China. The protocol included provisions on transparency, requiring China to publish all laws, regulations and other measures related to intellectual property rights. China agreed to eliminate any export performance, local content, foreign exchange balancing, technology transfer, and local sourcing requirements as conditions for investment approvals or import licenses. This was intended to address concerns about forced technology transfers. The protocol required China to provide national treatment to foreign rights holders, ensuring they receive the same level of intellectual property protection as domestic entities. Lastly, China committed to participating fully in the TRIPS Council and other WTO bodies dealing with intellectual property issues.

It is important to acknowledge that while these commitments were made in the Accession Protocol, their implementation and enforcement have been subjects of ongoing debate and trade disputes between China and other WTO members, particularly the United States and the European Union. The specific allegations of non-compliance or inadequate enforcement have evolved over time since China's accession in 2001.

One of the primary concerns raised by Western countries is China's alleged failure to adequately protect foreign intellectual property rights. Critics argue that China has not fully implemented or enforced its commitments under the TRIPS Agreement, which sets minimum standards for IP protection among WTO members. For instance, the Office of the United States Trade Representative (USTR) has consistently identified China as a Priority Watch List country in its annual Special 301 Report, citing issues such as trade secret theft, online piracy, counterfeit goods, and forced technology transfer.

The issue of forced technology transfer has been particularly contentious. Western companies have long complained that China requires them to transfer technology to local partners as a condition of market access, a practice that they argue violates WTO rules. While China denies that such policies are officially mandated, critics contend that they are often implemented through informal channels or regulatory requirements. The controversy over forced technology transfer in China has become one of the most challenging issues in the United States-China trade negotiations.

China's alleged cyber-espionage activities targeting foreign companies' intellectual property have also been a major source of tension. The United States and other Western countries have accused China of engaging in state-sponsored hacking to acquire valuable trade secrets and technological know-how. Cyber espionage has become a central issue in the larger debate over China's compliance with international norms and its commitments as a WTO member, including those relating to intellectual property.[55]

55 KE Maskus, "Intellectual Property Rights and International Innovation in the Era of Deepening Economic Integration" in BA Blonigen and WW Wilson (Eds.), *Handbook of International Trade and Transportation* (Elgar, 2020)

The Chinese government, for its part, has consistently denied many of these allegations and argues that it has made significant progress in strengthening intellectual property protection. China points to reforms in its intellectual property laws, the establishment of specialized intellectual property courts, and increased enforcement actions against intellectual property infringement. However, Western countries argue that implementation and enforcement remain inadequate. These tensions have led to various trade actions and retaliatory measures. Most notably, the United States initiated an investigation into China's intellectual property practices in 2017 which ultimately led to the imposition of tariffs on Chinese goods.

The difficulty in resolving these intellectual property-related tensions are compounded by several factors. First, there are fundamental differences in how China and Western countries view the role of the state in economic development and innovation. China's state-led model of economic development often clashes with Western notions of free-market capitalism and limited government intervention. Second, the rapid pace of technological change and the emergence of new industries have created challenges for existing intellectual property frameworks and WTO rules. Some of these issues will be revisited in the chapter on digital trade. The implications of these tensions are far-reaching. They have disrupted global supply chains, increased uncertainty for businesses, and potentially slowed the pace of innovation and technology diffusion. Moreover, they have contributed to a broader geopolitical rivalry between China and the West, with some observers warning of a potential "de-coupling" of the world's two largest economies.

Looking forward, resolving these intellectual property-related trade tensions will likely require a combination of continued dialogue, targeted reforms, and potentially new international agreements. Some experts have called for updating WTO rules to address issues like digital trade and state-owned enterprises more effectively. Others have suggested the need for more robust bilateral or plurilateral agreements to address specific intellectual property concerns. Digital trade agreements, to be explored in the next chapter, may ultimately achieve this.

9.6 Conclusion

Intellectual property has often been considered to be on the periphery of world trade law – a subject in its own right that only tangentially relates to trade. While the protection of intellectual property remains a matter of national law, the reality that goods and services linked to intellectual property cross international borders means that intellectual property is a vital aspect of world trade. By following the principle of harmonization, world trade law has attempted to foster trade in intellectual property-oriented goods and services by reducing the disparity in the recognition of these legal rights among the world's trading nations. Failure to protect intellectual property adequately is a restriction on trade because those who own intellectual property do not wish to risk exporting their goods or services to jurisdictions where they can be appropriated without compensation.

The WTO's TRIPS Agreement represents a significant milestone in international intellectual property law, establishing a comprehensive framework for the protection and enforcement of intellectual property rights within the global trading system. Its provisions cover a wide range of intellectual property categories and set minimum standards that all WTO members must implement in their national laws while also allowing for some flexibility to accommodate different legal systems and developmental needs. FTAs have adopted many of the rules found in TRIPS, in some cases granting stronger and wider protection.

Regardless of these successes in standardizing the treatment of intellectual property, the protection of intellectual property in the context of world trade law is not without its controversies. The precise scope of compulsory licensing under TRIPS, notably in the case of vaccines, remains uncertain. In the aftermath of a global pandemic, this remains a matter of much concern. More systemically, fundamental questions remain regarding differences in conceptualizing the nature of property that this is the product of human ingenuity that may differ from traditional Western categories and flowing from this, how best to strike a balance through the law between rewarding the discoverers of new knowledge and serving the needs of those who wish to benefit from it.

Discussion Questions

1. Why is the protection of intellectual property within the WTO's domain of activity?
2. What is harmonization and how is it achieved through the TRIPS Agreement?
3. Is compulsory licensing fair to the creators of intellectual property?
4. Is indigenous knowledge adequately protected by the TRIPS Agreement? If not what more could be done?
5. Does the protection of intellectual property feature prominently in bilateral/regional Free Trade Agreements? How does this differ from the TRIPS Agreement?

10 Digital Trade

10.1 Introduction

Digital trade is understood to mean the production, distribution, marketing, sale or delivery of goods and services by electronic means. The term digital trade is often used synonymously with electronic or e-commerce, although those terms are better viewed as sub-categories within the larger umbrella. E-commerce more aptly refers to the private, transactional elements of digital trade (i.e., contract formation and enforcement) whereas digital trade encompasses the broader state-level obligations and public policy issues that apply to governments and the private sector. Digital trade is, therefore, the appropriate term to use to identify a subject of enquiry within world trade law.

However, it is defined, economic activity taking place online has expanded significantly in the past decade, accelerating at an even greater pace during the Covid-19 pandemic. Sometimes described as the Fourth Industrial Revolution, digital trade now comprises 15 per cent of global GDP.[1] Intensifying competition to the benefit of worldwide consumers, digital trade covers not only the delivery of services with an international dimension but also the sale of goods through the Internet. Digital trade also creates important challenges in relation to the management of data, cybersecurity, the protection of intellectual property and the facilitation of new technologies designed to enhance innovation and engender greater efficiencies. Today, Artificial Intelligence has become the pre-eminent of these.

Building upon legal principles established in other contexts, many of which were explored throughout this book, world trade law has slowly begun to adapt to digital trade, in some cases breaking new ground. On the multilateral front, the WTO's Joint Statement Initiative aims to establish common principles on digital trade such as non-discrimination and the elimination of customs duties on electronic transactions. Pushing the agenda further, FTAs have taken the lead in the regulation of the international digital economy. In addition to including specialized chapters in FTAs, some countries have begun to conclude digital-only FTAs,

1 "Digital trust: How to unleash the trillion-dollar opportunity for our global economy" World Economic Forum (17 August 2022) citing statistics from the World Bank

DOI: 10.4324/9781003465676-10

known as Digital Economy Agreements (DEAs). Typically consisting primarily of best-efforts style language rather than binding commitments, these agreements focus on interoperability and encourage domestic regulatory reform.

This chapter will identify the importance of digital trade to the modern economy, noting the WTO's slow progress in this area contrasted with extensive developments in FTAs. Concentrating on the text of agreements such as the USMCA and the innovative Digital Economic Partnership Agreement (DEPA), this chapter will illustrate the emerging principles of digital trade law such as interoperability and the ban on data localization requirements as well as persistent impediments including data retention and privacy requirements.

10.2 The WTO and Digital Trade

WTO efforts to facilitate digital trade have been slow, reflecting in part the ongoing difficulties in making progress in trade liberalization at the multilateral level. The modern era of digital commerce took hold after the WTO was established and as such it is no surprise that the WTO does not contain specific articles covering digital trade. Nevertheless, there are several WTO agreements which are indirectly related to digital trade. These include, most importantly, GATS, TRIPS, and the plurilateral Information Technology Agreement (ITA).

10.2.1 General Agreement on Trade in Services (GATS)

GATS is highly relevant for digital trade and electronic commerce, despite being negotiated before the widespread adoption of the Internet and digital technologies. GATS provides a foundational framework that applies to trade in services delivered electronically. One of the ways GATS is relevant is through its technological neutrality principle. This means that the commitments made by WTO members under GATS apply regardless of the technological means by which a service is delivered. Therefore, services that can now be provided digitally, such as consulting, financial services, or education, are covered by existing GATS commitments even if they were not originally envisioned as being delivered electronically.

This issue arose in *the China – Publications and Audiovisual Products*[2] dispute. Brought by the United States against China, the dispute primarily focused on China's measures affecting trading rights and distribution services for magazines and audiovisual entertainment products. The Appellate Body upheld the panel's finding that China's GATS commitments on "sound recording distribution services" encompassed the electronic distribution of sound recordings. This interpretation is significant because it suggests that GATS commitments can be technology-neutral and thus applicable to new forms of digital distribution that may not have existed when the commitments were made. This reasoning potentially extends the reach of

2 China – Measures Affecting Trading Rights and Distribution Services for Certain Publications and Audiovisual Entertainment Products, WT/DS363/AB/R, adopted 19 January 2010

existing GATS commitments to cover various forms of digital trade, even if they were not explicitly contemplated at the time of scheduling.

The Appellate Body's approach to interpreting the ordinary meaning of "sound recording distribution services" in light of the object and purpose of the GATS provides a blueprint for how other digital services might be classified under existing commitments. This interpretative approach opens the door for applying traditional services commitments to new digital services, potentially bringing a wide range of digital trade activities under the purview of existing WTO rules. Another critical aspect of the case relevant to digital trade was the Appellate Body's treatment of China's argument that its measures were necessary to protect public morals, as noted in Chapter 6. While the Appellate Body ultimately found that China had not demonstrated the necessity of its measures, it did confirm that the protection of public morals could, in principle, justify certain trade restrictions. This finding is relevant for digital trade, as many countries have cited public morals, cultural sensitivities, or national security as reasons for restricting digital content or services.

The *China – Periodicals* dispute also touched upon the issue of how to classify and treat products that can be delivered both physically and electronically. While the focus was on audiovisual products and publications, the reasoning could potentially be extended to other types of digital goods and services. This aspect of the case highlights the ongoing challenge of determining whether digital products should be treated as goods (under GATT) or services (under GATS), a distinction that has significant implications for the applicable trade rules.

GATS's capacity to liberalize digital trade has been limited in part because of this problem of categorization. WTO members differ on whether products which were usually sold as goods due to their link to a physical carrier and which can now be delivered online over the Internet (e.g., music or movies) should be treated as goods under GATT or as services under GATS.[3] If goods delivered online were considered goods, they could be subject to tariffs or non-tariff barriers. On the other hand, if these products were considered services, they would be subject to trade restrictions under GATS such as market access barriers and discriminatory domestic regulations, which would depend on whether such "services" featured in the relevant WTO members' GATS schedule. The execution of an electronic transaction further necessitates infrastructure services including distribution and payment, which equally fall under GATS.

The GATS classification of services into four modes of supply also remains applicable to digital trade. Mode 1 (cross-border supply) is especially relevant since it covers services supplied from the territory of one member into the territory of another. This mode encompasses many forms of digital trade, including cloud computing services, online professional services, and digital content streaming. Mode 2 (consumption abroad) can apply to situations where consumers access

3 See KL Bergemann, "A Digital Free Trade Zone and Necessarily-Regulated Self-Governance for Electronic Commerce: The World Trade Organization, International Law, and Classical Liberalism in Cyberspace" 20 Marshall Journal of Computer and Information Law 595 (2002)

digital services while travelling internationally. Furthermore, the GATS principles of market access and national treatment are crucial for digital trade. Market access commitments ensure that WTO members do not impose quantitative restrictions on service suppliers from other members, which is important for digital businesses that can easily scale across borders. National treatment obligations require members to treat foreign digital service providers no less favourably than domestic ones, promoting a level playing field in the digital economy.

GATS is vitally important to digital trade also because the Internet itself is a communication service. Access to public telecommunication networks was incorporated into GATS via a separate Telecommunication Annex. The annex states that any service supplier of any other WTO member must be accorded access to and use of public telecommunication networks and services on reasonable and non-discriminatory terms and according to conditions for the supply of a service included in the country schedule. This is essential for the functioning of cross-border digital services, which rely on telecommunications infrastructure to reach customers in foreign markets.

10.2.2 The Trade-Related Aspects of Intellectual Property (TRIPS) Agreement

The TRIPS Agreement, discussed in detail in the previous chapter, plays a key, albeit indirect, role in the regulation of digital trade. While TRIPS was negotiated and came into force before the explosive growth of the digital economy, its provisions have important implications for various aspects of digital trade.

One of the most relevant aspects of TRIPS for digital trade is its provisions on copyright protection. The agreement requires member countries to comply with the substantive provisions of the Berne Convention for the Protection of Literary and Artistic Works. This protection extends to computer programs which are protected as literary works under the Berne Convention. In the context of digital trade, this means that software, which is a crucial component of many digital products and services, enjoys copyright protection across WTO member countries. This protection is vital for companies engaged in the development and trade of software and digital content.

Moreover, TRIPS addresses the protection of compilations of data. Article 10.2 of TRIPS stipulates that compilations of data or other material, whether in machine-readable or other form, which by reason of the selection or arrangement of their contents constitute intellectual creations, shall be protected as such. This provision is particularly relevant in the age of big data and data-driven business models, offering some level of protection for databases and other compilations of information that are increasingly valuable in the digital economy.

The agreement's provisions on trademarks also have implications for digital trade. TRIPS requires the protection of trademarks, including service marks, which is crucial in the online marketplace where brand recognition plays a significant role. This protection extends to domain names, which are often closely tied to trademarks and are essential for businesses operating in the digital space. TRIPS also addresses the issue of trade secrets, which is increasingly important in the digital economy. The agreement requires member countries to protect undisclosed information against unauthorized use "in a manner contrary to honest commercial practices." This provision is important for digital trade, where proprietary algorithms, customer data, and other forms of confidential business information are crucial assets. Furthermore, TRIPS include provisions for the enforcement of intellectual property rights, which are applicable in the digital realm. These include civil and administrative procedures and remedies, provisional measures, and border measures. While these were primarily designed with physical goods in mind, they have been increasingly applied to digital goods and services, though not without challenges.

TRIPS' provisions on patents also have implications for digital trade, particularly in areas such as software patents and business method patents. While the patentability of software and business methods varies across jurisdictions, TRIPS provides a framework for patent protection that has been applied to various digital innovations. Recall, however, that TRIPS was negotiated in the early 1990s, before the rise of many modern digital technologies and business models. As a result, it does not directly address many of the specific challenges posed by digital trade. Issues such as the protection of non-personal data, the regulation of cross-border data flows, and the treatment of new forms of digital intellectual property (like AI-generated works) are not explicitly covered by TRIPS. Despite these limitations, TRIPS has shown some flexibility in adapting to technological changes. The Doha Declaration of 2001, while primarily focused on public health issues, affirmed that TRIPS should be interpreted and implemented in a manner supportive of WTO members' right to protect public health and promote access to medicines. This principle of flexible interpretation could potentially be applied to emerging issues in digital trade. Moreover, the ongoing discussions within the WTO about e-commerce and digital trade often touch upon intellectual property issues covered by TRIPS. For instance, debates about the temporary copy exception in copyright law, which is crucial for the functioning of the Internet, often reference TRIPS provisions.

10.2.3 The Information Technology Agreement (ITA)

Discussed earlier in this book, the WTO's Information Technology Agreement (ITA) has played a crucial role in shaping the landscape of digital trade regulation since its inception in 1996. This plurilateral agreement, which has been expanded over the years, has significantly contributed to the growth of the global digital economy by reducing tariffs on a wide range of information and communication technology (ICT) products. By reducing the cost of importing and exporting ICT products, the agreement has fostered innovation, increased market access, and promoted the adoption of new technologies worldwide. This tariff elimination has been particularly beneficial for developing countries, allowing them to more easily access advanced technologies and participate in global value chains.

One of the most significant aspects of the ITA is its product coverage. Initially, the agreement covered a range of ICT products including computers, telecommunication equipment, semiconductors, software, and scientific instruments. The expansion of the ITA in 2015 (known as ITA-II) further broadened this coverage to include more advanced products such as new-generation semiconductors, GPS navigation equipment, medical equipment, and sophisticated testing instruments. This expanded coverage reflects the evolution of technology and ensures that the agreement remains relevant in the face of rapid technological advancements.

The ITA's impact on digital trade extends beyond mere tariff reduction. By lowering the costs of ICT products, the agreement has indirectly supported the growth of digital services and e-commerce. For instance, the reduced costs of computers and networking equipment have made it easier for businesses to digitize their operations and engage in cross-border digital trade. This has been particularly important for small- and medium-sized enterprises (SMEs), which can now more easily participate in global markets through digital platforms. The ITA has moreover played a crucial role in promoting regulatory coherence in the ICT sector. The agreement has encouraged countries to align their product classifications and customs procedures for IT products which has helped to reduce non-tariff barriers to trade. This harmonization has been particularly important in the context of rapidly evolving technology, where new products may not easily fit into existing categories.

The ITA has also contributed to the development of global value chains in the ICT sector. By reducing trade barriers, the agreement has allowed companies to distribute their production processes across different countries, taking advantage of comparative advantages in various stages of production. This has led to increased efficiency and lower costs for ICT products, ultimately benefiting consumers and businesses alike.

The ITA has indirectly influenced discussions on digital trade regulation. The success of the agreement in reducing tariffs and promoting trade in ICT goods has served as a model for potential future agreements focused on digital services and data flows. The collaborative approach used in negotiating and expanding the ITA has demonstrated the potential for plurilateral agreements to address specific trade issues, even when consensus among all WTO members is difficult to achieve. Furthermore, the ITA has highlighted the importance of technological neutrality in trade agreements. The agreement's approach of covering products based on their characteristics rather than specific technologies has allowed it to remain relevant despite rapid technological change.

10.2.4 Work Program and Joint Statement Initiative on Electronic Commerce (JSI)

Largely at the insistence of the United States at the WTO Ministerial Conference in 1998, WTO members decided to develop a work program covering digital trade. Very little progress was made on this front until recently. The most important contribution the WTO has made to digital trade is the plurilateral Joint Statement Initiative (JSI) on E-Commerce. This agreement represents a significant effort to establish global rules for digital trade. Launched in 2017, the initiative has progressed to the point where participants achieved a stabilized text in July 2024, marking a major milestone in the negotiations. The JSI covers a wide range of digital trade issues, organized into six main themes: enabling electronic commerce, openness and electronic commerce, trust and digital trade, cross-cutting issues, telecommunications, and market access. As of June 2024, the initiative includes WTO members accounting for over 90 per cent of global trade, highlighting its broad support and potential impact.

One of the key provisions is Article 19.3, which prohibits customs duties and other discriminatory measures on digital products distributed electronically between parties. This article aims to ensure the free flow of digital goods and services across borders without tariff barriers. Article 19.8 addresses the critical issue of personal information protection. It requires participating countries to adopt and maintain legal frameworks for protecting personal data, taking into account principles from international bodies like the APEC Privacy Framework and OECD Guidelines. This provision is crucial for building trust in digital trade, but its implementation may pose challenges for countries with less developed data protection regimes. Article 19.11 prohibits restrictions on cross-border transfers of information, including personal data, for business purposes. While this provision is essential for enabling the free flow of data that underpins digital trade, it has been a contentious issue due to concerns about data privacy and national security.

Parties are prohibited from requiring the use or location of computing facilities in their territory as a condition for conducting business.[4] This provision aims to minimize data localization requirements, which can act as significant barriers to digital trade. Data localization requirements are laws or regulations that mandate data about a country's citizens or residents be stored, processed, or handled within that country's borders. They can increase costs and reduce efficiency for multinational enterprises by requiring them to build or use local data centres in each country they operate in, rather than centralizing data storage. In so doing, they may impede innovation and the development of new digital services that rely on cross-border data flows. In that sense, they favour domestic companies over foreign competitors. On the other hand, data localization is thought to enhance data protection, privacy, and national security by keeping sensitive data within a country's borders and legal jurisdiction. Some countries view it as a way to assert "data sovereignty" and maintain control over their citizens' information.[5]

Article 19.15 of the JSI addresses cybersecurity, promoting cooperation between parties in tackling cybersecurity challenges. This provision recognizes the importance of cybersecurity in maintaining trust in digital trade, but effective implementation may require significant capacity building in some countries.

JSI parties are prohibited from requiring the disclosure of proprietary source code or algorithms as a condition for import, distribution, sale, or use of software.[6] Source code can be a key differentiator from competitors, containing innovative

4 Article 19.12

5 S Peng, *International Economic Law in the Era of Datafication* (Cambridge University Press, 2024) Ch 3

6 Article 19.16

features or efficient implementations that give their products an edge in the market. While this provision protects intellectual property in the software industry, it may face resistance from countries that view access to source code as necessary for security audits.

Article 19.17 of the JSI limits the liability of Internet platforms for third-party content, aiming to foster innovation and free expression online. Limiting the liability of Internet platforms for third-party content refers to legal provisions that protect online service providers, such as social media platforms, e-commerce websites, and content-sharing sites, from being held legally responsible for the content posted or shared by their users. This concept is often embodied in "safe harbour" provisions found in various countries' laws. These provisions typically shield platforms from liability for user-generated content, provided they meet certain conditions, such as promptly removing illegal content when notified. The rationale behind such limitations is to foster innovation and free expression online by preventing platforms from being overwhelmed by potential legal risks associated with user content. This approach allows platforms to operate without the need to pre-screen or heavily censor all user submissions, which would be impractical and potentially stifling to online communication and commerce. These protections are often balanced with requirements for platforms to implement content moderation systems and cooperate with law enforcement when necessary.

One ongoing challenge with the adoption of the JSI is the participation of developing countries and Least Developed Countries (LDCs) in the initiative. While the JSI is open to all WTO members, there are concerns about the capacity of some countries to implement and benefit from the proposed rules. To address this, the initiative includes provisions on capacity building and technical assistance, but their effectiveness remains to be seen.

Another uncertainty relates to the relationship between the JSI and the broader WTO framework. As a plurilateral initiative, the JSI's legal status within the WTO system is not fully clear, and there are questions about how its outcomes will be integrated into the multilateral trading system. Despite these challenges, the WTO e-commerce JSI represents a significant step towards establishing a comprehensive framework for digital trade.

The JSI on e-commerce has sparked significant debate since its inception in 2017. It has been argued that the JSI represents a departure from traditional WTO negotiating practices and there are consequently questions about its compatibility with the WTO's consensus-based decision-making process. While the JSI may offer a more flexible approach to rule-making, it could potentially undermine the multilateral trading system's integrity.[7] Others have suggested that the JSI reflects a broader trend towards "variable geometry" in trade negotiations, where subsets of WTO members pursue agreements on specific issues. Although this approach may lead to more rapid progress on digital trade rules, it risks creating a fragmented

7 M Burri, "Digital Trade Rulemaking in Free Trade Agreements" in D Collins and M Geist (Eds.), *Research Handbook on Digital Trade* (Elgar, 2023)

regulatory landscape that could disadvantage developing countries.[8] Concern has also been expressed that the JSI could undermine existing flexibilities for developing countries under GATS. In particular, the JSI's proposed rules on data flows and localization could limit developing countries' policy space for digital industrialization strategies.[9] On the other hand, the JSI could provide an opportunity for developing countries to shape global digital trade rules. Participation in the JSI could help developing countries build capacity in digital policymaking and ensure their interests are reflected in emerging norms.[10]

10.3 Digital Trade and FTAs

The number of FTAs dealing with digital trade (or e-commerce) has increased significantly in recent years. There have been more than 370 concluded since 2000.[11] The use of FTAs to deal with the rapidly growing issue of digital trade may be due to the slow pace at which the WTO has approached digital trade. Digital trade or e-commerce chapters are now commonplace in FTAs, although the most innovative trade treaties are now the digital-only Digital Economy Agreements (DEA), notably the Digital Economy Partnership Agreement (DEPA).

10.3.1 The USMCA's Digital Trade Chapter

The digital trade chapter of the USMCA is among the most comprehensive treatments of digital trade in any FTA. It goes further than the CPTPP's chapter on electronic commerce as such, the CPTPP represents the cutting-edge of digital trade coverage contained in a conventional FTA. Article 19.3 prohibits customs duties and other discriminatory measures on digital products distributed electronically between the parties. This provision ensures that digital goods and services can flow freely across borders without being subject to tariffs or taxes that could impede trade by raising prices.

Article 19.8 requires each party to adopt and maintain a legal framework for the protection of personal information of digital trade users. It specifies that this framework should take into account principles and guidelines of relevant international bodies, such as the APEC Privacy Framework and OECD Guidelines. The article also outlines key data protection principles that should be included, such as limitation on collection, choice, data quality, purpose specification, use limitation, security safeguards, transparency, individual participation, and accountability. This

8 H Gao, "China and WTO E-Commerce Negotiations" in D Collins and M Geist (Eds.), *Research Handbook on Digital Trade* (Elgar, 2023)

9 J Kelsey, "How a TPP-Style E-commerce Outcome in the WTO would Endanger the Development Dimension of the GATS Acquis" 21:1 Journal of International Economic Law 273 (2018)

10 N Mishra, "The Role of the Trans-Pacific Partnership Agreement in the Internet Ecosystem: Uneasy Liaison or Synergistic Alliance?" 20:1 Journal of International Economic Law 31 (2017)

11 M Burri and R Polanco, "Digital Trade Agreements in Preferential Trade Agreements: Introducing a New Dataset" 23:1 Journal of International Economic Law (2020)

is the essence of the principle of harmonization that features prominently in world trade law.

Restrictions on cross-border transfers of information, including personal information, if the transfer is for the conduct of business are prohibited.[12] This provision is crucial for enabling the free flow of data that underpins digital trade and the modern economy. Data localization is covered by Article 19.12 which prevents parties from requiring the use or location of computing facilities in their territory as a condition for conducting business. As noted above, this provision aims to minimize how data localization requirements can act as barriers to digital trade, discouraging protectionism in favour of local firms.

Article 19.15 addresses cybersecurity, promoting cooperation between the parties in tackling cybersecurity challenges and encouraging the use of risk-based approaches and industry best practices. This provision recognizes the importance of cybersecurity in maintaining trust in digital trade. The growing threat of cybercrime is believed to be one of the main impediments to consumers shifting to an online marketplace, even if this offers greater selection and lower prices.

USMCA parties are prohibited from requiring the disclosure of proprietary source code or algorithms as a condition for import, distribution, sale, or use of software in their territories is prohibited.[13] This provision protects intellectual property and trade secrets in the software industry. Article 19.17 limits the liability of Internet platforms for third-party content, aiming to foster innovation and free expression online. The chapter also includes provisions on electronic authentication and signatures,[14] online consumer protection,[15] and open government data.[16] These articles aim to facilitate digital transactions, protect consumers, and promote innovation through access to government information.

The USMCA's digital trade chapter contains several public policy exceptions that allow parties to deviate from certain obligations in order to pursue legitimate policy objectives. These exceptions are designed to provide flexibility while still maintaining the overall goals of the agreement. One of the key exceptions is found in Article 19.11, which deals with cross-border transfer of information by electronic means. While this article generally prohibits restrictions on data flows, paragraph 2 provides an exception for measures that are necessary to achieve a legitimate public policy objective. Such measures must not be applied in a manner that would constitute arbitrary or unjustifiable discrimination or a disguised restriction on trade. Additionally, the restrictions imposed must not be greater than necessary to achieve the objective. This exception allows parties to implement data protection or privacy laws, for example, provided that they meet these criteria.

12 Article 19.11
13 Article 19.16
14 Article 19.6
15 Article 19.7
16 Article 19.18

Similarly, USMCA Article 19.12, which prohibits data localization requirements, contains an analogous exception in paragraph 3. This allows parties to require the use or location of computing facilities in their territory to achieve a legitimate public policy objective, subject to the same conditions as in Article 19.11. This exception could potentially be used to justify certain cybersecurity or national security measures that require local data storage. USMCA also includes broader exceptions in Chapter 32 (Exceptions and General Provisions). Article 32.1 incorporates by reference the general exceptions from the General GATS, discussed in Chapter 5. These exceptions could potentially be invoked to justify measures that might otherwise violate digital trade provisions.

Additionally, Article 19.8, which requires parties to adopt legal frameworks for personal information protection, includes flexibility in paragraph 2. It states that in developing these frameworks, parties should take into account the principles and guidelines of relevant international bodies. This allows for some variation in approaches to data protection while still encouraging alignment with international standards. While not strictly an exception, Article 19.15 on cybersecurity encourages cooperation and risk-based approaches rather than prescribing specific measures. This provides parties with some policy space in how they address cybersecurity concerns, reflecting a balance between promoting digital trade and preserving policy space for legitimate public objectives. However, the specific language requiring measures to be "necessary" and not more trade-restrictive than required sets a high bar for invoking these exceptions, potentially limiting their use in practice.

USMCA's provisions on data flows and localization represent a significant step forward in digital trade governance, going beyond previous agreements in their scope and enforceability. Some hold that the broad exceptions allowed under the agreement could potentially undermine its effectiveness.[17] It has also been suggested that while USMCA's digital chapter may benefit large technology companies, it could potentially disadvantage smaller firms and developing countries participating in the digital economy.[18]

It is worthwhile to draw some comparisons between USMCA's digital trade chapter and the CPTPP's e-commerce chapter. While the agreements share many similarities there are some key differences in their approaches and provisions. One significant difference is in the language used regarding cross-border data flows. The USMCA prohibits restrictions on cross-border transfers of information, while the CPTPP requires parties to allow cross-border information transfer. This subtle distinction means the USMCA takes a more restrictive stance against government interference in data flows compared to the CPTPP.

Another important difference is in how the agreements justify exceptions for public policy objectives. USMCA applies a necessity test, requiring that any

17 M Burri, "The Governance of Data and Data Flows in Trade Agreements: The Pitfalls of Legal Adaptation" 51 UC Davis Law Review 65 (2017)

18 SA Aaronson and P Leblond, "Another Digital Divide: The Rise of Data Realms and Its Implications for the WTO" 21:2 Journal of International Economic Law 245 (2018)

restrictions on data flows or localization requirements be necessary to achieve a legitimate public policy objective. In contrast, CPTPP does not include such a necessity test, potentially allowing for broader exceptions. USMCA also lacks an explicit recognition of parties' regulatory requirements, which is present in the CPTPP. This omission in USMCA could be interpreted as providing less flexibility for national regulations compared to CPTPP.

Regarding source code protection, both agreements prohibit requiring the transfer or access to source code as a condition for market entry. However, USMCA extends this protection to algorithms expressed in source code, which is not explicitly mentioned in CPTPP. USMCA includes more detailed provisions on interactive computer services,[19] limiting the liability of Internet platforms for third-party content. This provision, which reflects United States law in this area, is not present in CPTPP.

While both agreements address personal information protection, USMCA provides more specific guidance on the principles that should be included in data protection frameworks, referencing international standards such as the APEC Privacy Framework and OECD Guidelines. USMCA includes provisions on open government data,[20] encouraging the publication of government information as open data. This topic is not addressed in CPTPP's e-commerce chapter, reflecting the USMCA's broader approach to digital governance issues.

Turning to the digital trade chapters in other leading FTAs, the EU-Japan Economic Partnership Agreement (EPA) takes a different approach to digital trade than USMCA or CPTPP. While it includes provisions on electronic commerce, it does not contain explicit rules on cross-border data flows or data localization. Instead, it focuses on cooperation in areas such as consumer protection, spam regulation, and the recognition of electronic authentication methods. This reflects the European Union's more cautious approach to data governance, influenced by its strong data protection regulations. The United Kingdom-Japan Comprehensive Economic Partnership Agreement (CEPA) includes a dedicated chapter on digital trade that goes beyond the provisions in the EU-Japan EPA. It includes commitments on the free flow of data, prohibition of data localization requirements, and protection of source code. This reflects the United Kingdom's post-Brexit approach to digital trade, which aligns more closely with the CPTPP model than with the European Union's approach.

Some FTAs have unique provisions that set them apart. For instance, the United States-Korea Free Trade Agreement (KORUS) includes provisions on interactive computer services that limit the liability of Internet platforms for third-party content. This provision, also influenced by United States law, is not commonly found in other FTAs and reflects the specific interests of the United States tech industry.

RCEP, while less ambitious than some other FTAs in its digital trade provisions, includes commitments on electronic authentication and signatures, online consumer protection, and personal information protection. However, it does not

19 Article 19.17
20 Article 19.18

include binding commitments on cross-border data flows or prohibitions on data localization reflecting the diverse approaches to digital trade among its member countries, including China with its strong focus on national security.

10.3.2 Digital Economy Agreements (DEAs) and the Digital Economy Partnership Agreement (DEPA)

FTAs granting favourable treatment to parties have become more complex and deeper, covering multiple policy areas. In one respect Digital Economy Agreements (DEAs) are a new trend in this movement, revealing a preference for signatories to separate digital issues away from other classic trade areas, such as trade remedies or tariffs. In another way, DEAs embody greater specialization, omitting many of the classic fields of economic integration associated with FTAs, such as tariffs and market access for services.

The rapidly changing nature of digital trade, driven by new technologies and the exigency of a pandemic, has necessitated a higher degree of flexibility than in traditional trade areas. This is illustrated in the emerging practice of concluding DEAs, with the United States-Japan Digital Trade Agreement of 2019 as the first to be concluded. Singapore has concluded several DEAs, establishing itself as a world leader in the field.

The United Kingdom-Singapore Digital Economy Agreement (UKSDEA), which entered into force in June 2022, represents another significant development in digital trade agreements. As the first digital-only agreement between an Asian and a European country, the UKSDEA aims to facilitate a more secure digital environment, enable trusted data flows, and support end-to-end digital trade. It includes provisions on cybersecurity, data protection, and digital identities, reflecting the priorities of two highly developed digital economies. The Singapore-Australia Digital Economy Agreement (SADEA), which entered into force in December 2020, builds on the existing free trade agreement between the two countries. It includes provisions on cross-border data flows, prohibition of data localization requirements, and cooperation on emerging technologies such as artificial intelligence and digital identities. SADEA demonstrates how countries are updating their existing trade relationships to address digital economy issues. The Korea-Singapore Digital Partnership Agreement (KSDPA), which entered into force in January 2023, is another example of how countries are forming bilateral digital economy agreements. This agreement covers areas such as data innovation, artificial intelligence, and digital identities, reflecting the shared interests of two technologically advanced economies in promoting digital trade and innovation.

These DEAs share several common features, including commitments to enable cross-border data flows, prohibit data localization requirements, and protect personal information. However, they also reflect the specific priorities and regulatory approaches of the participating countries. For instance, the UKSDEA places a strong emphasis on cybersecurity and online consumer protection, reflecting the United Kingdom's focus on these areas. One key aspect of these agreements is their focus on regulatory cooperation and interoperability. They often include provisions for collaboration on emerging technologies, digital identities, and e-invoicing systems, aiming to create a more seamless digital trading environment. Another important feature is their approach to digital inclusion, particularly for SMEs.

The geographically disparate mid-sized economies of Singapore, Chile, and New Zealand signed the Digital Economy Partnership Agreement (DEPA) in 2020. South Korea joined in May of 2024. Entering into force in January 2021, DEPA is a first-of-its-kind agreement because it is exclusively focused on digital trade, as a typical DEA, but is plurilateral in nature – specifically designed to bring in other countries. DEPA sets out new approaches to digital trade issues, promotes interoperability between different regimes and addresses several new issues arising from digitalisation including privacy, electronic contracting and Artificial Intelligence (AI).

The intention is that DEPA will complement the WTO negotiations on e-commerce (the JSI, discussed above) and build on the digital economy work underway within the Asia Pacific Economic Cooperation (APEC) and the OECD. DEPA could also be seen as an important step towards a broader multilateral agreement. As a stand-alone, open plurilateral agreement to which other WTO members are eligible to join through a self-contained accession process, DEPA is conceived as a "living agreement" which allows for continual updates and modernization as required. This approach is vital for an FTA with a rapidly changed field where technological innovation often precedes legal understanding.

The chapters of DEPA (which it terms "modules") of the agreement refine existing rules, particularly those of the CPTPP. DEPA also includes two e-commerce areas not covered by other FTAs: e-invoicing and e-payments, also found in Module 2. Although DEPA does not go as far as prescribing regulations for its signatories, the agreement acknowledges the growing significance of these features of the global economy and establishes interoperable standards through collaboration, building on a common set of e-commerce principles.

In that sense, DEPA embodies an approach of harmonization, a term which conveys a similar meaning to that of interoperability in other contexts such as Sanitary and Phytosanitary Standards and Technical Barriers to Trade, outlined in Chapter 7. The specific "modular" elements of the DEPA include Business and Trade Facilitation; Treatment of Digital Products and Related Issues; Data Issues; Wider Trust Environment; Business and Consumer Trust; Digital Identities; Emerging Trends and Technologies; Innovation and the Digital Economy; Small and Medium Enterprises Cooperation; Digital Inclusion; Transparency and Dispute Settlement.

The use of the term "modular" in DEPA is itself unusual and conspicuous. It conveys the notion that the agreement is a sum of component parts rather than an integrated whole and, by implication, that some of the various elements may be disassociated from the text, perhaps with a view to maximizing policy flexibility of future accessors. Many elements of DEPA are "soft" laws comprising best-efforts obligations rather than binding ones which lead to enforceable rights. These include "new initiatives which promote data exchange systems" in Article 2.2.9 and the requirement that parties "Endeavour to take into account electronic payment systems." The word "endeavour" plays a critical role in the agreement, appearing 28 times. Indeed, DEPA does not prescribe regulations but establishes basic principles through collaboration emphasizing interoperability.

The flexibility inherent in DEPA is captured by Module 4 on privacy which declares that "each party shall adopt or maintain a legal framework that provides for the protection of the personal information of the users of electronic commerce and digital trade." Yet each party may take different "legal approaches" to protecting personal information. This is followed by a set of guiding principles for promoting the interoperability of standards. There is also a commitment that parties will "promote innovation and competition."[21] This is classic harmonization in world trade law, enabling each party to choose its own way of reaching shared goals.

DEPA's preamble discloses a progressive aspect to the agreement that stands out among many modern FTAs. Parties:

> REAFFIRM the importance of promoting corporate social responsibility, cultural identity and diversity, environmental protection and conservation, gender equality, indigenous rights, labour rights, inclusive trade, sustainable development and traditional knowledge, as well as the importance of preserving their right to regulate in the public interest.

Inclusion of the Right to Regulate is becoming standard in FTAs, indicative of the shift towards recognition of signatory states' sovereignty over important matters of public interest where in the past this may have been subordinated to the needs of multinational enterprises. It underscores the importance of addressing the needs of a range of stakeholders, rather than merely the commercial entity operating in an international environment. The express reference to culture and Indigenous rights is still uncommon in FTAs and was unheard of ten years ago.

Module 2 on business and trade facilitation has some useful elements, including allowing trade documentation to be paperless and establishing legal frameworks at the domestic level to allow electronic submissions of documents like certificates of origin, import, and export documentation as well as SPS certificates (Article 2.2). Electronic invoicing is to be encouraged and made interoperable (Article 2.5). The module also includes specific rules on express shipments and clearance times (Article 2.6). It further commits parties to deeper cooperation on other new approaches for logistics (Article 2.4). This reflects enhanced trade facilitation, a topic covered in Chapter 2.

The provisions on electronic payments (Article 2.7) are especially important because it is exceedingly difficult for firms, especially smaller ones, to engage in cross-border trade if they cannot be paid electronically over the Internet. Again, it is noteworthy that some of the current language in this module, as with other parts of DEPA are hortatory rather than binding (best efforts). This embeds flexibility into the text of DEPA, potentially attracting additional signatories concerned about the effects of binding international commitments on economic sovereignty as well as social matters such as data privacy.

21 For example, Article 2.7(f)

As with many digital trade chapters of modern free trade agreements, like CPTPP and USMCA, DEPA's Article 3.2 prohibits customs duties on digital transmissions. Interestingly though, internal taxes on digital transmission are expressly permitted. This would appear to allow for the imposition of digital services taxes, of which more will be discussed below.

There is also a national treatment provision in DEPA (Article 3.3) preventing nationality-based discrimination. The rules on non-discrimination of digital products (Article 3.3) could become critically important as the digital economy continues to expand into areas that have not yet been conceived. Non-discrimination is relevant primarily for newer categories of digital products set out in the agreement as "computer programme, text, video, image, sound recording or other product that is digitally encoded, produced for commercial sale or distribution, and that can be transmitted electronically." There is a key exception for the broadcasting industry, reflecting the historical sensitivity of cultural industries.

Module 4 on data issues builds on the commitments of CPTPP, which prohibits data localization requirements (i.e., restricting the collection, processing, and/or storage of data within a country) to ensure free data flows. On the controversial topic of data protection, Article 4.2 of DEPA clarifies that Parties must have a data protection framework, but the specific nature of that framework is not specified. This grants fairly wide latitude for countries to apply their own data protection rules rather than being bound by strict rules such as the EU's General Data Protection Regulation (GDPR).

DEPA establishes that its signatories will cooperate on the vitally important issue of cybersecurity and online safety (Article 5) and on consumer protection. These obligations are coupled with a requirement to have consumer protection laws, although again no particular regime is proscribed. As suggested earlier, this enables regulatory flexibility amongst signatories both past and present. The module on business trust contains two features drawn from CPTPP, including the promise to stop unsolicited messages or "spam" (Article 6.2) and to provide online consumer protection (Article 6.3). These commitments are binding, reflecting the fundamental importance of these issues as non-negotiable elements of a functioning digital economy.

Parties promise to cooperate on Digital Identities via Article 7. Digital Identities have emerged as a somewhat controversial topic in recent years given the potential threat to civil liberties associated with "vaccine passports" which led to political tensions in a number of countries during the Covid-19 pandemic. On the other hand, digital identities enable so-called verifiable credentials, enabling individuals to satisfy regulatory authentication and authorization for various purposes, eliminating many of the burdens associated with carrying sensitive personal identification in the form of documents or electronic copies thereof. They are seen by some as "convenient, secure, and privacy-oriented alternative to current physical and digital identity management systems."[22] This has important implications for the

22 J Sedlmeir, et al., "Digital Identities and Verifiable Credentials" 63 Business & Information Systems Engineering 603–613 (2021)

streamlining of identification for the purpose of digital trade, including payment authorization.

Module 8 on emerging trends and technologies and Module 9 on innovation and the digital economy go further than any other FTA. While these sections also lack binding rules, they do create important nodes of collaboration in emerging areas where the needs of the private sector are bound to change. Module 8 sets out several topics that are poised to become even more important in terms of underpinning economic activity generally in the coming years including fintech and AI. Signatories not only set out standards but commit to actively "promote development of fintech solutions" and "promote cooperation between firms" in the sector, including with start-ups, a business entity that is rarely referenced explicitly in trade agreements.

On AI, a topic also typically not referenced in FTAs, even those with digital chapters,[23] cooperation is also required using accepted principles of AI Governance. This acknowledges that, with AI having become widespread, efforts to mitigate the potential risks arising from its use on a larger scale may have a bearing on international trade as well as economic activity generally. International alignment of AI governance frameworks is believed to be crucial in enabling the adoption of AI technologies across different jurisdictions.[24]

There is also a requirement for the parties to cooperate in relation to Innovation (Article 9) generally with a view to promoting creativity and cooperation. The Innovation module highlights areas that require state coordination to foster greater innovation, such as the use of public domains and open government data. There is a commitment to data innovation through open government data and data and regulatory "sandboxes" (something not typically found in FTAs) implying a willingness to entertain creative approaches to regulation, as first tested in low-risk environments before broader application. This enables the updating and modernization of the agreement as its membership grows and technology changes – precisely what makes DEPA a living agreement. The generality of this language reveals a broad sense of openness to ideas rather than a specific path which must be followed.

Parties further pledge to cooperate in relation to SMEs. The inclusion of material on SMEs has become commonplace in recent FTAs, recognizing the importance of these firms in the global economy, especially where digitization tends to enable firms of smaller size to enter foreign markets in a manner that would have previously been impossible. This is a regulatory agenda that is increasingly attracting the attention of global trade governance.[25] The promotion of interoperability may be of greatest advantage to SMEs since it helps reduce compliance costs associated with multiple jurisdictions.

23 Exceptions include the United Kingdom-Australia FTA Chapter 20 (on Innovation)

24 L Zhao, "Artificial Intelligence and Law: Emerging Divergent National Regulatory Approaches in a Changing Landscape of Fast-Evolving AI Technologies" in D Collins and M Geist (Eds.), *Research Handbook on Digital Trade* (Elgar, 2023)

25 D Collins, "Digital Trade and the WTO: Opportunities and Challenges for SMEs" in J Chaisse (Ed.), *Elgar Companion to WTO* (Elgar, 2023)

The Digital Inclusion material found in Article 11 of DEPA is also highly innovative and progressive, addressing the needs of women and Indigenous people. This commitment works towards fulfilling the UN's Sustainable Development Goals.[26] Disciplines on digital inclusion, which are also framed in hortatory language, may have also been designed to serve a signalling purpose, much as the preamble in a conventional FTA. The aspirational material reflects DEPA parties' concerns that the advantages of the digital economy need to be available to all.[27]

The requirement of access to technology, including Internet connectivity, to derive benefits from digital trade underscores the reality that efforts will be needed to ensure that historically deprived groups are not marginalized. This is key to tackling the so-called "digital divide" that prevents developing countries from deriving the economic benefits of the digital economy. Regulatory agility is not sufficient to stimulate progress in the digital economy on its own – digital infrastructure must be correspondingly built up if DEPA is to result in concrete benefits to its signatories.[28]

DEPA contains general exceptions which are modelled on those of GATT Article XX and GATS Article XIV. Interestingly, DEPA includes the specific addition of "environmental" measures, which is missing from the old GATT language.[29] There is also a self-judging essential security exception, now standard in modern FTAs, despite the possibility of abuse associated with the use of essential security to justify economic treaty breaches. WTO practice now suggests that such provisions are indeed justiciable by arbitral tribunals.[30]

Lastly, in terms of its institutional structure for the purposes of administration, as with many modern FTAs, DEPA establishes a Joint Committee to enable further dialogue among the parties, recognizing that it is a living agreement designed to adapt as new technologies and innovations emerge.[31] These kinds of permanent bodies are essential to facilitate the renegotiation of the treaty text, which is inevitably incomplete, ensuring the longevity of the instrument.[32]

DEPA is envisioned as an agreement to which other countries would be able to accede – expanding its reach well beyond the original three signatories. The authority to consider and approve the terms of accession, including the period for the deposit of an instrument of accession, vests in the Joint Committee, a body established under Article 12.1 which consists of government representatives of each party. Aspiring members will be required to demonstrate their efforts to date and the changes that will need to be made to their domestic laws and regulations – if any – to meet the obligations under the agreement.

DEPA disciplines have not yet been embedded into other FTAs, as anticipated by its modular nature although the momentum for doing so might be more

26 In particular Goal #5 on Gender Equality

27 Soprana, n 6 at 162

28 H Gao, "Digital Provisions Play a Key Role in Asia Pacific Agreements" East Asia Forum (2022)

29 Article 15

30 Russia – Measures Concerning Traffic in Transit, WT/DS512/7 (29 April 2019)

31 Article 12

32 TJ Park, *Incomplete International Investment Agreements* (Elgar, 2022)

compelling as the agreement itself expands.[33] While new countries can accede to the agreement, each chapter of DEPA can easily be inserted into other trade agreements – hence the use of the term "module" which implies ready re-application from one context to another. It is not precisely clear how this would work in practice but it may envisage a kind of DEPA *a-la-carte* through which potential signatories can pick and choose which sections they are prepared to accept, much as new signatories to CPTPP set out their market access offers in schedules. This is thoughtfully described as a way of putting in place building blocks stacked up in different combinations by different countries through which a global framework may be established incrementally.[34]

DEPA does not contain material on "capacity building" would be needed if any developing countries want to join. There is a pressing need to address the digital divide which DEPA arguably fails to address. This suggests that DEPA will be most appealing to developed economies that are not large enough to deliver principle-building standards on a global level, as in the case of the United States, the European Union, and China.

The long-term success of DEPA and other DEAs will require ongoing participation by firms which engage in digital trade in order to ensure that the regulations remain useful and relevant.[35] FTAs covering digital matters only but omit commitments in conventional areas such as tariff reductions and market access for services, is an untested approach in world trade law. The fact that digitization touches on so many economic issues indirectly, including, for example, trade facilitation in goods, suggests it may be uniquely suited to treatment in isolation.

Although DEPA contains clauses such as non-discriminatory treatment of digital products, information and communication technology products using cryptography, cross-border transfer of information electronically and prohibition of location of computing facilities, its Annex I states that various of the core elements of DEPA do not create any rights or obligations between the parties. This provision is essential to understanding DEPA's approach to digital trade regulation – it is expressly designed to foster collaboration and discussion with a view to building consensus. It contains very few binding obligations. Future signatories might find this attractive in one way in that it preserves regulatory sovereignty. This captures the importance of "soft law" or diplomacy as a principle of world trade law.

DEAs like DEPA enable negotiators to focus on the specific needs of trade in the digital economy, extending the scope of negotiations beyond the traditional, and arguably outdated, goods and services dichotomy under the WTO framework and enabling the incorporation of WTO-plus issues (e.g., data localization) that may otherwise have been omitted. This enables the generation of new ideas, for

33 D Elms, China Applies to Join DEPA (Talking Trade, Asian Trade Centre, 2022)

34 J Baccus, The Digital Decide: How to Agree WTO Rules on Digital Trade (Centre for International Governance Innovation (CIGI), 2020) at 1

35 D Elms, Talking Trade: Unpacking the Digital Economic Partnership Agreement (Asian Trade Centre, 28 January 2020)

example in relation to e-invoicing and AI, and offers insight into subjects which are evolving at a rapid pace, typically by encouraging cooperation rather than setting proscriptive rules which could end up being restrictive.

One of the drawbacks to a subject-specific agreement like DEPA is the potential for overlap and inconsistency with existing FTAs. This is especially since the distinction between trade in services and digital trade can often be blurred. Many services are delivered digitally, often yielding the (arguably redundant) provision in FTAs that obligations contained in digital trade chapters incorporate obligations found in services chapters.[36] The lack of concurrent negotiations on aspects of digital trade typically addressed in the trade in services chapters of FTAs could prove problematic since digital trade and trade in services, especially of the Mode 1 cross-border supply variety, are inevitably intertwined. This could be exacerbated in countries which have limited negotiating capacity or lack the ability to fully assess the impact new disciplines on digital trade introduced with a single-topic agreement could have on commitments and obligations arising from other existing trade agreements they have signed. In many respects, this is a modern recapitulation of the infamous "noodle bowl" problem in the era of the proliferation of regional agreements.[37]

10.3.3 DEAs and WTO Compatibility

As subject-specific preferential FTAs, DEAs raise some questions about their legal interaction with the WTO framework as an exception to MFN non-discrimination. Recall from Chapter 2 that GATT Article XXIV requires that FTAs eliminate duties and other restrictive regulations of commerce on "substantially all the trade" between constituent territories. For digital trade agreements that only cover digital products/services, it's questionable whether this meets the "substantially all trade" threshold.[38] It is further unclear whether DEAs sufficiently address non-tariff barriers to satisfy this requirement of GATT Article XXIV. Data localization requirements and other digital trade barriers could qualify.[39] With regard to the categorization as services, GATS Article V requires "substantial sectoral coverage" for services FTAs. Digital trade agreements may meet this for digital/electronic services, but likely not for services overall.[40] GATS Article V requires the elimination of substantially all discrimination between parties. Digital trade agreements often aim to do this for digital services, but the scope may be too narrow to satisfy GATS requirements fully. It should be noted that the WTO has generally taken a permissive approach to FTAs. DEPA would need to be assessed in

36 For example, USMCA Article 19.2.4

37 J Bhagwati, *Termites in the Trading System* (Oxford University Press, 2008)

38 H Gao, "Digital or Trade? The Contrasting Approaches of China and United States to Digital Trade" 21:2 Journal of International Economic Law 297 (2018)

39 M Burri, "Towards a New Treaty on Digital Trade" 55:1 Journal of World Trade 77 (2021)

40 AD Mitchell and N Mishra, "Regulating Cross-Border Data Flows in a Data-Driven World: How WTO Law Can Contribute" 22:3 Journal of International Economic Law 389 (2020)

terms of the number of sectors, volume of trade affected, and modes of supply to evaluate whether the agreement meets this requirement and whether it eliminates substantially all discrimination, particularly when DEPA parties do not engage in the negotiation of specific commitments.[41]

It may be that some of DEPA's provisions will need to be listed by the parties in their GATS schedules as additional commitments under Article XVIII. This article covers a wide range of measures affecting trade in services that are not subject to scheduling obligations under market access and National Treatment contained in Articles XVI and XVII of the GATS. Several of the disciplines negotiated under DEPA arguably fall under the scope of application of Article XVIII of the GATS.[42] It is quite possible that, were a dispute to arise between the parties, some of these issues could surface, particularly if there were corresponding allegations of GATS commitments breached and a WTO panel were to be appointed for the resolution of the matter. Recall that the dispute settlement chapter of DEPA enables claims to be brought through the WTO DSS.

The uncertain legal status of DEPA, as with other DEAs reflects other developments in international economic law in favour of trade "mini-deals" which fall short of fully binding treaties but nevertheless set the groundwork for meaningful economic cooperation.[43] These types of agreements have become popular in recent years, with over 1200 having been concluded involving 130 countries. In some cases, such "deals" are concluded between national and sub-central governments (which are not traditional subjects of international law), such as United States states. It is clear that trade departments are becoming more creative when attempting to address practical problems of coordination across multiple levels of government both horizontally (across countries) and vertically (within countries).

10.4 Digital Services Taxes (DSTs)

Digital Services Taxes (DSTs) are designed to address the widespread perception that multinational tech companies do not pay their fair share of tax. A global moratorium on DSTs was put in place while a multilateral DST convention is planned under the auspices of the OECD, but since this has not materialized, some countries will pursue their own DST regime unilaterally. Canada, for example, implemented a DST in 2024.

Based on the OECD model, DSTs consist of a 3 per cent tax on domestically-sourced digital services revenue earned by large domestic and foreign companies. It will apply to revenue generally arising from online marketplace services (e.g., Amazon), online targeted advertising services (such as those offered by Google),

41 M Soprana, "The Digital Economy Partnership Agreement (DEPA): Assessing the Significance of the New Trade Agreement on the Block" XIII:1 Trade Law and Development 143 (2021)

42 Ibid., at 167

43 K Claussen, "Trade's Mini-Deals" 62:2 Virginia Journal of International Law 315 (2022)

and social media services (as on Facebook). It also applies to the sale or licensing of user data obtained from these services. Since DSTs were conceived to combat the tax avoidance schemes of the big tech companies operating online while registered in low-tax jurisdictions, DSTs Act tend to apply only to businesses that meet high revenue thresholds. For example, under the Canadian DST, companies must earn global revenue from all sources of €750 million or more per year as well as Canadian digital services revenue of more than CAD$20 million per year. The 3 per cent tax would be levied on the amount by which Canadian digital services revenue for the particular calendar year exceeds CAD$20 million, prorated among company group members)

Like most taxes imposed on businesses, there is a strong likelihood that DSTs will simply be passed on to consumers, raising costs, and lowering living standards commensurately. They will also chill investment and employment, acting as a drag on economic activity generally. In addition to bad economic policy, DSTs also run the risk of violating world trade law.[44]

Although WTO rules do not impose obligations regarding the imposition or collection of tax, there are a few facets of WTO law that the DST Act could transgress. First is the WTO-wide moratorium on the imposition of customs duties on electronic transmissions, extended on a temporary basis most recently at the last WTO Ministerial Conference in 2022. It is not clear whether the current moratorium is enforceable under the WTO's dispute settlement process, as it is often thought of as a "political" commitment rather than a legally binding one. Still, there is a strong claim that the Canadian DST is not in keeping with the spirit of the moratorium which was designed to promote the free flow of data for the purposes of commercial activity.

More importantly, since DSTs will affect trade in Internet advertising and digital intermediation services, they fall within the scope of the GATS. As discussed in Chapter 8, GATS prohibits discrimination between "like" services or services suppliers, either foreign versus local or among foreign companies from different countries. In the case of a DST, the discrimination would probably be against American companies in favour of their equivalent domestic counterparts. It is difficult to anticipate whether digital services would be viewed as "like" their traditional domestic equivalents by a WTO panel. Digital advertising is arguably not "like" classic print advertising. On the other hand, digital intermediation services, such as those provided by Uber and Airbnb could be viewed as "like" taxi and hotel services, respectively, because they are in competition with each other. Competition between digital services providers of the same kinds of services but at different scales would be significantly easier to demonstrate.

Whether a violates the non-discrimination rules of the GATS depends on the commitments that the WTO member imposing it has made in its schedule of specific commitments. Many developed countries enacting DSTs made very broad

44 D Collins, "The Compatibility of Digital Services Taxes with World Trade Organization Law" in D Collins and M Geist (Eds.), *Research Handbook on Digital Trade* (Elgar, 2023)

commitments in relation to computer services and telecommunications, the two most relevant sectors. Still, in assessing whether a WTO member has made a specific commitment under GATS there is still much disagreement regarding whether various kinds of digital services, such as search engines, Internet advertising, streaming and cloud computing, that did not exist when commitments were scheduled in the mid-1990s, are covered by existing commitments. Based on WTO case law such as *China – Periodicals*, it would seem that GATS schedules extend to services that were not technically feasible or commercially available at the time the commitments were made. The interpretation of WTO agreements was arguably intended to be flexible enabling adaptation to new technologies. Consequently, a DST imposed on the cross-border supply of Internet advertising or digital intermediation services, but not on the supply of similar services domestically, could be viewed as the imposition of a tax on imported electronic transmissions.

DSTs do not formally distinguish between domestic and foreign services and service suppliers. The design of the DST could be problematic here because of its high thresholds, which appear to target the United States tech giants as well as the types of services covered, effectively excluding domestic suppliers. There are very few if any, non-United States companies which will be caught by the DST. In this regard, it would not be a defence for a country such as Canada to claim that the DST Act was imposed to address the under-taxation of digital platforms. Since the DST only applies to firms above a certain size, the tax will likely be *de facto* discriminatory if the only firms that are subject to the tax are foreign firms, almost all of which are American.

As discussed in Chapter 5, GATS contains general exceptions which enable WTO members to violate its rules under certain circumstances. But GATS general exceptions will likely not save a DST. The most relevant exception, for direct taxes and designed to address tax evasion,[45] is not relevant because DSTs are not income taxes, and are more aptly characterized as indirect taxes (meaning ones charged on services rather than on income). DSTs are also probably not "necessary" to secure compliance with income tax – necessity having a very high threshold under international law. It is noteworthy that DSTs are also not covered by double taxation agreements, taking them outside the scope of another exception to GATS rules.[46]

DSTs could also transgress obligations contained in FTAs. For example, the non-discrimination rule in the USMCA has a more open-ended prohibition of less favourable treatment accorded to other services and service suppliers in "like circumstances." Whether treatment is accorded in "like circumstances" depends on the totality of the circumstances, including whether the relevant treatment distinguishes between services or service suppliers on the basis of legitimate public welfare objectives. It is arguable that the equitable and effective imposition and collection of taxes on digital service suppliers is such a legitimate public welfare objective. But again, the design of DSTs as promulgated by the OECD, which

45 Article XIV(d)
46 Article XIV(e)

appears to single out American companies, undermines this claim. Some might assert that large tech firms put greater strain on public infrastructure, for example, electricity and telecommunication networks, but that would be difficult to quantify and would likely merit an assessment of their corresponding contributions to the economy. It is doubtful that a USMCA-appointed arbitration panel would support this conclusion.

As with any other kind of tariff, DSTs will ultimately be passed on to their customers in the form of higher prices. In the case of social media platforms which are notionally free, this would be paid by advertisers. Online streaming companies like Netflix will simply charge more for their subscriptions. Alternatively, it may transpire that these digital services companies may withdraw from jurisdictions which implement DSTs, resulting in a loss of choice for consumers in those countries.

10.5 Conclusion

Trade has come a long way since the days of spices packed on dusty camels' backs or stored in the dank holds of creaking sailing ships. Today, digital trade is mediated above the Earth by satellites in the blink of an eye.

Much as the Silk Road and later the great canals opened up a world of riches to society, the people of today have witnessed an explosion in digital trade. It has become a central pillar of the modern global economy, much as the shipping of raw materials was in bygone centuries. Although the WTO has not addressed digital trade directly, as a forum for the negotiation of principles of world trade law, it is well suited to facilitate digital trade by eliminating emerging forms of protectionism in this sphere, like data localization. Existing principles of world trade law such as non-discrimination, transparency, and harmonization have shown themselves to be equally important to the digital sphere.

The approach of the parties negotiating digital trade chapters in FTAs, especially the groundbreaking USMCA, was based on the premise that digital trade is trade; it is only the form through which the commercial transaction is performed which may be new, not its substance. Parties merely extended existing principles of world trade law or applied them to the digital marketplace.

As digital trade matures requiring greater adaptive capacity and specialist committees, DEAs have the potential to be transformative sources of world trade law, setting the agenda for rulemaking across the rapidly expanding global digital economy. The digital focus of DEAs sets them apart from many of the modern FTAs from which they draw inspiration, notably the USMCA and CPTPP. DEPA goes further, delving into innovative fields such as AI and breaking new ground in matters such as electronic trade facilitation. DEPA's status as a living, plurilateral agreement open to modification in line with changes in technology is further reflected in its intention to encompass new signatories willing to take on various of the agreement's modules on an optional basis.

This approach may itself reflect a new iteration of an established principle of world trade law – one premised on flexibility and optionality. Much as tariff commitments and market access obligations can be set by each WTO member, these new DEAs apply "variable geometry," enabling countries to bind themselves under international law only to the extent that they are capable given their unique needs at a given moment. Given the tumultuous history of global economic relations, since the first civilizations began to barter their surpluses millennia ago, these are essential features of a legal system well-adapted to the rapidly progressing and unpredictable nature of the modern economy.

Discussion Questions

1. What is meant by the concept of digital trade? What does it encompass?
2. What kinds of trade barriers exist in the sphere of digital trade?
3. Has the WTO done enough to liberalize digital trade? What more could it do?
4. What are the main features of digital trade/e-commerce chapters of FTAs?
5. What role can be played by Digital Economy Agreements (DEAs) regarding the future of digital trade?

Index

Note: Page numbers in *italics* indicate figures.

Kolibri 360 GmbH
Ferdinand-Jühlke-Straße 7
99095 Erfurt, Deutschland
produktsicherheit@kolibri360.de